Enduring Conquests

Publication of this book and the SAR seminar from which it resulted were made possible with the generous support of The Annenberg Foundation and The Brown Foundation, Inc., of Houston, Texas.

**School for Advanced Research
Advanced Seminar Series**

James F. Brooks
General Editor

Enduring Conquests

Contributors

Robin A. Beck Jr.
Department of Anthropology, University of Michigan

Kira Blaisdell-Sloan
Department of Anthropology, University of California, Berkeley

Thomas H. Charlton
Department of Anthropology, University of Iowa

Minette C. Church
Department of Anthropology, University of Colorado, Colorado Springs

Guillermo Cock
Consultores Patrimonio Cultural, Peru

Kathleen Deagan
Florida Museum of Natural History, University of Florida

Jennifer L. Dornan
University Programs, St. Edward's University

Patricia Fournier
Escuela Nacional de Antropología e Historia-INAH, Mexico

Elena Goycochea
Killa Inti Arqueología, Peru

Rosemary A. Joyce
Department of Anthropology, University of California, Berkeley

Matthew Liebmann
Department of Anthropology, Harvard University

David G. Moore
Department of Sociology and Anthropology, Warren Wilson College

Melissa S. Murphy
Department of Anthropology, University of Wyoming

Robert W. Preucel
Department of Anthropology, University of Pennsylvania

Jeffrey Quilter
Peabody Museum of Archaeology and Ethnology, Harvard University

Christopher B. Rodning
Department of Anthropology, Tulane University

Russell N. Sheptak
Archaeological Research Facility, University of California, Berkeley

Barbara L. Voss
Department of Anthropology, Stanford University

Steven A. Wernke
Department of Anthropology, Vanderbilt University

Jason Yaeger
Department of Anthropology, University of Texas at San Antonio

Enduring Conquests
*Rethinking the Archaeology of Resistance
to Spanish Colonialism in the Americas*

Edited by Matthew Liebmann and Melissa S. Murphy

SAR
PRESS

School for Advanced Research Press
Santa Fe

School for Advanced Research Press
Post Office Box 2188
Santa Fe, New Mexico 87504-2188
www.sarpress.sarweb.org

Managing Editor: Lisa Pacheco
Editorial Assistant: Ellen Goldberg
Designer and Production Manager: Cynthia Dyer
Manuscript Editor: Valerie Larkin
Proofreader: Carol Leyba
Indexer: Margaret Moore Booker

Library of Congress Cataloging-in-Publication Data

Enduring conquests : rethinking the archaeology of resistance to Spanish colonialism in the Americas / edited by Matthew Liebmann and Melissa S. Murphy. — 1st ed.
    p. cm. — (Advanced seminar series)
 Includes bibliographical references and index.
 ISBN 978-1-934691-41-0 (alk. paper)
1. Indians—Colonization. 2. Government, Resistance to—America—History. 3. Indians—First contact with Europeans. 4. Indians, Treatment of—America—History. 5. Indians—Material culture. 6. Indians—Antiquities. 7. Spain—Colonies—America. I. Liebmann, Matthew, 1973- II. Murphy, Melissa Scott.
 E65.E58 2011
 980'.013—dc22

                    2010051501

Copyright © 2010 by the School for Advanced Research. All rights reserved.
Manufactured in the United States of America.
Library of Congress Catalog Card Number 2010051501
International Standard Book Number 978-1-934691-41-0
First edition 2011.

All chapter illustrations by individual authors unless otherwise noted.

Cover illustration: Detail of title page engraving from the *Historia general de los hechos de los castellanos en las islas i tierra firme del mar oceano* by Antonio de Herrera y Ordesillas and Andrés González de Barcía Carballido y Zúñiga, 1726. Madrid, Spain: Imprento real de Nicolas Rodiguea [sic] Franco. Courtesy the P.K. Yonge Library of Florida History, University of Florida (image provided from the library's copy).

Contents

	List of Figures	ix
	List of Tables	xi
	Acknowledgments	xiii
1.	Rethinking the Archaeology of "Rebels, Backsliders, and Idolaters" *Matthew Liebmann and Melissa S. Murphy*	3
2.	Limiting Resistance: Juan Pardo and the Shrinking of Spanish La Florida, 1566–68 *Robin A. Beck Jr., Christopher B. Rodning, and David G. Moore*	19
3.	Native American Resistance to Spanish Presence in Hispaniola and La Florida, ca. 1492–1650 *Kathleen Deagan*	41
4.	Resistance, Persistence, and Accommodation at Puruchuco-Huaquerones, Peru *Melissa S. Murphy, Elena Goycochea, and Guillermo Cock*	57
5.	Convergences: Producing Early Colonial Hybridity at a *Doctrina* in Highland Peru *Steven A. Wernke*	77
6.	Cultural Encounters at Magdalena de Cao Viejo in the Early Colonial Period *Jeffrey Quilter*	103

CONTENTS

7. Pots and Plots: The Multiple Roles of Early Colonial Red Wares in the Basin of Mexico (Identity, Resistance, Negotiation, Accommodation, Aesthetic Creativity, or Just Plain Economics?)   127
   Thomas H. Charlton and Patricia Fournier

8. Pragmatic Choices, Colonial Lives: Resistance, Ambivalence, and Appropriation in Northern Honduras   149
   Russell N. Sheptak, Rosemary A. Joyce, and Kira Blaisdell-Sloan

9. The San Pedro Maya and the British Colonial Enterprise in British Honduras: "We may have a perfectly harmless and well affected inhabitant turned into a designing and troublesome neighbor"   173
   Minette C. Church, Jason Yaeger, and Jennifer L. Dornan

10. The Best of Times, the Worst of Times: Pueblo Resistance and Accommodation during the Spanish *Reconquista* of New Mexico   199
    Matthew Liebmann

11. Becoming Navajo: Refugees, Pueblitos, and Identity in the Dinétah   223
    Robert W. Preucel

12. The Archaeology of Indigenous Heritage at Spanish-Colonial Military Settlements   243
    Barbara L. Voss

    References   267
    Index   315

Figures

1.1	Locations discussed in this volume	13
2.1	Native towns visited by Juan Pardo, 1566–68	22
2.2	Excavations at the Berry site, 1986–2007	29
2.3	Excavations in Structure 1, showing center posts, wall posts, and entry trenches	35
2.4	Possible wrought iron shim in posthole, Structure 5	36
3.1	Detail of title page engraving from the *Historia general de los hechos de los castellanos en las islas i tierra firme del mar oceano*	42
3.2	Locations of principal Native American polities and Spanish settlements in La Florida, ca. 1565–1650	50
3.3	Drawing from a 1676 manuscript of an Apalache Indian ballgame pole	53
3.4	Massacre of Jesuits by Indians	55
4.1	Location of 57AS03 and Huaquerones within the archaeological zone of Puruchuco-Huaquerones	59
4.2	Early colonial stretcher burial from Huaquerones	72
5.1	The central and upper Colca Valley, showing locations of reducción villages and early doctrinas	84
5.2	Architectural map of Malata	88
5.3	Overview photos of Malata	90
5.4	Two views of the chapel entry, atrium, and plaza area	92
5.5	Architectural map of Malata	96
6.1	Map of Magdalena de Cao Viejo	104
6.2	View of the Huaca Cao Viejo	105
6.3	Two details of painted textiles from Magdalena de Cao	114
6.4	An offering in a cut gourd from a lower floor in House (Unit) 1	116
6.5	Cut paper from Magdalena de Cao	121
7.1	Central Mexican symbiotic region and Basin of Mexico with relevant sites	128
7.2	Tenochtitlan, Tlatelolco, and La Traza	129

Figures

7.3	Sections I–III of the *Códice de los Alfareros de Cuauhtitlán*	137
7.4	Symbol of the Crown and Monogram (R-Rex) used on Colonial Red Ware vessels from Cuauhtitlán by Alonso de Avila Alvarado	142
8.1	Selected Spanish and Indian towns in northwestern Honduras	151
8.2	Copper fishhook excavated at Ticamaya	153
8.3	Nolasco Bichrome vessel	154
8.4	Obsidian dart point recovered in colonial context at Omoa	155
8.5	Ruins of church of the colonial pueblo de indios of Yamala	162
9.1	Map of region showing San Pedro Sirís and surrounding village clusters	179
9.2	Muzzle-loading, rifled gun barrels from San Pedro Sirís	183
9.3	Incendiary rocket casings from the burning of San Pedro Sirís in 1867	184
9.4	Example of English bowl from San Pedro Sirís	186
9.5	Porcelain doll parts recovered from San Pedro Sirís	190
10.1	Pueblo villages of the Revolt and Reconquest eras	203
10.2	Box-and-whisker plot comparison of room sizes at pre- and post-1600 Zia settlements	205
10.3	Cerro Colorado, 1689–94	209
10.4	Architectural layouts of Patokwa, Boletsakwa, and Cerro Colorado, 1689–94	211
10.5	Histogram and scatterplot of room sizes at Cerro Colorado	212
10.6	Tewa wares as a percentage of the total ceramic assemblages of Jemez and Zia Pueblos	217
11.1	Three Corn Pueblito	227
11.2	Pueblito tree ring dates	229
11.3	Largo Canyon rock art panel showing a group of female Yé'i figures	239
12.1	Artist's conception of El Presidio de San Francisco as it may have appeared in 1792	247
12.2	Relative locations of the 1792 quadrangle and the expanded 1815 quadrangle	248
12.3	Size-based comparison of El Presidio de San Francisco's quadrangles	249
12.4	Detail of *View of the Presidio of San Francisco* by Louis Choris, 1816	254
12.5	Diagram of the recursive relationship between colonial military aggression and colonial architectural expansion	257

Tables

4.1	Sample composition from Puruchuco-Huaquerones by age, sex, and burial type	60
4.2	Individuals with perimortem injuries by burial type	63
4.3	Perimortem trauma by cases and individuals in both cemeteries	64
4.4	Perimortem trauma by skeletal element	66
11.1	Pueblo demographic data reported by fray Juan Agustín de Morfi in 1782	235
12.1	Architectural trends at El Presidio de San Francisco	250

Acknowledgments

Enduring Conquests would not have been possible without the dedication and hard work of many people. We offer our thanks first and foremost to the staff of the School for Advanced Research: to James Brooks, president of SAR, for his support of this project through all its phases, from initial planning of the seminar to the final publication of the manuscript; to Nancy Owen Lewis for her help in organizing the seminar; to Leslie Shipman and her staff for keeping us well fed and comfortable in Santa Fe; and to Lynn Thompson Baca, Lisa Pacheco, Ellen Goldberg, and Valerie Larkin at SAR Press for shepherding the manuscript through the publication process. Jason Ur provided essential expertise in drafting figures for Chapters 1 and 3, and Adam Stack aided in the bibliographic editing. We would also like to thank two anonymous reviewers for their insightful comments on the manuscript, which improved the final product greatly. Last but certainly not least, we are grateful to our fellow contributors for their participation in the seminar and the hard work that went into producing the pages that follow.

We would like to especially commemorate the contribution of Thomas H. Charlton, who passed away as the manuscript was being prepared to go to press. Tom's contribution was vital to this volume, and he and his coauthor, Patricia Fournier, performed a yeoman's service by agreeing to participate in the seminar on short notice. Tom's renowned scholarship helped to shape the field of historical archaeology in Mesoamerica, and his knowledge and insights into postconquest developments in New Spain will be sorely missed.

Enduring Conquests

1

Rethinking the Archaeology of "Rebels, Backsliders, and Idolaters"

Matthew Liebmann and Melissa S. Murphy

In the midnight shadows of Christmas Eve in 1492, the keel of the Spanish ship *Santa María* ground to a halt on a coral reef off the coast of an island known to its Taíno inhabitants as Ayiti. The loss of don Cristóbal Colón's flagship forced him to leave a contingent of thirty-nine crewmembers behind to construct a fortified settlement they dubbed Villa de la Navidad, while the admiral and the rest of his fleet departed to report to their sovereign patrons in Europe. When Colón returned to the island nine months later, he found the corpses of his men strewn along the coast, their fort burned to the ground. The colonists' possessions were scattered about the remains of the settlement, with the *Santa María*'s anchor and remnants of European clothing discovered in the houses of a nearby village. None of the thirty-nine Spaniards had survived. They had been killed, the island's native inhabitants reported, at the hands of neighboring Taíno warriors (Cohen 1969:90–91, 144–50).

The fate of this abortive initial attempt at Spanish settlement in the "New World" calls attention to the fact that indigenous peoples resisted the European colonization of the Americas from the very beginning (Deagan, Chapter 3). This was not an anomalous incident, but merely the first episode in a long pattern of native opposition to Spanish colonialism that spanned more than three centuries and ranged across two continents. Historical documents record repeated challenges to colonial authority by

American Indians between the sixteenth and nineteenth centuries: La Noche Triste in Tenochtitlan, the Guale Revolt in Florida, the Mixtón War in northern Mexico, the Taki Onqoy movement in the Andes, the Pueblo Revolt of 1680, and the Caste War of Yucatán are just a few of the most famous examples. Yet while these legendary acts of resistance have been celebrated by contemporary scholars as influential in shaping the colonial program throughout the Americas from 1492 to the present day, armed confrontation is but one of an array of strategies employed by indigenous peoples in their interactions with the hirsute foreigners who began appearing in their homelands five hundred years ago. As the contributions in this volume document, aside from direct opposition, indigenous peoples throughout the Americas navigated the colonial encounter at various times by means of cooperation, compliance, collusion, mimicry, mockery, ambivalence, flight, feigned ignorance, dissimulation, and a host of other calculated tactics. In the incident at La Navidad, for example, Taínos both destroyed the settlement and allied with the Spaniards, serving as informants, trading partners, servants, laborers, and brothers-in-arms for the colonial forces.

Much of what we think we know about the native negotiation of Spanish colonialism is founded upon modern readings of historical texts—and rightly so, as these documents provide an unparalleled level of detail (Church et al., Chapter 9; Sheptak et al., Chapter 8). Yet basing our understanding of Indian life in the Spanish colonies solely upon the written record can be problematic. The primary historical sources regarding this era tend to have been authored by Spanish officials, colonists, and missionaries, providing reports that have been filtered through the eyes and inkwells of nonnative interlocutors, in which indigenous perspectives were systematically excluded. Moreover, the masses of un- and underrepresented persons in Spanish colonial texts included not only native persons but also the multitudes whose identities fell into the ambiguous interstices between Indian and Spaniard. On the rare occasions that these "persons of little note" did create texts, they were commonly penned by elites and nearly always by males. Clearly these records must be considered with a critical eye, and even then they provide only partial versions of subaltern experiences in Spanish Colonial America. Furthermore, primary documents from this era tend to detail only the most overt, public, and seemingly exotic behaviors of native actors (Graham 1998:28–29), making it a challenge to discern the more mundane aspects of daily life within (and outside) the missions, villas, and *reducciones* of the New World, particularly those of nonelite persons.

Archaeology can help remedy these issues by providing new data with which we can investigate the various ways subaltern peoples navigated their lives under the yoke of Spanish colonialism. Archaeology complements historical studies of post-1492 life in the Americas (and vice versa) in many ways, providing a more nuanced and sophisticated understanding of the diversity of indigenous, mestizo, and criollo practices during the colonial era than that afforded by documents alone. The study of material culture can act as a corrective against inaccuracies in the historical canon, as well as corroborate ambiguous elements of the documentary record. More importantly, archaeology has the advantage of documenting the actions of "common" people independent of colonial-produced texts, because the bits and pieces of daily life they left behind reveal subtleties not recorded in historical documents. As a result, archaeology is not constrained by the same partialities as the historical record. Thus material culture can aid in representing the silent masses that have been muted via omission in colonial texts, helping to rescue native voices from what historian E. P. Thompson famously called "the enormous condescension of posterity" (1963:12).

Archaeology, however, is by no means a more objective or straightforward way of knowing the past than traditional text-based histories. To be sure, interpretations that build upon material culture suffer from vagaries and biases all their own. This is particularly true of archaeological studies concerned with how and what people in the past were *thinking* (Renfrew and Zubrow 1994:xiii), a category into which the archaeology of resistance often falls. Resistance is not always observable in and of itself, but rather can be an intent, a state of mind, and a rationale (Hodder 2004:32). An act characterized as resistance by one person can be classified as something else entirely by another—be it coercion, vandalism, ineptitude, or some other motivation. Furthermore, while resistance is often manifested in behavior, it can just as easily yield inaction. As a result, resistance is an inherently difficult topic to study archaeologically (Quilter, Chapter 6). The contributors to this volume are not the first to concern themselves with the motivations behind native acts during the colonial era. As historian Inga Clendinnen observes (2003:131), the missionaries who participated in the evangelization of the Americas were interested in discerning indigenous intentions too. "But they arrived at those 'intentions,'" she notes, "less by observation and enquiry than by imputation."

The challenge for archaeologists is to not fall into this same trap. Unfortunately, by their very nature many everyday acts of resistance leave no material signature (Singleton 1998:179; Spielmann et al. 2009:104), such as refusal, foot dragging, feigned ignorance, and dissimulation (Scott

1985:xvi). Those that do leave material traces are often equivocal at best. Consequently, the identification and interpretation of resistance in the archaeological record is often more art than science and can be heavily dependent upon historical and material contexts (Schurr 2010:57). Nonetheless, the studies assembled here take indigenous resistance to the Spanish Conquest as their starting point, examining not only the problems with this endeavor but also possible alternative interpretations that will improve our collective understanding of Native American lives under European colonialism.

ROMANCING THE CONQUEST

For most of the nineteenth and twentieth centuries, two opposed (but equally Spanish-centered) perspectives dominated depictions of the colonial period. On the one hand, pro-Spanish artists and scholars glorified their heroes' Conquest-era accomplishments, praising the conquistadores and missionaries as "harbingers of civilization" in a "realm of heathendom" (Bolton quoted in Keen 1985:662; Restall 2008:94). No less than the patriarch of Anglophone Conquest-era scholarship, William H. Prescott, commented in 1843 that "the remarkable achievements of the Spaniards in the sixteenth century...[have] the air of romance rather than sober history" (2000[1843]:4). On the other hand, this rosy view of Spanish colonialism has traditionally been countered by purveyors of the "Black Legend," who envisioned the Spaniards of the Conquest era as exceptionally backward, cruel, and "priest-ridden" (Keen 1985:658). The lack of attention to native agency that characterizes both of these Eurocentric perspectives has had repercussions down to the present day, with the persistence of popular imaginings of the Spanish Conquest as a history of forceful invasion, decisive subjugation, and the ultimate conversion (or extinction) of native populations (Cummins 2002:199).

With the flowering of ethnohistory as a distinct field in the latter twentieth century, new perspectives emerged emphasizing the combined use of anthropological and historical approaches to the study of Spanish colonialism, fostering a shift from investigations of colonial elites to an explicit focus on Native Americans (Spicer 1962; Gibson 1964; Wachtel 1977). Many of these studies abandoned the feigned neutrality of earlier histories, adopting an explicitly pro-Indian stance. Even so, they often perpetuated a view of indigenous peoples as passive subjects caught in a process of acculturation that they had no ability to shape (Keen 1985:672–73). That trend began to change in the 1980s as historians paid increasing attention to native resistance to Spanish control, making, in their words, "a mockery of the notion of 'the passive Indian'" (Spalding 1984:334). These studies examined the creative adaptations of indigenous actors to colonial rule, highlighting not only the instances of armed rebellion, but also the ways in which native actors manipulated legal proceedings, production, and systems of labor on a daily basis (Stern 1982; Borah 1983; Farriss 1984).

In recent years archaeological studies have followed suit, using material culture as a tool for documenting indigenous resistance (e.g., Deagan 2004; Dillehay 2007; Kepecs and Alexander 2005; Milanich 1999; Palka 2005; Preucel 2002; Rodríguez-Alegría 2008; Silliman 2001a, 2004; Spielmann et al. 2006, 2009). As Van Buren (2010:151–52) notes, these studies exemplify the fundamental shift that occurred following the Columbian Quincentenary (see Thomas 1989, 1990; Thomas, ed., 1991), with subsequent archaeological investigations underscoring the importance of a "bottom-up" understanding of colonialism and the recognition of the fundamental role of agency in the constitution of social life (see Beck et al., Chapter 2). In the past decade archaeologists have increasingly emphasized the fact that while the conquest of the Americas was indubitably brutal and exploitative, it was not uncontested by the indigenous populace, nor was it the swift, wholesale blitzkrieg it is sometimes made out to be (Rodríguez-Alegría 2008:33–35). Rather the colonial landscape was a patchwork of domination, resistance, accommodation, and negotiation, as indigenous peoples exerted a variety of strategies in their attempts to adapt to the colonizing and evangelizing efforts of the Spaniards (Wernke, Chapter 5; Liebmann, Chapter 10). This volume strives to continue the dialogue initiated by these recent archaeological and historical studies of indigenous resistance, and to further explore the multiplicity of tactics native peoples employed under Spanish colonialism.

THE DOMINATION OF RESISTANCE

Few topics have occupied the attention of anthropologists in recent years like that of resistance (Hollander and Einwohner 2004:533). Over the past two decades resistance has taken center stage in the investigation of social life, becoming increasingly popular—some would say trendy (Given 2004:11)—in part because the concept appears to be almost infinitely malleable. Building upon the works of Michel Foucault (1975, 1978, 1980) and James C. Scott (1985, 1990, 1998), anthropologists have found resistance seemingly everywhere in recent years, from white-collar bloggers (Schoneboom 2007) to fur-clad hunter-gatherers (Sassaman 2001). Indeed, in the landscape of twenty-first-century anthropology, resistance dominates. Nowhere is this domination more conspicuous than in contemporary archaeology, where the prominence of practice theory (and the concomitant emphasis on the role of agency in social life), the rise of household/domestic archaeology, and interest in the archaeology of enslaved and colonized peoples have combined to focus heretofore unprecedented attention on resistance among subaltern peoples.

This proliferation of interest has had both positive and negative consequences for the study of resistance. On the plus side, the consideration of opposition to power in its many forms has fostered investigations of the micropolitics of daily life, building upon the contributions of feminist approaches in anthropology (Geller and Stockett 2006). Focusing on resistance has led to a rethinking of long-held Marxist perspectives that denied agency to subordinate groups and viewed them as hapless victims and dupes (Giddens 1979). Attention to defiance (both active and passive) has also encouraged anthropology to broaden its horizons beyond a restricted focus on normative patterns, shared cultural traits, and social solidarity (Brown 1996:733). Maybe most significantly, the identification of "hidden transcripts" of resistance (Scott 1990) in their many forms has forced a general rethinking of hegemony (Greenhouse 2005; Sivaramakrishnan 2005), breaking down traditional binary understandings of domination and resistance. As a result, contemporary anthropologists recognize that not only are both power and resistance much more pervasive than had generally been acknowledged by previous generations (Ortner 1995:174–75), but also that rigid binary conceptions of colonialism mask considerable diversity within the supposedly polarized groups of colonizer and colonized (van Dommelen 2002, 2005).

Resistance is Futile...

In other ways, however, resistance has become a victim of its own success. Critics complain that the concept is overused and underanalyzed (Brown 1996:729–30; Ortner 1995:175–77). They argue that the notions of resistance that anthropologists commonly deploy are so vague as to undermine their utility. The assumption that resistance is the natural response to domination—and the concomitant identification of resistance in seemingly every social interaction (Foucault 1978:95–96)—dilutes its analytical value, say its critics. Resistance thus becomes "a seductive but ultimately infertile subject when promiscuously applied" (Holland and Eisenhart 1990:57). By homogenizing the varieties of opposition to power under the single umbrella term of *resistance*, archaeologists not only neglect important variations among its multiplicity of forms but also equate relatively minor power imbalances with attempts of the "truly oppressed" to ensure their very survival. This "savage leveling" can have the unintended consequence of diminishing, rather than assisting, our ability to identify inequities in social relations (Brown 1996:730).

In a similar vein, Hodder (2004:32) points out that archaeological studies of resistance often homogenize the intentions of past actors, implying that social groups operate as a unitary whole and overlooking the cross-cutting divisions that may have characterized them. While in most cases it is not practical (or even possible) for archaeologists to discern the intentions of specific individuals, there has often been a lack of consideration of the variability of intragroup intentionality when investigating resistance in the archaeological record. The assumption of social unanimity has directed attention away not only from the variety of responses to domination that might be manifested in the archaeological record, but also from the multiple social processes used to coordinate communal action in the past.

A related problem stemming from the abundant attention to resistance in recent decades has been a degree of disciplinary myopia, with anthropologists focusing overwhelmingly upon conflict and opposition at the expense of collaboration and reciprocity (as predicted by Ortner 1984:157). This problem has been particularly acute in archaeological analyses of colonial encounters. Yet as we know from ethnographic observations, cooperation, compliance, and collusion should be as much in evidence in the archaeological record as are resistance and domination (White 1986:56). This lopsided concentration undoubtedly stems in part from the romanticization of resistance characteristic of modern life in the West (Abu-Lughod 1990). In an age of unprecedented institutionalized hegemony, we live vicariously through the would-be resisters of the past, celebrating the underdogs who valiantly defied oppression (a romantic impulse stoked by Hollywood through an endless parade of movies such as *Avatar, Amistad, Apocalypto, Braveheart,* and *Dances with Wolves,* to name but a few). Yet this romantic yearning for the triumph of the human spirit over domination can blind us to the other forms of social interaction frequently employed by colonized peoples in their struggles for survival, including accommodation, collusion, and cooperation (Liebmann, Chapter 10; Voss, Chapter 12).

The cottage industry of resistance studies in archaeology has been buoyed by the ever-expanding influence of theories of practice and structuration in recent years (Bourdieu 1977; Giddens 1984) and the concomitant recognition of agency's role in social life. By acknowledging that cultural formations are not wholly determined by restraining structures and that human actors are not simply "dupes" of forces beyond their control (Meskell 1999:4), Bourdieu and Giddens opened a theoretical space for archaeologists to examine how individuals and groups can exert opposition to power. As studies invoking agency in the past became more common during the 1990s and 2000s, so too has the identification of resistance. Ironically, however, invoking resistance as a cause to explain indigenous actions can have the opposite of the intended effect. Rather than emphasizing agency, native peoples can be seen as merely responding to external stimuli, as knee-jerk re-actors rather than dynamic participants in the structuration of the colonial encounter.

If left unchecked, the problems provoked by the popularity of resistance studies—homogenization, myopia, romanticization, and the denial of agency—can lead to an unintentional "flattening" of the past, producing histories that are superficial, or worse, inaccurate. In the past, archaeological investigations have sometimes deployed resistance to explain aberrant patterns in material culture, invoking it as a conclusion. "The reason this artifact/feature/assemblage is different from the others," we are told, "is because it is a product of resistance." In the process, the documentation of resistance can become a conversation-ender rather than an invitation for further analysis. Thus, rather than developing the richer, more nuanced, and more complete understandings of the past that should be one of the primary goals of archaeology, cursory studies of resistance can force past actors into rigidly predetermined roles in which the colonizers dominate, the colonized resist, and never the twain shall meet. The reality of colonial experiences is, of course, never quite so simple.

Some of the problems identified here undoubtedly stem from the fact that archaeological studies of resistance are still in a relatively nascent stage. As with any intellectual endeavor, initial studies lead to further questions and deeper understandings of the complexity of social phenomena. Earlier studies were crucial in the establishment of resistance as a viable topic of investigation in archaeology, and as we build upon them, resistance can become a point of departure for investigation. The chapters assembled herein attempt to address some of these critiques through nuanced studies of resistance, acknowledging the complexities and problems associated with this topic while also contending with related social phenomena in their study of the colonized subjects of the Spanish Empire throughout the Americas.

RETHINKING RESISTANCE: CASE STUDIES

This volume originated with a session held at the 2007 Society for American Archaeology annual meetings titled "The Archaeology of

"Rebels, Backsliders, and Idolaters"

Indigenous Resistance to Spanish Colonization in the New World," which brought together archaeologists working in contexts throughout North, Central, and South America. Following that symposium, the contributors reconvened in Santa Fe for a short seminar at the School for Advanced Research in November 2008 to continue our discussions and reexamine our individual case studies from a variety of new perspectives. Initially, contributors were tasked with investigating the archaeology of indigenous resistance; however, by the time of the SAR seminar, it became clear that framing our investigations in this way was problematic for multiple reasons. Aside from focusing attention on seemingly obligatory responses rather than the active negotiation of colonial life, concentrating on resistance alone seemed to overlook and mischaracterize many crucial aspects of native experiences under colonial rule. For this reason we chose to broaden the focus of this volume, and thus while the chapters collected here take resistance as a starting point, they go on to investigate a multiplicity of actions and tactics other than overt opposition alone.

A related issue concerns the archaeology of "indigeneity." As many contributors note, the identification of indigeneity in the complex, hybrid forms of material culture that resulted from conquest and colonization in the Americas is no simple task. Indeed, in the post-1492 world the opposed categories of "indigenous" versus "European" were quickly found to be inadequate for describing the assorted ethnic and racial identities forged from colonial miscegenation. Contributors to this volume explore some of these thorny issues in their chapters, including the ways in which Spanish colonialism created and shaped ethnogenesis among indigenous populations.

The title of the volume, *Enduring Conquests: Rethinking the Archaeology of Resistance to Spanish Colonialism in the Americas*, reflects the variety of contexts and insights presented in the studies collected here. We chose the term *enduring* precisely because of its multiple meanings. According to the *Oxford English Dictionary*, in its transitive form the verb *endure* means "to undergo without succumbing or giving way." In this sense, *Enduring Conquests* emphasizes the experiences of native and subaltern peoples under the yoke of Spanish colonialism, a period that they faced, suffered, and ultimately outlasted. As an adjective, however, *enduring* can also mean "lasting or persisting." In this light, *Enduring Conquests* emphasizes the protracted nature of Spanish attempts to control the Americas. As the chapters in this volume demonstrate, this was not a swift and uncontested takeover, but rather a long and drawn-out series of engagements with ramifications that persist to the present day. Furthermore, the use of the plural form of *conquest* in the title is deliberate as well, reflecting a prominent theme running throughout the chapters of this volume: the fact that the Spanish invasion of the Americas was not a single monolithic event. Rather, *Enduring Conquests* emphasizes that Spanish colonialism in the Americas was variegated and diverse and was manifested in various ways according to differences in the culture, geography, and sociopolitical complexity of local conditions throughout the "New World."

In organizing this volume we have consciously chosen to cast the net wide, bringing together studies from urban and rural contexts, coastal and inland areas, deserts and swamps, and highlands as well as lowlands throughout the Spanish colonial Americas. In some of these regions the archaeology of Spanish colonialism has been studied for more than a century (Graham 1998; Fowler and Wilcox 1999; Ivey and Thomas 2005), while in others it is still in its nascent stages (Rice 1996a & b; Gasco et al. 1997; Jamieson 2005; Wernke 2007b:131). The contributions assembled here explore a wide range of temporal contexts as well, spanning the colonial era from 1492 to the mid-1800s, with some examining the very early contact/entrada period, while others look at the denouement of Spanish colonialism and how it has been memorialized. The volume is loosely organized geographically (Figure 1.1) with studies focusing on the Caribbean and southeastern United States (Beck et al., Chapter 2; Deagan, Chapter 3); the central Andes (Murphy et al., Chapter 4; Wernke, Chapter 5; Quilter, Chapter 6); Mesoamerica (Charlton and Fournier, Chapter 7; Sheptak et al., Chapter 8; Church et al., Chapter 9); and the western United States (Liebmann, Chapter 10; Preucel, Chapter 11; Voss, Chapter 12). By taking this pan-American perspective, we hope to draw out the local forces that shaped the implementation of Spanish colonialism, as well as break down the illusion that Spain's imperial system was monolithic, with identical policies (and results) throughout the Western Hemisphere (Weber 2005:xiii).

In Chapter 2, Robin Beck, Christopher Rodning, and David Moore examine domination and resistance in the encounters among members of the Juan Pardo expedition (1566–68) and native polities at the Spanish garrison of Fort San Juan de Joara (located in present-day North Carolina). They explore the shifting and changing nature of these encounters, from cooperation to the destruction of Pardo's garrison. Using Sewell's (2005) perspective on agency, their chapter examines several types of relations between native polities and the Spaniards (including labor mobilization, gift exchange, and military support), arguing that indigenous peoples used these relations to advance their own agendas. They point out that different polities advanced varying programs, and for some, the successful execution

"REBELS, BACKSLIDERS, AND IDOLATERS"

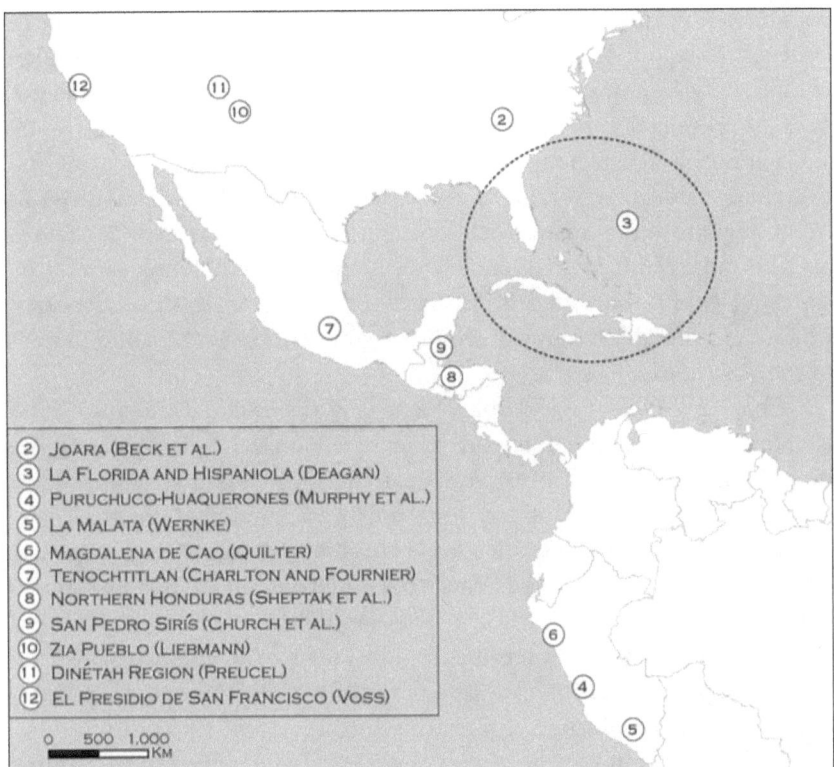

FIGURE 1.1.
Locations discussed in this volume. Labels correspond to chapter numbers.

of these agendas resulted in arguably higher prestige and social standing and the concomitant intimidation or elimination of political rivals. Their chapter demonstrates the critical need to situate colonizer–native interactions within both the local sociopolitical context and the nature of the colonial presence (in this case, with little institutional support). They caution against reliance upon the domination–resistance dichotomy in developing improved understandings of the relationship between polities of what became the southeastern United States and the Pardo expeditions.

In Kathleen Deagan's contribution (Chapter 3), "Native American Resistance to Spanish Presence in Hispaniola and La Florida, ca. 1492–1650," she notes that resistance to Spanish control appeared early in the circum-Caribbean and was not restricted solely to indigenous peoples, but was also enacted by enslaved and free Africans, white criollos, and mixed-race peoples throughout the region. She argues that the concept of resistance is problematic and ambiguous, and advocates flexibility in its conceptualization. Deagan reviews examples of organized, overt violent resistance by Taínos, mestizos, and Africans, as well as cases of ambivalence or outright rejection of Spanish cultural and religious elements both outside and within Spanish missions. Most notably, this chapter teases out how overt and organized resistance and accommodation followed class divisions in the regions under Spanish influence and how the absence of European artifacts in nonelite contexts could reflect rejection, indifference, or exclusion, but could also indicate the biases of archaeological investigations, which have tended to emphasize missions over non-Spanish communities of the post-Columbian era.

Chapter 4, by Melissa Murphy, Elena Goycochea, and Guillermo Cock, is unique to this volume in its use of bioarchaeological evidence to explore the colonial encounter. Through two bioarchaeological data sets, the authors trace the reconfiguration of traditional mortuary practices at the Inca cemetery of Puruchuco-Huaquerones (ca. 1470–1540) shortly after the Spanish Conquest and explore its significance for understanding indigenous entanglements with the Spanish in Peru. They argue that a subsample of burials from the cemetery likely represents individuals who fought against the Spaniards, perhaps during the Siege of Lima in 1536. The nature and location of traumatic injuries suggest armed conflict, and several individuals exhibit injuries from European weapons. Their chapter goes on to examine an idiosyncratic Early Colonial burial that likely represents a reinterment after Christian burial. Murphy and her coauthors propose that the burials of Puruchuco-Huaquerones can be interpreted in multiple ways—as resistance, persistence, accommodation, and/or complicity—pointing to the difficulties of assessing resistance in the archaeological record.

From the theoretical perspective of semiotic ideology, Steven Wernke (Chapter 5) examines Spanish evangelization at the early Franciscan *doctrina* (doctrinal settlement) at Malata in the Colca Valley of southern highland Peru and sketches its transition from an Inca administrative outpost to a locus of early Spanish colonial rule. Wernke argues that the organization of domestic, public, and ritual spaces at Malata reflects the convergence of Inca imperial structures with the materialization of the semiotic ideology of the Franciscan friars as they strove to impose a new Christian order. Rather than viewing this convergence through the lens of domination and resistance, Wernke sees negotiation in new domestic and ritual spaces and practices under Spanish colonial rule.

In Chapter 6, Jeffrey Quilter engages with the problematic identification and differentiation of resistance, accommodation, and ambivalence (among other [re]actions) in archaeological contexts through an investigation of architecture and landscape, textiles, religious material culture, and paper from the reducción of Magdalena de Cao, in the Chicama Valley of northern Peru. Like the contributions of Deagan (Chapter 3) and Murphy and her colleagues (Chapter 4), Quilter lays bare the difficulties of discerning resistance from the archaeological record without knowledge regarding the rationales of the would-be "resisters," as well as the problems of uncovering domination, accommodation, or ambivalence without understanding the intents of those in power. Quilter's rich and varied data set highlights the complexities involved in interpreting the colonial experience, as well as the many nuanced and perhaps contradictory meanings that can be ascribed to material remains and the built environment.

Drawing upon Spanish documents and the Codex of the Potters, Thomas Charlton and Patricia Fournier (Chapter 7) investigate the significance of indigenously produced Early Colonial Red Ware ceramics recovered from two ethnically distinct and socially stratified areas in the Basin of Mexico in the century following the Spanish conquest of Tenochtitlan. In the production of these ceramics, potters retained prehispanic techniques and some design elements, but they also incorporated new Spanish forms. Charlton and Fournier consider whether these vessels resulted from creative invention on the part of the indigenous potters or whether they represented their makers' recognition of an economic opportunity in the growing demand for these ceramics. They explore the possibility that the Red Wares represent resistance, but not that of the indigenous producers. Rather, these ceramics may have been used by their young colonial *consumers* in challenging and rejecting the Spanish metropole. Their contribution calls attention to the ambiguity of the colonial project and the diverse interests often subsumed under the monolithic categories of "Spaniard" and "colonizer" in the American colonies.

In Chapter 8, Russell Sheptak, Rosemary Joyce, and Kira Blaisdell-Sloan examine colonial resistance, appropriation, and "making do" among indigenous communities in northern Honduras through the lens of Michel de Certeau's (1984) concept of "tactics." They present evidence for both violent resistance and the reconfiguration of social relationships through ordinary acts. In one example, Sheptak and his colleagues describe how local Roman Catholic churches were built, maintained, and controlled by *indios* who then tactically appropriated these spaces for their own meaningful rituals and other newly emerging activities. This illustrates how a structure that might at first blush be viewed as an obvious locus of Spanish power and control can also serve to maintain and perpetuate indigenous cultural formations. This contribution thus explores the sophisticated ways in which indigenous peoples and their descendants redefined and appropriated Spanish colonial spaces, institutions, discourse, and material objects to perpetuate their own identities and histories.

Minette Church, Jason Yaeger, and Jennifer Dornan (Chapter 9) examine colonial encounters in nineteenth-century British Honduras between Maya peoples and colonial populations after the Caste Wars. Their study complements the others in this volume by contrasting British colonial policies with those of the Spaniards. Marshalling information about military operations, commerce and subsistence, religion, and education from archival records, oral histories, and material culture, they expose the often competing and conflicting agendas of the British authorities, loggers, and merchants, as well as the shifting and complicated relationships among Maya communities and between those communities and the colony. Their contribution underscores the fluidity of the relationships that occur among the varied constituents of the colonized groups and colonizers, as well as the complicated and tangled interpretive frameworks that accompany resistance studies.

Chapter 10, by Matthew Liebmann, examines the events of the Pueblo Revolt and Spanish Reconquest era (1680–94) in New Mexico, investigating the various strategies the people of the Zia Pueblo employed during this period. By focusing not only on resistance but also on the ambivalence, cooperation, and complicity that characterized Pueblo–Spanish relations during this tumultuous period, he "de-centers" resistance, an exercise that highlights the importance of relations within native communities in these events. His study also argues for the recognition of the importance of individual actors in fomenting resistance and complicity to colonial power. Ultimately, Liebmann suggests that archaeology can play a crucial role in countering the myopia, homogenization, and romanticism that have previously characterized studies of Spanish colonialism through the construction of new histories that give voice to the subalterns of the past.

In "Becoming Navajo: Refugees, Pueblitos, and Identity in the Dinétah" (Chapter 11), Robert Preucel examines interactions among multiple indigenous groups in northern New Mexico during the seventeenth and eighteenth centuries, and how Spanish colonialism in part shaped the changes in these interactions. Taking Navajo ethnogenesis as his starting point, Preucel frames his case study of the "Pueblito phenomenon" through ecclesiastical and governmental correspondence coupled with demographic records of Pueblo families and "souls." In a reexamination of previous interpretations of this phenomenon that relied upon rapid acculturation as an explanation for Navajo ethnogenesis, Preucel takes a practice-based approach to considering the distinctive material forms that were forged during this period in architecture, ceramics, and refuse disposal. His study concludes by rejecting essentialized notions of ethnic identity at the *pueblitos* and argues that ethnogenesis and hybridity resulted in the reconfiguration of practices that cannot be considered exclusively Navajo or Pueblo.

The final chapter, by Barbara Voss, focuses on labor relations at El Presidio de San Francisco, Spain's northernmost military outpost in the Americas. She critically reexamines the conventional interpretation that the colonial core, in this case the military fort, represents the material remains of the colonists' social history alone. Voss attends to the ways in which the heritage of native Californians might also be visible in the archaeological remains traditionally classified as "colonial." She foregrounds the coercion and subjugation of native Californians as laborers and the escalation of colonial violence in her diachronic view of the construction phases of the presidio, especially as they are manifested in the nineteenth-century expansion of the fort. Her chapter concludes with a discussion of heritage practices at the site, detailing how the inclusion of indigenous communities in archaeological research and interpretation at Spanish-colonial military sites allows a multitude of perspectives and gives visibility to unseen, hidden, and/or disenfranchised groups at colonial settlements.

EMERGENT THEMES: NEGOTIATING THE CONQUEST

The chapters in this volume present a host of new interpretations, providing more complex, nuanced pictures of Native American experiences under Spanish colonialism. In doing so, they also challenge us to reexamine our assumptions about the Spanish Conquest of the Americas. These studies push back against a grand narrative that views this era as a clash of civilizations—a narrative produced centuries after the fact—to construct more comprehensive and complex social histories of Native American life after 1492. Most saliently, they de-center traditional understandings of this period through at least two means: first, by employing the perspective of archaeology, they shift the focus of scholarship from the point of contact to the diachronic processes that shaped the Americas before and after 1492. This de-centering helps to emphasize the ambiguity of the colonial encounter, a time when European domination was neither complete nor viewed as inevitable. Second, by focusing explicitly upon the native side of the colonial equation, these studies highlight the importance of indigenous politics in the creation of the Spanish colonial world.

Furthermore, the contributions to this volume critically confront the application of theories of resistance to archaeological contexts. Many note the difficulties associated with the identification of resistance via material culture, and rightly so. But they also move the dialogue beyond oversimplified notions of domination and resistance in colonial contexts, drawing out the problems associated with seemingly self-evident notions of (dominant) cores and (dominated) peripheries, active colonizers and passive colonized, and the false dichotomy of indigenous survival versus extinction. Through the identification and examination of the central roles not only of resistance, but also of accommodation, alliance, ambiguity, and ambivalence, the authors emphasize the agency of indigenous life in the Spanish colonies, encouraging us to view Native Americans not as merely responding to colonialism, but as active players, shaping and negotiating the world around them. Native, criollo, and mestizo peoples generated new social forms from the Spanish colonial experience through creative processes such as ethnogenesis, nativism, revivalism, and the production of hybrid material culture. The studies collected here document a variety of these processes, testifying to the crucial roles played by all these groups in the formation not only of the Spanish American Empire, but of the modern world.

2

Limiting Resistance

*Juan Pardo and the Shrinking
of Spanish La Florida, 1566–68*

**Robin A. Beck Jr., Christopher B. Rodning,
and David G. Moore**

In May 1568, native peoples of the Carolinas and eastern Tennessee—at towns named Canos (or Cofitachequi), Joara, Guatari, Cauchi, and Chiaha—obliterated a string of Spanish forts that stretched from the Atlantic coast across the Appalachian Mountains. This would seem to be an act of resistance par excellence: indigenous peoples rising together to defeat the world's most powerful empire (see also Church et al., Chapter 9; Liebmann, Chapter 10; and Murphy et al., Chapter 4). Indeed, never again did Spain attempt to impose its colonial ambition upon the interior of the American Southeast. Yet we suggest that the concept of resistance—along with its regular partner, domination—may obfuscate rather than clarify the events that we seek to understand (Quilter, Chapter 6).

The themes of domination and resistance are fundamental to most theoretical articulations of the colonial experience. For many cases of Spanish and indigenous interactions in the Americas, they provide a solid framework on which to build insightful models of culture change and colonial entanglements. In our paper, we examine Juan Pardo's expeditions of 1566–68, focusing on relations between this expedition and the native polities of the western Carolina Piedmont and eastern Tennessee. Pardo twice led more than a hundred men into the interior Southeast and built half a dozen small forts. We have identified one of these garrisons, Fort San Juan de Joara, at the Berry site in what is now Burke County, North Carolina. Thirty soldiers occupied Fort San Juan—situated at the northern end of Joara, a large native town—for eighteen months. While our excavations have yielded evidence of cooperation between these Spaniards and their native hosts, the destruction of the fort's buildings by fire indicates that this cooperation ultimately failed.

Thinking about our case in terms of a domination–resistance dichotomy creates a dilemma: is it realistic to speak of the small group of Spaniards who manned this isolated garrison, or even of Pardo's combined force of 125 men, as the "dominant" side of the dichotomy simply because they were Europeans? Does such a dichotomy improve or inhibit our understanding of either Spanish or indigenous experience in the early colonial Southeast, where Spain so often—and often so spectacularly—failed to achieve much more than a tentative toehold? Here, we draw upon a conception of agency offered by William Sewell Jr. (2005) to propose that native polities on the Carolina Piedmont actively used the Pardo expedition as a structural resource to advance their own political and economic ends. Such an approach helps us understand the gamut of social actions that constitute this encounter, from early cooperation to the ultimate destruction of Pardo's forts.

First we offer a summary of the Pardo expeditions, which are little known outside the Southeast. In summarizing the historical context of this colonial entanglement, we draw attention to three distinct kinds of relationships between expedition members and indigenous peoples on the piedmont. At each of the major towns that Pardo visited, he and his men were received by numerous native leaders, some of whom traveled long distances to meet with the Spaniards. Invariably, two things occurred during these encounters: Pardo made gifts to the visiting dignitaries, and they in turn agreed to support the expedition by providing the Spaniards food and housing, including the construction of new buildings in their respective towns. And, on at least two occasions, a native leader apparently drew the Spaniards into military confrontation against his enemies. Each of these three kinds of interaction resists the simple dichotomous tropes of domination and resistance. Indeed, in each case we may profitably ask who was using whom. After summarizing the expeditions we turn to examine these interactions—including labor mobilization, gifting, and military support—under the lens of Sewell's approach to agency. Finding this perspective more nuanced in its approach to indigenous motivations and actions, we use it to shed interpretive light on the failure and destruction of Pardo's forts. Our point, again, is not to deny the significance of either domination or resistance for understanding colonial entanglements, but to illustrate that in cases such as ours these terms may unnecessarily constrain our interpretation of events.

THE JUAN PARDO EXPEDITIONS, 1566–68

During the first half of the sixteenth century, Spain launched many failed attempts to claim the American Southeast. Perhaps the most famous (or infamous) of these was Hernando de Soto's, which cut its ravenous swath across the Southeast from 1539 to 1543. But of the more than six hundred soldiers who began the expedition, more than half, including Soto himself, perished in La Florida. Other similarly disastrous ventures include those of Juan Ponce de León (1521), Lucas Vásquez de Ayllón (1526), Pánfilo de Narváez (1528), and Tristán de Luna y Arellano (1559–60). Although largely forgotten today, these were the first European attempts to explore the American South.

In 1565–66, after his successful expulsion of the French from La Florida, Pedro Menéndez de Avilés founded a pair of small colonies on the southern Atlantic coast: St. Augustine, established September 1565 in northern Florida, and Santa Elena, founded April 1566 on Parris Island, South Carolina; the latter was to be the principal site of Menéndez's colonial ambitions (Hoffman 1990; Hudson 1990; Lyon 1976; Paar 1999). When Spain's king, Philip II, received news of these developments, he ordered immediate reinforcement for Menéndez's colony. In July 1566, Captain Juan Pardo, a member of the king's private guard, arrived at Santa Elena with a company of 250 men and quickly began to fortify the settlement. As the Santa Elena colony was ill prepared to feed this contingent of soldiers for very long, Menéndez ordered Pardo to prepare half of his army for an expedition into the interior regions that lay behind the Atlantic coast. His task was to explore the area, claim its lands for Spain while pacifying local Indians, and find an overland route from Santa Elena to silver mines in Zacatecas, Mexico. Pardo left with 125 men on December 1, 1566. Over the following months they would revisit a small part of the path that Hernando de Soto's party had taken across the Carolinas in 1540 (Figure 2.1).

Of the first of Pardo's two expeditions into the interior, we have but a single eyewitness account—a brief and rather inattentive *relación* written by Pardo himself. This document provides few details about social relations on the Carolina Piedmont during the post-Soto era, other than the names of the places that the expedition visited and how their leaders received Pardo and his men. By combining this document with records of the second expedition, however, it has been possible to reconstruct a basic itinerary for

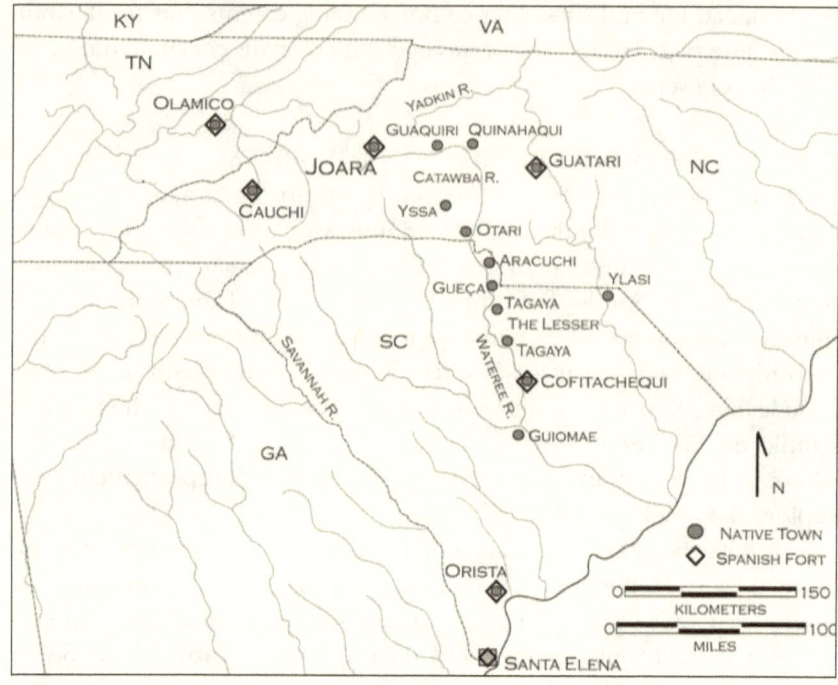

FIGURE 2.1.
Native towns visited by Juan Pardo, 1566–68.

the first (e.g., DePratter et al. 1983; Hudson 1990). After leaving Santa Elena, Pardo and his men went north for a few days across South Carolina's lightly populated inner coastal plain. The first town of note was called Guiomae, the same name as Soto's Himahi (Hudson et al. 1984:72; Hudson 1990:34). Two days later, they came to the important town of Canos, where Pardo reported that he "found a great number of caciques and Indians" (Pardo 1990:311). Fortunately, Juan de la Bandera, the expedition's notary, made two records of the second expedition and noted in the shorter of these that the Indians called this town "Canosi and, for another name, Cofetazque" (1990b:301). Thus, the place named Canos in the Pardo accounts is likely the same as Soto's Cofitachequi, one of the most powerful polities that Soto encountered east of the Appalachian Mountains (DePratter 1994; Hudson 1997:146–84; Hudson et al. 2008). Here, as at most of the important places that Pardo entered, he told the cacique and his subjects to construct a house for the expedition and to fill it with a quantity of maize for the soldiers' use.

When Pardo and his men crossed the Carolina Piedmont, it was in ferment and transition. More than two decades earlier, when Soto's army crossed this ground, Cofitachequi cast a long shadow from its location along the Wateree. During the century prior to Soto's arrival, this town appears to have precluded the growth of regional polities or chiefdoms in neighboring parts of the piedmont. Indeed, Cofitachequi was the only town where Soto encountered a chief—the famous "lady" or *cacica*—with any degree of regional, multicommunity authority. But, by the time of Pardo's arrival, Cofitachequi's power was on the wane, and as Pardo and his men would soon find, a pair of new polities were starting to coalesce just to its north. The accounts of Pardo's expeditions thus capture this social landscape at a moment of political instability, a fact that we must remember as we later seek to understand why its native peoples engaged Pardo and his men with the particular actions and strategies they did.

Pardo continued north from Canos through the Wateree-Catawba Valley, pausing at several small villages before arriving at Joara—Soto's Xualla—situated along a tributary of the upper Catawba River near the base of the Appalachian Mountains. In the fifteenth and sixteenth centuries, the upper Catawba River was among the most densely populated regions of the North Carolina Piedmont (Beck and Moore 2002; Moore 2002). More than fifty archaeological sites with Burke phase components (1400–1600) have been identified in this area and range in size from 500 m^2 to nearly 5 ha. The political center of the Joara chiefdom was the Berry site, located near modern Morganton. Berry is the largest known Burke phase site and one of the only sites in the valley with a platform mound.

Pardo's command from Menéndez had been to press over the mountains and forge a route to Mexico. At Joara, however, he could see that there was snow on the peaks that lay ahead (Martinez 1990:320), so he halted his westward push through the piedmont region. Pardo was at Joara for fifteen days, writing that its people "demanded Christians from me to catechize them" (Pardo 1990:312). Here, he built a small fort christened Fort San Juan de Joara, leaving it with thirty soldiers under the command of his sergeant, Hernando Moyano; this small outpost was the earliest European colony in the interior of what is now the United States (Beck et al. 2006:66). Our ongoing research at the Berry site, to which we will return, has identified the burned remains of Fort San Juan de Joara flanking the northern periphery of the Berry site (Beck et al. 2006).

The remainder of the army traveled northeast through the upper Catawba Valley, and after passing through an unoccupied region between the Catawba and Yadkin basins, arrived at Guatari, located in the central Yadkin Valley near present-day Salisbury, North Carolina. Pardo (1990:312) found thirty caciques and many Indians waiting to meet with him at Guatari, a clear indication of the town's prominence in 1567. Pardo stayed for just over two weeks, quickly departing for Santa Elena when he learned of a possible French military threat to the colony. He left four soldiers and a cleric, Father Sebastian Montero, to catechize the Indians, and it was here that Montero founded the first mission within the interior of North America (Hudson 1990:26).

During the six months that Pardo was at Santa Elena, Moyano, his sergeant at Fort San Juan de Joara, became enmeshed in conflicts between Joara and its adversaries across the Appalachians (Beck 1997). Francisco Martinez, who recorded testimony from four of Pardo's men at Santa Elena in July 1567, stated that Moyano left Fort San Juan on at least two occasions (Martinez 1990). On the first of these, he took twenty soldiers and perhaps a group of warriors from Joara into southern Virginia, where they attacked and destroyed a native village. Afterward, another mountain chief sent Moyano a message threatening to eat the Spaniard and his dog (probably a large mastiff). Moyano and his soldiers went back into the mountains and destroyed this chief's village too. Martinez's four informants claimed that more than two thousand Indians were killed during the attacks, but this is likely an exaggeration. Putting off their return to Joara, Moyano and his small company continued on to Chiaha, also known as Olamico, a powerful polity in eastern Tennessee. At Chiaha, they built a small fort and waited for Pardo's reinforcement.

Pardo left Santa Elena at Menéndez's command on September 1, 1567, taking 120 soldiers. As already noted, this second expedition was accompanied by an official scribe named Juan de la Bandera who kept two detailed accounts of the journey. The longer of these is particularly useful because of the data it offers on interpolity relations across the Carolina Piedmont. Pardo returned to Canos (or Cofitachequi) on September 10. Bandera notes that an impressive group of *orata* was awaiting the army at Canos, and that all of these had helped to build a large house for the Spaniards there or else had provided some maize. In the longer of his two documents, Bandera carefully distinguishes between the terms *mico* and *orata*: while the latter apparently refers to village headmen—he recorded the names of more than 120 orata during the second expedition—the former applied only to those chiefs with regional authority (e.g., Hudson 1990:63). In fact, Bandera explicitly stated that *mico* was the term used for great lords (*un gran señor*) and that *orata* was used for lesser lords (*un menor señor*) (Bandera 1990a:215). He recorded but three micos in the longer account: Joara Mico, Guatari Mico, and Olamico (Chiaha).

Thus, there was no mico present at Cofitachequi in 1567, though this was the only place in the Carolina Piedmont to which Soto applied the term in 1540. Still, Canos remained an important place, given that at least thirteen orata met there to receive Pardo; these included the leaders of Ylasi, Vehidi, Yssa, and Cataba (Bandera 1990a:260). Ylasi is probably the Ylapi of the Soto accounts, where Baltasar de Gallegos employed most of Soto's army to take some maize belonging to the cacica of Cofitachequi. Ylasi seems not to have been a subject of Canos in 1567, for while its orata did want credit for helping to build the house for the Spaniards there, he kept his maize contribution in a house he had built for that purpose in his own village (Bandera 1990a:261). Pardo continued north from Canos and visited several towns—Tagaya, Gueça, Aracuchi, and Otari—on the lower reaches of the Catawba River. Each of these towns was certainly subject to Cofitachequi in 1540, though it is unclear whether any remained so in 1567, but each had built its own wooden house for Pardo. All of the towns along the Wateree-Catawba, in fact, built such houses, a point to which we will return.

On September 24, 1567, Pardo arrived at Joara and Fort San Juan, where he learned that his sergeant, Moyano, "was gone from the fort...and that the Indians had him under siege" (Pardo 1990:313–14). Pardo and his company left at once for Chiaha, likely crossing the Appalachians through the Swannanoa Gap and then into eastern Tennessee via the Pigeon River Gap. On October 7, they arrived at Olamico, the main town of Chiaha, where they found Moyano and his men "hard pressed" but safe (Pardo 1990:314). From Chiaha they continued southwest for three days, but at Satapo, Pardo learned of a plot to ambush the expedition and decided to turn back. At Olamico, the company built Fort San Pedro, where Pardo left twenty-seven men. At Cauchi, west of present-day Asheville, North Carolina, they built another fort, San Pablo, garrisoned with eleven men (Bandera 1990a:278). On November 6, the rest of the army returned to Joara.

While the company rested, no fewer than twenty-five orata and their *mandadores* or principal men came to see Pardo at Joara, a clear consequence of the burgeoning status enjoyed by this chiefdom and its leader, Joara Mico. Some of these leaders had met with Pardo at Cauchi as he was returning across the mountains, and Hudson suggests that they may have represented Cherokee towns (Hudson 1990:88–89). Some also likely came from Burke phase communities on the upper Catawba and nearby Yadkin rivers. Bandera does report that five were "*caciques of*" Joara Mico (Bandera 1990a:278, italics added), and that their towns likely formed the core of the Joara polity (Beck and Moore 2002:201). Finally, just before Pardo left Joara, two chiefs called Chara Orata and Adini Orata—though nominally subjects of Guatari—came to switch their allegiance to Joara. To prevent hostility between Guatari and Joara, Pardo persuaded these men to continue giving their obedience in the place they were accustomed.

Leaving thirty men at Fort San Juan, Pardo and the rest of the expedition departed Joara on November 24 and arrived at Guatari on December 15. As at Cofitachequi when Soto passed through the Carolinas in 1540, the mico at Guatari was a woman; thus, two of the three micos whom Soto and Pardo met in the Carolinas were women. This is rather extraordinary given the lack of complementary evidence (archaeological or documentary) for women holding these highest seats of political leadership in other southern chiefdoms. In his account of the first expedition, Pardo states that thirty caciques met him at Guatari, the most at any town during the two expeditions. Bandera does not say how many visited during this later occasion, but the number was far less impressive. Pardo told the mico to summon her subjects to help the Spaniards build a fort, and from Bandera's list of formal gifts that Pardo made that day, it appears that about seven of the subject orata came at the mico's behest (Bandera 1990a:284). While at first this number seems low, it is close to the number that Bandera describes as "caciques of" Joara Mico.

Pardo completed Fort Santiago at Guatari on January 6, 1568. Leaving a corporal named Lucas de Canizares in command of the fort and its sixteen men, he departed on the following day with the rest of his army and arrived at Canos (or Cofitachequi) on January 23. Pardo remained at Canos for eighteen days, building another fort called Santo Tomás where he left thirty men (Bandera 1990a:292). Leaving Canos and the Carolina Piedmont, he made a strong house at the coastal-plain village of Orista and then returned to Santa Elena with fewer than a dozen men on March 2, 1568.

Shortly after Pardo's return to Santa Elena, relations between these garrisons and their indigenous hosts took a calamitous turn. By May, news reached Santa Elena that Indians had attacked all of the forts, including Fort San Juan, and that all were destroyed. Only one soldier, Juan Martín de Badajoz, is known to have escaped from the destruction by walking native trails at night and taking cover during the day. Although it is not known whether all the forts were attacked at the same time—in a strategy similar to the better-known Pueblo Revolt of 1680 (Liebmann, Chapter 10)—it is clear that none remained by June 1568. With this episode, the native peoples of the southern Appalachians emphatically rebuffed Pardo's attempt to extend Spanish ambitions into their domains, bringing to a tumultuous close Spain's last effort to claim the northern interior of its La Florida venture.

ENTANGLED AGENTS AND THE CONTEXT OF COLONIAL ACTION

It is easy to conceive these events as native resistance to a Spanish attempt at domination. Indeed, this violent rejection of Spain's presence offers a gift-wrapped package for such treatment. However, such an approach also perpetuates an insidious assumption that in any colonial interaction it was inevitably the Indians seeking to resist the might of the Europeans, and, moreover, that the arrival of Europeans on the North American continent was inevitably disastrous for all Native Americans. While this claim is certainly true when applied to the macronarrative of the Columbian Exchange, it is less helpful for understanding any particular context of colonial entanglement. Indeed, it may obfuscate variability in the kinds of interactions between native peoples and Europeans in different times and places. In some cases, as in the expeditions of Juan Pardo, the arrival of Europeans played into the hands of native peoples engaged in their own local contexts of competition, alliance, and exchange (Preucel, Chapter 11). An approach based in agency—rather than based on resistance per se—offers a more nuanced understanding of colonial entanglements and allows us to focus on these local contexts of action. We are not suggesting that resistance and agency are contradictory concepts, but rather that framing this particular engagement in terms of agency might better direct our attention to the indigenous perspective, thereby helping us to avoid treating native motivation as mere reaction or response.

Here we adopt a perspective on agency advocated by sociologist William Sewell Jr. (2005). This is not the place to present a fuller explication of Sewell's theory (see Beck et al. 2007), but we do need to briefly summarize his approach. At the heart of Sewell's theory is the concept of structure. Expanding the work of Anthony Giddens, Sewell makes an explicit case that social structures consist of material or actual resources and virtual schemas. Sewell's schemas, like Giddens's rules, are "generalizable procedures applied in the enactment/reproduction of social life" (Sewell 2005:131). Schemas are not context dependent (i.e., they are generalizable) and can be transposed to cultural contexts beyond those for which they were originally learned; this makes schemas virtual, as "they can be actualized in a potentially broad and unpredetermined range of situations" (Sewell 2005:131). Resources are actual in that any opportunity to mobilize them in social action is fixed to place, time, and quantity (Sewell 2005:133). Resources therefore implicate, as they are recursively implicated by, their associated schemas:

> A factory is not an inert pile of bricks, wood, and metal. It incorporates or actualizes schemas, and this means that the schemas can be inferred from the material form of the factory. The factory gate, the punching-in station, the design of the assembly line: all of these features of the factory teach and validate the rules of the capitalist contract. (Sewell 2005:136)

He uses this relationship to define agency as the "capacity to reinterpret and mobilize an array of resources in terms of cultural schemas other than those that initially constituted the array" (2005:142–43). Not only is structural change the outcome of human agency, but agency itself is defined as the capacity to effect structural change.

With Sewell's perspective in mind, and from the viewpoint of native polities such as Joara, Canos, or Guatari, we may imagine that the Pardo expeditions themselves were an array of resources, one with the potential to be mobilized by indigenous peoples toward a range of political, economic, and military ends. We believe it is especially important to keep in mind that the people of Joara—from Joara Mico down—had no knowledge of what Spain's colonial machinery had accomplished in other parts of the Americas. They had no reason to fear Juan Pardo and his men as representatives of the greatest empire in the world or to gauge their own actions accordingly. Instead, they understood the Spanish occupation of their town in terms of their own cultural knowledge and experience, their social structures for integrating resources and schemas. Thus, we will only understand the motivations of leaders such as Joara Mico by focusing on the local, indigenous contexts of their political action (see Liebmann, Chapter 10; Preucel, Chapter 11; Sheptak et al., Chapter 8, for the analytical value of situating colonial entanglements within the realm of intraindigenous politics). We now turn to examine three kinds of interaction between Spanish soldiers and their Indian hosts—labor mobilization, gift exchange, and military support—to see if our approach casts a different light on these entanglements than the concepts of resistance or domination may cast alone.

Labor Mobilization

First is the native practice of building houses for the Pardo expedition, which could easily fit within a narrative of Spanish domination, or at least of indigenous acquiescence to Spanish authority. At many of the towns where Pardo stopped during his first expedition, he commanded native inhabitants to build structures, presumably as way stations along his proposed road to Mexico, and to subsequently fill some portion of them with

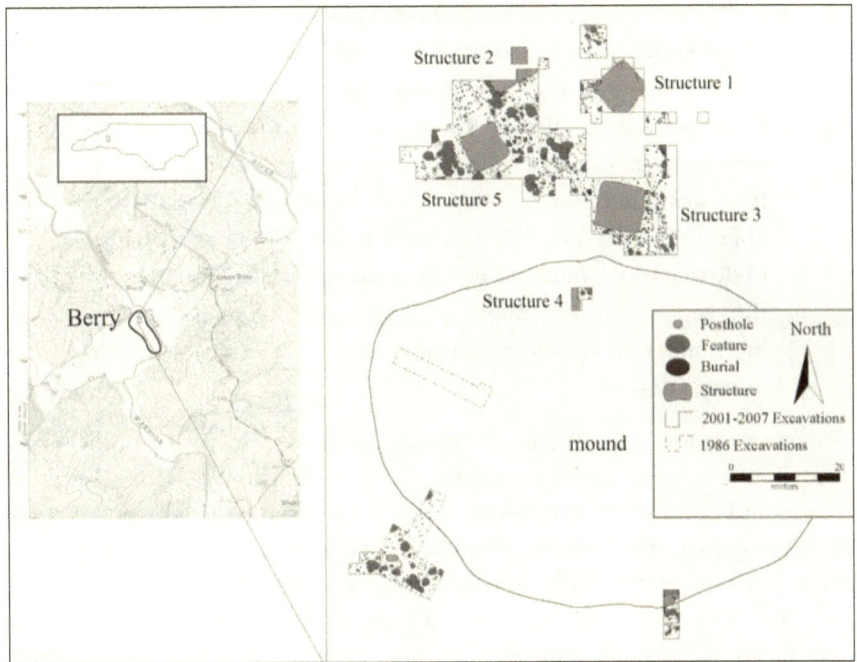

FIGURE 2.2.
Excavations at the Berry site, 1986–2007.

maize. When Pardo retraced his route several months later, Bandera noted that large new houses awaited the company in all of the native towns where Pardo had made such a request, and even in a few where he apparently had not. At the Berry site, the five burned structures associated with Fort San Juan (Figure 2.2) may be typical in size and form of the houses that native leaders at other towns and villages built for the expedition. These five are all quite large by piedmont standards and would clearly have represented an outlay of labor and resources. Many of the buildings also held stores of maize, nominally collected for use by the expedition, but likewise requiring an investment of time and labor.

Pardo and Bandera interpreted the construction of these buildings as evidence of indigenous submission to Spanish authority (cf. Voss, Chapter 12). Pardo indicates as much, writing that when his first expedition came to Canos, "I found a great number of caciques and Indians and I made them the customary speech on behalf of God and His Majesty. They were very content and obedient to the service of God and His Majesty" (1990:311). And when Pardo returned to Canos several months later, Bandera (1990a:260) noted that:

> before now it had been declared and said unto them by the captain how they were to make the house and maize which they had for His Majesty, and that it was suitable for them to turn Christian and be under his dominion...and...now that His Grace saw that they actually fulfill the things stated above, it is necessary that in the presence of me, the notary, they ratify and approve it. They...declared and said that they will be very happy to do that which has been commanded and declared to them by the captain in His Majesty's name and as such, remaining...under the said dominion, they made the "Yaa," which I, the notary, attest.

Later events would emphatically reveal the degree to which both Pardo and Bandera were mistaken about native submission to His Majesty at Canos and other piedmont towns. In fact, for us to use the concept of resistance to explain the Indians' ultimate rejection of the Spaniards is to reify the latter's line of thought. That is, resistance suggests that the act of building one of these houses represents a temporary loss or a ceding of local autonomy to Spanish authority, an acquiescence that was, in the end, rescinded. Instead, we might need to look more broadly at the indigenous political context for these actions.

Canos—better known as Cofitachequi—was one of the most important places where Pardo requested that a house be built for the Spaniards. As many as a dozen chiefs from nearby towns met with Pardo while he rested there during his first expedition, and it was expected that all of these orata would assist in building the house at Canos and help fill a portion of it with maize. When Pardo returned here during the second expedition, he met again with most of these leaders, all of whom wanted credit for having done their part in making the house. One of these, Ylasi Orata, wanted credit for helping build the house at Canos but was holding his maize contribution in a house he had built for that purpose in his own town. In 1540, when Soto crossed the same region, Ylasi was subject to Canos (the latter keeping a corncrib there to store its tribute), but by making his own structure and filling it with maize, Ylasi Orata was demonstrating—both to Pardo and to Canos—that he was no longer obligated to pay tribute at another town. We suggest that such a motivation likely applied to other peoples along Pardo's path; specifically, making a house for Pardo's expedition became a means for expressing one's autonomy relative to other indigenous towns and polities, and was more a statement about long-simmering and contested local relations than a temporary bow to Spanish authority.

Beyond the opportunity to demonstrate autonomy with respect to other towns and polities, building a house and providing it with a store of maize also allowed some chiefs to coordinate labor on a regional scale and to show their capacity for such expenditures to other leaders and to the Spaniards. At Guatari, Joara, and Canos, for example, it is clear that labor was drawn from neighboring towns and villages. Bandera again reports that seven orata and their associates came when summoned by Guatari Mico. This capacity was not shared by all of the towns that built houses for the expedition—for example, smaller villages such as Ylasi, Tagaya, Otari, and Aracuchi. Thus the act of building a house for these Spaniards also gave some emerging leaders—especially those such as Joara Mico and Guatari Mico, who seem to have lacked regional stature at the time of the Soto expedition—the opportunity to improve their positions at the multicommunity scale.

Gift Exchange

Initially at least, the Pardo expeditions afforded many native leaders an opportunity to acquire exotic European trade goods. Pardo made formal presentations of these goods to the chiefs who came to visit with him and appears to have been particularly generous, not surprisingly, to the leaders of those towns where he garrisoned a fort. Bandera made very meticulous notes about the materials that Pardo presented as gifts, including necklaces of beads (probably glass and brass or copper); small iron chisels, wedges, and knives; pieces of taffeta cloth, silk, and satin; iron axes of various sizes; ball buttons; and small mirrors. During his second expedition, Pardo gave away twenty-nine necklaces, 126 chisels and wedges, thirty-two knives, thirty-five plain or socketed axes, six mirrors, several ball buttons, and many swatches of fabric or textile (Hudson 1990:135–38). These materials were quickly distributed across a wide swath of the Carolinas and nearby areas, as it is clear from the Pardo accounts that many chiefs traveled large distances, sometimes more than one hundred miles, to meet with Pardo and receive a gift for their efforts. Pardo seems to have taken care to distribute these gifts through proper channels of local authority so that native leaders could use these exotic resources to bolster relations with their subjects and with one another. It is significant in this respect that the detailed lists of supplies that Bandera recorded for each of Pardo's six garrisons included no specific trade materials, a point to which we will return.

Numerous examples of such European trade items, all or most of which are likely associated with the Pardo expeditions, are known from Burke phase contexts. During the late 1880s, Smithsonian archaeologists excavating at several burial mounds in the Happy Valley section of the upper Yadkin River—about twenty miles from the Berry site, as the crow flies—recovered two iron chisels, a small iron axe, an iron spike set in a bone handle, and a piece of an iron blade from Burke phase burials (Moore 2002; Thomas 1894). Moore's (2002) analysis of upper Yadkin ceramics indicates a very close relationship between the people of this area and those of the upper Catawba during the mid-sixteenth century, and the individuals buried with these European items in the upper Yadkin were likely among the orata who visited Juan Pardo at Joara in 1567. Significantly, these individuals were also buried with items of native manufacture usually interpreted as markers of status in Late Mississippian societies, including stone spatulate celts and engraved shell gorgets. At Berry, we have recovered more than two dozen glass and rolled brass beads—probably lost from necklaces intended for exchange—since 2001. Also, David Moore recovered an iron knife from a burial that he excavated as part of his dissertation work in 1986 (Moore 2002:235–36). The knife lay across the upper chest of a male individual and may have been worn suspended from the neck.

In summary, the Pardo expeditions provided local leaders over a wide swath of the Carolina Piedmont access to exotic materials that easily fit within native contexts for status and exchange relations. Moreover, the opportunity to receive such goods attracted many leaders to those towns situated along Pardo's path, particularly those where he built forts. From this perspective, hosting such a garrison was likely far from an imposition to mico and orata—at least at first—but appears instead to have offered a means of increasing one's stature at the local and regional scale, particularly in relation to those chiefs lacking such direct access to the Spaniards and forced to make long treks to participate in these Spanish–native exchange relations.

Military Support

During the six months between Pardo's first and second expeditions, Hernando Moyano, the sergeant whom Pardo placed in charge of Fort San Juan, became embroiled in the violent conflicts between Joara and its adversaries across the Appalachians. According to the statement of Francisco Martinez, Moyano left Fort San Juan on at least two occasions to attack unfriendly villages in present-day southwestern Virginia and eastern Tennessee. Each time, Moyano took twenty of his men across the mountains, and though it is unstated in Martinez's account, the Spaniards were probably accompanied by a contingent of warriors from Joara. It is unclear what events precipitated the first of these excursions, although it seems most likely that there were long-standing hostilities between these mountain towns and the people of Joara. With the second case, it is clear from Martinez that another chief personally threatened Moyano, with the result that his village was destroyed by the Spaniards and their allies. Unfortunately, while the Martinez document is brief and provides little explicit detail about relationships between Joara and its neighbors, it seems quite likely, if we read between the lines, that Joara Mico successfully entangled Moyano in his own local politics, using the Spanish presence as a resource to intimidate or remove potential rivals. We therefore need to envision Moyano's forays across the Appalachians as more than a simple case of Spanish malfeasance. Instead, Joara Mico may have successfully used the Spaniards—whether they knew it or not—to further his own political and military ends. We suggest that Joara Mico's actions are more easily understood through Sewell's concept of agency than within a framework of domination and resistance.

THE FAILURE OF PARDO'S FORTS

Finally, we would like to consider the destruction of Fort San Juan and the rest of Pardo's undermanned garrisons during the spring of 1568. As we noted at the beginning of this chapter, it is all too easy to interpret this series of events as the ultimate act of resistance—the violent rejection of Spain's colonial enterprise. And yet the people of Joara and other towns had little knowledge of Spain's broader ambitions and indeed had no way of knowing that they were challenging the mightiest empire in the world at the time. We believe that such an understanding of indigenous actions, while not necessarily inaccurate, does misleadingly imply that the only relationships of consequence here were those between the Spaniards and their resisting native hosts. On the contrary, and as our previous discussion suggests, actions the native leaders undertook in their entanglements with the Pardo expedition often had more to do with political positioning relative to other native leaders and towns than to the Spaniards themselves. This is not to suggest that the soldiers at Pardo's forts had not worn out their welcome, but rather that the native attacks on these forts and their aftermath are not reducible to such a tidy interpretation. Evidence from the Berry site may offer dramatic evidence of a more thickly layered set of aims and motivations on the part of Joarans when they destroyed Fort San Juan.

The Weakening of Spanish–Native Relations at Joara

Even before the fall of the Spanish occupation at Joara, there is new evidence that relations between the Spaniards and Joarans had already begun to fray. We have thus far excavated two of the burned buildings associated with the Spanish compound, Structure 1 and Structure 5. As is evident in Figure 2.2, Structure 5 was built atop a mass of large pit features. There are at least six such pits in the area under or immediately around this building, and most of these pits we have excavated contain Spanish artifacts (Beck et al. 2006: table 1). There are no such pit features in the area under or immediately around Structure 1. Looking at the broader scale of the entire compound, these large features are concentrated in the western section with Structures 2 and 5, while the eastern section with Structures 1 and 3 is relatively free of these pits. We believe that Structures 1 and 3 were probably built first, and that the mass of pits in the western section of the compound were dug in association with the construction and use of these first two buildings. Structures 2 and 5 were built later and are thus intrusive into those pits that define this area. Since we believe that all of these buildings were burned at the same time, when the people of Joara burned Fort San Juan, this interpretation of a construction sequence implies that Structure 1 was used for longer than Structure 5, an implication borne out by recent work.

Our excavations in 2007 and 2008, supported by funds from the National Science Foundation, have revealed that Structure 1 had two superimposed hearths located at the center of the building, one associated with its original floor surface and the other associated with the surface in use when the building burned. Structure 5, by contrast, had only one hearth stage and no evidence of multiple floor surfaces. We feel confident suggesting, then, that Structure 1 saw longer use than Structure 5. We should also point out, though, that neither building appears to have been in use for an extended period. Neither exhibits any evidence of rebuilding and neither was rebuilt after being consumed by fire.

A more obvious difference between the buildings is the time expended in the preparation of the structural surfaces and entryways. While Structure 1 (Figure 2.3) exhibited a clearly defined house basin, a pair of deep entrance trenches, and four central support posts—all typical of native-style Mississippian houses in the South Appalachian area—Structure 5 is more ephemeral in comparison, lacking a clearly defined house basin, entrance trenches, or central support posts. In fact, the posts themselves bring up another point of comparison. Many of the wall posts in Structure 5 display an unusual pattern, in that the postholes are quite large in relation to the actual posts. This would undoubtedly have caused problems with stability, and indeed one of these postholes contained a large fragment of wrought iron jammed between the edge of the post and its posthole as a possible

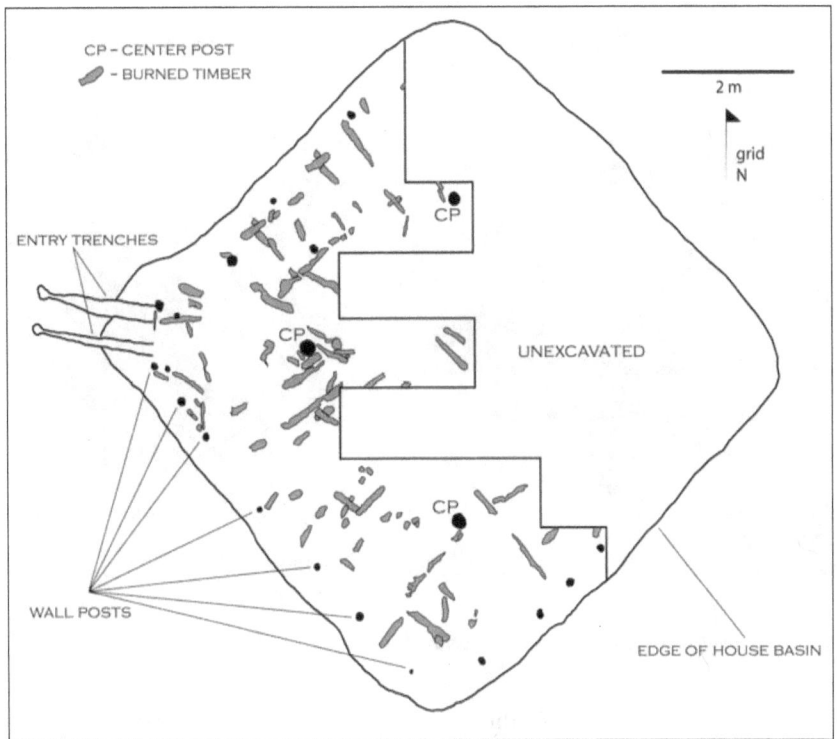

FIGURE 2.3.
Excavations in Structure 1, showing center posts, wall posts, and entry trenches.

shim (Figure 2.4). In Structure 1, however, all of the posts were rammed into place. We believe that the postholes of Structure 5 were dug with metal tools, perhaps with the shovels we know that Pardo left for his soldiers at Fort San Juan.

What can these architectural details tell us about relations between Spaniards and Indians at Fort San Juan? Here we will offer some preliminary observations. Structure 1 was built in a manner typical of Mississippian buildings in our study area. This in no way contradicts our interpretation of the building as a house for Pardo's soldiers because the Pardo documents evince that Late Mississippian people built such structures for the expedition at many towns in the Carolina Piedmont, including Joara. Structure 5 is an interesting comparison, in that it seems to be much more of an expedient construction. If Structure 1 were built at the beginning of the Spanish occupation of Joara—during the first winter—then both its style and the techniques of its construction indicate a high degree of cooperation

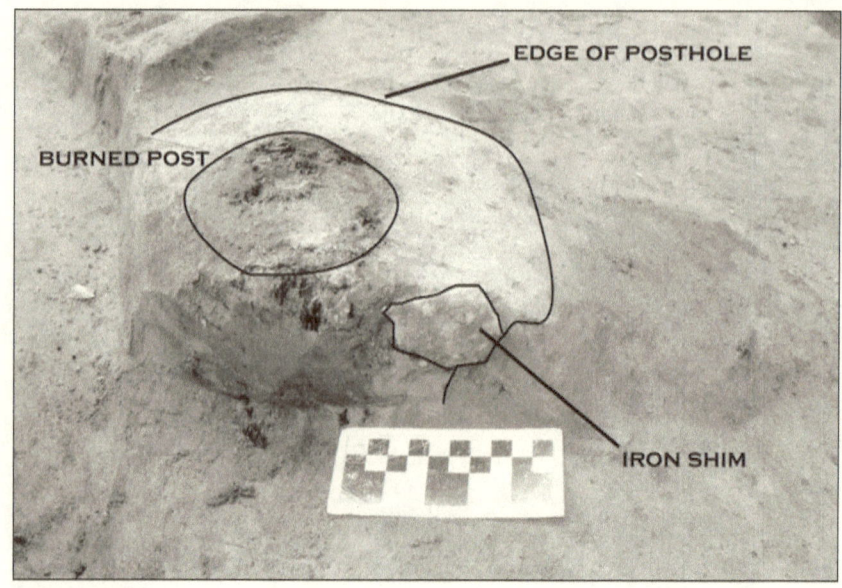

FIGURE 2.4.
Possible wrought iron shim in posthole, Structure 5.

between the Spaniards and the native Joarans. While we have yet to conduct excavations in Structure 3, its location in the eastern part of the compound suggests that a similar interpretation may be warranted. By the time that Structure 5 was built—probably prior to the second winter—it appears that Joarans were supplying the Spaniards with little expertise or support. Rather, its flimsy or expedient character suggests that it and perhaps Structure 2 were built by people with less skill at the construction of such houses. The archaeology of the Spanish compound tells us as much about the fluid and changing native perceptions of the Spaniards in their midst as it does about the Spaniards themselves. As Barbara Voss shows (Chapter 12), the architecture of a colonial encounter is more than just an architecture of the colonizer: it situates in time and space the dynamic relationships between—in our case—would-be colonizers and the indigenous peoples who brought their own agendas to the encounter.

The Destruction of Fort San Juan

By late May 1568, news arrived at Santa Elena that Indians had attacked all the interior forts, and that all had fallen. It is unclear whether every fort was surprised at the same time, in an action prefiguring the better-known Pueblo Revolt of 1680 (see Liebmann, Chapter 10), but it is clear that none remained by June 1568 (Hudson 1990:176). Several factors appear to have played a role in the Indians' decision to destroy the forts, but two stand out: Spanish demands for food and the soldiers' improprieties with native women. With respect to the provisioning of Pardo's forts, there was probably a great deal of miscommunication between Spaniards and Indians about the presentation of food. By the spring of 1568, the soldiers at the forts may have had few trade goods left to offer in exchange for maize and the other foodstuffs they received from their native hosts. From the Spaniards' perspective, this was fair and just, as the Indians of the Carolina Piedmont were now their subjects, having formally made the "Yaa," and they therefore owed the Spanish Crown—and the men who served as its military stand-ins—continued sustenance as tax or tribute. And yet from the indigenous perspective, the soldiers were no longer fulfilling their part of an exchange relationship, such that they owed the Spaniards nothing (e.g., Mallios 2006).

Sexual politics seem to have played a significant role in the forts' destruction. At the town of Guatari, for example, Bandera (1990a:285) recorded that "the captain commanded him [the corporal placed in charge of Fort Santiago] in the name of His Majesty...that no one should dare bring any woman into the fort at night and that he should not depart from the command under pain of being severely punished." However, Teresa Martín, a native woman taken to Santa Elena on Pardo's second expedition and wife of Juan Martín de Badajoz (believed to be the only survivor of the attack on the forts), testified to Governor Canço in 1600 that the men waited "three of four moons" for Pardo to return to the interior, and that when he had failed to do so they began to commit improprieties with native women, angering their men (Hudson 1990:176). We recognize that there are many ways to interpret these "improprieties" and acknowledge that sexual violence may have played a role in the ultimate destruction of Pardo's forts. But we should not generalize all such relationships without better documentary support. During the early 1700s, for example, indigenous women across the piedmont actively sought and maintained sexual relations with English traders, and we see no reason to assume that native women lacked such agency during the occupation of Fort San Juan. In fact, Indian women from the interior later married two of Pardo's soldiers. So while it is possible that sexual violence occurred at Joara, we have no direct historical evidence for it and some good reasons for believing that native–Spanish sexual relations here were more complex than this. As with other aspects of the entanglement, we must situate sex in its appropriate social-historical context.

In any event, 130 soldiers and all six of the forts were lost, and with them Spain's only attempt to colonize the deep interior of northern La Florida. Indeed, the destruction of Pardo's forts precipitated the shrinking of Spain's claims in the American Southeast. Virginia, known as Ajacán, was abandoned in 1571 after a brief, disastrous mission attempt. Santa Elena, too, was finally abandoned in 1587, after which time Spain's territorial holdings in the Southeast were largely limited to modern-day Florida. Even so, no Europeans penetrated as far into the southern interior as Soto and Pardo until the second half of the seventeenth century.

The failure of Fort San Juan also may have changed the native political landscape more durably than we might expect, given the brief span of its occupation. At Berry, much of the mound's construction may have postdated the burning of the fort. Evidence from David Moore's 1986 excavations offers intriguing support for this possibility. Two fragments of olive jars and one piece of lead sprue were recovered from a partially intact humus zone overlaying moundfill on the south margin of the mound. During the time that the zone was forming, this part of the mound was only about 1 m high (Moore 2002:220, Figure 2.3), suggesting a low earthen feature similar to those that Cyrus Thomas described in Caldwell County in his reports on the Smithsonian's Yadkin River fieldwork. If so, then most of the mound's volume was added *after* the humus zone formed—and thus after these olive jar sherds and lead sprue were deposited—as we know that the Berry mound eventually attained a height of at least 4 m (Thomas 1891:151). While careful stratigraphic analysis is needed to resolve the temporal context of the mound, it is possible that the people of Joara used the destruction of Fort San Juan to consolidate political authority in the upper Catawba and neighboring regions, a triumph they celebrated in the expansion of their mound into a true platform.

If we may assume then that the Spaniards had already worn out their welcome by sometime in the spring of 1568, and that the material resources they demanded from Joarans (namely food and native women) were no longer matched by the resources they offered in return, then Joara Mico may have used his attack as a demonstration of strength—not to the Spaniards, of course, but to his neighbors. Platform mounds are quite uncommon here, and it may only have been in the aftermath of the fort's destruction that Joara Mico earned the political capital to sponsor such a monument's enlargement. Documents from the Pardo expeditions suggest that Joara Mico was actively trying to consolidate or expand his authority at the time of the expeditions, and we believe that the destruction of Fort San Juan may have offered him an opportunity to do so.

CONCLUSION

In summary, we find the concepts of domination and resistance too restrictive for the context of the Juan Pardo expeditions. We do not doubt that there are many parts of the Americas where these terms provide a solid foundation for understanding indigenous interactions with Spain. However, it may be the case that these concepts fare less well in areas where Spain fared less well, in areas where the duration of the entanglement was relatively brief and where Spain failed to establish a long-term institutional presence. Rather, we have tried to show how native polities of the Carolina Piedmont mobilized resources of the Pardo expeditions—human and non-human alike—for their own political, economic, and military ends. This approach turns our focus away from mere reaction and onto the native context of motivated action or agency.

3

Native American Resistance to Spanish Presence in Hispaniola and La Florida, ca. 1492–1650

Kathleen Deagan

The Spanish invasion of the Caribbean in 1492 and Florida in 1513 provoked the earliest episodes of Native American resistance to European presence in the Americas. In both areas, native military resistance to the Spanish arrival was immediate, organized, and sustained, and played out as a struggle between two sovereign powers—one indigenous and one invading. The goal of the native people of the Caribbean and Florida in this struggle was to destroy and drive out the Spaniards, and the goal of the Spaniards was to conquer, claim, and control the indigenous American people and their territory (Figure 3.1).

Despite early successes, however, the Spaniards ultimately defeated the organized military resistance of the native people in these regions through a combination of introduced disease, technology, and cultural patterns of warfare (Cook 1998; Dobyns 1983; Sauer 1966; Wilson 1990), giving way to different, essentially nonmilitary forms of coercion, resistance, and accommodation. From a Spanish perspective, "pacification" had occurred by 1500 in Hispaniola, and by about 1650 in La Florida (the region of what is now the southeastern United States that was initially claimed by Spain, extending southward from the Chesapeake Bay and eastward from the Mississippi River).

FIGURE 3.1.
Detail of title page engraving from the Historia general de los hechos de los castellanos en las islas i tierra firme del mar oceano, *by Antonio de Herrera y Ordesillas and Andrés González de Barcía Carballido y Zúñiga (1726), depicting the 1495 Battle of the Vega Real in Hispaniola between Spaniards and Taínos. Madrid, Spain: Imprento real de Nicolas Rodiguea [sic] Franco. Courtesy the P.K. Yonge Library of Florida History, University of Florida (image provided from the library's copy).*

Resistance to Spanish presence and policy nevertheless continued throughout the colonial period, shifting, however, from a scenario of open conflict between two acknowledged enemies to one of an occupied people confronting a newly imposed ruling regime through both overt rebellion and covert resistance.

NATIVE AMERICAN RESISTANCE IN HISPANIOLA AND LA FLORIDA

The nature of Spanish engagement with indigenous people of the Caribbean and La Florida also changed after political and military domination by Spain was claimed. Instead of concentrating on gaining political and territorial control through force, Spanish policy became explicit in its goal to control and change the lives and minds of the people they saw as their newly acquired subjects and *peones* (peasant laborers). Central to this intention was religious conversion to Catholicism, life in settled towns, and "hispanicization"—living like Spaniards in matters both material and spiritual. Christianity and social identity were inextricably linked in the Spanish world view, and this position was explicitly codified in the Spanish imperial project (see, for example, discussions by Elliot 2006:133–44; Hanke 1949; and MacAlister 1984:391–97).

Because of this very explicit social agenda for dominance, it has been possible for archaeologists and historians in some settings to assess the degree to which these mandates were embraced, accommodated, altered, and rejected in daily practice by conquered people in America. This chapter considers (with emphasis on archaeologically generated insights) some of the expressions of Native American resistance to Spanish presence in Hispaniola and La Florida between 1492 and about 1650, and the new forms of cultural engagement generated as a consequence.

INDIGENEITY AND RESISTANCE

Resistance to Spanish imperial mandates and colonization practice was manifested in America quite rapidly by many other ethnic/racial groups, both in concert with and independently from Native Americans. This was particularly evident after Spanish forms of dominance and political dominion shifted from military to social and ideological. Both overt resistance and "everyday forms of resistance" (Scott 1985) to the Spanish mandate to live like Spaniards and to obey Spanish laws were in many ways manifested along class (rather than racial or ethnic) divisions in the regions of Florida and Hispaniola and, as historians such as David Weber (1992) and John Kessell (1997) suggest, in many other frontier regions as well. I would argue (and am certainly not the first to do so for this region; e.g., Guitar 1998; Landers 1990, 2006) that alliances among indigenous people, enslaved and free Africans, white creoles, and mixed-race people proved to be among the most potent forces in successfully subverting the ruling Spanish intentions. Considered from a material practice perspective, it was nonviolent resistance to the proscribed Spanish intent by all of these people who lacked formal authority that ultimately recast the Spanish American Empire and its policies.

This observation underscores the difficulty of counterposing *indigenous* with *Spanish* as analytical categories for purposes of studying resistance, which Murphy and Liebmann pointed out in the symposium on which this volume is based. Conflating the notion of indigeneity with *Native American* potentially confines the discussion to racial rather than social terms, in that it excludes many second and third generation black and white creole residents of the Americas who, as Charlton and Fournier illustrate (Chapter 7) did not consider themselves to be either Spaniards or Native Americans. They nevertheless effectively resisted Spanish hegemony, often in concert with indigenous Americans. Considering Native Americans in isolation artificially fragments the landscape of resistance to Spanish domination during the colonial era.

OPERATIONALIZING RESISTANCE

As most scholars recognize, the concept of resistance itself is also highly problematic, despite its popularity as a research focus over the past twenty years. Critiques of resistance studies (e.g., Brown 1996; Hollander and Einwohner 2004; Hoffman 1999; Ortner 1995; Schaffer 1995) have pointed out that notions of resistance, like power, are social constructs and are multidimensional, multiscalar, contextual, and fluid, both on the parts of those performing resistance and by those interpreting it. A focus on resistance and domination is sometimes accused of being "ethnographically thin," based on essentialized oppositions, and without a full consideration of the internal complexities and power relations in both the dominant and subaltern groups (Ortner 1995). It is difficult to resist imputing intentional resistance to practices that appear not to conform to hegemonic norms, particularly when we work through material culture. Ethnographic work with living people has, however, shown that subjects studied and characterized as practicing resistance to imposed power often disagree with ethnographers about their roles as "resisters" (Hoffman 1999; Brown 1996).

What is resistance in one setting is conformity to cultural mores in another. Lip piercing on a teenager may display resistance to parental wishes but may also display a need to conform to teen peer group values and norms. Tattoos on neo-Nazi youths display resistance to government-sanctioned American values of racial tolerance and diversity but also conformance to neo-Nazi peer group identity and values. The delineation of resistance in symbolic terms therefore depends greatly on context, which poses special concerns for archaeologists.

Tension often exists between accommodation and resistance, in that resistance is often ambiguous and rarely expressed in a pure form, as nearly all of the contributors to this volume point out from their distinct contextual perspectives. For example, as Melissa Murphy and her colleagues (Chapter 4) and Jeffrey Quilter (Chapter 6) suggest, Native American Christian burial in a Catholic church accompanied by traditional grave goods may imply elements of both accommodation and resistance. We might also consider the ambivalence inherent in a Native American woman marrying a Spanish man but insisting on retaining traditional indigenous household practices.

Such concerns led Michael Brown to suggest that "lingering uncertainty about the rules by which one makes valid analytical claims" exists in studies of resistance, and that they therefore often devolve into romanticized accounts of struggle in which the researcher becomes the hero (Brown 1996:731-33). Little seems to have been resolved analytically over the past decade. In 2004, still perplexed by the ambiguity of much of the work on resistance, sociologists Jocelyn Hollander and Rachel Einwohner surveyed social science literature to learn how the notion of resistance is conceptualized across disciplines (Hollander and Einwohner 2004). They found "considerable agreement about two core elements of resistance (action and opposition) and about what we have called 'overt' resistance, which is intended by the actor and recognized by both targets and observers. We found disagreement, however, about the limits of the concept, prompted by various writers' attempts to extend the concept in different ways. We have argued that two issues—recognition and intent—lie at the heart of these disagreements" (Hollander and Einwohner 2004:547).

This concern about whether "resistance" must incorporate or can be separated either from intentionality on the part of a "resister" or recognition on the part of a "dominator" is unresolved and perhaps should remain so. Different historical and cultural contexts and different questions about them may require flexible approaches to conceptualizing resistance. The suggestion that "cultural resistance can be located within any contrary practice where knowledge exists of the alternatives" (Pauketat 2001:13), for example, may be useful in understanding how cultural traditions, constructed through often unconscious practice and often with unintended consequences, persist in a context of change. In circumstances of overt, externally imposed power asymmetry, however, such as those presented by invasion and colonization, such a broadly constructed notion of resistance is less useful. In this discussion of Spaniards and Native Americans in the Caribbean and Florida, I refer to resistance as a conscious decision to oppose the imposition of ideas, practices, or beliefs by a dominant entity.

In this sense, "resistance" is not equated either with survival or with agency. Forms of conscious resistance range from overt and often violent confrontations to the covert "everyday forms of resistance" as made explicit by James Scott (1985). Everyday or covert resistance does not seek the overthrow of the power-imposing entity but rather to mitigate or subvert its mandates, intentions, and effects. I would include within this the notion of resistance by indifference—choosing to ignore the imposition of ideas, practices, or beliefs, despite a mandate on the part of the powerful to embrace them.

HISPANIOLA

The first Spaniards to arrive in America—the 150 men who crewed Columbus's three ships in 1492—were met by the people of the Caribbean with amazement, hospitality, and suspicion, but not with overt resistance. That changed in 1493. The wreck of the *Santa María* on Christmas Eve of 1492 forced Columbus to leave thirty-nine Spaniards in the village of the Taíno cacique Guacanagarí, which Columbus claimed to have renamed "La Navidad." Guacanagarí's town is thought to correspond to the archaeological site in Haiti known as "En Bas Saline" (Deagan 1987, 2004). Within nine months, all of the Spaniards had been killed and their settlement destroyed (Deagan 1987).

The violent suppression of the Spaniards at La Navidad was the first known instance of overt resistance to Spanish presence by American Indians, and it was successful. Columbus, on his return journey in 1493, abandoned his plan to establish a settlement at La Navidad and instead sailed westward to build the town of La Isabela, which he fortified heavily against the Taíno (Deagan and Cruxent 2002).

The Taíno's first organized military confrontation with the Spaniards under Columbus took place in 1495, in the central Vega Real of Hispaniola (today the Dominican Republic). By 1498, the allied Taíno forces had been vanquished by Spanish attacks, famine, and devastating population losses through epidemic disease, and as a consequence Columbus imposed tribute on the Taíno. (See Wilson 1990 and Sauer 1966 for comprehensive treatments of these events.)

The institution of *encomienda* was formally implemented in America in 1503. Spanish governors assigned tracts of land and all of the Taínos who lived on it to individual Spaniards (*encomenderos*), who retained hereditary rights to their encomiendas. The Taíno residents of the encomienda lands were obliged to exchange their labor for instruction in Christianity and "civilization." Hereditary encomiendas were outlawed in 1542, although the use of Indian labor was continued through the *repartimiento* system, whereby the government could temporarily assign Indians (but not their lands) to individual Spaniards for periodic labor (Kirkpatrick 1939; MacAlister 1984:157–66). Under both encomienda and repartimiento, labor drafts were imposed on Indian towns, and workers were assigned Spanish mines and plantations for several months at a time, returning to their home villages after their work periods. These labor exploitation patterns were distinct from the practice of *reducción*, in which entire towns were relocated and combined at new locations. Reducciones in Florida and the Caribbean were most often implemented under the guise of religious instruction and indoctrination, but convenience of labor consolidation was not ignored.

Under all of these systems, however, labor was organized and mediated through the Taíno caciques (Arranz Marquéz 1991; Moya Pons 1992). Spanish acknowledgment and respect for chiefly status was explicitly articulated from the first days of contact in 1492 onward and quickly became a central element of Spanish policy regarding the American Indians (see, for example, Ramos Gómez 1993:124–67; Hanke 1949; Hussey 1932). This elite alliance helped to forge and underscore the class-based nature of postpacification resistance, in that resistance to labor regimes by Native Americans was resistance to both Spanish and elite Taíno domination. This is expressed archaeologically in the very nonrandom distribution of European (that is, "exotic") materials in the few post-Columbian Taíno sites that have been excavated, with European objects clearly concentrated in elite residential or burial contexts (Deagan 2004; García Arévalo 1990; Vega 1979a).

Despite the military and political subjugation of the Taíno, overt resistance to Spanish invasion and occupation persisted for decades in the Caribbean. After about 1518, when the importation of African slaves to the Caribbean began, Indian rebels were joined by escaped Africans (Altman 2007; Deive 1989; Landers 2006). Many Taínos and Africans simply left their sites of labor and fled to mountainous regions or to other islands to live in isolated, illicit *cimarrón* communities (that is, illicit refuges from Spanish control).

The most important and effective indigenous uprising against the Spaniards in the Caribbean, which was known as the "Bahoruco War," took place from 1519 until 1532 (Altman 2007; Las Casas 1951 (II): 259–61; Mira Caballos 1997:312–29). It was organized and led by the charismatic Taíno leader known as Enriquillo, who was a Taíno cacique in Hispaniola. He had been taken as a child by the Franciscan friars, who raised and educated him as a literate Christian. After an attack on his wife by the encomendero to whom his town had been assigned, Enriquillo organized a force of more than 100 Taínos and established a settlement in the remote

Bahoruco Mountains. They were soon joined by escaped African slaves, who had just arrived in the Caribbean, as well as other Taíno caciques and their subjects, who included a number of mestizos (people of mixed European and American Indian parentage). Enriquillo's guerilla forces attacked Spanish settlements for fourteen years, and in 1532 the Spanish authorities finally offered a peace treaty. It gave Enriquillo freedom, lands, and an encomienda but unfortunately did nothing to alter the abusive labor and race-based power practices that had provoked the rebellion (see Altman 2007; Mira Caballos 1997:316).

The treaty agreement with Enriquillo was, however, an important precedent for what would become a not infrequent Spanish policy for dealing with trenchant Indian and African guerilla resistance. Legal recognition, freedom, and often land were granted as terms of peace to rebels in Mexico, Venezuela, Florida, Panama, Colombia, and Ecuador when Spanish authorities were unable to defeat them (see Landers 2006). This reflected a certain pragmatic, if reluctant, willingness on the part of imperial authority to accommodate local resistance and to change in response to it. This Spanish compliance in adjusting their asserted demands and expectations to accommodate American Indians and avoid violent resistance was also exercised regularly in the southeastern United States.

Very little is known archaeologically about these early Indian and African resistance movements in the Caribbean. The places in which the rebels lived were well hidden and apparently equally inaccessible to both sixteenth-century Spanish authorities and twentieth-century archaeologists (see Vega 1979b; Arrom and García Arévalo 1986; Weik 2004).

Not all resistance to Spaniards in Hispaniola, of course, was overt, violent, or organized. There is some archaeological suggestion that many, if not the majority, of nonelite Taíno were indifferent toward and possibly rejected Spanish cultural elements and values, and particularly the Spanish agenda of imposing civilization and Christianity. The site of En Bas Saline in northern Haiti is one of the largest Taíno sites recorded on the island, and it is thought to have been the seat of the *cacicazco* (chiefdom) of the Taíno cacique Guacanagarí and the town in which Columbus left his men in 1492. The site was occupied from about 1200 until about 1530, with a substantial postencounter occupation indicated by radiometric dates, European rat and pig bones, and tiny fragments of glass, metal, and Spanish pottery (Deagan 2004).

During the first decades of the sixteenth century, the Taíno town at En Bas Saline was located within 2 km of the Spanish town of Puerto Real and was undoubtedly subjected to an encomienda labor draft. Nevertheless, the people at En Bas Saline only rarely incorporated Spanish items into their material life, and these were typically food items rather than material culture (Deagan 2004). Recent work by James VanderVeen (2007) at Taíno sites in the vicinity of La Isabela, Columbus's second settlement in the Dominican Republic, suggests a similar pattern. Although no European artifacts have been recovered, the post-1492 occupation of these sites has been established through VanderVeen's analysis of residues on the interior of Taíno cooking vessels, suggesting that European plant and animal species were being used (VanderVeen 2007).

The scarcity of European artifacts at Taíno sites in Hispaniola—other than elite burial contexts (García Arévalo 1990; Vega 1979a)—is conspicuous, and traditionally it has been accepted that the Taíno were decimated by disease and subjugation so quickly that no archaeological record of their historic-era occupation was generated. As more recent archaeological and ethnohistorical work in the Caribbean (and particularly in Cuba, see Yaremko 2006) has shown, however, it is likely that many post-Columbian indigenous sites have simply not been recognized, owing to the assumption by archaeologists that post-Columbian Taíno sites should have incorporated European materials. The suggestion that the Taíno may have been disinterested in adopting European materials other than food items is a proposition worth investigating through more fine-grained recovery and assessment of these sites. Both Taíno men and women were subject to the labor drafts and alleged conversion efforts imposed by encomienda and repartimiento, and had ample experience of the Spaniards and their ways, if not explicit instruction in Christianity and "civilization." The examples of En Bas Saline and La Isabela suggest, however, that they may have returned to their villages when the draft was complete with little or no adoption of Spanish materials.

LA FLORIDA

When Juan Ponce de León reached Florida in 1513, resistance to Spanish incursion by the indigenous people was immediate and decisive. Following Ponce's death from an Indian-inflicted arrow wound, it would take more than another half century of repeatedly failed pacification attempts for Spain to gain even a tenuous foothold in Florida. Even then, most of the Florida peninsula south of St. Augustine and most of the interior Southeast never came under either Spanish control or mission conversion (Figure 3.2) (see Hann 2003; Smith 1989). Two Spanish towns, Santa Elena among the Guale and St. Augustine among the Timucua, were established in 1565–66; however, Santa Elena was repeatedly attacked by

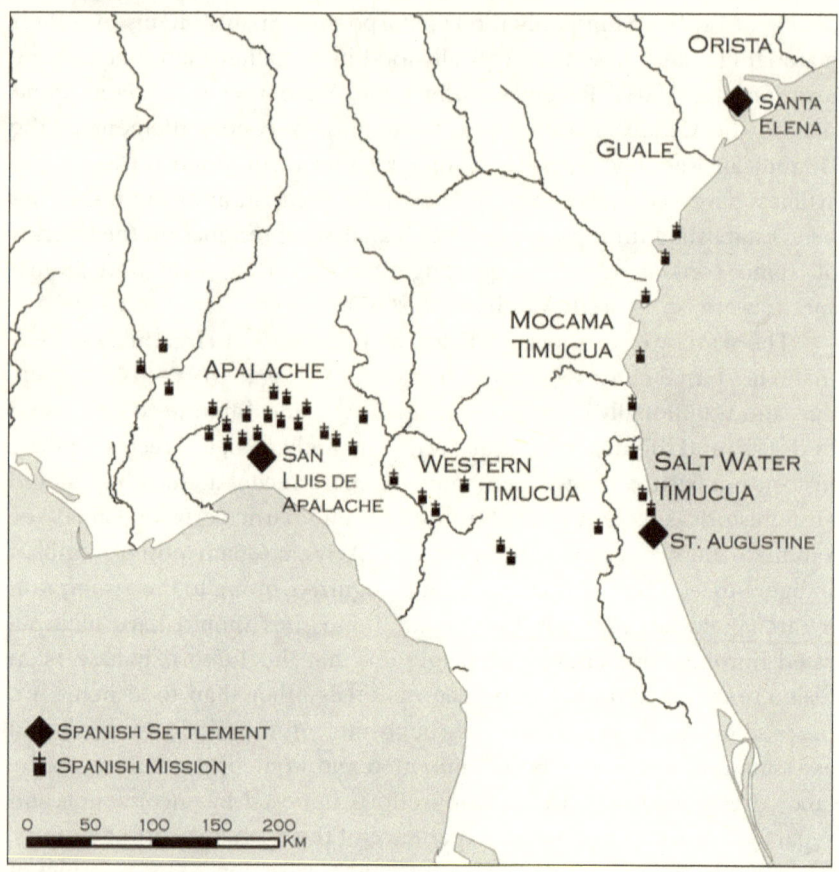

FIGURE 3.2.
Locations of principal Native American polities and Spanish settlements in La Florida, ca. 1565–1650.

the Guale and was abandoned in 1587. The Jesuits attempted conversions in Florida between 1568 and 1572, but violent native resistance caused them to abandon the mission field within five years (Gannon 1965).

By the time Florida was colonized, the New Laws of 1542 had outlawed the institution of encomienda and the individual ownership of rights to native labor service (Bushnell 1994:121–24). Florida was a fortified presidio (a community with a permanent garrison of Crown-supported soldiers), in which soldiers were paid a salary by the Crown and had no legal right to booty, captives, or personal labor service. The effort to control La Florida and its inhabitants was undertaken principally through the Franciscan mission system, in which friars went as supplicants to the Indians and were dependent on native cooperation and goodwill for survival. In those

NATIVE AMERICAN RESISTANCE IN HISPANIOLA AND LA FLORIDA

parts of the frontier in which the indigenous people accepted Christianity, missions served as buffer zones against invasion from foreign European powers and sources of food and labor. But "where the Indians rejected Christianity, the frontier did not advance" (Bushnell 1996:63; see also Weber 1992).

In La Florida the frontier never advanced beyond a narrow stretch of the Georgia and north Florida coastlines, and a narrow strip across north Florida. The rest of the area claimed by Spain as La Florida was populated throughout the entire colonial period by an unknown number of indigenous communities that rejected Christianity and the Spaniards, and were referred to by Spaniards as *infieles* or *indios bárbaros*. Archaeological and documentary research (as well as the written Spanish accounts of the era) have tended to concentrate on the Spanish mission communities and their Native American residents. Consequently, little is known about the communities of infieles or indios bárbaros other than the threat they posed as refuges for slaves and former Christian Indians.

As with the encomiendas of Hispaniola, the success of the mission effort was essentially dependent on the native caciques who sanctioned not only the presence of the missionaries but also the allocation of their subjects' labor. Nonelite indigenous people produced food for the Spaniards, built mission structures, served as long-distance bearers, and eventually (during the seventeenth century) filled annual labor drafts for work on the public defenses of St. Augustine. As reward for this, the caciques were acknowledged as privileged leaders, allied with the Spaniards in the regional political balance of power, and gained access to exotic and useful European goods such as tools, blankets, ornaments, European garments, and cloth. Like their Spanish counterparts, the *hidalgos* (those with claim to nobility), native caciques were exempt from manual labor, taxation, corporal punishment and were permitted to carry swords and ride horses (Bushnell 1989).

There is little evidence that the *indios peones* (Indian laborers) of Florida received or incorporated significant amounts of European materials in their domestic lives, and possibly few changes in their daily practices other than additional labor requirements. The limited archaeological investigations carried out in Native American contexts at mission sites in Florida do, in fact, suggest that the distribution of European elements is highly nonrandom, occurring in areas interpreted as having been elite residences (Scarry 2001:54; Shapiro and McEwan 1992; Loucks 1993). In the context of mission communities, resistance to the Spaniards was effectively, for nonelite natives, also resistance to their cacique.

Such resistance on the part of indios peones did occur, principally by leaving the mission community to join other natives who rejected conversion and Christianity—those referred to in documents as pagans, infieles, or *gente bárbara*. Despite the potential punishment of public whippings if they returned or were caught, people regularly departed from the missions, a fact that the Spanish missionaries and officials regularly complained about. As disease and British encroachment threatened the Spanish mission system in seventeenth-century Florida, "natives without privilege or status were deciding that the kinds of society that suited God, the king, the españoles and the chiefs did not suit them. It offered a common Indian too little, and asked too much" (Bushnell 1994:145). As in the Caribbean a century earlier, these pagan communities often included escaped African slaves, and all were considered to be cimarrones (see Hann 2003:78–82; Bushnell 1994:145–46).

As in Hispaniola, very few if any of these communities have been investigated by archaeologists, partly because the focus of much historical archaeology, as noted above, has been on the missions themselves. But it is also possible that, as in Hispaniola, such sites have gone unrecognized because of an absence of visible European materials. Whether such an absence of European material reflects indifference, choice, or exclusion cannot yet be assessed.

Curiously, some of these unconverted groups eventually sought refuge in Spanish mission communities and in St. Augustine, as the Native American social landscape of the Southeast came under severe demographic and international political stress during the seventeenth century. Even then, although the native inhabitants voluntarily submitted to the annual labor draft to work on the fortifications in St. Augustine, many refused conversion to Christianity (Bushnell 1994:144–45, 165–66; Hann 2003; Worth 1995:101–2).

Subtler forms of resistance to Spanish mandates played out in the missions themselves. Historical and archaeological research in Spanish-American missions documents the many ways in which elements of Catholic ritual were selected, rejected, and transformed by people throughout the Spanish Americas, either through everyday forms of resistance or direct negotiation (see, for a few of the many available examples, Clendinnen 1987; Thomas 1990:357–58; Gutiérrez 1991:82–91; Ortíz 1969:51–52; Weber 1992:105–21; McEwan 2001; Murphy et al., Chapter 4; Wernke, Chapter 5; Quilter, Chapter 6; Sheptak et al., Chapter 8). Excavations in the Florida missions have documented, for example, the inclusion of indigenous as well as European grave goods with Christian Indian burials inside mission churches, contrary to proscribed rules for burial, as well as the incorporation of charnel house remains and bundle burials inside churches (Deagan 2008:40–44; Larsen 1993:325; Larsen et al.

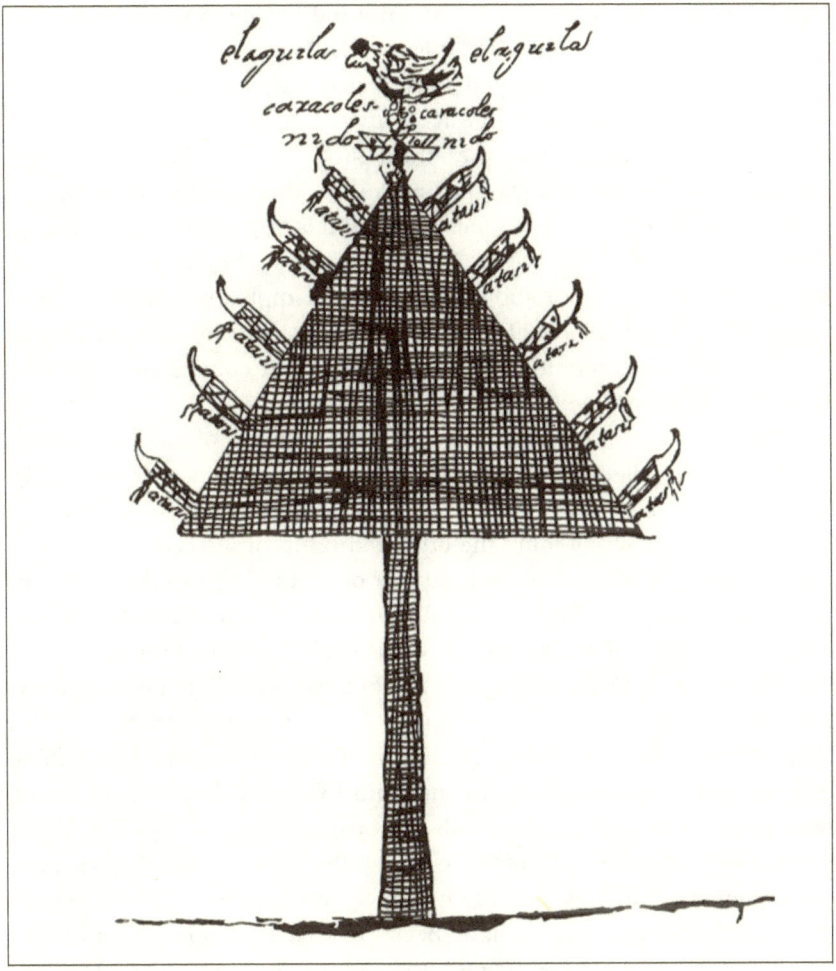

FIGURE 3.3.
1676 manuscript drawing of an Apalache Indians ballgame pole by Franciscan Friar Juan de Paiva (Paiva 1676). Courtesy P.K. Yonge Library of Florida History, George A. Smathers Library, University of Florida.

2001; McEwan 2001:637; Milanich 1999:139; Thomas 1988:120–22, 1990:357).

Native American council houses—traditional and highly important ritual and symbolic indigenous spaces—were incorporated into the mission complex at nearly every Florida mission site that has been documented (see essays in McEwan 1993). In the Apalache province, the traditional ballgame was played in the plaza (Figure 3.3), accompanied by public pagan ritual that was reprehensible to (but endured by) the Spanish friars (see Bushnell 1978; Hann 1988:331–33; Paiva 1676).

Much of this was undoubtedly negotiated resistance between caciques and Spaniards, with refusal and accommodation on both sides (see, for example, Scarry 2001). Caciques throughout La Florida did, however, openly resist Spanish actions and intentions when grievances were perceived. In some cases, the caciques achieved this through the Spanish legal system by exercising their right to communicate and lodge complaints in writing with the governor and the king (for examples, see Bushnell 1979; Hann 1993; Worth 1998:190–211; Scarry 2001). African slaves in Florida also used written communication to protest unjust conditions or enslavement (see Landers 1999:27–28, 39–40).

On a number of occasions, however, the caciques of La Florida organized formal, violent resistance against mission presence (Figure 3.4). Virtually all of these events were provoked by Spanish actions interpreted as insulting to or threatening the inherited rights of the caciques. One of the earliest of these acts was the Guale Revolt of 1576 against the Spaniards at Santa Elena, provoked specifically by Spanish punishment of Guale caciques accused of murdering a "Christian." The rebellion forced the abandonment of the Spanish town. The Spaniards retaliated with a vengeful scorched-earth campaign, resulting in the reestablishment of Santa Elena three years later and a famine in the Guale region. The famine brought about Spanish peace treaties with fifteen of the Guale caciques, who agreed to ally themselves with the Spaniards and accept Franciscan missionaries (Bushnell 1994:60–63; Paar 1999). The Guale caciques, however, again allied and revolted against the Spanish presence in 1597, a four-year retaliation thought to have been provoked by Spanish efforts to interfere with the rights of caciques to polygyny (Bushnell 1994:65).

One of the fiercest and bloodiest indigenous resistance movements against Spanish presence took place among the interior Florida Timucua region in 1656, after Spaniards had attempted to make caciques carry burdens and contribute their own labor in the annual draft (Worth 1998). Like most of the other rebellions, it was provoked by Spanish disrespect of the cacique elite.

CONCLUSION

The incidents recounted above represent only a portion of the many accounts of violent Native American resistance to Spanish presence in Hispaniola and La Florida provided by a wonderfully rich documentary record (and increasingly rich archaeological record). Among the people

Native American Resistance in Hispaniola and La Florida

FIGURE 3.4.
Massacre of Jesuits by Indians. *Engraving by Theodore de Bry, America, part 4, plate 16. ca. 1594. Courtesy the University of Florida Smathers Library Special Collections.*

who lived under the sphere of Spanish Christian influence, overt, violent resistance seems to have been aligned along class divisions. Caciques organized and mediated both overt resistance in the form of rebellions and overt accommodation by arranging the provision of food and labor to the Spanish governors in exchange for privilege, military alliance, and goods. The ways in which everyday forms of resistance were practiced by nonelite natives have not yet been documented, except to the extent that there was little incorporation of Spanish material elements in their daily lives. Whether this was a consequence of rejection or exclusion is unknown. We also do not yet understand the extent to which nonelite Native Americans resisted their own caciques and their policies, other than by fleeing. Such resistance, particularly covert resistance, must surely have occurred.

I remain fascinated, however, by similar forms of resistance that immigrant Spanish residents of the region practiced against their own "great caciques" in Spain (see also Charlton and Fournier's [Chapter 7] discussion of criollo resistance to the Spanish metropole). Exploring this topic is neither central to the focus of this volume nor possible for reasons of space, but it is germane to the larger issue of Spanish colonization of the

Americas and the many forms of resistance to it. Nonelite colonial residents of Spanish descent also resisted imperial intentions in ways that forced imperial accommodation and change. One of the most visible examples was their refusal to conform to mercantilist prohibitions against trade with foreigners. The acquisition of contraband goods was regularized by the mid-sixteenth century, and Spanish-American colonists incorporated prohibited non-Spanish goods into their households regularly, despite the overt and often violent reprisals by the Spanish authorities, which were generally unsuccessful (Deagan 2007).

In matters of "living like Spaniards and civilized people," colonial residents of all ethnic and racial backgrounds made their own decisions about what that meant. They married one another, incorporated one another's domestic practices into their daily lives, and claimed a separate identity as criollo Americans. Although Spanish authorities (as well as the indigenous Indian caciques) did not change much either in personhood or policy, the nonelite people of both republics did.

Ultimately, I would suggest, the overt and covert forms of resistance to Spanish mandates practiced by Native American, white criollo, and African residents of Spanish America were successful. As historian David Weber reminds us, nearly three centuries after Spain's initial invasion, most of the area that composes Spanish-speaking America today was occupied and controlled by Native American people. And today the majority of people living in that region claim a connection to, if not descent from, American Indians. If Spanish and Native American resistance and accommodation to one another in the colonial period resulted in the transformation of indigenous American society, so too did it transform Spanish society in America.

4

Resistance, Persistence, and Accommodation at Puruchuco-Huaquerones, Peru

Melissa S. Murphy, Elena Goycochea, and Guillermo Cock

Embodied by their material remains, the Andean deceased remained physically present and spiritually alive as continuing and more permanent members of Andean society in the sixteenth century. Lineages known as *ayllus* were believed to have descended from one or several sacred ancestors (*mallquis*) who were interred in the community's symbolic site of origin, the ancestral burial place (Doyle 1988; Isbell 1997; Salomon 1995).[1] Rituals honoring the dead marked the passage of the recently deceased from the world of the living to the place of the sacred ancestors, and interment in the ancestral burial place was the only way for this journey to be completed and the only way to be buried (Doyle 1988:258; Salomon 1995). The sacred ancestors were venerated and commemorated in most aspects of everyday life (Doyle 1988; Salomon 1995:324), and they were closely connected with food and agriculture (Doyle 1988:67–69; Salomon 1995). Although local deities were partially supplanted by the Inca religious cults and icons during the apogee of the Inca Empire, Andean religious practices retained their regional and local character, and local deities continued to play important roles in traditional native beliefs (MacCormack 1991:98; Mills 1997:3). Worship focused on a mythicized genealogy and geography that were particular to a community (Salomon 1991:4). Through the protracted mortuary rituals and celebrations, the deceased were transformed into ancestors, and this transformative process may be glimpsed through the material investigation of the deceased and their mortuary contexts from the perspectives of bioarchaeology and mortuary archaeology.

Spanish invasion and conquest ruptured traditional religious and cosmological geographies through chaotic plunder, violence, repression, and the introduction of new epidemic diseases, followed by decades of territorial occupation and Spanish imperial rule (Abercrombie 1998; Cook 1998; D'Altroy 2005a; Del Busto Duthurburu 1966, 1978; MacCormack 1991; Rowe 1957; Spalding 1999; Stern 1982; Wachtel 1977). While acknowledging the destruction and disaster brought by the Spanish and experienced by Andean peoples, this study attempts to examine the fluid and variable reactions of communities on the central coast of Peru to invasion and conquest through the comparison of the Late Horizon burials with the idiosyncratic burials that depart from the traditional Late Horizon burial patterns. These idiosyncratic burials give us a window into the splintering and redefinition of traditional mortuary practices at the community of Puruchuco-Huaquerones, and they offer a material perspective of indigenous responses to Spanish colonialism. The bioarchaeological analysis of two case studies allows us to explore resistance (violent and nonviolent), accommodation, persistence, and complicity among the multitude of responses and actions that may have been enacted by the colonized members of the community from Puruchuco-Huaquerones as well as by the Spanish colonizer. In the first case, we argue that people from Puruchuco-Huaquerones engaged in outright defiance and violence with the Spaniards and their indigenous allies at or around the time of the Siege of Lima (1536). In the second case study, we present an example of possible corpse removal and secondary interment in the community's cemetery and explore how this might be interpreted within studies of colonialism, domination, and resistance.

ARCHAEOLOGICAL SETTING

The archaeological zone of Puruchuco-Huaquerones is located on the central coast of Peru 12 km outside downtown Lima on the southern side of the middle region of the Rímac Valley (Figure 4.1). Several archaeologists have suggested that Puruchuco may have been involved in the Inca administration of the region during the Late Horizon due to the presence of imperial Inca architectural influences, such as trapezoidal features, triangular niches, and double-jambed doorways (Jiménez Borja 1973; Tabio 1965; Villacorta O. 2001; 2004:553).

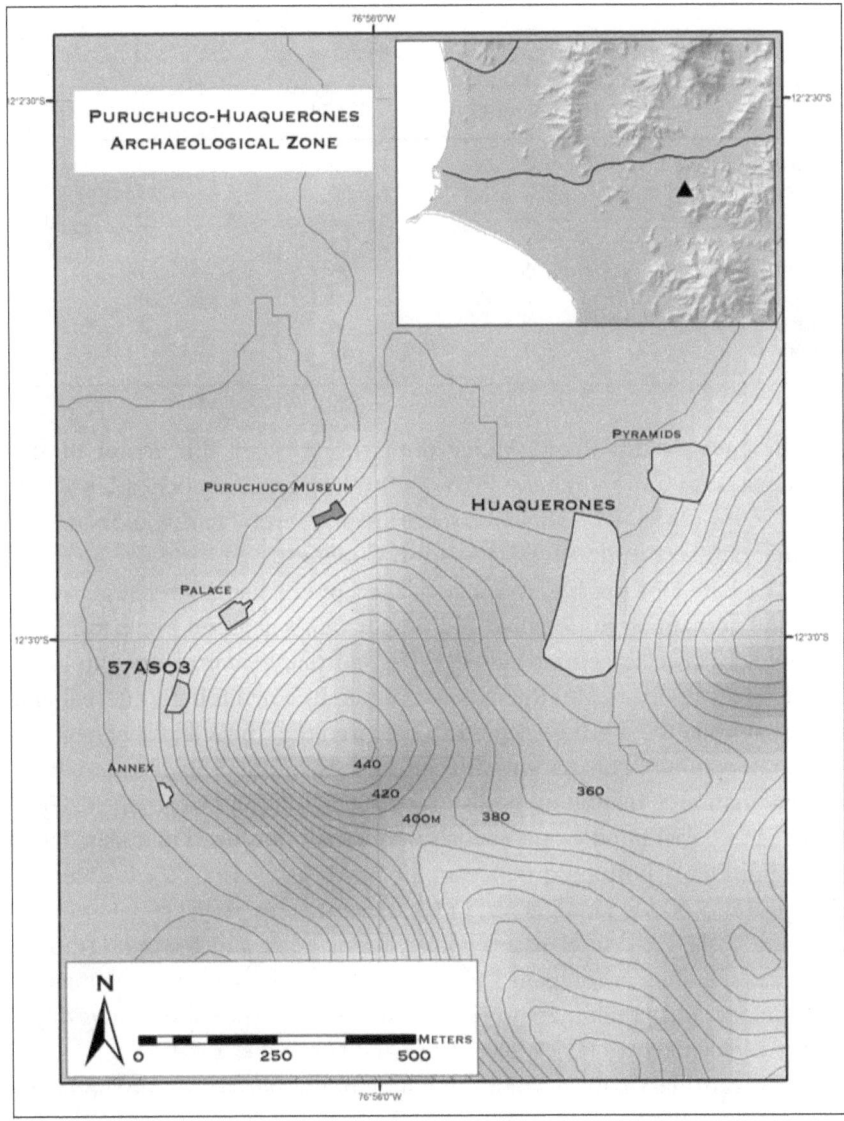

FIGURE 4.1.
Location of 57AS03 and Huaquerones within the archaeological zone of Puruchuco-Huaquerones.

The archaeological zone contains several cemeteries, two of which, Huaquerones and 57AS03, were excavated by Guillermo Cock and Elena Goycochea and are the subject of this study. Based on the ceramic chronology, it is estimated that the majority of burials in both cemeteries (Huaquerones and 57AS03) are Late Horizon and date to the early presence

TABLE 4.1.

Sample composition from Puruchuco-Huaquerones by age, sex, and burial type

	Huaquerones	57AS03	TOTAL
> 15 years of age	138	120	258
Males	72	60	132
Females	58	47	105
Indeterminate sex	8	13	21
Late Horizon	105	43	148
Atypical	0	69	69
Indeterminate type	23	8	31
Total	321	198	519

of the Inca in the Rímac Valley until shortly after the arrival of the Europeans, or approximately 1475–1540 (Cock and Goycochea 2004:185; Cock 2006) (Table 4.1). However, there are also several Early Colonial burials that date to shortly after the Spanish Conquest.

The Late Horizon burials range in their preservation from large textile bundles containing mummified individuals with soft tissue preservation to completely skeletonized individuals.[2] The mortuary contexts are extraordinarily well preserved, and the majority of burials contain both internal and external funerary offerings. Bundles were given their bulk and shape by textiles, raw cotton fill, raw cotton with cottonseeds, or other plant materials, or a combination of the different fills (Cock 2006; Cock and Goycochea 2004). Inside the burial bundles, individuals were usually arranged in a seated and flexed mortuary position oriented to the northeast. Various textiles, ceramics, gourds, wooden implements, musical instruments, staffs, metal artifacts, weaving baskets and implements, maize, beans, coca, and *Spondylus* (thorny oyster) shell often accompany the bundles as offerings, varying by quantity and quality, and preliminary work suggests that the types of offerings differ in the two cemeteries (Cock 2006; Cock and Goycochea 2004).

The mortuary patterns of a subsample of the burials from 57AS03 are distinct from the Late Horizon burials (Cock 2006). These unusual burials possess few, if any, mortuary offerings, and they lack the bundle fill encountered in the Late Horizon burials (Cock 2006). Typically, they possess a single textile layer or an outer textile layer and an inner shroud that surrounds the principal individual, who was usually interred alone (Cock 2006). The burial positions are also atypical and there appears to be more variability than consistency. Individuals were unearthed in a semiflexed position, a supine position, a combination of semiflexion and supination, and an extended prone position. Rarely were these burials oriented toward the northeast, as was the custom with the Late Horizon burials (Cock 2006). These atypical burials were mostly clustered in the most superficial stratigraphic layers of 57AS03 and at the periphery of the cemetery (Cock 2006). They do not represent a mass burial, but rather each burial constitutes a separate burial event that occurred within a short period of time. Based on these observations, Guillermo Cock and Elena Goycochea hypothesized that these burials might represent early contact period burials that were hastily prepared and interred due to the dangerous conditions surrounding the arrival of the Spaniards in the area. There is no obvious evidence for genetic differentiation or for a demographic shift (e.g., population immigration) between the two cemeteries, so we believe that the individuals who were interred atypically were members of the community at Puruchuco-Huaquerones (Murphy et al. 2008).

VIOLENCE AND CONFRONTATION: THE SIEGE OF LIMA, 1536

Following Francisco Pizarro's capture and the eventual execution of the Inca ruler Atahualpa (1532–33), the Spaniards installed a young noble named Manco Inca as a puppet emperor. Pizarro and his men then established new cities through the Inca realm, including a new capital city, Ciudad de los Reyes, in 1535, known today as Lima (D'Altroy 2005a; Del Busto Duthurburu 1978; Spalding 1999; Vega 1980). Throughout the realm they implemented the *encomienda* system with designated local lords, *kurakas*, serving as the leaders of each group of indigenous Andeans within the defined land grant area under the *encomendero* (Spalding 1999).

Manco Inca grew increasingly frustrated by his subjugated position under the Spanish and began to rebuild old alliances and mobilize the Inca generals and their troops outside Cuzco. Managing to escape from Cuzco in 1536, Manco Inca assembled his troops and ordered the attack on the former Inca capital and a siege of the city and its Spanish residents (D'Altroy 2005a; Del Busto Duthurburu 1978; Cieza de León 1985[1553]; Guaman Poma 1980[1615]; Vega 1980). On Saturday, May 6, 1536, an Inca army attacked Cuzco and almost succeeded in defeating the Spaniards. The siege lasted over a year and resulted in isolating Cuzco from the rest of the Spanish-controlled territories and in preventing the reinforcements sent by Pizarro from reaching the Spanish trapped in the city (D'Altroy 2005a; Del Busto Duthurburu 1978; Cieza de León 1985[1553]; Guaman Poma 1980[1615]; Vega 1980).

Because of these initial victories in mid-August 1536, Manco Inca ordered one of his generals to march to Lima and launch a simultaneous siege of the new Spanish capital. The general, with several other Inca captains and perhaps as many as 30,000 troops, stationed themselves strategically by surrounding Lima from three different fronts (Del Busto Duthurburu 1978; Vega 1980). From these vantage points, the Incas controlled the city and could observe all the movements of the Spanish troops, specifically the measures that Pizarro and his followers were taking both to protect the city and to attack the Inca forces (Del Busto Duthurburu 1978; Vega 1980). Although there were not many Spanish forces in Lima, they were reinforced by some lords of the Andean polities from the central coast (Spalding 1999; Rostworowski 1977). These indigenous allies took the opportunity to defend the Spanish capital, fighting alongside the Spaniards and thereby rejecting the possible future imposition of power and control by Manco Inca and his forces (Rostworowski 1977, 2002; Spalding 1999).

About six days after the beginning of the siege—and afraid that Pizarro would receive reinforcements from Panama, Santo Domingo, Nicaragua, and Guatemala—the Inca general ordered the attack of Lima, and his troops descended onto the coastal region to take control of the city (Del Busto Duthurburu 1978; Vega 1980). During the battle, he was purportedly killed by a lance or spear injury, and he died along with forty of his captains and thousands of his troops (Del Busto Duthurburu 1978; Guaman Poma 1980[1615]; Vega 1980). The Spaniards had targeted the military leaders because they knew that the Inca military was not composed of a standing army and that the troops would likely abandon the battlefield without their leaders (D'Altroy 2005a; Del Busto Duthurburu 1978; Vega 1980). As skirmishes and battles continued, the Inca troops were severely demoralized by the death of their general and their failure to recapture Lima. Two Inca leaders and their forces reportedly fled the Rímac Valley to return to the highlands along the Chillón River Valley to the north (to Canta) and the Lurín River Valley to the south (to Huarochirí) (Del Busto Duthurburu 1978; Vega 1980). The troops that took the southerly route along the Lurín Valley may have passed very close to Puruchuco-Huaquerones (Figure 4.1).

The siege of Cuzco lasted for several more months but was eventually quelled by the Spanish and their reinforcements. Manco Inca and his followers fled to Vilcabamba, on the eastern side of the Andes, where Manco Inca established a neo-Inca state that practiced guerilla warfare tactics for the next few years (D'Altroy 2005a).

The Siege of Lima is the only known historical battle between the Spaniards and the neo-Inca forces in the central coast region, and it

TABLE 4.2.
Individuals with perimortem injuries by burial type

	Huaquerones (N=138)	57AS03 (N=120)	TOTAL
Late Horizon	17/105 (16.2%)	4/43 (9.3%)	21/148 (14.2%)
Atypical	0/0 (0.0%)	26/69 (37.7%)	26/69 (37.7%)*
Indeterminate	1/23 (4.3%)	0/8 (0.0%)	1/31 (3.2%)
Total	18/138 (13.0%)	30/120 (25.0%)	48/258 (18.6%)

* Statistically significant differences in frequency of perimortem trauma between atypical and Late Horizon burials ($p < 0.001$)

occurred approximately 12 km from the archaeological zone of Puruchuco-Huaquerones. Here, we argue that members of this community engaged in violent encounters with the Spaniards at or around the time of the Siege of Lima because of the community's close proximity to the battle's location. Furthermore, many of the individuals from the 57AS03 cemetery at Puruchuco-Huaquerones exhibited high rates of perimortem traumatic injuries and possible injuries from European weapons (Murphy et al. 2010) (Table 4.2).[3] For the combined sample (Huaquerones and 57AS03), approximately 18.6 percent (48/258) of the sample possessed perimortem injuries. At 57AS03, 25.0 percent (30/120) of the sample possessed perimortem injuries (versus 13.0 percent of the Huaquerones sample).

Within the context of other studies of warfare and conflict-related trauma, the frequency of perimortem traumatic injuries is relatively high, particularly at 57AS03. Except in cases of human sacrifice, massacres, or battlefield cemeteries, few bioarchaeological investigations report frequencies of deliberate violent trauma above 25 percent (Milner 2005; Novak 2000; Smith 2003; Willey and Emerson 1993; Willey and Scott 1996). Comparable bioarchaeological investigations of violence in the central Andes report low frequencies of perimortem injuries (e.g., Altamirano et al. 2006; Andrushko 2007; Kellner 2002; Torres-Rouff and Costa Junqueira 2006; Tung 2007) and the frequency of perimortem injuries from Huaquerones is consistent with these studies. The atypical burials from 57AS03 show the highest frequency of perimortem injuries, and when compared to the traditional Late Horizon burials, these differences are statistically significant ($\chi 2 = 5.55$, $df = 1$, $p \leq 0.05$) (Murphy et al. 2010) (Table 4.2).

In both cemeteries, males possessed higher frequencies of perimortem traumatic injuries than females, which suggests that the males were more

TABLE 4.3.
Perimortem trauma by cases and individuals in both cemeteries

	Huaquerones (N = 138)	57AS03 (N = 120)	TOTAL (N = 258)
Cases (cranium + postcranium)	24	167	191
Individuals	18 (13.0%)	30 (25.0%)	48 (18.6%)
Males	12	19	31
Females	6	9	15
Indeterminate	0	2	2
Cases (cranium)	13	40	53
Individuals	13 (9.4%)	21 (17.5%)	34 (13.2%)
Males	9	13	22
Females	4	7	11
Indeterminate	0	1	1
Cases (postcranium)	11	127	138
Individuals	6 (4.4%)	18 (15.0%)	24 (9.3%)
Males	4	14	18
Females	2	4	6
Indeterminate	0	0	0

often engaged as combatants or that they were targeted as potential threats (Table 4.3), but, in general, males are more often the victims of violence (Walker 2001). At 57AS03, males were also more often victims of multiple injuries, with multiple injuries to their cranial and axial skeletons (Murphy et al. 2010). Although we do not report on these injuries here, a surprising number of children were also victims of violence, and several young children possessed lethal injuries to their crania (Gaither et al. 2007).[4]

In the pooled sample, a total of thirty-four individuals over fifteen years of age sustained perimortem cranial injuries, and several of these individuals possessed more than one perimortem cranial injury (34/258; 13.2 percent). The frequency of perimortem cranial injuries is higher at 57AS03 than at Huaquerones, particularly among the atypical burials (17.5 percent versus 9.4 percent, respectively). The majority of these perimortem injuries to the cranium exhibit characteristics that are consistent with injuries from blunt force trauma with evidence of a point of impact, radiating fractures, and concentric fractures (Berryman and Symes 1998; Berryman and Haun 1996). A preponderance of these cranial injuries was sustained on the anterior cranial vault and on the left side of the cranium, which suggests that the victims were facing their attackers and that the assailants may have been right-handed.

Resistance, Persistence, and Accommodation in Peru

These blunt force traumatic injuries are not diagnostic of a particular type or class of European or indigenous weapon, and it is widely known that native warriors and former enemies of the Incas supplemented the Spanish forces (D'Altroy 2005a; Del Busto Duthurburu 1978; Vega 1980). The Spaniards who accompanied Pizarro were not particularly well armed and likely used the weapons they brought with them or whatever was available (Lockhart 1972; Restall 2003). The blunt force injuries could have been caused by European maces or clubs used by the Spanish, or indigenous maces or clubs used by their indigenous allies. Since the Spaniards' forces included their indigenous allies, a combination of indigenous weapons and European clubs likely caused these injuries, but it is extremely difficult to match an injury to a corresponding weapon (Boylston 2000). We also cannot rule out the possibility that some indigenous warriors may have been armed with Spanish weapons.

In the combined sample from both 57AS03 and Huaquerones, twenty-four individuals sustained perimortem injuries to the postcranial skeleton (Table 4.3) (Murphy et al. 2010). The cases of perimortem injuries to the postcranial skeleton are much more numerous in 57AS03 than in Huaquerones (15.0 percent versus 4.4 percent) (Tables 4.3, 4.4). In Huaquerones, perimortem traumatic injuries to the postcranial skeleton were only observed on ribs. In contrast, from 57AS03 many elements in the axial skeleton show high frequencies of perimortem injuries, with the most frequently fractured elements being the ribs, followed by the scapula, and then the radius and tibia (Table 4.4). The combination of the high frequency of perimortem injuries to the cranium and postcranium, particularly the ribs and thorax region, is compelling evidence for warfare and deliberate interpersonal violence, as suggested by other studies (Lovell 2008:376; Brickley 2006). People who served in the Inca military reportedly wore lightweight cotton padding as armor, so the high frequency of fractures to the ribs and other postcranial skeletal elements suggests that the thorax region was particularly vulnerable due to inadequate protection. Trampling by horses may also have caused the high frequency of injuries to the thorax region.

From 57AS03, several individuals possess injuries that are anomalous and unlike perimortem injuries observed in studies of prehispanic violence from the central Andes (e.g., Andrushko 2007; Murphy 2004; Tung 2007; Verano 2003, 2007, 2008). Two individuals merit particular attention because we believe they possess injuries consistent with European weaponry (Burial 248, Burial 123). Burial 248 possessed three quadrangular-shaped defects to the left parietal and occipital that likely represent sharp force

TABLE 4.4.
Perimortem trauma by skeletal element

Element	Huaquerones		57AS03	
	Total # Elements	Perimortem # (% of total)	Total # Elements	Perimortem # (% of total)
Cranium	129	13 (10.1%)	99	40 (40.4%)
Clavicle	245	0	203	2 (1.0%)
Scapula	241	0	203	8 (3.9%)
Sternum	115	0	102	2 (2.0%)
Innominate	249	0	204	2 (1.0%)
Ribs	2847	11 (0.4%)	2382	98 (4.1%)
Humerus	189	0	207	0
Radius	180	0	196	3 (1.5%)
Ulna	178	0	193	0
Femur	176	0	203	2 (1.0%)
Tibia	173	0	199	2 (1.0%)
Fibula	175	0	199	1 (0.5%)

trauma inflicted by a steel-edged weapon. The quadrangular defects measure approximately 8.78 x 5.24 mm (average), and they each appear to be separate perforating injuries. Burial 248 also sustained multiple perimortem injuries to the postcranial skeleton, including perimortem fractures to the left first rib, to the proximal tibia, and to the left third and fourth metacarpals.

Clubs and maces, slings with sling stones, large axelike implements, bolas, tumi knives, and large wooden spears were the types of weapons in the Inca arsenal (D'Altroy 2005a; Rowe 1946). The Inca attached metal heads made of copper, silver, or bronze to their maces and axes (Rowe 1946), but steel weaponry was not introduced until after the Spanish Conquest. The quadrangular injuries on Burial 248 are similar to injuries on human remains from the battlefield cemetery of Towton, England (1461). In her study of these human remains, Novak argues that many of the quadrangular injuries were likely caused by the top spike of a polearm or the beak of a war hammer (Novak 2000), weapons that the Spaniards also carried (Del Busto Duthurburu 1978; Salas 1950). The similarities of these injuries to one another suggest that a European weapon may also have caused the quadrangular defects on Burial 248. None of the published studies of prehispanic violence in the central Andes report quadrangular defects of this nature (Andrushko 2007; Klaus 2008; Klaus et al. n.d.; Tung 2007; Verano 2003, 2007, 2008).

The second individual with unusual perimortem injuries, Burial 123, possesses several cranial injuries that are consistent with gunshot wounds reported in modern forensic cases (Berryman and Symes 1998; DiMaio 1999). We believe that the circular injury on the left parietal of Burial 123 is consistent with descriptions of firearm injuries from modern forensic cases, as well as from historical accounts of low velocity firearms (Berryman and Symes 1998; DiMaio 1999; Gross 1861; Longmore 2006; Magee 1995). The circular defect on the parietal has internal beveling (Murphy et al. 2010), which is one of the typical characteristics of modern firearm injuries (Berryman and Symes 1998; DiMaio 1999). The anterior cranial vault possesses extensive perimortem damage and an area of external beveling, which is often observed in modern gunshot exit wounds and which could have been caused by the exit of the projectile (Murphy et al. 2010). A plug of bone was recovered among the facial fragments that we believe was pushed into the cranium by the impact and force of the projectile (Murphy et al. 2010). The plug is compressed on its ectocranial surfaces, and it has several fine-line radiating fractures on its endocranial surface (Murphy et al. 2010). The Spaniards were likely armed with several types of firearms, such as the arquebus, some pistols, and a small cannon (falconet) (Guilmartin 1991; Salas 1950). In comparison to modern firearms, these early firearms were of low velocity and were considered clumsy, unreliable, and inaccurate (Gross 1861; Guilmartin 1991; Longmore 2006; Magee 1995). Surgical accounts from the American Civil War describe how the round musket ball and other projectiles sometimes came apart upon impact (Gross 1861:377–82; Longmore 2006:40; Magee 1995), which may explain the extensive perimortem fracturing and damage to the anterior cranial vault of Burial 123.

These traumatic injuries on Burials 123 and 248 possess characteristics that are comparable with injuries reported from other studies of medieval weaponry or with modern forensic investigations, and these injuries were likely inflicted by individuals carrying sixteenth-century European weapons (Berryman and Symes 1998, DiMaio 1999; Novak 2000). The results from this analysis of perimortem injuries in the 57AS03 burials indicate that these individuals experienced interpersonal violence that resulted in their deaths. A comparison of the nature and pattern of the injuries between the two cemeteries reveals some stark differences and suggests different contexts of violence. The number of individuals from Huaquerones who possess perimortem injuries is consistent with other studies of prehispanic violence from the central Andes (e.g., Altamirano et al. 2006; Andrushko 2007; Tung 2007). At 57AS03, the frequency of perimortem injuries is significantly higher, particularly among the atypical burials, with individuals possessing multiple injuries and with injuries that may have been caused by European weapons. The high prevalence of lethal injuries and the atypical burials from 57AS03 may have occurred during the Siege of Lima or afterward, as a result of escalating violence and chaos in the early postconquest period.

Numerous scholars have described how coastal populations did not serve in the Inca military because they were not considered trustworthy and because they were not well adapted to high-altitude environments (D'Altroy 2005a; Murra 1986). Historical accounts emphasize that it was mostly highland communities who assisted the Incas during the Siege of Lima and that coastal communities did not participate or fight with the Incas (D'Altroy 2005a:221; Del Busto Duthurburu 1978; Vega 1980). However, the high frequency of perimortem injuries, the pattern of these injuries, and the possible injuries from European weapons suggest that people from the community at Puruchuco-Huaquerones engaged in violent encounters with the Spaniards and may have participated in the siege.

After the Spanish invasion, abundant opportunities existed for individual elites to advance themselves amidst the chaos and confusion of conquest, as well as within the context of the precarious positions held by the local lords (kurakas) (Rostworowski 1977, 1978; Spalding 1999:945; Ramírez 1996). At the time of Spanish control of the central coast, the lords of the Rímac Valley had different agendas and interests, and some of the lords aided the Spanish in the construction of the city of Lima and fought with them against Manco Inca's forces during the Siege of Lima (Rostworowski 1978, 2002). In one instance, a local lord, Don Gonzalo, had served the Spaniards since the founding of Lima, and he compelled his subjects to attend Catholic Mass (Rostworowski 2002:220, 244–45). He represents one local lord's political initiative to advance his own interests under Spanish rule, as well as an attempt to resist the reemergence of Inca domination on the central coast (see also Beck and colleagues, Chapter 2, and Church and colleagues, Chapter 8). However, not all of the ethnic communities from the Rímac Valley allied themselves with the Spanish. People from Puruchuco-Huaquerones were part of a different ethnic community in the Rímac Valley (see Rostworowski 2002:219) that existed at the periphery of the political and religious center of Spanish control. People from Puruchuco-Huaquerones may have fought in the battle against the Spaniards. Alternatively, members of this community could have defied Spanish domination by failing to ally themselves with the Spanish and, in so doing, may have been victims of violent retribution at the hands of the Spaniards and their indigenous allies. So although Puruchuco-Huaquerones is in close geographic proximity to the location of the uprising, the cemetery itself is not a battlefield cemetery, and people from the community could have fallen victim to Spanish violence for other reasons. Here we report about violent encounters and the possibility of violent resistance against the Spaniards from the perspective of those who experienced the violence, but the contributions by Beck and colleagues (Chapter 2) and Voss (Chapter 12) tease out the different forms of violence and how the archaeological remains of these might be read and interpreted.

We believe that the atypical burial treatment at Puruchuco-Huaquerones reflects the recalibration and perpetuation of traditional mortuary rituals during the chaos and uncertainty surrounding the Spanish invasion. Prehispanic funerary rites were usually protracted affairs involving the entire community, and a corpse was usually interred on the fourth or fifth day of mourning after death (Cobo 1979[1653]; Doyle 1988; Salomon 1995; Salomon and Urioste 1991). The Late Horizon (typical) burials from Puruchuco-Huaquerones likely reflect the traditional funerary rites and interment as they were performed prior to the Spanish Conquest, when the entire community could mourn, celebrate, and make offerings to the deceased. Both of these young adult males (Burial 248, Burial 123) were among the atypical burials and were buried without offerings, without burial fill, and in an unusual position. Both individuals were interred with textiles that are consistent with prehispanic textiles from the central coast of Peru, and Burial 123 possessed a fragmentary prehispanic undergarment. We believe that after the violent encounters with the Spaniards and their forces, the surviving community members hastily interred those who had perished from the violent conflict.

CLANDESTINE DISINTERMENT AND COVERT RESISTANCE OR COMPLICITY AND OVERT RESISTANCE?

Viceroy Francisco de Toledo's policy of settlement relocation and consolidation into Spanish-style towns (*reducciones*) in 1569–70 represented the first systematic approach to extirpation (Mills 1994), whereby all indigenous practices and forms were repressed and replaced with Spanish ones (Gose 2003). Two contributions to this volume, by Wernke and by Quilter (Chapters 5 and 6, respectively), explore archaeological case studies of some of these early Spanish-style towns and native responses and actions within these communities.

Toledo's stringent measures resulted in the replacement of traditional cultural practices with Spanish institutions, all under the supervision of parish priests and civil authorities. Toledo's policies marked the end of Spanish occupation as a liminal condition that had persisted for several decades because they resulted in the crystallization of Spanish governance with religious policies and with the capture and execution of the exiled Inca rulers (Rowe 1957). Christian church burials were considered important elements for settlement consolidation and for the establishment of the church as the ritual center of the settlement (Cummins 2002; Gose 2003:152–53). Church burials would occur when rural clergy or a priest connected to the community supervised the placement of the corpse in an extended position and the corpse was interred in a church grave (Doyle 1988:203). Usually the church burial occurred underneath the church's floor, but some outdoor cemeteries were associated with churches (Gose 2003:153).

The late sixteenth century witnessed intensified evangelization efforts (1583–85) (Duviols 1986, 2002). However, Indians had not relinquished their native religions, and these efforts were also deemed unsuccessful (Gose 2003; Mills 1997). The extirpation campaigns in the seventeenth century were the most repressive and involved inquisitorial investigations of idolaters, individual confessions, and the condemnation of other offending idolaters (Duviols 1986; Mills 1994, 1997).

The majority of the written sources about indigenous mortuary rituals are outgrowths of the Toledan and post-Toledan viceregal policies to eradicate native religious practices in the middle to late sixteenth century and the campaign to extirpate idolatries during the seventeenth century (see Duviols 1986). These documents provide details across a broad geographic sampling; however, they were written several decades after Spanish conquest and Christianization and after native practices were undoubtedly altered and assimilated by Christian realities, terms, and ideas (Mills 1997:4; Salomon and Urioste 1991). A rich and textured early-seventeenth-century (1607–60) record of ancestor worship and traditional mortuary rituals exists from the southern Ancash and Lima regions, especially in Cajatambo (see Duviols 1986 and Doyle 1988). The Huarochirí manuscript (1608) reveals and enriches the record of native beliefs, but the influence of compulsory Christian conversion and its accompanying assumptions is pervasive (Salomon 1995:319; Salomon and Urioste 1991). Early soldiers and chroniclers described traditional Andean mortuary rituals as they were practiced in Cuzco until 1551, but the later writings of Guaman Poma de Ayala and Pedro Cieza de León show the most interest and concern for mortuary customs in the Inca capital and provinces (MacCormack 1991).

Despite several decades of evangelization, traditional mortuary practices and the ancestor cult persisted in many regions of the Andes, hidden from Spanish authorities after Spanish invasion and conquest. The ancestor cult was viewed as the main impediment to Christian indoctrination because of the connection between the ancestral mummies and a community's origins, as well as their role in agricultural and religious cycles (Doyle 1988; Gose 2003). The testimonies, proceedings, and investigations during the idolatries campaigns are extraordinarily detailed in the sources from the Archive of the Archbishopric of Lima and in the writings of the parish priests and religious authorities (e.g., Cabello Valboa, Acosta, Murúa, Cobo, and Arriaga), so much can be said about the indigenous religious beliefs, particularly regarding the ancestor cult and mortuary rites, as well as the strategies of Spanish ecclesiastical inspectors and local priests who targeted what they perceived as idolatrous beliefs and practices from 1610 to 1850.

As early as 1541, the Spanish church was aware of the Andean practice of corpse removal from church graves as AAL notes (Doyle 1988:246; Arriaga 1920[1621]:61, 70, 75, 142, 147; Doyle 1988:205; Duviols 1986, 2002; Millones et al. 1990; Gose 2003:157). Relatives or family members disinterred the dead at night, when the ecclesiastical authorities or the devout Christians in the community could not observe these activities according to Toledo (Gose 2003:153; Doyle 1988:205).

When interrogated by the ecclesiastical investigator about why the dead were removed from the Christian burials, witnesses in the idolatries campaigns testified that the recently deceased spoke to the living, warning that they would "curse their relatives" if they were not removed and subsequently buried in the sacred community burial structure and that the extended supine burial position prevented the deceased from "breathing and moving" (Doyle 1988:205). To these witnesses, the church burial was considered anathema because the location was not the symbolic place of origin for the community and the deceased would not join the sacred ancestors in the ancestor burial place.

We believe that an Early Colonial burial from Puruchuco-Huaquerones provides a second point of departure to explore the myriad indigenous responses to Spanish evangelization. An adult female was recovered in the deepest level of the Huaquerones cemetery (approximately 2 m below the surface), which was intrusive into Late Horizon burials. She was placed on a wooden/cane stretcher in an extended supine position, but upright in the burial pit (Figure 4.2). She was accompanied by an Early Colonial ceramic vessel (Figure 4.2), but she was not buried with any items of European manufacture such as clothing or glass beads. The tattoos on her forearms were preserved because of her mummified state. Two children were also interred inside the outer funerary shroud, and at least one of the

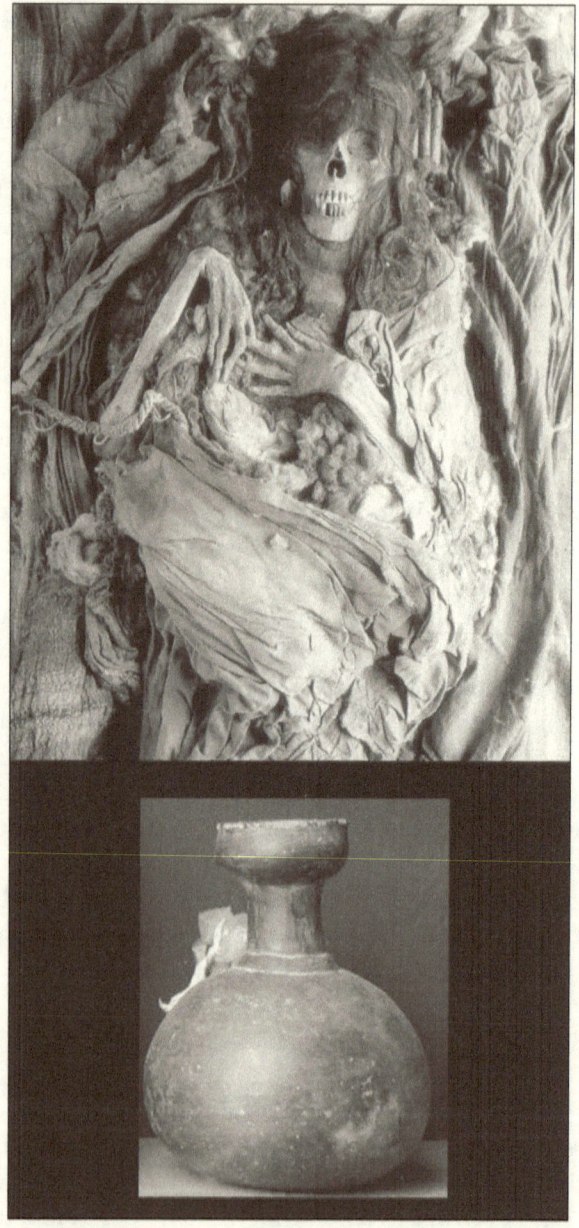

FIGURE 4.2.

(Top) *Adult female from Huaquerones interred in an extended position on her back (supine) on a stretcher with two children and an Early Colonial ceramic vessel (below). She was interred upright in a burial pit that was intrusive into the Late Horizon deposits. Photo: Proyecto Puruchuco-Huaquerones.*

children was added after the initial funerary preparations. The original textile covered the principal female and her internal mortuary offerings; however, with the addition of one of the children, a textile panel was added to expand the size of the original funerary shroud.

This burial may represent an early example of corpse removal from a church cemetery because of the presence of an Early Colonial ceramic vessel, its intrusion into the Late Horizon burials below it, and its extended burial position, rather than the usual seated and flexed burial position, which is the customary position in the Late Horizon burials from Puruchuco-Huaquerones. The addition of one of the child burials into the funerary bundle and the consequent modification of the original funerary shroud suggest that the funerary preparations may have extended beyond the original church burial, and perhaps occurred afterward, a phenomenon that is described in the idolatries sources. Andean mortuary rituals were typically elaborate and protracted, occurring over several days after death, and the first anniversary of the death was often a celebrated event that involved the repetition of the funerary rites and the addition of funerary offerings (Cobo 1990[1653]; Doyle 1988), but in this example the unusual burial position and the inclusion of the Early Colonial vessel lead us to believe that this was more than a celebration of the first anniversary of death.

After the woman's interment in the church grave, it is likely that her family and community members disinterred her corpse. Either one or both children were added to the funerary bundle and then the entire stretcher was interred in the community cemetery. Although we cannot pinpoint whether these activities were nocturnal and clandestine, if we accept the testimonies that traditional mortuary rituals and corpse disinterment were concealed from religious authorities, then this example may represent indigenous covert resistance to the Spanish policy of church burial. Members of the community likely accommodated many of the other Christian saints and rituals because they were not contradictory to the traditional pantheon and practices; however, church burial ruptured the connection between the sacred ancestors and the origin of the community. Therefore, some members of this community recalibrated the Late Horizon practice through the disinterment and reinterment of the church burial and thereby continued their prehispanic beliefs about death, the ancestors, and the social reproduction of society under the new Christian regime.

In this case study, we must also interrogate our use of covert resistance as an explanation and explore other actions and responses of both the colonized and colonizer during the Christianization efforts of Spanish colonization. We believe this Early Colonial burial is an early example of corpse removal before the establishment of the reducción period, and it is likely that, at the time, the relatives of the deceased were not deliberately subverting or resisting Christian doctrine. Since we believe this reinterment occurred shortly after the Spanish Conquest, people from Puruchuco-Huaquerones could have accommodated Christian burial rituals with the intention of reburial afterward, without viewing this reburial as an impediment to Christian conversion. Given the variability in early evangelization efforts and the small numbers of parish priests during the Early Colonial period, it is difficult to assess whether the local religious authorities knew about the reinterment and whether they were complicit in, or accommodating of, these indigenous practices within the community of Puruchuco-Huaquerones. Prior to the Toledan reforms, the parish priests appropriated Andean beliefs and forms as part of their Christian conversion efforts, and the ancestor cult was not viewed as an impediment to these efforts until several decades later.

RESISTANCE, PERSISTENCE, AND ACCOMMODATION

Bioarchaeological analysis of the breakdown and reconfiguration of the traditional mortuary practices at Puruchuco-Huaquerones offers evidence of how indigenous resistance was enacted on the central coast of Peru and how these responses differed from, or were in concordance with, what is known about early indigenous resistance and responses to Spanish invasion and conquest of the Inca Empire. These data are the only ones that evince the violent encounters between indigenous communities and the Spaniards in Andean South America, as well as the material evidence of disinterment and reburial.

In our case studies, the written accounts of Spanish invasion and conquest both handcuff and liberate our investigation of indigenous resistance to Spanish colonization. As D'Altroy (2005b) has noted, the view of conquest and colonization is biased toward the written record as well as the perceptions of these texts' authors. For example, although some coastal communities allied themselves with the Spaniards against the neo-Inca state, our case study demonstrates that some people from Puruchuco-Huaquerones fought against the Spaniards and their allies at some point, which underscores the limitations of the written texts and the importance of archaeological/bioarchaeological case studies in illuminating the variability of local responses to Spanish colonization. Although other possibilities are explored, the written accounts allowed us to infer that these violent encounters with the Spanish occurred at or around the Siege of

Lima because of the site's proximity to the location of the uprising and the southerly escape route and because of the physical evidence of injuries from European weaponry.

Further, the ethnohistorical sources for the Spanish invasion of the Inca Empire are extremely limited in their temporal and geographic scope. For instance, the ethnohistorical literature that describes the ancestor cult and the importance of the sacred ancestors is temporally and geographically widespread; however, most of the published materials that describe the ancestor burial place and the practice of corpse disinterment are from highland regions, are not specific to the central coast, and date to the intensification of the idolatries campaigns. At Puruchuco-Huaquerones, a large sample of burials has been unearthed and recovered from several cemeteries within the archaeological zone, which is a different mortuary pattern from what has been observed of burial locations in the highlands. However, there may be a distinction between how and where the sacred ancestors were interred in coastal regions prior to and after the Spanish Conquest. Although we believe that the cemetery was sacred and symbolically important to the people from Puruchuco-Huaquerones, to date we have not recovered any burials that would qualify as the one or two sacred ancestors who would have connected this physical location with the symbolic origin place of the community, and we are not aware of ethnohistorical sources that deal specifically with this area of the central coast and with this question. However, without the recorded testimonies of the clandestine disinterment from the idolatries literature, the Early Colonial burial from Huaquerones would appear as an idiosyncratic burial without association with indigenous resistance, persistence, or accommodation. If we understand the Andean cemetery of Puruchuco-Huaquerones as part of a community's "built environment" (Silverman 2002), and further, part of its religious and cosmological geography and connection with the community's ancestors (Doyle 1988; Salomon 1995), then the atypical burials and the Early Colonial burial reflect the breakdown of the normative mortuary practices but also the persistence and perpetuation of the most important component of these beliefs and practices: the interment in the community's cemetery with fellow community members and the sacred ancestors.

ACKNOWLEDGMENTS

This research was made possible by grants from the National Geographic Society, Bryn Mawr College, Wenner-Gren (#6791 to Murphy), and the National Science Foundation (#0618192 to Murphy). The authors would like to thank the numerous students from Haverford College, Bryn

Mawr College, Universidad de San Marcos, and Pontificia Universidad Católica del Perú who assisted and participated in the laboratory research. Special kudos to Maria Fernanda Boza and Jason Toohey for their valuable assistance and insight. We would also extend our gratitude to the other seminar participants and the anonymous reviewers, as this work was greatly improved by their constructive and insightful feedback.

Notes

1. Spalding (1984:28–29) defines an *ayllu* as "a group—family, lineage, or generation—whose members were related to one another through their descent from a common ancestor." This chapter follows Spalding's definition, but discussions abound over how to define and identify the ayllu in archaeology (see Isbell 1997). In this text, we use the general terms *ancestral burial place* as an English translation of the numerous indigenous terms, including *machay, chullpa, pucullo,* and *ayahuasi. Mallqui* describes the one or two *specific* sacred ancestors who were the founders of a particular ayllu (see discussion in Doyle 1988:47–87; Salomon 1995:321–23).

2. Out of respect for SAR's policy on the publication of images of Native American human remains and images of mortuary offerings, the authors have removed those images that have been published elsewhere. To view images described in this chapter, the reader is referred to the publication by Murphy and colleagues (2010) in the American Journal of Physical Anthropology 142(4):636–50.

3. Perimortem trauma refers to trauma that was sustained at or around the time of death.

4. For intersample comparability (following Milner et al. 1991; Steadman 2008), this study focuses on the trauma rates for individuals fifteen years of age and older (n = 119). Trauma rates for individuals less than fifteen years of age are reported elsewhere (Gaither et al. 2007).

5

Convergences

Producing Early Colonial Hybridity at a Doctrina *in Highland Peru*

Steven A. Wernke

> The habit, the crucifix, the routines of prayer, the protocols of fraternal speech and conduct marked and made those who possessed them "Franciscan." How to be a Franciscan missionary they discovered and invented in the doing of it. Written texts had little part here: they would carve out of their own days the texts by which they would live....They mapped the slow making of a Christian landscape out of the events of their daily work....
> (Clendinnen 1987:50)

This passage from Inga Clendinnen's perennially influential *Ambivalent Conquests* evokes the everyday life of routine, ritual, and observance that formed the core of early Franciscan evangelization in the Yucatán. It is fitting in its emphasis on the primacy of practice over doctrine—early missionization throughout the Spanish Americas did not emphasize uniform or rigorous doctrinal instruction per se, but rather the implantation of a civilizing cultural package through the mission settlement (Graham 1998; Hanson 1995). Equally telling, however, is how Clendinnen frames the missionary encounter through an evocative realist style to fill the gaps left by ecclesiastical documents and evoke the daily rhythms of life in

77

early Franciscan missions. But how else are we to know of the day-to-day negotiations between the missionaries and missionized in the "slow making of a Christian landscape"? Indeed, as Clendinnen observes, written texts played little role in that process. The documentary corpus of early Spanish evangelization in the Americas is dominated by high-level prescriptive texts, extirpation trials, and ecclesiastical memorials. These church texts were oriented by discourses of regimentation and triumphalist narratives of mass conversion. Earlier histories of the "spiritual conquest" of the Americas (the ur text here being Ricard 1966), more or less accepting this top-down perspective, shed light on the institutional development of early Spanish Catholicism in the Americas, but they provided few insights into how evangelization was practiced in the field, let alone indigenous engagements with it. The subsequent generation of emphasis on indigenous resistance to Spanish pretensions to religious conversion was an appropriate historiographical intervention, though "resistance" is but one of many forms of indigenous engagement, and, as this and several other contributions to this volume argue (Beck et al., Chapter 2; Liebmann, Chapter 10; Preucel, Chapter 11; Sheptak et al., Chapter 8; Voss, Chapter 12), limits indigenous agency to conflictive and reactive, rather than proactive or cocreative roles in missionary encounters (see Ortner 1995).

Basic and critical questions thus remain: how did indigenous communities perceive, interpret, and act on early missionary interventions into their most deeply inculcated cultural practices and beliefs? How did pastoral agents negotiate their mandate of instilling a uniform faith with the vastly diverse realities of the indigenous communities they encountered? Addressing these questions draws attention to how mutual accommodation, negotiation, and appropriation of religious beliefs and practices must have characterized the concerns of evangelical encounters at least as much as the drive for doctrinal purity through religious eradication and replacement of idolatry. Ecclesiastical authorities were loathe to acknowledge negotiation and heterodoxy in writing, so documentary researchers—as exemplified by Clendinnen above—have developed innovative and critical modes of reading and writing against the grain and between the lines of their sources. As necessary and valuable as these hermeneutics have been to gaining insights into the everyday negotiations of early evangelical encounters in the Spanish Americas, they necessarily chafe at the edges of the observable in documentary research.

This is where archaeology can make an important contribution. Through archaeology, we can further "excavate between the lines" to recover the residues and media of religious transformation in the Spanish

Americas. But neither should it be considered only a blunt instrument of last resort. By focusing on how the material world itself emerged from and structured daily practices, archaeology is uniquely equipped to analyze a primary medium and outcome through which religious negotiations occurred. This requires a move toward approaches that explore the structuring and even agential aspects of material culture and the built environment—how they were shapers of, and not only reflections of, past behaviors (see, e.g., Appadurai 1986; DeMarrais et al. 2004; Soja 1989). Through such a vantage, mission settlements can be seen as emergent stage sets that were produced by (and for) novel forms of worship, daily life, and subjectivity.

Archaeologists and architectural historians working in North America and Mesoamerica have made major strides in identifying the built configurations and conditions of life and worship in missions. Sequences of missionization in the Spanish borderlands and Mesoamerica have been proposed with identifiable archaeological correlates (Hanson 1995; Thomas 1988). But in the Andean region, mission archaeology—and colonial archaeology in general—remains in its infancy (see Jamieson 2005; Klaus et al. 2005; Quilter, Chapter 6; Quilter et al. 2005; Rice 1996a, 1996b; Van Buren 1999, 2005; deFrance 2003; Wernke 2003, 2007a).

Accordingly, the research discussed here starts at the beginning, by providing a view of the transition from Inca to Spanish colonial rule, and of the very earliest evangelical forays in the Andean highlands, through excavations at an early Franciscan *doctrina* (doctrinal settlement) in the Colca Valley of southern highland Peru. This settlement, known today as Malata (site number TU-170), was initially a small Inca administrative outpost during terminal prehispanic times. In the early decades following the Spanish invasion—between the 1540s and 1560s—Malata was transformed into a doctrina when a group of Franciscan friars established a series of chapels at settlements throughout the Colca Valley (Cook 2002, 2007; Wernke 2007a). These doctrinas were then forcibly abandoned or built over with the institution of the viceroyalty-wide *reducción* (Indian "reduction" village) program in the 1570s (see Quilter, Chapter 6). Malata thus provides an ideal, chronologically controlled window into the transition from Inca to colonial rule and the first wave of evangelization in the Andes. To date, it is the only such early evangelical complex to be extensively excavated in the Peruvian highlands.

By analyzing the sequence of architectural remodeling at the site, the spatial organization of its domestic compounds, and connectivity between domestic compounds and the larger site layout, I will show that Malata underwent significant growth and reordering of its architectonic spaces during its short life as a doctrina. I argue that the plan of Malata integrated preexisting domestic and Inca imperial structures but was also transformed according to specific Spanish concepts of urban order centered on the household, church, and plaza. By extension, I suggest that the site plan was reorganized to inculcate a Christian lifestyle—to interpellate Christian subjects through newly habituated rhythms of daily practice. Ironically, however, the effectiveness of this project must have depended on its legibility to the site's inhabitants, and thus would have been initially understood and acted on through ideologies of space and the material world that were not of the friars' making. On the eve of the Spanish invasion of the Andes, Inca imperial consolidation was an ongoing process, and Inca imperialism was negotiated in many social dimensions and material media analogous to those of Spanish evangelization—especially through elaborately staged, public ritual in open plazas (see Coben 2006; Morris and Thompson 1985; Moore 1996). The inhabitants of Malata, many of whom were born before the conquest, thus brought distinct sensibilities and practices regarding the sacred, public, and domestic spaces that they constructed and inhabited during the site's brief use life as a doctrina. Built spaces intended to effect religious conversion instead produced what Jaime Lara (2004) has called "convergence"—a hybrid built and social arrangement that was not entirely conceived of or controlled by the friars or their charges. I thus argue that new forms of colonial religious practices emerged at least as much from these processes of mutual appropriation and accommodation as from indigenous "resistance" to Catholicism.

SPANISH COLONIAL SEMIOTIC IDEOLOGY AND MISSION ARCHAEOLOGY IN THE ANDES

As in other areas of the Americas, Spanish administrators and clergy emphasized from the very beginning the importance of reshaping the built environment to transform Andean communities; in fact, much colonial social engineering and evangelization was rather deterministic about it. Spanish thinking in the sixteenth century held that orderly urban settlement (*civitas*) was not just reflective of or a necessary precondition for social order (*policia*), but actually generated it (Kagan 2000; Cummins 2002; Gose 2003). This ideology informed the work of early missionaries and reached its maximum expression in the institution of the *reducciones*, a massive program of forced resettlement in the 1570s that moved some 1.5 million native Andeans into gridded, European-style villages centered on the church and plaza (Hemming 1983:393). Long advocated by the Crown and colonial magistrates, and finally implemented by the Viceroy Francisco de Toledo in the 1570s, the idea of "reducing" people was also semantically related to ordering, rationalizing, rendering intelligible, subjugating, and converting (Cummins 2002; Durston 1999; Gose 2003; Mumford 2005). Conversion had always been linked to a larger Spanish civilizing project, whereby living "like a Christian" in planned, orderly urban settlements was thought to literally transform pagans into Christians. This is made explicit in the writings of the colonial jurist Juan de Matienzo, whose blueprint for the colonial state in the Andes (*Gobierno del Perú*) (1910[1567]) was implemented by Toledo, and in Toledo's own instructions for resettlement (Levillier 1935).

Early Spanish evangelization was in this sense guided by, to borrow from Webb Keane, a particular "semiotic ideology": a set of "basic assumptions about what signs are and how they function in the world" (Keane 2003:419). Semiotic ideology is an especially useful concept for archaeologists because it expands the domain of ideology beyond the realm of discourse to consider how ideologies are enacted and transformed through practice and material manifestation. It also situates inquiry of ideologies of the material in a wider framework for understanding relationships between signs, meaning, and materiality. Building on the semiotics of Charles Sanders Peirce (and in contrast to, in particular, Saussurean models of sign systems), the concept of semiotic ideology starts from the premise that sign systems in practice cannot be separated from concrete instantiation—whether linguistic, performative, or material. Seemingly abstract qualities—what Peirce calls *qualisigns*—must, in order to have meaning or social efficacy, become somehow materialized. Such is the case with the semantic range of "reducción" and its material embodiments discussed above. In the process of materialization, associated qualities of words, things, and actions become bound with other qualities, since no concrete token can have only one meaning or quality. Words, things, and actions thus enter into complex articulations with one another in particular historical and social conjunctures, which Keane (2003:410) refers to as "representational economies." It is thus through materialization and the ongoing exchanges of representational economies that meaning and efficacy become at once possible and contingent—a process Keane (2003:414) calls "bundling." In contrast to more instrumentalist models of materialization (DeMarrais et al. 1996), in which elites strategically materialize (whether through portable media, feasts, monumentalism, or other forms) their dominant ideology to further their interests, materialization in this sense is the process through which semiotic ideologies are at once constituted and potentially destabilized.

STEVEN A. WERNKE

Here I am concerned specifically with how such polysemy emerges through (and in) the built environment as a medium of religious inculcation in the colonial Andes. This is not to claim flatly that the "architecture of conquest" (Fraser 1990) was ineffectual. Rather, it is to point out that while buildings generally "stabilize social life...[they] stabilize *imperfectly*" (Gieryn 2002:35, emphasis in the original). Rather than being mute impositions on social life, buildings occupy the middle ground between structure and agent—they structure interaction even as they are subject to remodeling, repurposing, dereliction, and demolition—all the while remaining objects of interpretation and representation. Such indeterminacy is especially acute in early colonial encounters, where often radically different semiotic ideologies come into articulation, generating—as postcolonial scholars such as Bhabha (1994) and Chatterjee (1993) point out—profound ambiguity and ambivalence, rather than clearly drawn dialectics of domination and resistance (see also Liebmann, Chapter 10). Despite the best-laid colonial plans, then, in practice, new kinds of "third spaces" (*sensu* Bhabha 1994) of reflexivity, ambiguity, and possibly contestation, emerge through built forms.

A focus on the negotiation of semiotic ideologies through representational economies thus provides a model for how the material world is integral to the negotiation of power and meaning. At issue is how the material world is inherently bound up in and thus constitutive of discourse and practice—what Ingold (1993) refers to as "dwelling." On the one hand, being mindful of these possible relationships highlights how materiality places limits on how humans can endow their world with meaning. Certainly, clerics in early colonial times had to reckon with this fact. Often lacking personnel or strong coercive means, they were forced to build in and around existing settlements, often directly within existing temple complexes. As Barbara Voss points out in this volume, the construction of even the most "Spanish" of Spanish colonial settlements was itself necessarily a collaborative affair between the Spanish and indigenous communities, and new built forms once introduced must have been apperceived, interpreted, and acted upon through extant semiotic ideologies. On the other hand, the material world can also generate new possibilities of meaning. Indeed, the ideology that motivated the construction of early evangelical complexes, or, on a grander scale, the Toledan colonial project of reducción resettlement, was premised on the notion that restructuring the built environment of everyday life would generate Christian subjects. But by the same token, it did not (and could not) account for how these new built environments would articulate with existing material arrangements. More conventional symbolic approaches cannot account adequately for how the material world can also trip up people's conventions in this way, "as if the world could hold no further surprises for them" (Keane 2007:18). And certainly the material world of early Spanish missions in the Americas was full of surprises (to say the least) for missionary and missionized alike.

But if the material world and practice are central to understanding early evangelical encounters in the Andes, we are far from understanding how transformations of the material world and everyday practices played out in the actual spaces where they occurred. Our ignorance of the spatial, material, and practical dimensions of the first wave of evangelization in the Andes, between the 1530s and the 1560s, is doubly regrettable, since it also remains almost entirely undocumented in written texts. No published pastoral texts from the period exist, and no manuscript versions of early catechetical guides have been identified (Durston 2004; Estenssoro 2003). Instead, most of what is known comes from Church policy decrees of the First and Second Ecclesiastical Councils of Lima (1551–52 and 1567–68) and from a scattering of accounts in provincial archives. Ecclesiastical memorials recount the works of early missionaries, but these were often written after the deaths of their subjects and were shaped as much by hagiographic tropes as by their lived realities. This is true of the Colca Valley in particular, the site of one of the earliest Franciscan interventions in the Peruvian highlands.

THE EARLY FRANCISCAN PRESENCE IN THE COLCA VALLEY

The province of the Collagua ethnic group, centered in the Colca Valley, was quickly identified by the Pizarros as a key demographic, economic, and political center in the south-central Andean highlands (Málaga Medina 1977; Pease 1977). Situated in the semiarid western cordillera, the Colca Valley forms part of the largest drainage of the southern Peruvian Pacific watershed, and was home to two large ethnic groups: the Quechua-speaking Cabanas of the lower end of the valley (ca. 2,800–3,200 m.a.s.l.) and the Aymara-speaking Collaguas of the central and upper reaches of the valley (ca. 3,200–4,000 m.a.s.l.). With a combined population estimated in the range of 60,000 to 70,000 inhabitants on the eve of conquest (Cook 1982), the province was considered one of the richest *encomiendas* (trusteeships of indigenous labor) in Peru, and the Collaguas were first granted by Francisco Pizarro to his half-brother Gonzalo in 1540 (Málaga Medina 1977).

Less than a decade following the sieges of Cuzco and Lima (see Murphy et al., Chapter 4), a small group of friars entered the Colca Valley probably around 1545, making it one of the earliest locales of Franciscan pastoral activity in the southern highlands (Tibesar 1953:65). No ecclesiastical

Steven A. Wernke

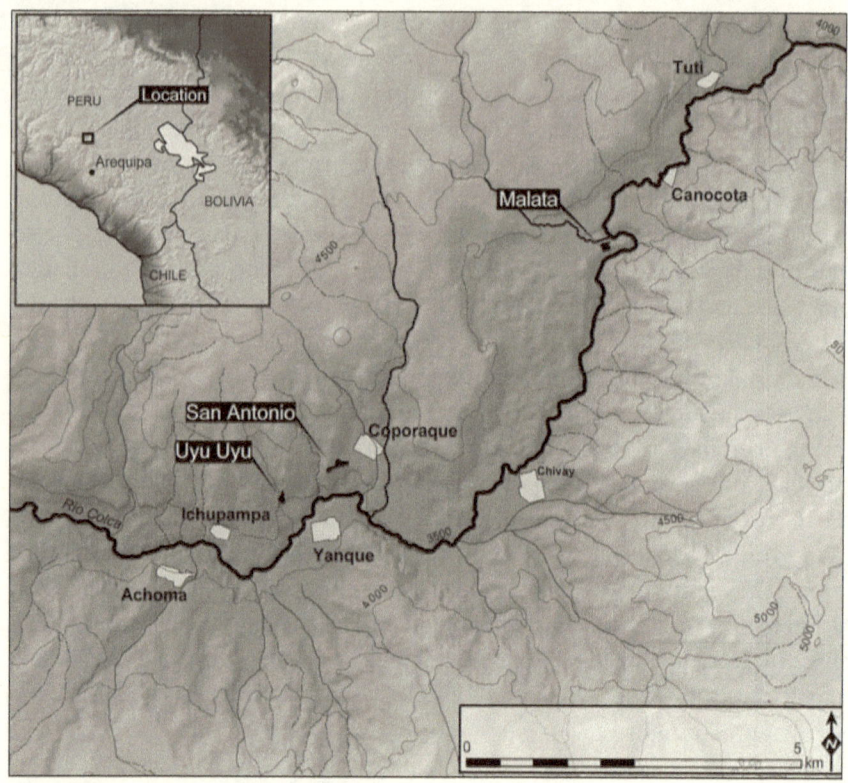

Figure 5.1.
The central and upper Colca Valley, showing locations of reducción villages and early doctrinas discussed in the text.

documents from this initial period of evangelization have been identified, but a report from 1585 housed in the archive of the Franciscan convent in Lima states that "forty years ago the friars [of Our Father Saint Francis] entered the province of the Collaguas" (AFSL, registro 15, parte 5 [ca. 1585], f477r). The group was headed by one fray Juan de Monzón, of whom little is known, although he was said to have accompanied fray Marcos de Niza and the other members of the original group of Twelve Franciscans to enter Peru (Tibesar 1953:65). He and accompanying fray Juan de Ginés established a series of early doctrinas in the principal settlements of the valley. Almost nothing other than the names of some of these first doctrinas is described in the known documentary corpus.

What is described of this early foray, as is common to the genre of ecclesiastical memorials, are tales of the missionary zeal of Monzón in the heroic terms of a spiritual conquest. He was said to have carried out an extensive extirpation campaign, ridding the hilltops and peaks in and around the valley of their shrines, and publicly burning massive hauls of ancestral mummies and ritual paraphernalia (ASFL, registro 15, parte 5). This and other reports from the mid-1580s were written in response to petitions by Collagua native lords for the reinstatement of the Franciscans after they were replaced by parish priests from the Diocese of Cuzco in the early 1580s. They were produced in the context of a contentious case that pitted the diocesan priests—whom the Collagua lords claimed had engaged in commerce, overcharged for sacraments, and other abuses—against the Order (Cook 2002), and should be read accordingly, rather than as dispassionate registries of early Franciscan pastoral activities. For example, the 1585 report states flatly that the friars "baptized all the Indians that now live and also those that died Christian. They also built churches and convents in all the villages and with their synod and alms helped make many of the adornments of the sacristies" (AFSL, registro 15, parte 5, f477r). The few at-hand descriptions of the initial Franciscan presence in the valley are thus problematic for understanding the scale and methods of evangelization used by the friars, and are silent on the issue of indigenous engagements with it.

In prior research, I have identified rustic chapels at two Collagua-Inca administrative outposts in the central part of the valley (Wernke 2007a), as well as a possible early chapel at the provincial capital of Yanque (Figure 5.1). At one of these—the site of Uyu Uyu—the chapel is situated on the central plaza at the site, directly opposite a large (29 × 7 m) Inca great hall (a form often referred to as *kallanka*) structure that fronts the entire western side of the plaza. At the other—the site of San Antonio—the chapel is situated atop a prominent hilltop adjacent to an Inca hall and its plaza. Much as in Mesoamerica (Burkhart 1998; Edgerton and Pérez de Lara 2001; Hanson 1995; Lara 2004), the earliest missionary strategies in the Colca Valley seem to have been based on largely outdoor catechesis in recycled prehispanic ritual spaces (often using the same plaza spaces as during Inca times) in a participatory and performative pastoral approach. Such plaza/great hall couplets as those found in association with chapels in the Colca are omnipresent in the empire. Though multifunctional, one of their main uses was for staging elaborate processionals and commensal rituals, in which the state—through imperial representatives or local elites—reified an ideology of state magnanimity vis-à-vis subject populations (see Moore 1996; Morris and Thompson 1985; Coben 2006). Through the metaphor of "feeding," commensal ritual was a primary idiom of state–subject relations, as the Inca was presented as a living deity and father-provider to his subject "children" (see, e.g., Bray 2003; Ramírez 2005). The material and labor of state prestations in these rituals paled by comparison to the labor taxes that subject populations provided to the state, but such rituals evoked and (re)constituted archetypal constructs of Andean personhood and community, defined by varied conceptions of reciprocity between people, and between humans and the cosmological forces that animate the visible world (Murra 1980). Through standardized ritual programmatics and material forms, the great hall–plaza complex objectified a normative model of state–subject relations.

Elsewhere, I have argued that the close association between the locations of these chapels and their close spatial association with Inca administrative architecture and plaza spaces suggests a missionary strategy that piggybacked on such Incaic spaces of state integration (Wernke 2007a). Rather than the vision of eradication and conversion represented in the memorials, the archaeological evidence—at the scale of both settlement pattern and site layout—suggests a strategy of spatial analogy that linked and leveraged built-in spaces of Inca state-sponsored ceremonials with new forms of Christian ritual.

During the 1560s, Church institutions in Peru were expanding and formalizing, and Church policies pushed for increasingly uniform doctrine following the early period of experimentation (Durston 2007; Estenssoro 2001, 2003). Certainly this drive for orthodoxy was in line with the decrees issued from Rome at the height of the Counterreformation (the decrees of the Council of Trent were received in Lima in 1565), but more proximately the Church in Peru was reacting to increasingly alarming reports of apostasies in the provinces, reaching a fevered pitch in the central highlands, where a millenarian cult—the Taki Onqoy ("dancing sickness")—reportedly prophesized the expulsion of the Christian deity by Andean huacas and advocated the reinstatement of autochthonous rule (Millones et al. 1990; Stern 1982). Whether the Taki Onqoy resistance movement was as widespread and threatening as portrayed by ambitious provincial diocesan clergy is a matter of debate (Mumford 1998), but such reports of continued idolatry surely informed the policies outlined in the Second Lima Council (1567–68). Though true parish systems were not established outside the urban centers of the viceroyalty during this time, the Second Lima Council called for greater doctrinal uniformity.

Reflecting these changes, the Franciscan mission in the Colca Valley expanded and formalized during the 1560s. Four additional friars were assigned to the valley, and formal convents were established in the villages of Yanque, in the central part of the valley, and Callalli, in the valley's upper reaches, forming a hub-and-spoke system of primary and secondary doctrinas (Cook 2002, 2007). Malata was likely a small secondary doctrina in this network, serviced from the convent of Callalli.

There is also evidence that the friars had already begun congregating households from their dispersed prehispanic settlements during this time. For example, the friars were said to have congregated the dispersed *ayllus* (Andean kin-based corporate collectivities) of surrounding settlements to the doctrina of San Antonio (discussed above) (see Wernke 2007a). As I discuss below, the site of Malata exhibits marked growth and formalization during its brief use life as a doctrina.

THE DOCTRINA OF MALATA

The site of Malata, situated high in the Colca Valley at 3,850 m.a.s.l., occupies a draw immediately above the dramatic 200-m-deep gorge of the Colca River (Figures 5.1–5.3). The site is located just upvalley from a large bend in the river that separates the intensively terraced, agricultural core of the valley from the grazing lands of the valley's upper reaches. A major Inca road ran through this section of the upper valley, and Malata was situated on a short spur off the road.

The 1.6-ha residential area of the site houses eighty structures, most standing and well preserved. This habitational zone is surrounded by mortuary areas in the surrounding colluvial slopes, where we documented 201 rock-lined subterranean ovoid collar tombs (nearly all disturbed, some showing human remains and diagnostic Late Horizon ceramics), as well as two rectangular prehispanic *chullpas* (burial towers) overlooking the river gorge.

The occupational sequence of Malata has been defined with considerable precision. Our excavations opened a total area of about 300 m² in a variety of contexts (see Figure 5.2). The artifact assemblage clearly reflects a primary occupation from Inca times (the Late Horizon, ca. 1450–1532) that extends into immediate postconquest times. Of the 6,659 diagnostic sherds from all contexts at the site, 89 percent (n = 5,948) are of Late Horizon styles, while 9 percent (n = 580) are of Colonial styles.[1] The specific timeframe of the colonial occupation is well defined, since all diagnostic colonial artifacts pertain to the first half of the sixteenth century or earlier. Of the colonial ceramics, only two green glazed fragments (from a single bowl) were recovered. These appear to be of the Morisco Green type —a lead glaze ware corresponding to the late fifteenth to mid-sixteenth century (Lister and Lister 1987). Blue glass beads of the Nueva Cádiz type—a small, drawn bead of square cross section, sometimes helically

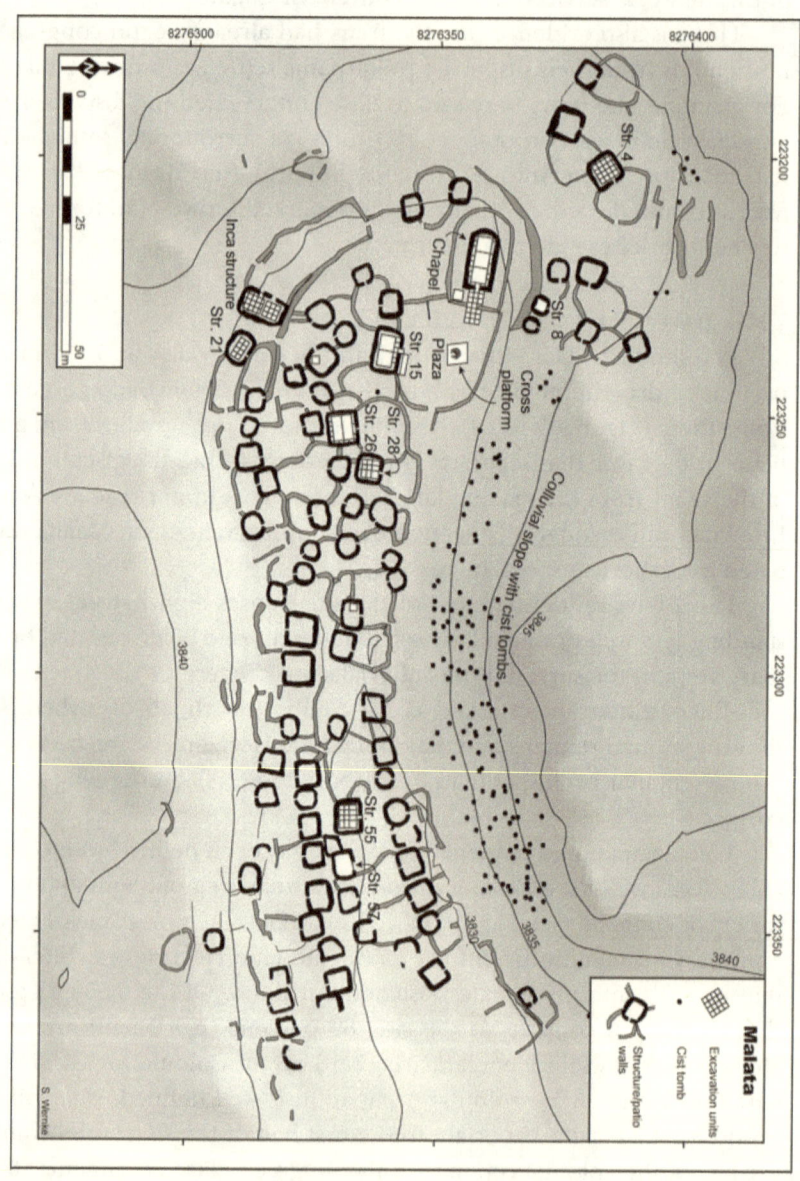

FIGURE 5.2.
Architectural map of Malata.

twisted—were recovered from the floors of several domestic structures. These beads were only produced during the first half of the sixteenth century, probably in coastal Venezuela (Smith and Good 1982). Distinctive "caret head" nails, also diagnostic of the first half of the sixteenth century, were recovered from domestic structures and from the Inca structure at the site (Flint and Flint 2003:253). No colonial artifacts diagnostic of later times were recovered. In short, all indices point conclusively to an early and short colonial occupation. This range is congruent with documentary descriptions of the sequence of doctrina construction and use in the valley during the 1540s to 1560s and their replacement by the reducciones in the 1570s.

The remarkable state of architectural preservation at the site allows a detailed reconstruction of its spatial organization and transformation through time. The site is divided between a residential sector in the eastern, lower end of the site, and public and ritual spaces and buildings in the higher, western end, including an Inca structure and plaza, and a chapel with curved apse and surrounding terraced atrium.

Malata during Inca Rule

Prior to becoming a doctrina, Malata appears to have functioned as a secondary- or tertiary-level outpost during the Inca occupation of the valley. This function is evident in the presence of a small (8.2 × 4.2 m), rustic Inca structure with two trapezoidal doors opening westward to a long (24.0 × 8.5 m) plaza atop a terrace on the higher, western end of the site. As discussed above, this kallanka-like Inca great hall structure and open plaza configuration is a recurring pattern at Late Horizon sites throughout the valley (Doutriaux 2002, 2004; Wernke 2006) and is generally consistent with Inca settlement planning. Such open plaza spaces and associated buildings were often used as staging grounds for a variety of commensal events (Coben 2006). This is the most parsimonious interpretation for the function of this structure as well, given the high proportions of finely crafted serving wares recovered from our excavations in it.

Unlike other such sites in the valley with such Inca architecture, however, there are no indices for a significant occupation of Malata during the preceding Late Intermediate period (CE 1100–1450). Of the fourteen structures we have excavated, none have produced Late Intermediate period (Collagua I and II) ceramics in primary contexts. The site thus appears to have originated as a prerogative of Inca administration, but it clearly would have been a relatively minor outpost, judging by its small size and expedient architecture.

FIGURE 5.3.
Overview photos of Malata. View A is from the west; note curved apse of the chapel and Inka structure with its two doors and plaza. View B is from the northeast.

The Chapel

To the adjacent north of the Inca structure and plaza, facing the opposite direction, are a chapel, enclosing atrium, and plaza. The chapel at Malata is similar in its diminutive size (maximum interior measurements of 10.3 × 4.5 m) and general form to those previously documented, but with a well-formed, curved apse (Figures 5.2 and 5.3). Like the others, its masonry and overall construction are rather expedient. The lightly dressed fieldstone walls are set in irregular courses in thick mortar, with a mud and rubble core between the facings. This probably reflects upon the early stage of evangelization, both in terms of the economistic and nonspecialized labor investment embodied in the chapel, and the small population it would have serviced. Services in the chapel would have been small-scale and rather intimate. Calculating an area of one to two individuals per square meter in the congregation area, it would have accommodated twenty to forty individuals. The orientation of the chapel does not adhere to Church conventions of an eastward-oriented chancel, but instead accommodates the existing settlement and topographical setting. The chapel's entry looks over the plaza and main residential area below, across to high craggy peaks on the other side of the river gorge.

Our excavations in the chapel encompassed virtually all the interior and revealed an almost entirely intact floor plan and altar platform. Although the entry side of the chapel is heavily deteriorated (perhaps due to mining of worked façade stones), clearing excavations around the entry revealed a surprisingly narrow doorway: at 63 cm, it was wide enough to admit only one person at a time (Figure 5.4A). Jambs on both sides of the base of the doorway indicate that its two small doors opened from the center, swinging inward. Entering the chapel, its floor plan changed considerably over its use life. There were two construction and use periods: initially, the floor was composed of a single level from the entry to the base of the altar in the rear; later a chancel platform (1 m deep, 21 cm high) with two fieldstone steps was built across the width of the structure in front of the altar (Figure 5.4A).

The altar platform itself was intact; it abuts the center of the apse (measuring 1.67 m wide × 0.80 m deep). During the first period of use, it would have stood 84 cm high off the floor, and after the chancel platform was built, it would have stood 53 cm high. Presumably, a small altar would have been placed on top of this altar platform. In both the first and second periods of use, the floor of the chapel was composed of packed earth—it was not paved with cobbles or flagstones. Inside the entry, in the northeast

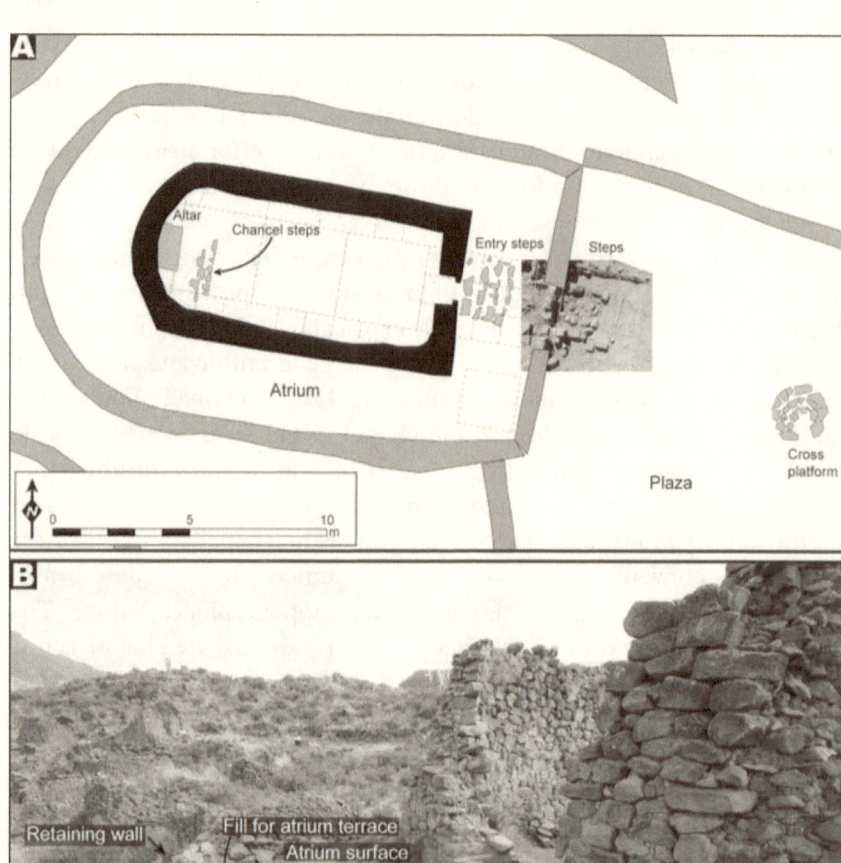

FIGURE 5.4.
Two views of the chapel entry, atrium, and plaza area. View A shows the alignment of the chapel entry, atrium entry, and cross platform. View B shows stratigraphy of atrium terrace fill overlying three of the four original steps, and atrium retaining wall, which separates the atrium from the plaza.

corner of the structure, there was an extremely compact ovoid feature of well-sorted silty clay, which, by analogy with known church floor plans, may have been the location of a baptismal or holy water font. Single courses of large fieldstones—perhaps the bases of transverse walls—were uncovered inside the entry and under the chancel platform, each about 20 to 30 cm below the level of the floor surface. Their function remains obscure because they would not have been visible, nor do they appear to be part of an earlier structure, since their ends abut cleanly with the side walls of the chapel and thus postdate them. In any case, the interior of the chapel shows significant remodeling through its use life with the installation of a platform, creating a chancel separate from the congregation area.

The Atrium and Plaza

Other clear attributes of Spanish urban planning are evident: the entries of the chapel and atrium face east, giving access to a larger plaza (20 × 16 m); all of these entries align with the remains of a circular fieldstone feature (2 m diameter) in the center of the plaza (see Figure 5.2). It is also roughly aligned with the doorway of a large colonial structure in the center of the plaza's south side. Excavations around the circular feature showed that it is a three-tiered platform with no discernable Inca attributes, ceramics, or underlying associated features. It was probably a platform for a central cross.

We also excavated the large structure (Structure 15) fronting the south side of the plaza (see Figures 5.2 and 5.3). This building can be definitively identified as colonial based on its low, wide doorway (a diagnostic colonial feature given local terminal prehispanic architectural conventions—see Wernke 2003, 2009) and prominent position in the plaza. The packed-earth floor in this structure was extremely clean, turning up only a handful of artifacts of any class (aside from small dispersed carbon fragments). The floors of the eight domestic structures we excavated, by contrast, all had much higher artifact densities. The only noteworthy artifact from the floor of this structure was a small silver fragment (most likely a small piece of ornamentation) inside the doorway. By all indications, this colonial building was used for some formal—most likely civic or administrative—function given its location in the plaza.

Core elements of a Spanish colonial settlement were thus inserted into the site plan of Malata: church, atrium, and plaza with central cross and civic building. However, there is clear evidence that this layout was not planned or constructed in a single episode. Rather, it was the end state of considerable remodeling over the brief use life of the site as a doctrina. Clearing excavations in front of the chapel show unambiguously that it was originally fronted by four entry steps, three of which were subsequently buried by the fill of the artificially leveled, terraced atrium around the chapel (Figure 5.4B). The eastern wall of the atrium, which functions as a retaining wall for the atrium fill, also forms the western wall of the central plaza. Steps were built from the plaza up to the entry of the atrium formed by this retaining wall (see Figure 5.4B). Thus, the atrium, plaza, and steps leading up to the atrium from the plaza, most likely along with the large colonial structure in the center of the plaza's south side, were added subsequent to the construction of the chapel with its original four steps.

The public Spanish urban design elements at the site were therefore part of a significant remodeling episode, signaling the growth and formalization of the doctrina over its short life. Two scenarios are most likely, then; either (1) Malata was established as a doctrina during the first wave of evangelization in the 1540s and was subsequently modified during the expansion of the Franciscan mission in the valley in the 1560s, or (2) Malata was established during the second wave of evangelization in the 1560s, and was modified sometime shortly after—that is, during the following decade but prior to the forced abandonment of this and other sites like it in the early 1570s with the establishment of the reducciones. The kinds of alterations we documented seem more compatible with the longer scenario of establishment in the 1540s, followed by remodeling as part of the general growth and formalization of the Franciscan presence in the valley during the 1560s. It seems unlikely that the modifications could have predated the 1560s, because before that there were only a handful of friars in the valley. But in any case, the doctrina underwent significant remodeling during its ten to thirty years of use as a doctrina. Moreover, as discussed below, this remodeling appears to have been part of a general expansion and growth of the doctrina.

Domestic Structures and Compounds

Evidence from the site's residential areas also points to significant growth and the addition of newly configured domestic compounds during Malata's doctrina occupation. Domestic architecture at the site is composed of a mix of circular/ovoid (n = 30) and rectilinear (n = 42) fieldstone structures arranged in compounds around patio areas delimited by low fieldstone walls. Our working hypothesis prior to excavation was that the rectilinear structures were built and used during colonial times, while the circular/ovoid buildings most likely dated to the Late Horizon, some or most of which continued to be occupied through the doctrina occupation. This expectation was based on the distinctive organization of the domestic compounds of the two forms, the presence of diagnostic colonial features among the rectilinear buildings, and the distinct distributions of the two forms within the site. First, rectilinear domestic buildings with few exceptions are situated singly within walled patio areas, while circular buildings are situated in groups of two or more around a shared patio space. Several rectilinear buildings also have colonial architectural details, such as floor-level arched niches, a distinct angle change at the union of gables and lateral walls, and their wide, short doorways (the doorways of prehispanic Collagua domestic buildings are extremely narrow and tall—a diagnostic trait; see Wernke 2003, 2006). Our excavation results are consistent with this hypothesis. The interiors of eight rectilinear buildings (excluding the Inca structure) were excavated, and all but one produced diagnostic colonial artifacts (including ceramics, nails, and glass beads) in subfloor contexts. Though we have excavated in only one circular structure, it produced no colonial artifacts. This does not preclude the possibility that it was built or used during colonial times, but judging against the presence of colonial artifacts in the rectilinear structures, it is a reasonable assumption.

Also, rectilinear structures are markedly concentrated on the western and eastern ends of the site, suggesting they were added onto an older residential core. At the high, western end, away from the rest of the residential area and just behind the chapel, are a handful of domestic compounds of quadrangular domestic structures situated singly in patio areas. One of these (Structure 4) is among the largest domestic structures at the site (only three equal or exceed it in area). It also has a large arched niche in its northern wall (a colonial feature). Given its isolation, proximity to the chapel, and form, it seemed the most likely structure to have been used by a visiting friar. Our excavations in it indeed revealed unique features that set it apart from all other domestic structures at the site. Unlike all other domestic structures, which were open, single-room buildings, Structure 4 was internally divided into two rooms. It also contained unusual artifacts, including the only fragments of colonial ceramics with colored glaze—the Morisco Green–style sherds mentioned above—and a large piece of iron that was probably a piece of door hardware. So it is the most likely quarters for the friar, near the chapel and overlooking the rest of the settlement from a distance.

At the opposite, eastern end of the site, where rectilinear buildings also predominate, there is a corresponding marked change in the organization of domestic compounds. While the core residential area near the Inca structure and plaza is composed of agglutinated patio groups of circular structures, at the eastern end, houses are laid out in rows facing one another across three roughly straight, parallel streets, forming a discrete neighborhood (see Figure 5.5).

STEVEN A. WERNKE

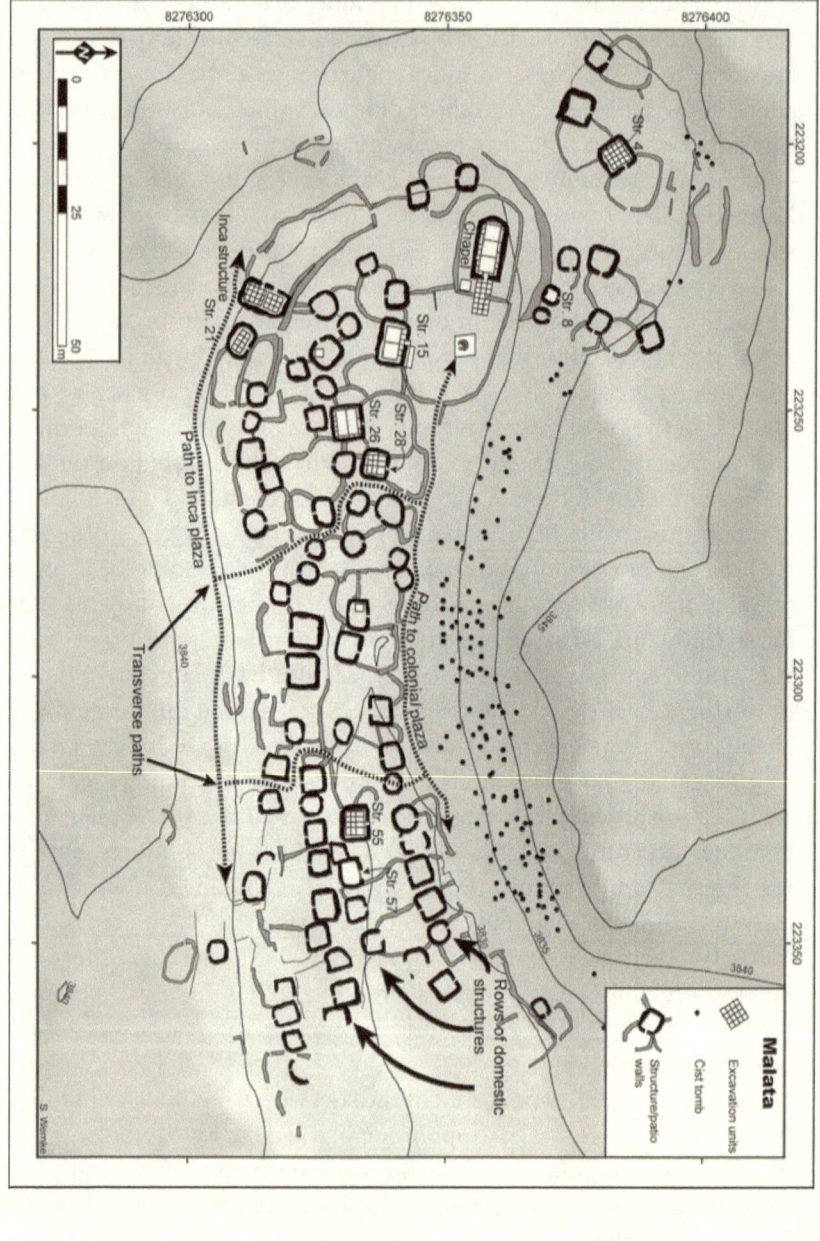

FIGURE 5-5.
Architectural map of Malata showing rows of domestic structures at eastern extreme of the site and single path entering the plaza.

96

We excavated two buildings from a single domestic compound in this part of the site. One of these (Structure 57) was a small (4.4 × 3.3 m) special-function colonial building used for a range of craft production activities. It is unique in form for its high, ungabled walls (such a shed-style roof has never been registered in the large database of prehispanic domestic architecture in the valley), with many small niches at different levels and a floor-level arched niche in the center of its rear (south) wall, opposite the doorway (another colonial feature). A large ash lens in front of the arched niche indicates it functioned as a hearth or perhaps a kiln. In both the southeast and southwest corners, round features of thin fieldstones most likely functioned as platforms for production activities. We recovered yellow, red, white, cream, and brown pigments and a well-sorted, fine clay from discrete lens features in its floor. A range of rolled river cobbles of various sizes was also recovered, perhaps for burnishing ceramics. Weaving tools—in particular, loom picks, or *wichuñas*, made of camelid metatarsals—were also found in this structure. While analysis is ongoing, these are clear indications of diverse craft activities, probably related to ceramic and textile production.

To the adjacent west, Structure 55 is a larger (5.3 × 4.3 m) gabled building that appears to have been used for a range of domestic and production activities, including cooking, weaving, and perhaps metallurgy. A hearth was located in the northeast corner, associated with a mixed midden of domestic refuse (abundant macrobotanicals, faunal bone fragments, utilitarian ceramics, debitage), and semicircular "platforms" similar to those found in Structure 57 were fitted into the northeast, southeast, and southwest corners. Notably also, we recovered the largest collection of colonial glass beads from floor level contexts in Structure 55: 11 Nueva Cádiz beads (Earle 1994). These two structures were thus involved in a variety of production and domestic activities during the colonial occupation of the site.

In short, all indices suggest that this eastern neighborhood was a colonial addition. As discussed above, the friars are documented as having congregated ayllus in doctrinas elsewhere in the valley; it is likely that these households were similarly resettled to Malata from neighboring settlements. So it appears that the process of "reduction"—both in terms of the concentration of the population into fewer, larger settlements, and in the reordering of settlements according to Spanish urban ideals—was already under way prior to the establishment of the reducciones themselves.

Adjacent to the east of the colonial plaza is a notable exception to the pattern of peripherally situated quadrangular houses, but one that further reveals the structuring of space and movement through the doctrina

(Wernke n.d.). Here, Structures 26 and 28 form a single elite domestic compound at an important intersection of a transverse path that directed traffic to the main path into the colonial plaza (see Figure 5.5). This is almost certainly the paramount elite indigenous household compound, emplaced at a key site in the doctrina. They are the last two structures before reaching the single entry to the plaza, and thus command a view of all traffic or processionals entering it (Wernke n.d.). Structure 26 is the largest house at the site, and is also notable for its height and mass, with 80-cm-thick walls and 3.5-m-high gables. It is also fronted by the largest patio area of any domestic compound. Interestingly, to access Structure 26 requires passage through the patio and in front of Structure 28, a much smaller and more rustic structure. Structure 28 and its patio thus could have functioned to monitor visitors before being admitted to the large patio area of Structure 26.

Excavations in both structures revealed features and artifacts typical of indigenous houses at the site. Structure 28 revealed very high concentrations of domestic refuse on an irregular, pitted floor, a hearth, and a table-like circular fieldstone feature in its southwest corner. Structure 26 had a similar circular feature against the center of its rear wall but was much cleaner, with small fragments of a range of decorated and utilitarian ceramics embedded in its compact, level floor. Both structures produced colonial utilitarian wares intermixed with local variants of fine Inca polychrome ceramics. A Nueva Cádiz bead was recovered from the lowest depths of the floor in Structure 26, further indicating a colonial construction date for that structure.

All evidence thus points to this compound as being that of a high-ranking indigenous household. Indigenous political authority thus remained quite literally central even after the reordering of the doctrina. The location, forms, and spatial organization of this compound must have at once reinforced the authority of the indigenous elites who resided there, even as their authority became associated with the public and sacred spaces of colonial integration—the plaza and church (Wernke n.d.). A view of how pathways were routed to converge in front of this compound and into the plaza beyond illustrates how the built environment of the plaza was manipulated to affect the shape of ritual through the formation of processionals.

Proceeding through the Doctrina

The fieldstone walls that line paths, divide domestic compounds, and delineate the plaza and atrium are also well preserved. We mapped these walls in detail to gain a view of the connections between different areas of the site. Most of these walls are not tall. They did not physically preclude entry, but presumably their construction delineates a preferred routing, so deviations from it would have been considered transgressions. Quantitative network analysis of these routes is beyond the scope of this paper, but their most striking feature is how the plaza has only one legitimate entrance: through a single path leading from the north side of the residential area to the east (Figure 5.5). All traffic to the plaza and into the atrium and chapel—at least according to the ideal plan—was funneled to this single path. Two transverse paths cut across from the south side of the site to the main path, one passing near Structure 55 in the eastern neighborhood, and the other next to the elite domestic compound of Structures 26 and 28 adjacent to the plaza. Inhabitants of this elite compound thus would have been able to view every member of the community as they congregated and proceeded through the single entry to the central plaza.

Movement through the doctrina thus literally created a processional past that domestic compound and into the plaza, giving a view straight ahead to the central cross and chapel entry beyond. This can hardly be fortuitous. Moving forward through this sequence, the walker would go through a series of accesses, from the single plaza entry (1.6 m) looking straight ahead to the plaza cross and the entry to the atrium (2.2 m wide). Finally, participants would proceed up the steps and enter one by one through the narrow (63 cm) doorway of the chapel itself.

CONVERGENCES: SEMIOTIC IDEOLOGIES AND THE BUILT ENVIRONMENT AT MALATA

Though executed in rustic fashion, the introduced built forms and new connections between domestic, public, and sacred spaces at Malata materialized the semiotic ideology of the friars—one in which the daily rhythms of living and worshiping was to produce Christian subjects and a new social order. The friars attempted to institute a particular representational economy, in which the circulation of people was controlled and centripetal, centering on the civic plaza and the sacred space of the chapel. A new Christian community was to be constituted, as Clendinnen suggests in the opening passage, through the mapping out of daily rhythms of work and ritual, as movement through the doctrina created a processional from houses to the central plaza and chapel. This in itself is remarkable since it shows that even during the earliest period of evangelization at a small doctrina, the friars went to considerable lengths to restructure the built environment and create new patterns of interaction and rhythms of daily life among its inhabitants.

STEVEN A. WERNKE

It might be argued that this represents a straightforward expression (albeit on a diminutive scale) of the "architecture of conquest" (Fraser 1990)—a built imposition that stabilized new beliefs and practices. And there is little doubt that this was the intent, but in practice the stability of this materialization was surely not as unproblematic as the friars would have had it. Its effectiveness necessarily derived from its legibility to the local community, that is, from common material signs (plaza, processional), which in turn were "bundled" to quite different qualisigns, linked in turn to different semiotic ideologies. And indeed, material cognates were readily at hand: the spatial logic of processionals and public ritual in plaza spaces was a core aspect of the local experience of Inca imperial politics. To the extent that this restructuring took hold, it would have required—at least initially—apprehension through already established schema. The restructuring of the built environment at Malata thus produced vectors of convergence through the links between the outward similarities of material forms. The more rigid site planning that followed the original founding of the doctrina, part of a much broader retrenchment to a more uniform (and often violent) doctrinal regime in the 1560s, likely arose as a reaction to this emerging heterodoxy. In many ways, the reactionary response of the Church in the 1560s prefigures the much broader and repressive regime Toledo instituted a decade later.

These findings thus provide a view of the in situ negotiation of new domestic and ritual spaces and practices during the earliest phases of evangelization in the Andes—a perspective that is entirely absent in ecclesiastical written sources. I have tried to show how the friars' attempts to institute a new Christian Andean order through a new spatial order were both confronted by the material reality of the existing settlement itself, and dependent on their resonance with analogous indigenous spaces and conceptions. What was at issue, then, was not so much a dialectic of domination and resistance, but one of a mutual appropriation of forms and the power and meanings that emerged from them.

Acknowledgments

Research at Malata was funded by a National Science Foundation Senior Research Grant (# 0716883), a Vanderbilt University Center for the Americas Faculty Research Fellowship, a Vanderbilt University Research Scholar Fellowship, and a Vanderbilt University Undergraduate Research Supervision Grant. Spatial analysis and cartography were supported by the facilities of the Vanderbilt University Spatial Analysis Research Lab. Logistical support was provided by the Center for

Archaeological Research in Arequipa (CIARQ), the Parish of Chivay, the Irrigation Commission of Tuti, and the Municipality of the District of Tuti. Special thanks are owed to Mr. Jesús Quispe and the community of Tuti for their support and hospitality. Excavations at Malata, under the codirection of Ericka Guerra Santander, were conducted with the authorization of Resoluciones Directorales 1096 (July 11, 2006) and 828 (July 6, 2007) of the National Institute of Culture of Peru. I am especially grateful to Matthew Liebmann and Melissa Murphy for their invitation to participate in this exciting seminar and volume. They and the other seminar participants were extremely generous in their review and critique of earlier drafts of this chapter. The observations of anonymous reviewers were integral to further fortifying it. All errors of fact and interpretation are my own.

Note

1. A small sample of ceramics (n = 131, 2 percent of diagnostics) pertain to the pre-Incaic Late Intermediate period (1100–1450) and are likely a mix of antiques recovered from domestic contexts and secondary deposits in subfloor fill from earlier use of the site as an agricultural zone.

6

Cultural Encounters at Magdalena de Cao Viejo in the Early Colonial Period

Jeffrey Quilter

INTRODUCTION

Magdalena de Cao, in the Chicama Valley of northern Peru, may be the best available locale for testing the archaeological visibility of resistance and other indigenous responses to their circumstances in Early Colonial period Latin America (Figure 6.1). The reason for such a claim is the rich data set made available due to two circumstances. The first of these is the well-known remarkably preservative qualities of the Peruvian desert coast. The second is a catastrophic event that preserved and sealed materials that residents would have removed under more benign circumstances such as gradual site abandonment. Despite the extraordinary and diverse remains available for analysis and the numerous insights that may be gained through studying them, difficulties remain in attempting to clearly identify resistance, accommodation, ambivalence, and other social stances, in terms of both attitudes and behavior. This chapter briefly reviews the background and occupational history of the site, discusses four sources of information to examine social dynamics, and concludes by addressing the potentials and problems that they offer for interpretation of resistance and similar social attitudes and actions.

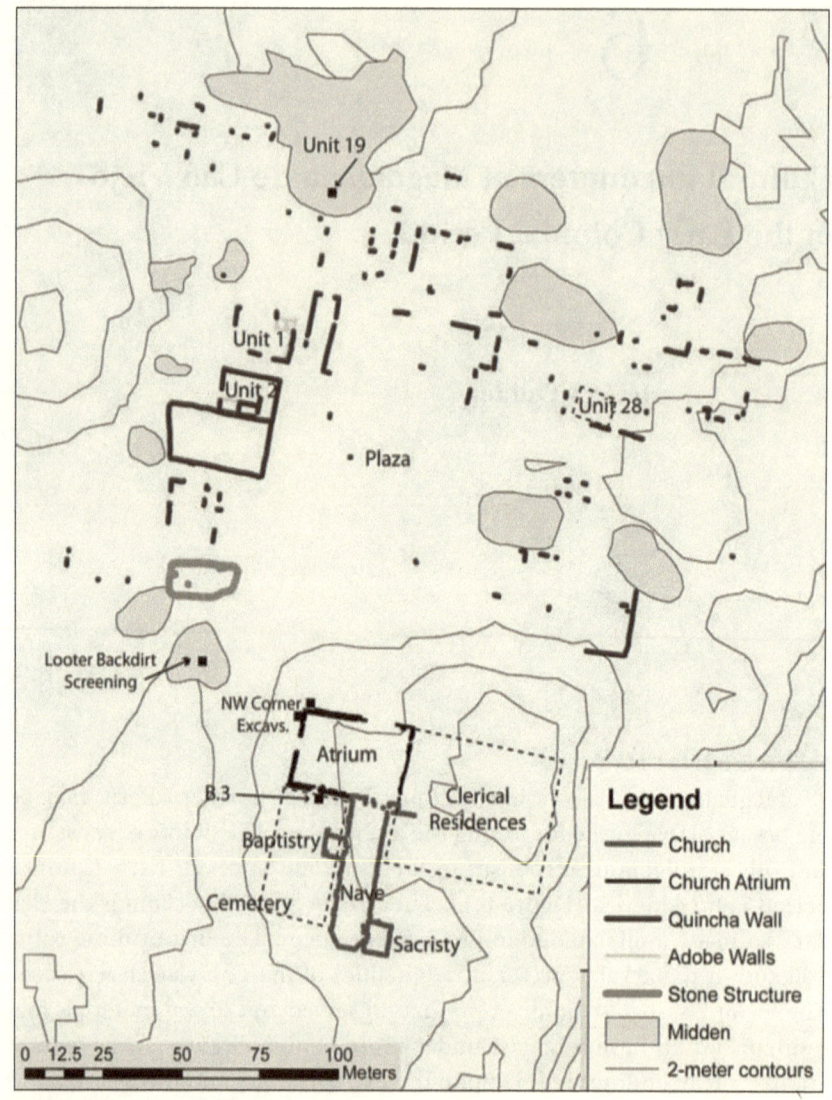

FIGURE 6.1.
Map of Magdalena de Cao Viejo based on archaeological research.

GENERAL BACKGROUND AND OCCUPATIONAL HISTORY OF MAGDALENA DE CAO VIEJO

Today, the Colonial period site of Magdalena de Cao Viejo is one component of the El Brujo Archaeological Complex, a 4-km2 triangle of ancient beach terrace next to the Pacific Ocean and the irrigated fields of

FIGURE 6.2.
View of the Huaca Cao Viejo from the ruins of the church nave. The standing wall, at left, is the east wall of the nave. The west wall can be seen in the middle of the photograph at far right.

Chicama Valley (Quilter 2007). Except for Junius Bird's (Bird et al. 1985) excavations at Huaca Prieta, the El Brujo Archaeological Complex received little archaeological attention until 1990. Since then, a long-term research project has been carried out by a team of Peruvian archaeologists working under an accord with the Peruvian National Institute of Culture and the Fundación Wiese of Lima, which has also provided most of the funds for research at the site. That research has focused mostly on one of the Moche huacas, the Huaca Cao Viejo, where a number of important finds have been made (Mujica Barreda 2007) (Figure 6.2) and which underwent at least four major construction phases during its use life between sometime prior to CE 200 and 650, after which it was abandoned. By CE 800, Moche culture was in a process of transformation and in the ensuing centuries was succeeded by the Lambayeque, Chimu, and Inca. Traces of these archaeological cultures at the site are successively lighter through time, with the next significant occupation being the colonial settlement of Magdalena de Cao.

Although local lore claims that Magdalena de Cao was founded in 1538, it more likely was established in 1566 when native people were forced to move from their ancestral settlements into four communities built and organized on Spanish plans (Cummins 2002), known as *reducciones* (sing.: *reducción*): Santa María Magdalena de Cao, Santiago de Cao, San Salvador de Paiján, and San Pedro y San Pablo de Chocope (Castañeda 2006, 2007). This first Magdalena was beside the mouth of a branch of the Chicama River and is not the site being discussed here. In 1578, a severe El Niño event brought massive floods that destroyed that first Magdalena de Cao and other towns close to the river. Testimonies recorded after the event included a statement that the Magdaleneros fled to "an old town that is next to the ocean on a height where they had stayed and which is inhabited to today…" (Huertas Vallejos 1987[1578]:131; translation by Quilter). As there is no other candidate for such a location, colonial remains are abundant at the El Brujo complex, and the residents of contemporary Magdalena de Cao claim the archaeological site as their previous settlement, it is fairly certain that the colonial sector at El Brujo is the settlement described and thus first occupied in 1578.

Established and run by members of the Dominican religious order, the church complex was built at the northern end of the Moche plaza. Buildings in the complex consisted of a church at its center, oriented north–south, with an open atrium (courtyard) and town cemetery to its west, and a suite of buildings that included residences, offices, a kitchen area, and other rooms on the east, mostly on a prehistoric platform in the northeast corner of the plaza.

North of the church complex and at a lower level, the Magdalena town was organized on a grid pattern with north–south streets, commonly 2.5 m in width, running on the same long axis as the huaca and its plaza, about 10 degrees east of north, with intersecting streets running east and west. A large (± 75 × 75 m) plaza was placed square with the atrium and nave sectors of the church complex.

The blocks of residences surrounding the plaza consisted of compounds defined by *quincha* (wattle-and-daub) walls. Although they may have ranged in size somewhat, these compounds appear to have been rectangular, measuring about 15 m on a short side and 20 to 25 m in length. They were internally divided, consisting of a large patio area where animals were kept and outdoor work was performed, and two or three small rooms for sleeping and indoor activities.

To date, two residential compounds have been excavated extensively and a third has been test excavated. All show the same sequence of occupation, beginning with an initial settlement directly on a land surface still retaining traces of prehistoric occupation. Through time, modifications to the structures occurred, including the building of hearths, the accretion of ash and other soil lenses on the floors, and mostly minor reorganization of rooms through the use of adobe bricks, some of which were salvaged from prehistoric, probably Moche-era, structures. The site's domestic area changed fairly dramatically, as evidenced by thick (≥ 10 cm) lenses of ashes that were later covered by even thicker (± 30 cm) deposits of animal dung and strawlike vegetal material. The residential nature of the town appears to have changed from a community of humans to a locale for relatively few people but great numbers of sheep and goats.

The church complex experienced an even more dramatic change of fortune than the town. We found large sections of the church nave walls collapsed to the east, into the kitchen area of the residential compound. Based on the pattern of wall fall, this likely was due to a significant seismic event. Whether this incident caused the abandonment of the church or if some time passed before the religious community left is not entirely clear.

The wall collapse trapped many objects, and if any attempt was made to retrieve items of importance, no great effort apparently was expended. The items left in the debris included various paper documents such as printed church announcements, religious and historical texts, and schedules of worship, and handwritten musical scores, letters, ledger accounts, and other records. Given that these materials, which can reasonably be considered to have been valuable, were left at the site, we believe that the Dominicans abandoned the church complex fairly soon after the wall collapse. The low quincha architecture of the town apparently suffered much less damage than the tall adobe walls of the church, however, and it remained occupied after the religious order left the area.

We found paper fragments in the floors of the domestic occupation of the town, suggesting that the church collapse occurred before the Magdaleneros shifted their economic activities to sheep and goats. The townspeople appear to have mined the abandoned church, evidenced by extensive deposits of old, mounded earth rich in artifacts in many areas. The dense, settled consistency of these deposits suggests that they were made many years ago, and we found virtually no remains indicative of the nineteenth century or later in them. Parts of the church complex also were used for hide processing, as indicated by great amounts of tara (also known as *taya* [*Caesalpinia spinosa*]) leaves and seeds, used for hide tanning, as well as a storage bin for the material with an associated wooden hide scraper nearby, built on the west atrium wall (Vásquez Sánchez and Rosales Tham 2008).

Alfonso Toribio de Mogrovejo (Benito 2006:52), second archbishop of Lima, provided the earliest description of Magdalena in 1593 when he visited the community. He noted that at the time there were 715 inhabitants, of which 169 were tributaries (*tributarios*), male heads of households. In a visit in 1599, Pedro Martínez, an agent of Toribio, reported 150 tributaries (Benito 2006:166). We may therefore infer that Magdalena was an active community at least as late as 1599. Dated paper documents found in the ruins of the church are secure for as late as 1612 and possibly as late as 1650. After that, we are uncertain as to how long the town was occupied. Magdalena was noted in 1730 in a report on a sea voyage along the north coast of Peru, and this suggests that the town was visible from the ocean (Castañeda 2006, citing Ortiz Sotelo 1993). In addition, a 1763 map by Miguel Feijoó de Sosa (1984[1763]) shows Magdalena on the littoral. At that time, Feijoó noted that sixty-nine indigenes and fifty-six mestizos lived at the site. This dramatic decrease in population size may indicate that by this time, or soon after, the town was primarily raising animals and processing their hides.

On a map prepared by the Archbishop of Trujillo, Martínez Compañón, ca. 1780, Magdalena is shown well inland, roughly where the modern town is located. It therefore seems reasonable to infer that Magdalena de Cao Viejo was abandoned and the new town, still occupied today, was established sometime between 1763 and 1780. No significant occupation of the Brujo terrace subsequently took place, save for the small number of archaeologists who have regularly spent their workdays there since 1990. A small fishing community on the beach next to Huaca Prieta likely has been there since the Preceramic period, however.

CASE STUDIES IN IDENTIFYING RESISTANCE

Here I present information on four aspects of the Colonial period occupation of Magdalena de Cao Viejo: architecture and landscape, textiles, religious material culture and practice, and paper. These progressively move from activities that were directed by the agenda of the Spanish to those increasingly subject to the agency of native peoples at the site, and then, with paper, I consider things that were first exclusively under Spanish control and then completely under control of local people.

The town presumably was laid out under the direction of the Dominicans. Textiles were made by native people using local materials, but they may have had to conform to Spanish demands for certain styles and products. At the same time, however, some elements of costume were imported from Europe. Religious rites were dominated by the Spanish, especially in public form, but private activities, occurring within domestic settings, had the potential to be performed away from foreigners' prying eyes. Paper documents were uniquely Spanish possessions and tools of

Cultural Encounters at Magdalena de Cao Viejo

control of native peoples but, once abandoned, they were gathered up and used by local people. Looking at these varying activities that had greater or lesser public aspects and potentially stronger or weaker control by Spanish overlords may offer the opportunity to examine the relative degree of imposition of foreign ways and resistance or accommodation to them by native people.

Architecture and Landscape

While the El Niño floods may have been the initial impetus for the colonial settlement on the El Brujo terrace, its long-term occupation was a deliberate choice rather than a necessity. Granted, the effects of a severe El Niño may have been prolonged over several months, and the high, dry El Brujo terrace would have remained an advantageous location, but, even considering this, there were various options regarding where to situate the settlement in the 4-km^2-area of the terrace, including more than half a dozen other mounds of varying sizes, some larger, some smaller, than the Huaca Cao Viejo.

The two largest mounds at El Brujo are Huaca Cao Viejo and Huaca Cortada (also known as Huaca El Brujo), both Moche and both roughly the same size. The Huaca Cortada is close to the ocean and only 150 m from the northwest edge of the terrace. This windswept location may have been avoided in favor of the Huaca Cao Viejo, on the eastern edge of the terrace, with more room downwind and in front of it where a town could be established. In addition, two Moche-era mounds to the west and north of the main town area, and the terrace edge to the east, would have worked to produce a distinct sense of place nestled within a well-defined area in an otherwise flat landscape. Furthermore, while the sea can be seen almost equally as well from Huaca Cao Viejo as from Huaca Cortada, the Huaca Cao Viejo and the adjacent plain offer a much better view of the agricultural fields east of the terrace than does Huaca Cortada.

How much such practical considerations figured into locating the town where it is may be conjectured without any clear resolution. The placement of the church in relation to Huaca Cao Viejo clearly suggests that ideological agendas were in operation, but, again, we may ask why one temple mound was selected and not the other. Although relatively little research has been carried out at Huaca Brujo, research at Huaca Cao Viejo has revealed that after the complex ceased to be an active Moche ceremonial center, people of the succeeding Lambayeque culture excavated into the collapsed and covered walls of the old temple to bury their dead there. Although both Moche huacas may have continued to be venerated, the

Huaca Cao Viejo may have retained or developed a heightened status of sanctity for it to have served as a cemetery for later people.

The Dominicans placed their church complex directly on the floor of the Huaca Cao Viejo plaza and on the platform at its northeast corner. The orientations of the complex and the town were the same as that of the huaca complex: ten degrees east of magnetic north. This orientation apparently was not simply a consequence of utilizing the old plaza walls because the nave of the church could have been built in any direction. Common Christian practice would have been to orient the complex east–west, so that the congregation and priest standing to face the altar would have been oriented toward the sunrise and the cardinal direction associated with Christ's return on Judgment Day. Instead, the church faced the huaca. Peruvian archaeologists report that they found a large posthole on the summit of Huaca Cao Viejo, which was interpreted as the locus of a large wooden cross.

Most scholars are now sensitive to the complexities of the dialogue between conquerors and conquered in the colonial experience. In the Magdalena case, as in so many, the imposition of a church and town on a pagan holy place may have been considered by the Spaniards as the triumph of Christianity, but natives almost certainly viewed it as recognition of the power of place, of the sacredness of the huaca. The archaeology of this landscape can be read as Spanish domination or accommodation or both. The problem of understanding which it might be is not interpretable from the archaeological remains because we cannot infer the intentions of the Dominican friars. Indeed, the friars themselves may have been divided or ambivalent in their attitudes, some firm in their belief of the triumph of Christianity, others cognizant of the recognition of a sacred place of historical importance, and still others ambivalent to these issues. It is quite clear that the Church as an institution saw its mission as clear cut, but even Church officials varied in their instructions to missionaries. There was a general recognition that conversion had to be done in steps, not all at once, and so some tolerance of non-Christian ideas should be followed. Indeed, if the Moche plaza was clear and open, it would have formed a perfect space for staging Christian rituals outdoors in a setting more aligned with native practice yet not directly contradictory to Christian ritual (see Lara 2004).

Architectural and landscape spaces are problematic in allowing easy interpretations of domination or resistance. Salient in this discussion are the differing concepts of landscape by local indigenous people in contrast to those of the colonizers, the degree to which each group recognized and responded to the other's perceptions, and the kinds of dialogues that occurred because of such perceptions and concerns. In some cases there was mutual accommodation (Wernke, Chapter 5), while in others evidence may be interpreted as defiance, especially when the colonizer departed and indigenous people had the opportunity to make an expressive statement by acting on the materiality of the intruder's former presence (Beck et al., Chapter 2; Church et al., Chapter 9). Based on architectural evidence alone, however, the Magdalena case is ambiguous. The Spaniards planting their cross, placing their church in the Moche plaza, and orienting the town plan to align with the ancient works all may be interpreted as Spanish and Christian triumphalism or as accommodation to an indigenous architectural plan that had cosmological significance.

Textiles and Related Crafts

Textiles at Magdalena offer views of social identities and the ways in which body space was restructured under the colonial regime (Brezine 2008). Given the excellent preservation at the site, we have recovered a great variety of fragments of garments and related items, including several different kinds of shoes and sandals. Fully studying these materials will take some time, especially in sorting various accessories such as sections of badges, belts, straps, and other items.

There are many textiles made of European materials such as linens, lace, and felt, as well as decorative techniques such as embroidery that were shared but rendered differently in the Old and New Worlds. While the two centuries of site occupation at Magdalena is relatively brief by prehistoric standards, considerable change took place from a historical perspective. Yet it is difficult to discern such changes archaeologically. Changes in weaving technology and clothing styles are well enough known, for Europe at least, and we know that separating earlier from later textiles and clothing is an important task that is feasible even if it remains to be done, though this is made more difficult by the fact that many such items have been found on the site surface, in trash deposits, and in looters' back dirt. We also must take into account the fact that changes in styles may have lagged in the colony, compared to the European homeland, and that there would have been a great incentive to wear and use pieces of clothing for a much longer period of time given their scarcity.

In general, analyses performed to date suggest that native men more rapidly adopted Spanish clothing styles than women, a common pattern in colonized societies in which men are more active in public affairs with foreigners than women. We may bear in mind, however, that few if any

European women likely were at the site, so there probably were few opportunities for native women to see foreign styles of female clothing.

We have recovered European-style men's singlets, leggings, gaiters, leggings or socks, and hats. Fabrics include silk and linen and textiles made by distinctive processes such as felt, damask, lace trim, and European embroidery styles. Many of the articles of clothing are fragmentary, which makes it difficult to determine if they are from men's or women's clothing, but many appear to be male items of dress. Women appear to have worn traditional-style clothing, including wrapping a large square cloth, or *manto*, over the shoulders. Any adaptations to European-style female dress remain to be documented.

While some men adopted items or aspects of European dress, prehispanic-style male tunics were also worn. There are two variations of these garments. The first, more traditional style has warp-patterned stripes of blue and different shades of brown, ranging from a light buff to a dark chocolate brown. The second style of male tunic has a general prehispanic appearance to the untrained modern eye. Its decoration consists of small dots of colored alpaca wool on a caramel-colored tunic with a bottom border of alpaca tapestry dyed in the same colors as the dots. Whether this is a new indigenous Colonial period style, a continuance of a previously undocumented prehispanic style, or a modification of a preconquest style remains to be determined.

Textile arts are one area in which we clearly see hybridity and syncretism at the site. Some wool fabric appears to have been dyed after it was woven, a rare Andean practice but a common European one, as was overdyeing. Scissors and shears were in use and curved seams are known, suggesting that European ideas of tailored fabric were adopted. Cloth buttons as fasteners also have been found on European-style garments.

Carrie Brezine's (2008) study of the Magdalena textiles shows evidence of the mixing of native and European technologies and styles. At least in the case of textiles, then, there are clear cases of hybridity as can be seen in other materials in other case studies, such as ceramics among the Navajo (Preucel, Chapter 11). On one textile, warp and wefts are traditionally spun in native cotton but the twill-based pattern of the garment mimics European damask and, furthermore, an anomaly in the fabric suggests that some automation technique, perhaps a European-style loom, may have been employed rather than traditional Andean technologies, which relied more on the manipulation of threads by fingers. Another textile consists of a ground cloth made in the indigenous tradition of paired cotton warps and single wefts but exhibits embroidery in European style.

European clothing was "tailored" with cloth cut by scissors to conform to or veer away from the body, while native textiles, for the most part, were formless. At Magdalena we see examples of Andean textiles that were modified or partly constructed through the use of cutting and sewing in European style. As studies continue, understanding which European technologies and styles were fully or partly embraced and which native practices were continued, discontinued, or modified will offer interesting views on cultural dynamics in Early Colonial period Peru.

We found many examples of painted textile fragments (Figure 6.3). Light and dark brown (as they now appear) were painted in geometric designs on cream or white cotton cloth. Although painted textiles are known from early times in Peru, continued in use, and were particularly popular in late prehistory, this style appears to be uniquely colonial. In the most complete burial we encountered, a woman interred with two small bags filled with balls of textile twine was wearing a manto of this style of cloth.

The designs on the textiles we have cleaned and studied so far appear to be geometrical patterns and have no direct antecedents in known prehistoric painted cloths from the north coast. At first view, there appears to be great complexity in the design fields of these textiles. On one fragment (Figure 6.3A), a design element consists of a large square, 50 cm on a side, with two rectangular frames at top and bottom, each filled in with different repeating elements, nested triangles in one, and step-motifs in the other, with added complexity in the form of multiple dark and light horizontal lines separating each rectangle. At the sides, a different border style was created through simple straight strokes that produced rectangles of varying sizes around the edge. Diagonal lines with small triangles creating a step- or toothlike design fill the center of the square defined by the rectangles. This elaborate design field is only one part of the larger composition, which, elsewhere on the fabric, includes large rectangles and other geometrical shapes, all of which are filled in with zigzags, triangles, wavy lines, and other elements.

The painted decorations, in part or in whole, do not partake of European artistic conventions, and while they appear to have a prehispanic gestalt, from a contemporary perspective, there are no motifs that could be cited as clearly or strongly linked to pre-Columbian symbolism. One textile (Figure 6.3B) has a repeating motif of a crosslike element with a circle at its center against a background of concentric circles, all of which are filled in with small dots. If anything, this may allude to the Christian cross, although the reference could be debated. It certainly seems more a Christian motif than one associated with precontact religions.

Jeffrey Quilter

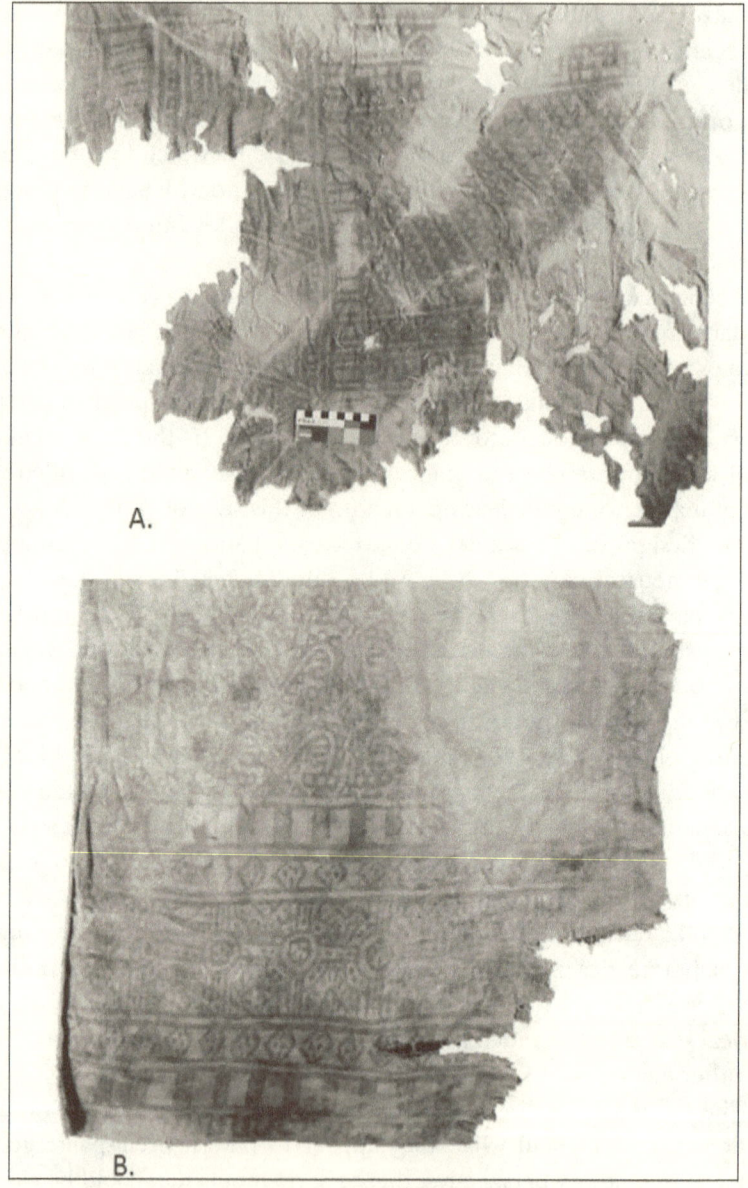

Figure 6.3.
Two details of painted textiles from Magdalena de Cao. A. Block design. B. Design that includes a row of crosses near the bottom.

The painted textiles raise several interesting issues. Because the textiles covered the female burial, they may have been seen by priests performing burial rites, and so the avoidance of motifs with prehispanic religious references may have been a deliberate strategy by the townspeople. We have only found one complete, undisturbed adult colonial burial, the woman previously noted. Interment with two bags filled with cotton twine would have been against strict Christian tenets, although such a practice may have been a small transgression that was tolerated or ignored.

Perhaps more likely, Dominican priests and friars may not have been present when the body was prepared and thus may not have seen the mantle of the woman or known that objects were included with the burial. Perhaps the priest saw the decorated cloth at a stage before the final wrapping, but this apparently minor issue could be critical in comprehending who was the audience viewing these textiles and who was not.

The painted textiles do appear to be a new form of decorated cloth garment or at least a style much more common than in previous eras. Painting is an economical, efficient way to rapidly decorate a large surface. If decorating textiles in this manner increased in the Colonial period, its origin may be partly due to the stressed circumstances of native people who had less time to weave for the dead than when they were independent. Overall, the colonial textiles suggest that native peoples were comfortable adopting many aspects of European dress and textile technologies while retaining their own clothing practices as they wished and, furthermore, that the Dominicans allowed them to do so. The painted textiles may have been developed under exploitative conditions, but there is no clear evidence of resistance in them.

Many of the more traditional-style woven textiles display seemingly innocuous images of stylized birds and fish that do not appear to carry heavy symbolic loads. If resistance was being expressed in these designs, we cannot see it, and of course it may be that they were used so that the Spanish friars could not see it either. But many of these designs appear to have been common and also relatively light in symbolism in precontact times as well. One major stumbling block to understanding patterns of resistance and even straightforward change is our relative lack of detailed knowledge of material culture and symbolic systems immediately prior to the conquest among common people.

Religious Material Culture and Practice

We excavated substantial areas of the living quarters in two domestic compounds, Houses 1 and 2, during our research and placed large test excavations in a third, House 28 (Van Valkenburgh 2007). This work included complete excavation of a 4 × 6 m room (Recinto 2) in House 2

FIGURE 6.4.
An offering in a cut gourd from a lower floor in House (Unit) 1.

and an area of the same size in House 1. In both cases, the floors of the early occupations contained several examples of offerings. These commonly consisted of cut gourds or gourd bowls filled with multiple layers of wrapped and folded cloths enclosing seeds, seedpods, leaves, and similar food items, mostly plant remains (Figure 6.4). Many of the textiles in these bundles often were torn and tattered. As in the case of clothing, a detailed study of these offerings remains to be carried out, but they appear to include textiles of more than only native style.

Perhaps the most interesting aspect of these household offerings is what they lack: figurines. Andean religious practice commonly included small figurines as offerings in Inca times, a practice that continues today. The Inca made small figurines of humans in gold, silver, and *Spondylus* shell and dressed them in miniature garments. These were miniature versions of human sacrifices and accompanied the victims in their graves (Rowe 1996:302–6). Continuing to today, agriculturalists and pastoralists bury small carved stone figurines of camelids, commonly with holes in their backs filled with animal fat, in fields and camelid corrals to ensure fertility. At Magdalena, however, such practices are not materially in evidence. To date we have found only one figurine, which is made of fired clay and fairly crude in manufacture. While generally indigenous in style, it has no clear prehispanic precedents and could just as likely have been a child's toy as anything else.

In House 1 we found two examples of Christian iconography: a small wooden cross and a metal crucifix. The wooden cross is small, only 3.6 cm in height. It was hand carved and its small base indicates that it was meant to be stable when placed on a surface. The crucifix is made of a metal alloy and is broken at the top so its length cannot be determined, but the cross bar measures 2.6 cm wide. The object appears to have been for personal adornment, probably worn on a chain around the neck or possibly pinned to clothing. The crucifix may have been made locally or imported; future metallurgical studies may clarify this point.

Both the cross and the crucifix were found in House 1 where traditional-style offerings had been placed in floors. Although the Christian items appear to have been deposited at a slightly later date than many of the offerings, we believe that at least some of the subfloor deposits could have been contemporary with the use lives of the cross and crucifix. While the filled gourds were deposited deliberately, the Christian artifacts appear to have been lost or discarded. Indeed, many objects such as a pair of inlaid finger rings in House 28, which we might expect to have been carefully curated, were found on house floors at Magdalena, as if they were either left deliberately or lost in the last moments of occupation. These patterns raise questions of the kinds of values placed on such objects. There seems to be a relatively cavalier attitude about them, as best these things can be judged, and while such an interpretation is highly subjective, perhaps it is indicative of native attitudes toward foreign goods as interesting but expendable.

A ritual involving smoldering materials in gourd bowls was carried out at the site, although this was possibly not a practice that occurred directly in a house. We found two clear examples of this practice, and in one case a large "Venetian" blue-and-white-with-red bead was found in the middle of the burnt matter. The excavation in which these offerings were found was a 1 × 2 m unit, so it was hard to determine the context of the deposits. It may have been a trash pile, although some levels indicate that residences were located in this area during the Colonial era. Whether a colonial garbage dump or residence, the location was at the back end of the town, as far away from the church as possible, and could have been carried out clandestinely.

Spondylus shells also were found in the strata in this excavation and they too were frequent in the houses. As one of the essential components of Andean ritual, their presence seems to suggest that traditional beliefs and rites were continued. But this evidence is open to more than one interpretation.

Prehispanic household and similar ritual practices in the town can be compared with evidence in the church that at least offers more than a simple, straightforward interpretation as Christian. A Spondylus shell was found lying on the floor of a square room adjacent to the sanctuary end of the nave of the church that we have interpreted as the sacristy, the priest's office, and, in this case, possibly his residence. The shell lay on a thin layer of soil just above the plaster floor. This suggests that the shell was placed in the sacristy after the end of the room's use, so it might be read as a form of resistance. Or was it simply a kind of resanctification of the place or simply a recognition of its sacred importance?

Less ambivalent in terms of the actions involved, but perhaps more perplexing regarding intent compared to the Spondylus in the sacristy, was the discovery of the lower leg and foot of an individual placed in the sacristy wall. The tibia and fibula with attached foot had been inserted or built into the adobe wall so that the sole of the foot was facing outward, jutting from the exterior of the wall, although some distortion of the ligaments was in evidence, making the sole not completely flat. The human remains had been placed directly behind a large balk of adobes built against the interior of the wall, possibly as a personal altar for the priest. Thus, the proximal end of the leg bones would not have been visible from inside the room and, with enough plaster, the foot would not have been visible on the exterior of the sacristy.

What are we to make of this foot and leg in the wall behind the altar? While Moche sacrifices dismembered victims and scattered them around plazas, later Andean rituals tended to emphasize complete bodies as sacrificial offerings. The inclusion of the leg and foot in a wall as an offering would have been understood by native residents of Magdalena, but the practice seems more in tune with the use of body parts as Christian relics rather than an Andean ritual. But Christian relics were of saints and none were extant in Peru in 1578, nor would have such holy remains, if present, have been crudely placed in an adobe wall. The priest may or may not have known of this deposit, and the townspeople may or may not have known either. The social vectors that led to the placement of the partial remains of a human being in this wall—domination, resistance, syncretism, or hybridity—are highly uncertain. Still, the insertion of this leg in the wall, possibly directly behind the priest's personal altar, is perhaps the strongest suggestion of the expression of resistance, or perhaps more accurately, subversion and defiance, at the site.

One final artifact to discuss that sheds light on issues of belief and practice at Magdalena is a small maize cob devoid of kernels and wrapped and tied in husk and fibers. One of these was recovered from a midden of materials that appear to have been tossed over the north wall of the church atrium when townspeople mined the destroyed ruins of the church structure; others have been found elsewhere as well. When the first wrapped maize cob was pulled from the sifting screens, the workers immediately recognized it and its purpose: these wrapped cobs are still used as ritual house cleansers. It is unlikely that this item was used anywhere other than in the church complex, given where it was found, so it appears that traditional practices were carried on within its sanctified precincts.

Paper

The difference between prehistory and history, between preliterate and literate societies, commonly has been seen as a profound divide between fundamentally different modes of life. Such distinctions are marked even when it is noted that literacy often is restricted to a narrow social class—Pizarro was illiterate—and not only by those with knowledge of the written word. In captivity, the Inca monarch Atahualpa was fascinated that a word (*Dios*, God) written on his fingernail by one Spaniard could be read and understood by another who had not seen the act of writing.

The propagation of the faith by Dominican friars and the implementation of regal rule by government officials were both carried out through written and printed documents. The pen and printing press were as mighty as the sword in many ways in the latter phases of the conquest of Peru. The Spaniards were particularly fond of keeping records for their own sake, such as the case of two shoemakers who in 1544 had an impressive document produced by a notary stating nothing more than that they had arrived in Lima (Lockhart 1968:68).

Spanish documents served to define, repress, and subjugate native people. But Andean peoples quickly learned to use the system that repressed them (juridical procedures, in particular) to fight back and to regain some of their losses (Stern 1982:114–37). The introduction of documents and the social action they carried with them was perhaps the most profound change in the lives of native Andeans in the transition from prehistory to the Colonial era. Given all this, we might expect native attitudes toward paper documents to be one area where resistance or some other profound social stance or action should be clearly evident, yet ambiguity reigns.

When the Magdalena church walls collapsed, they trapped a great variety of documents. If the friars retrieved any books or archives, they also left many behind, including what appear to be quite valuable tomes such as chant books written in gold leaf or ink and other hand-decorated volumes that would have been both spiritually and monetarily valuable. The manuscripts that we have found offer a unique view of the life of the monastic community and include not only chant and music scores but also ledger accounts, personal letters, notes, and "doodles" in handwritten documents, as well as pages from printed documents for holy offices, breviaries, lectionaries, church and secular histories, calendars of saints' days, and the like.

With the church complex abandoned, the townspeople mined paper as well as other materials from the ruins. They used this paper in various ways. In the town we found many small strips of paper for which we cannot determine any specific use. These paper fragments are often relatively small, measuring no more than about 2 × 3 or 4 cm on a side, while others are long, thin strips. There is no consistent pattern even in this, however, as some paper may be larger or smaller. Yet a common feature is that the papers are torn into small pieces, and there are few examples of whole pages of documents in the town. In the church area, by contrast, we often found larger pieces of paper and, in a couple of cases, several sheets of paper bound in a book or ledger. Apparently, larger sheets were procured from the church area and were then torn into smaller fragments at domestic sites in the town. The small pieces of paper in domestic settings showed no clear patterns of location that we have been able to detect.

Some of the paper in the church complex may have been partly exposed to the air, perhaps from being tossed aside in mining for more desirable materials: a large sheet of paper found next to a nave wall was stained with bird droppings, indicating exposure for some time. Another piece of paper was stained with human excrement, suggesting that it was used as toilet paper. While this certainly shows little regard for the value of the written word, it is hard to know whether the employment of the paper to such an end was an act of defiance or a mere (and perhaps novel?) convenience. Still, we can say that there was definitely a lack of reverence for the printed word by at least one Magdalenero. A similar apparent lack of appreciation is evinced by cigarette butts made of tobacco rolled in pieces of paper documents of various sorts (probably the earliest material evidence of cigarette smoking). While both the cigarette and toilet paper examples suggest a low esteem for documents, the possibility remains that someone thought biblical verses might cure hemorrhoids or that lighting a cigarette wrapped in a psalm produced holy smoke.

A frequent use of paper was the production of cutouts made either by tearing the paper by hand or, apparently, through the use of scissors or some other sharp-edged tool (Figure 6.5). Some of the papers were torn into long, thin strips, while others were made into forms of no particular shape. More often than not, the paper was simply folded in two and then

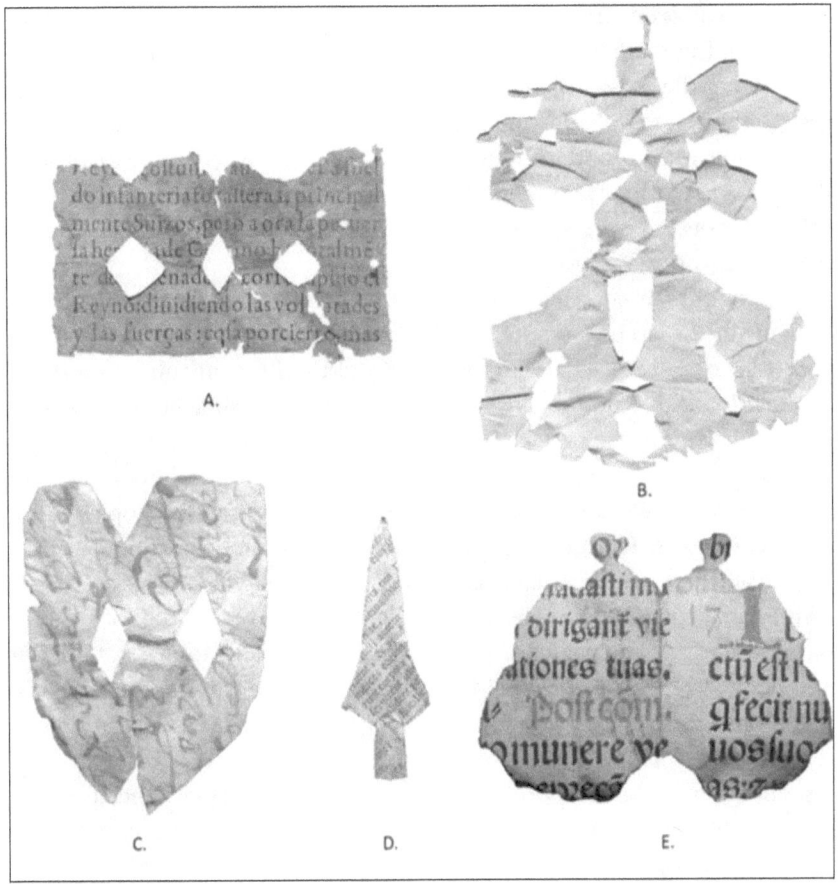

Figure 6.5.
Cut paper from Magdalena de Cao. Relative sizes in this montage not to scale. Maximum widths except where noted provided after description. A. Diamonds (7.3 cm). B. Elaborate geometric design (7.25 cm). C. Mask-like cutout (4 cm). D. Spear blade (5.2 cm tall). E. Butterfly (5.1 cm).

torn to produce a simple bisymmetrical and (to our eyes) abstract or simple geometrical shape. We have no accurate count on the number of examples of these because a detailed study of the papers remains to be done, but a rough estimate suggests that there are a dozen or fewer of the ambiguous but bisymmetrical forms. Other cut paper is more deliberately worked but lacks any clear iconographic content, such as a piece of printed page with three diamond shapes cut into it in a row (Figure 6.5A). At the other extreme are highly elaborate papers that were cut into repeating geometric shapes generally similar to snowflake patterns, as might be done today for a Christmas decoration (Figure 6.5B). Many of the cutouts that we have found are fragmentary, so their overall design pattern is not clear.

Among the most striking of the cutouts are those in what appear to be recognizable forms. Unfortunately, there are only three: a stylized face or mask, a spear blade, and a butterfly (Figure 6.5C–E). What are we to make of these? We could interpret them in many ways, from profound engagements with the tools of oppression (spear blade), to literal flights of fancy (butterfly), to an abstract face or mask.

We might consider the fact that if these things were made of cloth and securely in the prehistoric era, or if they were found in an undoubted historic European context, their meanings would still be difficult to interpret. Cloth cutouts are known to have served as decorations on prehispanic garments (T. Cummins, personal communication October 2008), but these papers did not serve that purpose. Cut paper figures played important roles in ethnographically documented shamanic rituals among the peoples of the sierra Otomí and Tepehua and the Nahua of southern Huasteca and are prehistorically evidenced among rituals practices of the Aztecs (Sandstrom and Effrein Sandstrom 1986). The Magdalena papers, however, do not seem to have been involved in similar rites. The fact that they are found scattered in a midden suggests that they held no aura of the sacred and were easily disposed of once their use was done. Again, however, we must tread carefully in such matters, for how and why such things were used and discarded is simply a difficult matter to approach from a strictly archaeological perspective.

The materiality of the social processes occurring in the Conquest and Early Colonial periods of the New World is thus not easy to identify (see Liebmann 2008a; Liebmann and Murphy, Chapter 1). Even overt resistance may leave few traces, just as the signatures of mighty battles may be evanescent on the landscape, given time and the fading of memory, not to mention the scavenging of equipment and the burial of bodies (but see Murphy et al., Chapter 4). Although the rich material record of the colonial occupation of Magdalena de Cao offers us the real possibility of tracing attitudes of accommodation, resistance, and the ambivalence of the subjugator and subjugated, identifying behaviors associated with such attitudes (which may have shifted in the minds of people living in those times, and through the decades so hard to tease out of the archaeology) will be difficult. But it will be well worth the effort.

A HANDSHAKE AWAY FROM ATAHUALPA

The archaeological record at Magdalena de Cao Viejo manifests the continuity of some precontact material culture, the adoption of European objects and practices, and the mixture of the two, to a greater or lesser extent, depending on the material in question. How these things were used and what was thought about them or how various social strategies were employed is much harder to discern, though we have some inklings of these as well. There are other aspects of early colonial life, such as the adoption of European domesticated plants and animals or the varying continuities and changes in the uses of ceramic vessels, which are not discussed here. Examining these and other artifacts should help to develop a fuller view of issues of resistance and other behaviors and attitudes.

A critical aspect in doing this, however, will be developing a better understanding of life in northern Peru immediately prior to the Spanish arrival, such as is available in the Colca Valley in southern Peru (see Wernke, Chapter 5), so that we can document change and continuity. At present, daily life in late prehispanic northern Peru—especially for common people—is poorly known. We see evidence of indigenous-style ceramics side by side with European glazed wares, for example, yet we face a harder task in discriminating the styles of the native ceramics in terms of their links to late prehistory than we do the European-style fine wares. Many more years of study are likely ahead of us to be able to make the kinds of finely tuned analyses of production and distribution of both indigenous and European styles of ceramics as are available for other areas of the early colonial New World (see Charlton and Fournier, Chapter 7).

Jaime Lara (2004) has pointed out that early Christian missionaries in Mexico recognized the coincidental similarities between Aztec beliefs and their own, including the symbolic powers of blood and sunlight: Jesus as the Light of the World and the Aztec Sun God; the Sacred Heart of Jesus and hearts of sacrifice, among others. While human sacrifice and sexual license were to be stopped, missionaries were advised by their superiors to tolerate some practices and redirect others such as singing and dancing. This was for practical purposes as much as anything else: it was recognized that wholesale change in behavior and beliefs could not occur overnight, especially when a few friars faced thousands of native people. But it also reflected an appreciation for the complexities of the conversion process. The missionaries recognized the ambivalences, ambiguities, and variability of Spanish and native interactions, and this was also true in Peru, especially before the Third Council of Lima (1582–83) when Church organization and evangelization were finally and definitively organized.

Such appreciation for the variability in native–Spanish relations constitutes a far cry from George Kubler's (1961:32; cf. Quilter 1996) view of a "total replacement in symbolic matters" of American Indian civilization by the Spanish. Indeed, for many scholars, we have moved beyond syncretism to see the native–Spanish encounter as a markedly pointed event but one that nevertheless was a moment in a continuing cultural process of change that included borrowing, absorption, hybridity as actions, and domination, resistance, accommodation, and ambivalence as some of the attitudes or cultural poses, sometimes overt, sometimes covert, sometimes conscious, and sometimes partly so. As language and culture can be understood as part of a single universe constantly in dialogic process (Tedlock and Mannheim 1995), so was the experience of Spaniard and native. As in Mexico (Lara 2004:204), much of prehispanic religion was recycled because it was relatively easily Christianized and, as much, Christianity was relatively easily indigenized.

How we balance this with the knowledge that native peoples also came to recognize that a distinct (kind of) historical moment had arrived—that led to an appreciation of "nativeness" or "indigeneity" as opposed to the "otherness" of the Spanish presence in Peru—is a delicate business. Steve Stern (1982) marks the historical watershed ca. 1564 when the Spanish priest Luis de Olivera stumbled upon the Taki Onqoy sect and movement that claimed that the ancient, pre-Inca, local huacas would rise up to destroy the Spanish and establish a golden age of Andean prosperity. By then, according to Stern, native peoples had put aside regional identities to embrace a common nativism.

It is a sobering thought that, in so many ways, the physical worlds and the moral universes of Spaniard and native in late sixteenth-century Peru were much more alike than either one is to those of contemporary Euro-Americans. They lived in a "world lit only by fire" (Manchester 1993), while we stare into the glow of computers and TVs, and the visions that they saw and that we see in those various lights are very different indeed. Shorter spans of time can still be significant, however. Many of the people who established the town on the El Brujo terrace were only a handshake away from Atahualpa; many of their parents could have known him. But only a very few of the oldest people could have remembered life before the arrival of the Spanish, and most would have only known of such times through the eyes of their childhoods.

This fading of memories is one of the reasons that the 1570s can be seen as the transition from the era of the Conquest to the Colonial period. The other reason, though bound up with the first, is the viceroyalty of Francisco de Toledo. For better and worse, he established order in a world that had been chaotic for more than two generations (Zimmerman 1938).

Academics tend to root for the natives. Personal biographies, field experiences, and perhaps the sense of marginalization of scholars by an increasingly anti-intellectual society, combined with the wonder of what the world would be like if "The Encounter" had never occurred or had been delayed, all make us root for the Incas against the Spaniards. But, ultimately, we have to take the world for what it is, not what we wish it would be. And so did the people at Magdalena de Cao. How they navigated that reality is what we are presently attempting to understand in our research at the site.

Acknowledgments

Many people made this work possible. Sincere thanks are extended to the National Science Foundation and the National Endowment for the Humanities for the majority of research funds. Dumbarton Oaks and the Peabody Museum of Archaeology and Ethnology, Harvard University, provided additional financial support. This work would not have been possible without the great generosity and support of the Fundación Wiese, Lima, and especially through the kindness and friendship of Mr. Marco Aveggio of that institution. So too, the Peruvian archaeologists of the El Brujo Archaeological Complex were essential in accomplishing this work, particularly Régulo Franco Jordán, César Gálvez, and Carmen Gamarra. The combined Peruvian-U.S. archaeological team was another essential element in this work. Jaime Jiménez S. was my co–field director, and I cannot fully express my gratitude to him for getting this work done and for his passion and love in doing it. Similarly, a great number of coinvestigators were essential to the project. They include Maria Fernanda Boza, Carrie Brezine, William Doonan, R. Jeffrey Frost, Catherine Gaither, Danielle Olga Mirabal, Melissa Murphy, Michele Koons, O. Gabriel Prieto, Hal Starratt, Jennie O. Sturm, Lisa Trever, and Nathaniel Van Valkenburgh. Tom Cummins very kindly provided helpful ideas on the paper cutouts from Magdalena de Cao. Thanks to Sarah Quilter for careful proofreading and interesting observations on this text. Two anonymous reviewers also greatly helped to sharpen the focus of this chapter, and I thank one, in particular, for the direction to the Sandstroms' most interesting book on paper cutouts of Mexico. All these are sincerely thanked as well as Matthew Liebmann and Melissa Murphy for inviting me to the SAR short seminar.

7

Pots and Plots

The Multiple Roles of Early Colonial Red Wares in the Basin of Mexico (Identity, Resistance, Negotiation, Accommodation, Aesthetic Creativity, or Just Plain Economics?)

Thomas H. Charlton and Patricia Fournier

PROLOGUE

The Spanish Conquest brought about drastic changes in the lives of the indigenous people in the Basin of Mexico (Figure 7.1). The immediate results of the carnage of war included multiple disruptions of indigenous life throughout the basin and at all levels of social, political, legal, religious, and economic organization. More pervasive, and of greater long-term impact, were the newly introduced hispanic institutions. Those areas of life would henceforth be organized on the basis of these institutions. There can be no greater symbol of such institutional presence than the construction of the capital of the Viceroyalty of New Spain on the ruins of the Mexica capital Tenochtitlan (compare with Voss, Chapter 12).

There the Spanish colonists established La Traza, an area covering some thirteen blocks in each direction from the central plaza. Today this area corresponds to the historic center of Mexico City (Charlton et al. 1995) (Figure 7.2). La Traza was designated as a living area in the center of the new capital for upper-class Europeans, including Spanish (*peninsulares*) and criollo elites. Lower-class Europeans, excluded from the noble class of the conquerors and their descendants, were forced to reside in the indigenous zones found in the outlying neighborhoods of the city (e.g., Fournier and Charlton 1996–97; Valero de García Lascuráin 1991).

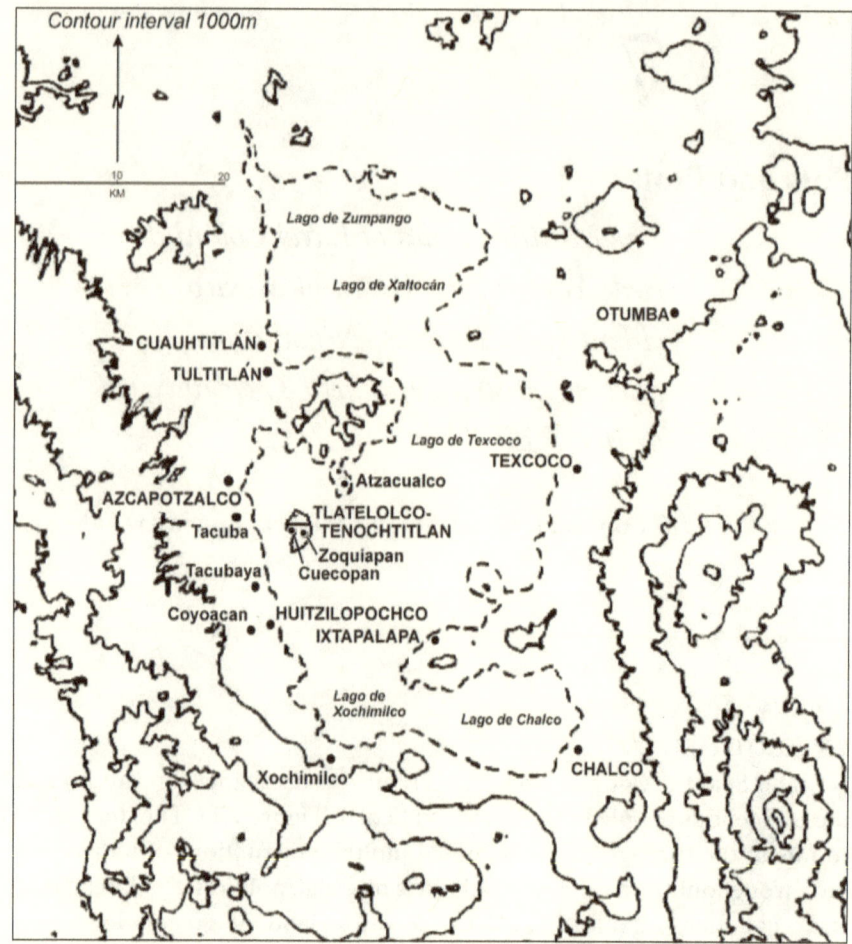

FIGURE 7.1.
Central Mexican symbiotic region and Basin of Mexico with relevant sites. Base map derived from Detenal 1:250,000 series maps NE 14-1 to NE 14-3 (1970), NE 14-4 to NE 14-6 (1979), and NE-10 to NE-12 (1970). Drafted by Cynthia L. Otis Charlton.

Residential areas for native inhabitants were designated throughout the city: to the north of La Traza, the *cabecera* of Santiago de Tlatelolco was established; to the west and south of the Spanish zone, San Juan; in the northeast, San Sebastián Atzacualco; San Pablo Zoquiapan (including Xochimilco) was located to the southeast; and Santa María Cuecopan (today called La Redonda) to the south. Other important centers (with a few Europeans but predominantly indigenous populations, some subject to either San Juan

POTS AND PLOTS IN THE BASIN OF MEXICO

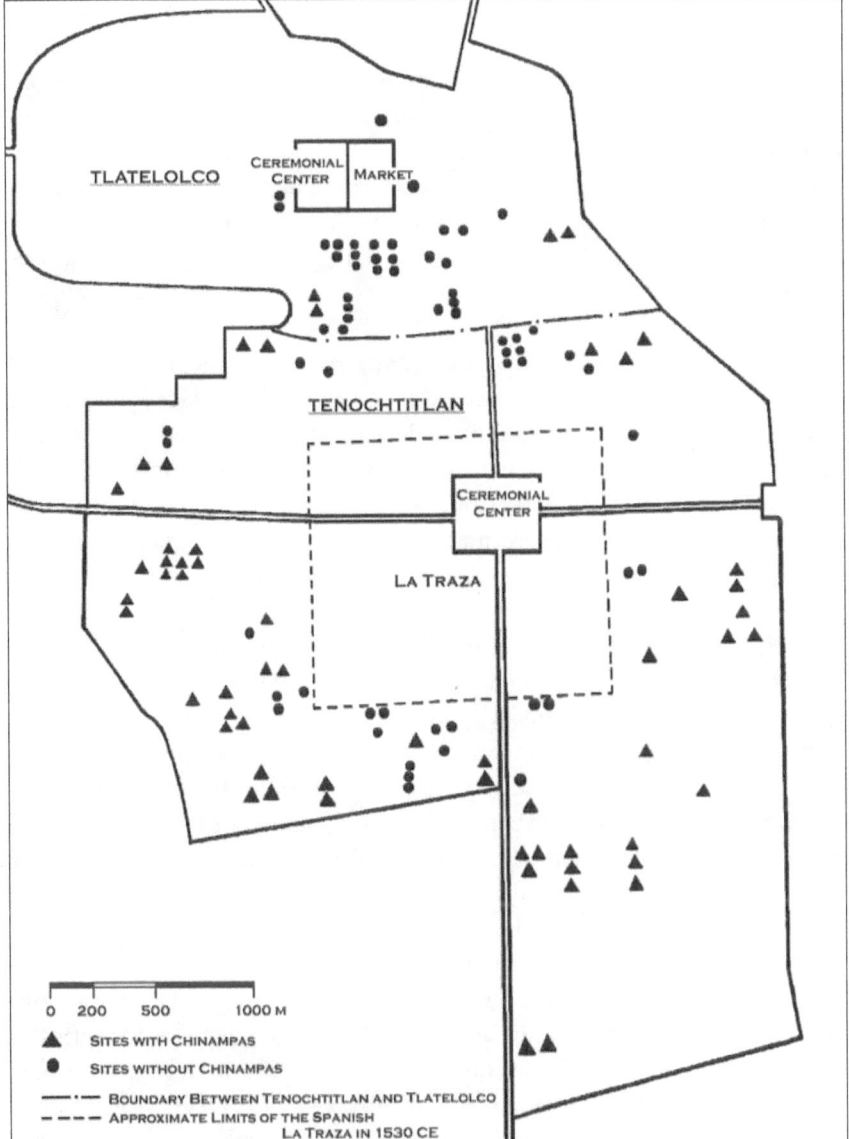

FIGURE 7.2.
Tenochtitlan, Tlatelolco, and La Traza. Drafted by Cynthia L. Otis Charlton based on Plano 2, Valero de García Lascuráin 1991:54.

Tenochtitlan or Santiago de Tlatelolco) included Cuauhtitlán, Tacuba, Azcapotzalco, Texcoco, Tacubaya, Chalco, Coyoacan, Huitzilopochco (Churubusco), and Ixtapalapa (see Figure 7.1).

The urban society of the viceroyalty was characterized by sharp social, economic, and ethnic divisions reflected in the arrangement of residential zones. Later, by about the middle of the seventeenth century, such divisions were further defined within a purportedly biologically based system of *castas*, involving in its simplest rendition *mestizaje*, Spanish/Indian miscegenation. Although the purported biological bases of such differences run as a leitmotif through the literature, the archaeological record suggests systematic differences in the distribution of material goods consumed by various socioeconomic and ethnic groups in their (ideally) physically separate residential zones.

One example of such systematic differences in the distribution of material culture is the frequency of postconquest ceramics found in La Traza on the one hand, and Santiago de Tlatelolco on the other. Given the presence of mostly indigenous occupants in Tlatelolco, and mostly elite Spaniards—peninsulares and criollos—in La Traza, it is not surprising that we find proportionately more majolicas, porcelains, and glazed earthenwares in La Traza than in Tlatelolco. What is surprising, however, is the significant presence in both areas of the same types of postconquest, indigenously produced Red Wares. What does the presence of indigenously produced Early Colonial period Red Ware consumed in two contrasting areas of the colonial city tell us about interactions between the indigenous people and their descendants, and the class-ridden society of their conquerors and related ethnic groups and their descendants?

Early Colonial period urban society was dynamic, stratified, and multiethnic. Is the development of Early Colonial Red Wares solely indicative of aesthetic exuberance and cultural elaboration resulting from the contact of two diverse societies? Are these vessels symbols of the development of an indigenous colonial identity accompanied by resistance to or accommodation of the conquerors? If so, was this symbolism recognized by the conquerors and their descendants and used to facilitate negotiations with the indigenous elites? Or did the indigenous potters simply recognize a new potential market and exploit it with Red Wares that were well received, and if so, was this acceptance by the new elites facilitated by the prior existence of an aesthetic preference among the Spaniards to which the indigenous potters catered? Fortunately, there exist not only the archaeological data but also documentary sources that provide us with contextual information on the social, economic, and political systems in which the middle and late sixteenth-century Red Ware ceramics produced in the basin were heavily used in Mexico-Tenochtitlan and Tlatelolco.

BACKGROUND: PRE-1521 CERAMIC TRADITIONS IN THE BASIN OF MEXICO AND THE IBERIAN PENINSULA

Before the conquest, several subregions in the Basin of Mexico produced ceramics, including Cuauhtitlán, Tultitlán, Otumba, Texcoco, Tenochtitlan, Ixtapalapa, and Chalco (see Figure 7.1). Such identifications are based on documents, instrumental neutron activation analyses (INAA), and archaeological studies of artisan production (Charlton et al. 1999; Charlton and Otis Charlton 1998; Elson 2006; Gibson 1980; Hodge et al. 1993; Otis-Charlton 1994). The technical and aesthetic qualities of the wares produced reflect the craftsmen's high degree of specialization. Within Tenochca society, many of these ceramic artisans had been in charge of producing earthenwares to embellish the ceremony celebrating the 1486 ascension to the throne of Huey Tlatoani Ahuízotl, the eighth Mexica king (Durán 1967).

Following Parsons's typology with some modifications (Parsons 1966), the preconquest Aztec ceramic complex included four trade wares (Huasteca, Central Gulf Coast, Chalco-Cholula, and Xochimilco) and four wares with specific functions (Texcoco Fabric—marked for salt manufacture, long-handled Incense Burners, loop-handled Incense Burners, and Braziers for cooking). In addition, there were two wares that numerically dominated service and utilitarian vessels in domestic households (Red Ware—service vessels; Orange Ware—utilitarian and service vessels). Additionally, archaeologists use the category of Miscellaneous Ware as a catchall term for a variety of wares not readily included in the other categories.

Of these, the most numerous are the Orange Ware vessels, which include the undecorated Plain Orange type, and the well-known decorated Black-on-Orange type, with numerous identified black line decorative variants on a variety of forms, usually service vessels, and less common decorated types. Orange Ware vessels are followed in frequency by Red Ware vessels, usually service vessels, including the Plain Red type and decorated types with painted decorations in various color combinations on a red background (black, white, yellow). In some cases there are identified decorative variants, such as the Black-on-Red and Black-and-White-on-Red types. These two wares composed the majority of the preconquest Aztec ceramics in a typical Late Postclassic household. All were made using molds and were finished, with or without decoration, by burnishing, occasionally done so well on the Red Ware as to be considered polishing. Forms were primarily flat-based hemispherical or flaring-walled bowls with simple rims (Parsons 1966). Hourglass-shaped *copas* occurred in low frequencies as did jars with vertical loop handles. These forms seem to be solely service vessels. Black, white, and yellow were used to paint designs, usually on the exterior surfaces alone, but at times on interior surfaces, and in various color combinations. Types include Plain Red, either without designs, or with designs in other colors being present (black, white, yellow) alone or together. In some types (e.g., Black-on-Red, Black-and-White-on-Red) design variations were classified as decorative variants within the type (Parsons 1966). Postfiring incisions also occur on some forms.

By contrast, ceramic production in Spain at the time of the conquest included lead-glazed earthenwares with utilitarian and service forms, and tin-glazed majolicas, primarily service wares. The potter's wheel and the closed-vault kiln were also present (Lister and Lister 1987). In addition, as we note below, a tradition of small, unglazed, polished red decorative vessels persisted in Spain (Trusted 2007).

EARLY COLONIAL CERAMICS IN THE BASIN OF MEXICO (1521–CA. 1620)

Ceramic acculturation and elaboration, technical and aesthetic, flourished during the Early Colonial period. The ceramics of New Spain reached a level of excellence in the sixteenth century, when two high-quality pottery traditions, the native and the Spanish, influenced each other. The native potters contributed a deep knowledge of local clays and techniques such as burnishing, which were new to the Spanish. The Spanish potters introduced the potter's wheel, lead or lead oxide and tin glazes, as well as the closed-vault kiln. The indigenous tradition provided burnished and polished earthenware types, at times with painted and molded decoration, along with some plain wares. The European tradition introduced *colorada* (red) smoothed wares, *amarilla* (yellow) glazed wares, and *blanca* (white) majolica wares. Occasionally, Spanish techniques such as glazing were applied to some indigenous wares.

Trade wares and those with specific functions do not show any post-conquest elaboration resulting from culture contact in the basin. However, the technical and decorative apogee of Mexica ceramics prior to the conquest—the well-burnished indigenous Orange Ware and the fine-polished Red Ware, with and without painted decorations—were elaborated further after 1521. These developments followed both preconquest formal and decorative conventions and new influences from the recently introduced Iberian ceramic tradition (Charlton et al. 2007).

Such wares came into Spanish hands in a number of ways. Early Colonial period registries (1521–1620) of appraisals and tribute lists indicate that some indigenous communities held in *encomienda* by various conquerors periodically provided their *encomenderos* with pitchers and *comales* as part of the tribute they were required to pay. Many of these vessels were the same forms that had met prehispanic needs (Paso y Troncoso 1905, 1940; *Libro de las Tasaciones* 1952; Valle 1993). In part, their uses were functionally related to the storage, preparation, and serving of new foods such as tortillas to which Europeans had become accustomed. Many of these persisting Plain Orange forms, such as comales, declined in surface finishing during this period. At the same time, changes in the form and style of Red Ware occurred (including the location of decorative attributes and surface finish). Some of these changes appear to result from the sixteenth-century relaxation of preconquest guildlike restrictions of forms and designs for practitioners of specific ceramic ware traditions.

The potters sold their products, directly or through intermediaries, in the most important markets in Mexico-Tenochtitlan such as Tlatelolco, the major preconquest market, and in El Volador in Tenochtitlan. The Tlatelolco market gradually lost importance after the fall of Tenochtitlan, and the El Volador market became more important. According to later registries of the middle seventeenth century, these markets also traded in the raw materials needed for the production of European tradition ceramics. In the markets all segments of the complex socioeconomic and ethnic hierarchical pyramid of the great city came together, where all the castas bought and sold what was necessary for daily life (e.g., Cervantes de Salazar 2000; Fournier and Charlton 1996–97; Mendieta 1945; Sahagún 1989).

BURNISHED/POLISHED RED WARE IN THE EARLY COLONIAL PERIOD

Salvage archaeology in Tlatelolco, carried out by the Dirección de Salvamento Arqueológico of the Instituto Nacional de Antropología e Historia (INAH) in the early 1990s, recovered substantial amounts of Colonial Red Ware in a sixteenth-century indigenous context (Charlton et al. 1995; Fournier et al. 1995). These ceramics revealed a complex pattern distinct from that of pre-1521 domestic households. Although there were some preconquest forms (bowls, copas, and jars) with pre- and postconquest designs on their exteriors, most exterior designs disappeared during this time. The bulk of these vessels differed from the indigenous ceramic assemblage in terms of new forms (plates and dishes), new styles of decoration (Aztec IV Black-on-Orange designs and new curvilinear floral motifs), new placement of decorations (on the interior of dishes and the upper surfaces of plates), and enhanced (but selectively applied) surface burnishing.

Some minor introductions made their initial appearances in the sixteenth century, only to become more prevalent and elaborate in the seventeenth and eighteenth centuries: incrustations of shell or stone pressed into the clay to form a design are one example; the appearance of a new form, a small Plain Red jar with fluting and a gourdlike appearance, is another. Another unusual form, the globular Plain Red incurved-rim goblet with an annular or low pedestal base (sometimes with black decoration over a burnished natural tan or a red painted surface) and rough surface treatment, is present in significant numbers as well.

At Tlatelolco the indigenous Red Ware ceramic tradition continued with modifications, including the incorporation of two new forms—plates and "dishes" (flat-based flaring-wall bowls with interior decoration and tripod supports, including effigies)—that were not present in preconquest Red Ware ceramics. The decorated interiors were probably borrowed from the preconquest and Early Colonial Black-on-Orange tradition. The exteriors of the molded effigy tripod supports are similarly painted and decorated, but the bases of the vessels and the backs of the supports lack any finishing (changes that only occur in low frequencies in rural occupations; Charlton et al. 2007).

By comparison, Enrique Rodríguez-Alegría (2002, 2005a, 2005b) has recently studied a similar complex of sixteenth-century Colonial Red Wares recovered from good contexts associated with households in La Traza. The associations of Colonial Red Wares with Asian porcelains provide a post-1573 date for those materials. Rodríguez-Alegría (2002:267–72) notes the presence of utilitarian Red Ware forms (basins and ollas) used in cooking and storage, as well as service vessels. The service vessels include preconquest forms such as hemispherical bowls, copas, small ollas in gourd-shaped forms, and jars, along with Colonial Red Ware forms such as plates and tripod dishes, which were borrowed from preconquest Orange Ware forms. He also notes the presence of feldspar inlay, zonal burnishing, and fluting as new decorative techniques, although these occurred infrequently (2002:276). The forms and designs change, but the preconquest techniques and colors used in painting persist.

The Colonial Red Ware ceramics found at Tlatelolco and La Traza are similar enough to consider both to represent subsets of the same late sixteenth-century urban Colonial Red Ware ceramic tradition. Unfortunately, the details of the provenience and associated wares in both settings are inadequate to carry out detailed statistical analyses of the materials. For the moment we shall make do with the qualitative descriptive analyses presented.

Within a half century after the conquest, some Black-on-Orange ceramic production had been moved to the Texcoco production zone

(Charlton et al. 1999). Some Red Ware production continued in the Tenochtitlan production zone (Rodríguez-Alegría 2002:365–69). Whatever preconquest guild restrictions had existed to maintain separate preconquest Orange Ware and Red Ware ceramic traditions in terms of forms, colors, and designs appear to have weakened so that the Colonial Red Wares incorporated plate and tripod dish forms and designs from the Orange Ware tradition. In addition, new forms and decorative techniques, possibly from Spanish sources, appear in small quantities. These are urban phenomena with little presence in rural areas.

How and why did the Red Ware ceramic tradition develop along these lines after the conquest? What might it tell us about the exceedingly complex and dynamic urban society in which it occurs? What factors influence the use of these changes by both the indigenous households in Tlatelolco and those of the hispanic elite in Mexico-Tenochtitlan? Let us look at several relevant developments after the conquest that might shed some light on these questions.

Spanish and Indigenous Aesthetic Preferences for Colonial Red Ware

It might be argued that in the late sixteenth-century urban occupations, the forms and color of the Colonial Red Ware vessels appealed to Spanish aesthetic tastes as well as maintained memories of the prehispanic, late Postclassic Red Ware ceramics among the indigenous people in the Basin of Mexico. The Colonial Red Ware is comparable to the bright red ceramics of Extremadura, the homeland of Hernando Cortés and of many of the other conquerors (Trusted 2007:146). The vessels graced the tables of the members of the nobility of New Spain (Rodríguez-Alegría 2002) and were used by Tlatelolco's indigenous residents. Their absence in the sixteenth-century rural Basin of Mexico is probably related to the limited presence there of Spaniards and other Europeans during the Early Colonial period.

There is substantial literature dealing with the presence among the Spanish (peninsulares and criollos) of a continuing desire for ceramics that seem to be Colonial Red Ware from the sixteenth to the eighteenth centuries. This would support the idea that the indigenous potters modified their ceramic production forms and decorations to appeal to the Spaniards or made them according to Spanish directions. Later the Red Wares could be found in distant territories and provinces in northern New Spain such as New Mexico and Texas. They were also exported to Florida and to Spain itself (Trusted 2007:99, 146). Various inventories of goods for Mexico City as well as for northern New Spain mention Mexican or red *jarrillos* that may well have been produced in the Basin of Mexico (e.g., Boyd-Bowman 1972; Fournier 1989; Muriel and Lozano 1995). A similar case is in the *lienzo* [canvas] of 1785, the work of Francisco Clapera, "De Chino e India, Genizara" (García Sáiz 1989; Katzew 2004).

Postconquest Developments: The Encomenderos of Cuauhtitlán

The community of Cuauhtitlán was a major preconquest and Colonial period pottery manufacturing center in the basin (Gibson 1964:350–51), although pottery was not listed among the tributes paid as recorded in the *Libro de las Tasaciones* (1952:149–50). INAA (Hodge et al. 1993; Elson 2006) indicates that there had been pottery production in the Cuauhtitlán region at least since the Early Postclassic period. In the Early Colonial period Cuauhtitlán was an important population center. Despite the multiple epidemics that had affected the area, there were still 5,200 indigenous tributaries in the *doctrina* in 1560 (Gibson 1980:100, 139), while in the region there were 10,600 indigenous tributaries (Gerhard 1986: 131).

After the conquest in 1521, Cortés assigned Indian tribute and labor to various conquerors through the private institution of the encomienda (Gibson 1964:58–59). He awarded Cuauhtitlán and other northern basin communities to Alonso de Avila, but for a variety of reasons (including his death around 1535) this encomienda was held first by his brother, Gil González de Avila (Benavides), and then by his nephew, Alonso de Avila (Alvarado) the younger (son of Gil González de Avila) (Gerhard 1972: 127–28; Gibson 1964:416; Thomas 2000: 17–19). The encomienda reverted to the Crown on August 3, 1566, with the executions of Alonso the younger and his brother, Gil González de Avila the younger (Gibson 1964:416–17; *Libro de las Tasaciones* 1952:149–50).

In 1525 the municipal government of Mexico-Tenochtitlan granted to Alonso de Avila the elder a lot located between Cortés's house and the monastery of San Francisco in the central part of La Traza (now the present-day street of Santa Teresa). In 1527 his brother received a contiguous lot on the street of the Relox (today Argentina) "that is in the third part where the temple of Huitzilopochtli was located" (Muriel 1978:6; authors' translation). Both house lots were bequeathed to the children of Gil González de Avila (Benavides). After the execution of Alonso the younger and Gil González the younger, the houses were torn down and the lots sown with salt. A plaque located near the Aztec Templo Mayor marked the approximate location of their residences along with their executions.

El Códice de los Alfareros

The best-known chronicle of Cuauhtitlán is the *Annales* or *Codex of Chimalpopoca*, written around 1570. However, there also exists another

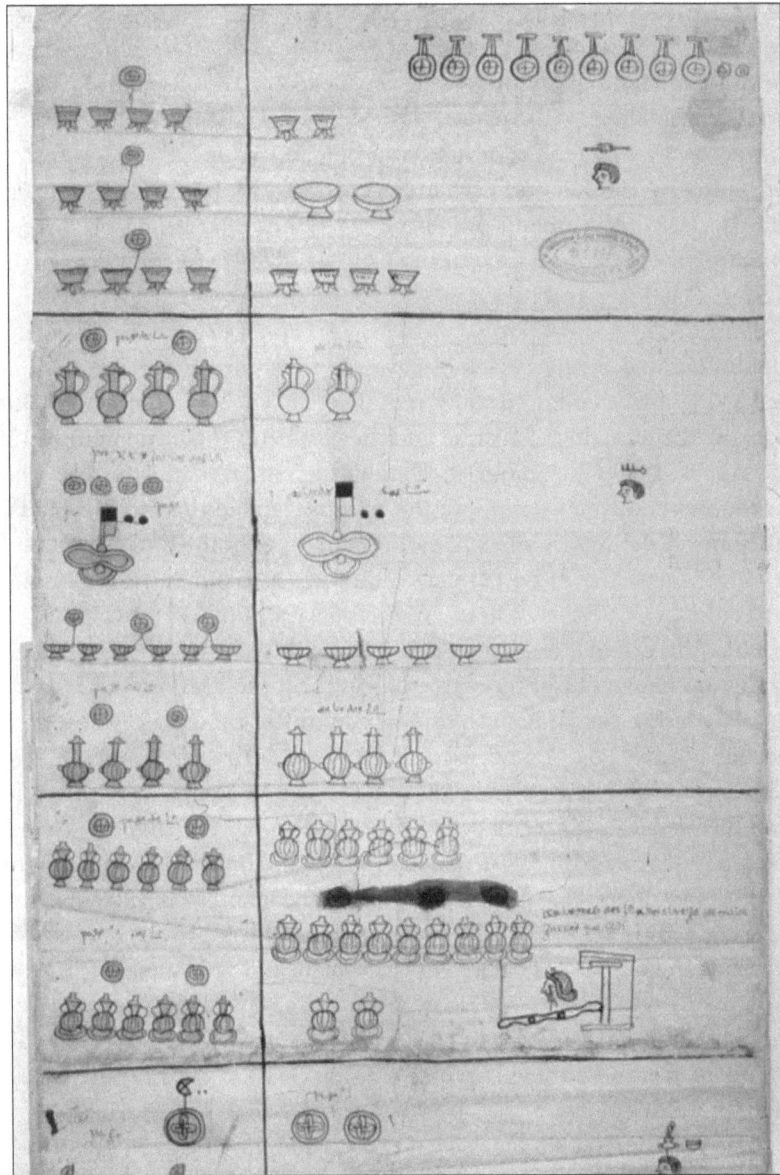

FIGURE 7.3.
Sections I–III of the Códice de los Alfareros de Cuauhtitlán. Used by permission of La Bibliothéque Nationale de France.

sixteenth-century document, the 1564 *Códice de los Alfareros* (or the *Codex of the Potters*) (Figure 7.3), which has received only limited attention (Barlow

1951; Charlton 1995; Charlton et al. 1995) but is relevant for archaeological investigations of the Early Colonial period. The codex incorporates images drawn in much-modified prehispanic stylistic conventions (Barlow 1951:6) and is supplemented with Spanish glosses. This document was either written/painted by the indigenous protagonists of a lawsuit in 1564 or was made at their initiative (Mohar and Fernández 2006:13–14). It is important for our study because it documents graphically the kinds of ceramics produced in Cuauhtitlán close to the time of the Colonial Red Ware ceramics encountered in Tlatelolco and La Traza.[1]

The *Códice de los Alfareros* presents a complaint by four potters from Cuauhtitlán concerning a lack of payment for some of the commissioned vessels they had made and delivered. The suit was directed against Juan Suárez de Peralta, the magistrate and the alcalde of Cuauhtitlán until 1567 (Silva Tena 1990:19). Suárez de Peralta had ordered the vessels, which were subsequently delivered, but the potters claimed that he had paid for only some of the vessels and still owed them for the others (a claim that he disputed). Juan Suárez de Peralta's father was a friend and brother-in-law of Hernando Cortés, as well as a close friend of Alonso and Gil González de Avila, the original encomenderos of Cuauhtitlán. Obviously Suárez de Peralta was a member of the sixteenth-century elite in New Spain.

Included in the codex are representations of the vessels whose forms and decorations correspond (for the most part) to those of archaeologically known Colonial Red Ware vessels. The vessels for which payment had been received are painted in red to the left side of a vertical line. Those for which payment was still due are to the right of the line and are not colored. In the codex there are images of drinking cups, tankards, pitchers, water jugs, ollas, bowls, tripod dishes, anthropomorphic effigy vessels of bearded Spaniards and of Africans painted in black, plain and decorated jars (stamped or painted eagle heads, "squash type fluting"), bowls with pedestal bases and plain or fluted bodies, and ollas with lids. Ollas with lids are decorated with geometric and undulating lines, possibly incisions. Missing are any representations of plates.

The vessels depicted far exceed the varieties and frequencies of vessel forms and decorations encountered in Tlatelolco and La Traza as described earlier. Many of the forms and decorations do occur archaeologically in greater frequencies in seventeenth- and eighteenth-century deposits, both urban and rural. In rural areas, the Colonial Red Ware type attains its greatest frequencies and varieties during the Middle and Late Colonial periods and is associated with the introduction and growth of ranches and haciendas. Colonial Red Ware was either not favored by or was not readily available to the indigenous people in the Otumba area in the sixteenth century and was present there only in relatively minor quantities during the seventeenth and eighteenth centuries (Charlton 1996; Charlton et al. 2007).

Nevertheless, the illustrations do include the tripod dishes mentioned earlier as well as some of the ollas, jars, and bowls with fluted bodies, which occur in low frequencies in the Tlatelolco and La Traza excavated collections. Some examples of the anthropomorphic effigy jars featuring African heads and painted in black were found in a shipwreck in Pensacola Bay. The wreck is believed to date from the ill-fated expedition of Tristán de Luna in 1559 (Smith 1999:109), which coincides nicely with the illustrations in the codex.

THE POLITICS OF RESISTANCE: NEW LAWS AND ENCOMIENDAS

The conquerors had divided and distributed between themselves the labor, lands, and tribute of the indigenous population in New Spain through encomiendas later inherited by their descendants and sought by the Crown. Among the privileged classes of late sixteenth-century Mexico—the conquistadores and their heirs—there was a profound resentment of the Crown in general and the viceroys in particular. This was due to a looming threat to enforce the New Laws of 1542 to "limit all *encomienda* grants to a single lifetime and to abolish Indian personal service" (Knight 2002:18). Those who had aspired, without success, to gain an encomienda, those who had already lost encomiendas, and those who were in danger of being dispossessed opposed implementation of the New Laws (Porras Muñoz 1968). Included, of course, would have been Alonso de Avila Alvarado the younger, the encomendero of Cuauhtitlán.

Luis de Velasco was the viceroy from 1550 to 1564. His unexpected death in 1564 left a power vacuum in New Spain for over two years before his replacement arrived in October 1566. The *audiencia* took the reins of government for two years but did not effectively fulfill its functions and failed to ensure that its orders were respected (Vincent 1993). In the absence of a viceroy, the situation became fertile soil for the young, disaffected encomenderos to forge ideas and to plan violent measures with the ultimate goal of separating Mexico from Spain. It is not clear that such a conspiracy was ever more than indiscreet talk, however. The audiencia's heavy-handed response could have been an attempt to cover its own ineptitude before the arrival of the newly appointed viceroy, Gastón de Peralta, Marqués de Falces (1566–68).

An additional factor aggravating the situation was the return of Martín Cortés de Zúñiga in 1563. He was the legitimate son and heir of Hernando Cortés from his marriage with Juana de Zúñiga, second Marquesa of the Valley of Oaxaca. Born in Cuernavaca in 1532, he lived in Europe from eight years of age and inherited his father's estate, title, and prestige, the equivalent of an aristocratic position and titles. His status was reinforced by his proximity to the Spanish court for several years. In his 1563 return to Mexico, Cortés de Zúñiga was accompanied not only by his wife but also by two of his half brothers, Luis and Martín, illegitimate sons of the conqueror, but both legitimized by Pope Clemente II in 1529. During his youth in Spain, the second Marqués of the Valley of Oaxaca had inherited a peculiar prideful demeanor in public, which was worthy of a king in ostentation and pretension. In New Spain, many viewed this as not only startling but above all threatening, due to the fact that he was at the time the only "nobleman" born in Mexico. As his holdings were also threatened by the Crown's intention to eliminate the encomienda system, some encomenderos (such as Alonso de Avila) saw him as a future king of an independent New Spain.

The attitudes of Martín Cortés, along with his occasional rivalry with the Spanish viceregal authorities, garnered him a great deal of hatred among those in high positions but much friendship among his fellow criollos, encomenderos, and fortune hunters eager to live the licentious life in the fashion of the Iberian courts and to capture absolute power over the lands and the natives of New Spain. After his arrival, the second Marqués del Valle promoted celebrations or was a cocontributor to these, common among the privileged classes of Mexico City. These galas were graced with indigenous ceramics made in the Basin of Mexico and indigenously prepared foods. It was at these galas that a plot was eventually hatched to declare Martín Cortés king of an independent New Spain.

THE HISTORICAL INTERSECTION OF POTS AND PLOTS

In various accounts and chronicles, the polished Red Ware of Cuauhtitlán appears at splendid celebrations organized in 1566 by the criollo Alonso de Avila the younger, an intimate friend of Martín Cortés. The Cuauhtitlán ceramics described in the *Códice de los Alfareros* of 1564 are linked to the Cuauhtitlán ceramics associated with the ostentatious feasting in La Traza and hence with the developing plot to crown Martín Cortés king of New Spain. There is a compendium of documents about the case of the "alzamiento con la tierra," or the so-called conspiracy of Martín Cortés, published by Orozco y Berra (1853b:193), which includes a good part of the testimony of the defendants and the witnesses in the legal process against the separatists, whose pretensions the audiencia frustrated in 1566.

Another account, perhaps based on hearsay, was written at the beginning of the seventeenth century by fray Juan de Torquemada (1969). He reviews some facts related to the conspiracy in his *Monarquía Indiana*. A further source of substantive importance is the *Tratado del Descubrimiento de las Yndias y de su Conquista* (Suárez de Peralta 1990), a manuscript authored by the same Juan Suárez de Peralta who was sued in 1564. (This manuscript was completed in 1589, but it was not published until 1878.) Juan Suárez de Peralta was born in Mexico around 1537 (1544 according to Thomas 2000:389) and was a witness to and a participant in the way of life of the criollo descendants of Hernando Cortés and the conquerors.

When these three sources are compared, some inconsistencies and contradictions regarding the nature and timing of the events become apparent. However, here we are mainly concerned with the late sixteenth-century Colonial Red Wares and their use by the elites of the Viceroyalty of New Spain, and not the precise details of the purported plot. Despite difficulties regarding the sequence of the events, the documentary information available on the presence and use of Cuauhtitlán Colonial Red Wares is clear and, in some cases, detailed. The late sixteenth-century Colonial Red Wares and indigenous foods may in this context be viewed as symbols reflecting the degree to which the children of the conquerors and other elite personages in Mexico-Tenochtitlan had adopted modified indigenous products and foods.

The chronicle by Juan Suárez de Peralta is of special importance to the purported insurrection of Martín Cortés and the young encomenderos who may have incited it. Suárez de Peralta relates that in June 1566 the recently born son of Martín Cortés, the second Marqués of the Valley of Oaxaca, was baptized as Pedro Cortés de Ramirez de Arellano. He would eventually inherit the *marquesado* from his father (Goldberg 1971; Orozco y Berra 1853a). The baptism festivities included mock battles, music, and the building of a passage from the house to the church covered with flowers and with triumphal arches. By this time rumors of a plot had spread and many participating in the baptismal festivities were armed. Viceregal personnel did not attend (Suárez de Peralta 1990:198–201). There was a sumptuous feast following the baptisms, described by Suárez de Peralta:

> Alonso de Avila invited the marchioness to a very superb dinner party prior to which there should be celebrated and was celebrated a masquerade on horseback.

FIGURE 7.4.
Symbol of the Crown and Monogram (R-Rex) used on Colonial Red Ware vessels from Cuauhtitlán by Alonso de Avila Alvarado. Drawn by Cynthia L. Otis Charlton based on Suárez de Peralta 1990:186.

In all these occasions they thought that arms would be taken up, and secretly the judges and those loyal to the king were armed and showed prudence. A merry masquerade was celebrated and afterwards the dinner, very expensive and abundant, served in pots known as *alcarrazas*, and clay mugs, all made in the town of Alonso de Avila, in Cuauhtitlán, where a lot of pottery is produced. And to decorate the pots, they ordered that all had signs as follows: A letter R and above it a crown [Figure 7.4]. All mugs and pots had them, and Alonso de Avila himself gave the marchioness a larger alcarraza with this sign. I believe as soon as the meal started that the *oidores* had one and said that the sign meant "you will reign." They kept the vessel and after the dinner everyone went home, and as I have said, nothing was said that the judges did not know and write down. (Suárez de Peralta 1990:198–201, authors' translation)

According to another source, great celebrations that were worthy of a king followed one another throughout one whole week: "Banquet followed banquet without interruption" (Orozco y Berra 1853a:47, authors' translation).

The Plot Unravels, The Pots Appear

While the feasting continued after the baptisms on June 30, Luis de Velasco, the former viceroy's son, and others presented testimony to the audiencia about the suspected conspiracy whose goal was to place Martín Cortés on the throne of an independent New Spain. The two brothers, accused as conspirators, were taken into custody at their residences (located on the present-day corner of Guatemala and Argentina streets). They and others, including Martín Cortés, were interrogated and their testimonies recorded.

Orozco y Berra (1853b) summarized additional data about the conspiratorial behavior of the two ill-fated encomenderos involving earlier festivities in which allusion in writing and behavior was made to the marqués and his wife as being rulers of New Spain (Orozco y Berra, 1853b:7–8). Torquemada (1969:629) concurs, and other data (Vincent 1993:133) from the Archivo General de Indias (AGI) agree with those recorded by fray Juan de Torquemada about the brothers' inappropriate regal references to the marqués and the marquesa at the fiesta in March.

Of particular relevance to our study is the testimony of a Pedro de Aguilar from Seville. He acted as a messenger between the conspirators (Vincent 1993:135). His declaration of April 1566 details what had happened in the festivities organized by Alonso de Avila the younger in honor of the Marqués and the Marquesa del Valle in March 1566, months before the festivities associated with the baptism of the Cortés twins as described by Suárez de Peralta. According to Pedro de Aguilar, Alonso de Avila had ordered:

> all the tasty dishes to be prepared the way the Indians do, so he ordered the prepared meal to be brought from his subject towns, with the complete dinner service of plates, pitchers, jugs, candlesticks, *tijeras*, and saltcellars. (Orozco y Berra 1853b:198)

Among the testimonies associated with the judicial process brought against the conspirators, several potters from Cuauhtitlán related that they had produced for the household of Alonso de Avila various water jugs and other vessels decorated with a crown as a coat of arms (see Figure 7.4). These were produced before the celebration of the masquerade in March 1566, although clearly pieces with the same coat of arms were made for that occasion as well (Vincent 1993:133).

CONSIDERATIONS OF CAUSALITY

The manufacture of late sixteenth-century Colonial Red Ware maintained the use of prehispanic techniques of vessel shaping (molds) and finish (surface burnishing and polishing), and retained some design elements as well. At the same time, the Colonial Red Ware potters incorporated forms and decorative elements previously associated only with the Black-on-Orange ceramic tradition. How should we understand these changes?

1. Economically Motivated Creation through Agency

One approach would be to consider these changes as evidence of a successful expression of creativity and originality on the part of the indigenous potters after the conquest. Within the new social, political, economic, and religious context of the viceroyalty, the artisans may be considered as active agents producing ceramics based on a complex combination of indigenous knowledge, skill, and aesthetics with an understanding of Spanish preferences for forms and colors of service wares. There does not seem to be any direct impact on the forms and designs of Colonial Red Ware from the European ceramic manufacturing tradition. Rather, the Black-on-Orange indigenous ceramics provided forms and decorations perhaps as a result of a breakdown in preconquest guild restrictions. At the same time, since the vessel forms and new designs are from within the indigenous form and design conventions, the urban indigenous people also used the same vessels.

An incentive to make these changes may simply have been economic. The potters were asked to produce certain vessel forms for which they were supposed to be paid an agreed-upon amount of money, as the *Códice de los Alfareros* indicates. What the indigenous Colonial Red Ware potters did was incorporate in their products formal and stylistic characteristics desired by both Spaniards and native peoples. These actions could be part of processes leading to the construction of new identities and value complexes. Thus they used new combinations of indigenous elements to accommodate the formal and aesthetic preferences of both their Spanish and indigenous customers (van Dommelen 2005).

Liebmann (Chapter 10) discusses Puebloan ceramic assemblages as indices to gauge Pueblo interactions following the 1680 revolt, suggesting that the adoption of technological and stylistic changes reflected social and political linkages between the interacting pueblos. This to some extent is comparable to our suggestion that in the Basin of Mexico the use of similar ceramics indicated a developing bond between the two groups, indigenous and criollos. Similarly, Beck et al. (Chapter 2) discuss the Juan Pardo expeditions in the southeast United States where creativity in response to Spanish presence and demands occurred. They suggest this is best viewed within the context of indigenous politics, which in turn could be understood as active native agency rather than simple dominance and a resistance response. The successful results for the indigenous people in their case, they argue, are related to the absence of a long-term hispanic presence and institutions, quite *unlike* the situation in Basin of Mexico.

2. Tools of Negotiation

The consumption of these wares by both the indigenous residents of Tlatelolco and the Spanish residents of La Traza is of particular interest. Obviously the wares were desirable to both ethnic groups, as noted above. Rodríguez-Alegría (2002, 2005a, 2005b) has suggested that Europeans, both peninsulares and criollos in New Spain, used these burnished Red Wares to reach out to indigenous leaders over meals served on native pottery. The meals would serve as situations in which power would be negotiated. Since the only historically documented instances of the use of this type of pottery are by Europeans alone, Rodríguez-Alegría's position does not seem to be supported.

From the documents relating to the Avila-Cortés "conspiracy," however, it readily becomes apparent that in late sixteenth-century Mexico-Tenochtitlan there was a strong interest in consuming native foods prepared by natives and served on "native" vessels. There were also masquerades and reenactments of the meeting of Cortés with Moctezuma and episodes of the conquest, carried out by Europeans—some dressed as natives were supposed to have dressed. So perhaps there was no use in negotiation, but surely there was use based on the criollos' demonstrated interest in things Indian. Such interest might indicate the development of a "national" identity, locally rooted and separate from the identity of the peninsulares (Berkhofer 1978).

3. Memories of Home

Why did the Spaniards and their descendants adopt the use of the modified Red Ware ceramics for grand occasions? Had they used similar pottery previously? In the sixteenth century, the Iberian region of Extremos-Estremoz as well as others in Portugal (Dias Diogo and Trindade 2002; Queirós 1987) were famous for their fine burnished pottery, which was vermillion or bright red and occasionally white. Archaeologists have called this ware *terra sigillata*, similar to pieces registered in seventeenth-century sources. This ware was esteemed in the Iberian Peninsula and other regions in Europe such as the Low Countries (e.g., Baart 1992; Casanovas 2001; Gaulton and Mathias 1998; Gutiérrez 2000:74–78; Gutiérrez et al. 2003; Veeckman 1994). The *búcaros* and other red vessels with highly polished surfaces were items consumed by the Iberian nobility during the first half of the sixteenth century. Some pieces were part of the dowry of Isabel of Portugal, who married Carlos V in 1526 (Vasconcellos 1921). The production of such burnished ceramics in the domains of the Spanish Crown and later those of Portugal was ongoing, according to archaeological information available for Central Mexico, the Province of Michoacan, New Vizcaya, New Santander, Sinaloa, New Mexico, Texas, Florida, and the Jesuit missions among the Guaraníes in South America (e.g., Brown et al. 2004; Fournier 1997; Fournier and Santos 2007; Fournier et al. 2007; Galindo 2003). Colonists would look to the indigenous ceramics for something similar to what they had known in the old country. There it would have been outside their daily lives and consumed by the Iberian nobility. Where no similar pre-Columbian pottery tradition existed, they established the production of red wares with highly burnished surfaces.

4. The Seeds and Symbols of Separatism and Local Patriotism in Sixteenth-Century New Spain: Resistance to the Crown

We like to attribute resistance to colonized native peoples (see Liebmann and Murphy, Chapter 1). However Deagan (Chapter 3) points out that resistance may be practiced not only by the conquered indigenous people but also by various other subordinate groups within heterogeneous multitiered conquest society. Such resistance may take various forms. The colonizers in the Basin of Mexico formed no simple homogeneous dominant group but rather were quite diverse in the social, economic, and political arenas. Such diversity harbored antagonism and resistance.

So it was in the capital of New Spain where the Crown was trying to take the encomiendas away from the heirs of the conquerors. The Spaniards and their descendants, the Avila brothers and the Marqués del Valle, in 1566 organized and participated in a masquerade with indigenous overtones in the house of Alonso de Avila. In this masquerade the emperor Moctezuma receives Hernando Cortés upon his arrival in Tenochtitlan in 1519. On the one hand, the son of the conqueror, the second Marqués del Valle, took the role of his father, while on the other hand, the young encomendero Alonso de Avila Alvarado adopted the persona of Moctezuma and dressed in Indian guise.

For the judges conducting the legal process against the insurrectionists, the procession organized by Avila Alvarado in the streets of Mexico

City, in which the participants dressed as Indians and gave Martín Cortés a crown, was a clear indication that the marqués intended to become the king of New Spain. In the ritual masquerade, the instigators of the revolt and the Marqués del Valle had presented a theatrical version of the submission of Tenochtitlan to Spain (Drake 2004) but with overtones of criollo resistance.

Events in 1566 demonstrated the use of a symbol of royalty on vessels from Cuauhtitlán, the crown and the letter R (see Figure 7.4), suggesting some resistance against the Crown further supported by the attempt to install Martín Cortés as the king of New Spain. This use of a European symbol on indigenous ceramics and the failed conspiracy provide early evidence of the construction of a form of patriotic ideology (e.g., Cañizares-Esguerra 2005; Mazzotti 2005). This is the first expression of a criollo patriotism that increased toward the end of the sixteenth century and continued during the seventeenth century, arising from the threat of the Crown to end the inheritance of encomiendas. Of interest in these interactions is the importance of how the sons of the conquerors constructed their identity with indigenous overtones and how they perceived the actual indigenous people, a subject worthy of further investigation (Berkhofer 1978).

If we examine suggestions made by Mazzotti (2005), in our case study it is possible to postulate that the commensurate scale of the festivities was considered equivalent to the style of the Iberian nobles and thus was a further demonstration that the criollos aligned themselves ideologically with the peninsulares. Yet at the same time, they incorporated indigenous traditions by employing indigenous foods and ceramics. Thus, in the setting of the conspiracy of 1566, the criollos presented characteristics of an elite group commemorating the honor and courage of their ancestors during the conquest, but incorporating indigenous foods and ceramics into those commemorations. This was a fundamental element in support of their demands for social and political recognition.

CONCLUSION

By the late sixteenth century, Colonial Aztec Red Ware had developed on the basis of an indigenous Red Ware tradition combined with indigenous forms originating in the Black-on-Orange ceramic tradition. Colonial Aztec Red Ware vessels were used by indigenous people in Tlatelolco and Europeans in La Traza. These developments occurred at least forty years after the conquest and were probably market based, the potters manufacturing indigenous-tradition vessels modified to appeal to both ethnic groups. Special orders are known to have been placed by Europeans, so these may have been purely economic transactions. Not all vessels illustrated in the *Códice de los Alfareros* occur in the deposits examined, which suggests that some forms and styles were uncommon at this time. European acceptance may have been due to memories of desirable pottery in Spain or due to a fascination with things "Indian" (similar to nineteenth-century American fascination with chinoiserie). This fascination may have underwritten the use of Colonial Red Ware ceramics to mark the identity of the criollos with symbols of resistance against the Crown marked on them.

Acknowledgments

We would like to thank Yuki Hueda for having located the *Códice de los Alfareros* and obtaining a color microfilm copy. John DeBry earlier had provided full-scale photocopies of the document to Thomas Charlton. Cynthia L. Otis-Charlton prepared the figures and translated an earlier version of this chapter from Spanish to English. She also provided proofreading assistance. We thank Luis Alberto López Wario, Director, and Margarita Carballal, Sub-Director of the Dirección de Salvamento Arqueológico of INAH, for permission to analyze the materials from Tlatelolco. We also thank Melissa Murphy and Matthew Liebmann for asking us to participate in the SAR symposium and for their helpful suggestions and editing while we rewrote the chapter for publication.

Note

1. The codex is now housed in the Mexican stacks of the Bibliothèque nationale de France (BnF) in volumes 103–18 with the catalog number Mex 109 ICR q1487 bis, a catalog reference that differs from that cited by Robert Barlow (1951). According to the BnF description, the codex is an "accounting record of a factory of indigenous ceramics subsequent to the conquest" and is "an original figurative manuscript on European paper 1.90 m in length and 0.32 m in width" (authors' translation).

8

Pragmatic Choices, Colonial Lives
Resistance, Ambivalence, and Appropriation in Northern Honduras

Russell N. Sheptak, Rosemary A. Joyce, and Kira Blaisdell-Sloan

Our focus is on the relational coproduction of the colonial order, which is a long-term historical process. For us, there was no singular Indian or Spanish experience, but rather a fracturing and multiplying of positions that could be occupied by the entire spectrum of actors. Reducing the scope of agency in this ongoing history to domination and resistance places a higher value on certain forms of action than on others, elevating aggressive, violent, oppositional, activities to a more significant position than the repeated actions of everyday life. It is arguable that many of the indigenous societies of the Americas persisted as historically continuous descendant peoples not just, or even primarily, because they actively opposed European colonization, but rather because they shaped the colonial situation into a context for perpetuating their own lives and communities through countless small acts, some even seeming to be acts of compliance (Sheptak 2005; Silliman 2001a, 2005a).

Michel de Certeau's (1984) concept of everyday practices as "tactics" is appropriate to this project because of its emphasis on dispersal of agency and contestation of centralizing power. Tactics are not extraordinary, but ordinary; they are the continuing ways that human subjects occupy social landscapes that they do not entirely control. Tactics can be conceived of as the "appropriation" of what is offered in places like the colonial settings we examine, exceeding the intentions of those who seek control, seizing the moment for one's pragmatic ends, bringing a "repertoire of practices... into a space designed for someone else" (Poster 1992:102).

Archaeologists need to draw on the entire gamut of material traces wherever they have been deposited. Too often, archaeologists insist that only the excavated material traces "count" as archaeological evidence. Documentary archives *are* a part of the archaeological record, and we insist on working seamlessly from the archive to the field site. Indeed, because of the richness of the archive and the still incipient nature of field archaeology of colonial sites in Honduras, documents are the strongest part of our evidence. Traditional disciplinary identities foster resistance to fully embracing the unity of the dispersed materiality of past experiences. Archaeologists are comfortable with flora and fauna like those discussed below as indicators of Indian, Spanish, and creole identities. The architectural plans we cite from excavations documenting abandoned churches also pass muster as "archaeological" data. But standing colonial churches and religious images still in use today may be excluded as archaeological data, understood as evidence for art historians or ethnographers (Sheptak and Joyce 2008). When it comes to documents, archaeologists may see these as the proper domain of historians.

We argue that all these phenomena are *archaeological* data. Following Wylie (2002:161–67), we understand archaeological models are strengthened by tacking back and forth between different forms of archaeological evidence. The dispersion of material traces itself is critical evidence of political and economic contexts, helping us to reinstate a broader landscape perspective on the processes through which indigenous communities persisted.

We thus understand the colonial landscape of northern Honduras (Figure 8.1) from a perspective that considers a range of tactics as evidence of an ongoing process of resistance to incorporation and erasure, through practices that often look like acquiescence to colonial authority. In this broader sense, *resistance* may be a useful term for us to think about how colonized people used the tools at their disposal to recreate meaningful worlds. Concepts like *tactics* serve better in disentangling indigenous histories from material remains of people's everyday actions, including colonial documents. Integration of documents with other material traces is indispensable to any assessment of the meaning of practices, without which we can never know if something was an act of resistance, domination, or persistence, what de Certeau (1984:29–42) called "making do," the primary way that people in everyday life engage with the world.

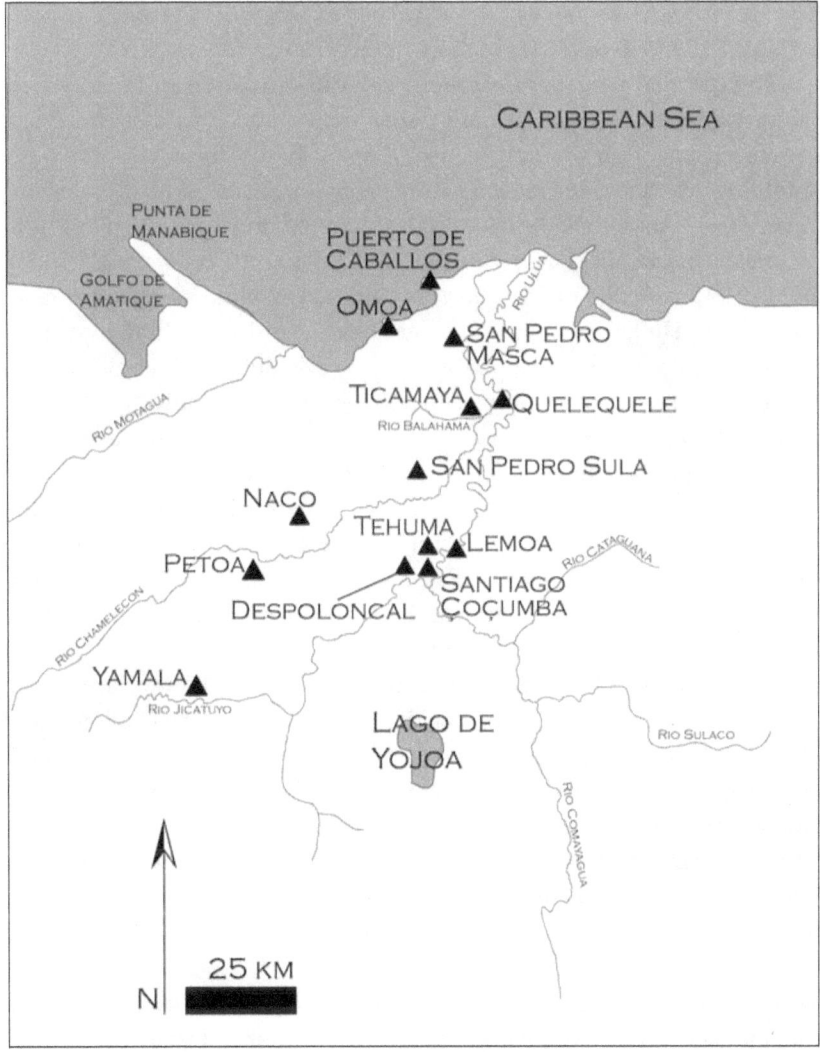

FIGURE 8.1.
Selected Spanish and Indian towns in northwestern Honduras.

In the pages that follow, we consider a series of examples of Honduran indigenous people "making do" that enabled them to persist from the initial period of colonization in the early sixteenth century well into the Republican era, after 1821. We select our examples of ways of making do to illustrate the range of tactics available to, and used by, these people, and to suggest how these left material traces that we today can interpret.

RESISTANCE AS MILITARY CAMPAIGN: THE DEFENSE OF THE RÍO DE ULÚA, 1520 TO 1536

The colonial process in northern Honduras began with military campaigns whose traces exist in both documentary and excavated materials. Letters written from the perspective of Spanish governors as events were unfolding describe a decade-long struggle by the people of the Río de Ulúa (Ulúa River), under the leadership of Çoçumba, to whom other towns in the valley owed allegiance (Gomez 2002; Sheptak 2004, 2006, 2008). Çoçumba reportedly fortified his riverbank towns with extensive palisades and ditches. He led raids on a town established in 1525, killing its officers and abducting at least one Spanish woman. Çoçumba and his allies maintained pressure on Spanish forces that attempted to pass through their territory, although they did not move against the established Spanish coastal town of Trujillo to the east. Their goal appears to have been to keep the Spanish from encroaching on a defined area in the northern Ulúa Valley. Spanish forces did not exercise similar restraint. In retaliation for one attack on a Spanish convoy that passed through Çoçumba's territory, Governor Andres de Cereceda captured two of Çoçumba's subordinate lords, mutilated them, and sent their bodies to Çoçumba.

The itinerary of this Spanish march suggests that the place where Çoçumba was then located was at the confluence of the Choloma and Chamelecon rivers. Remains of a settlement established before the mid-fourteenth century, occupied through the nineteenth century, are found at precisely this location. Invisible on the surface, this was a prosperous town with significant long-distance connections (Blaisdell-Sloan 2006; Wonderly 1984a). These include the highest proportion of obsidian of all known Honduran sites dating to the early sixteenth century, 91 percent from the Ixtepeque source, located far southwest (Blaisdell-Sloan 2006:239). A copper wire fishhook (Figure 8.2) recovered precisely matches examples from Lamanai and Chalancan, in northern Belize, a trace of material connections that extended north, through the Caribbean (Blaisdell-Sloan 2006:242–43; Oland 2004).

Archival documents allow us to identify this archaeological site as Ticamaya, a principal town of Çoçumba, described as a "great merchant" trading in cacao from Honduras to Maya cities in the Yucatán peninsula (Gomez 2002; Sheptak 2004, 2006, 2008). It would be easy to think of the shift from engagement in an active trading network to the military campaign against the initial Spanish invasion solely in terms of a paradigm of "resistance" to conquest. But this would reduce the actual events of a decade-long military struggle to an undue uniformity, concealing substantial

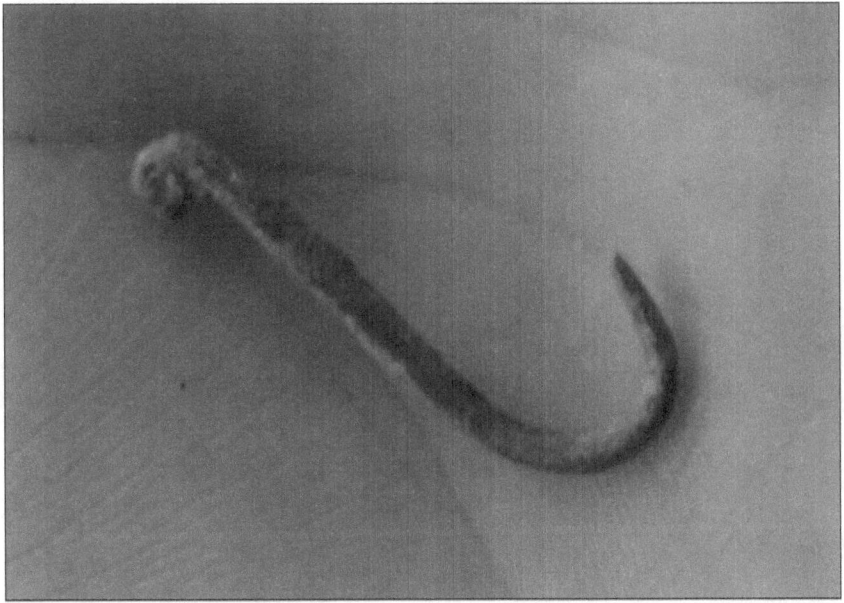

FIGURE 8.2.
Copper fishhook excavated at Ticamaya. Photo by Kira Blaisdell-Sloan.

complexity in the actual tactics and practices employed. Documents show us shifting factions among the Spanish, and alliances between Spanish and indigenous actors that helped to keep the Río Ulúa autonomous long after Cortés first declared it a Spanish colony (compare Beck et al., Chapter 2).

Çoçumba defined a sphere of action that probably corresponded to an existing indigenous territory, avoiding engaging the Spanish outside that area. Governor Cereceda complained that the *indios* (Indians) of towns in the nearby Naco Valley were apt to flee to the hills, leaving him without a labor force. But he did not blame Çoçumba.

Nor do excavated data suggest that Ticamaya had influence in this neighboring area. The Naco Valley had its own colonial settlements, represented today by the archaeological sites of Naco and Viejo Brisas del Valle (Henderson 1977; Henderson et al. 1979; Strong et al. 1938; Wonderly 1981, 1985, 1986a, b; Neff et al. 1990). Material culture suggests these two sites were distinct from Ticamaya. A style of painted serving vessels that make up 17.7 percent of the assemblage at Naco, Nolasco Bichrome (Figure 8.3), is extremely rare (1.67 percent) at Ticamaya, even though access to these vessels was not limited, as they are found in every household there (Blaisdell-Sloan 2006:271–72).

Figure 8.3.
Nolasco Bichrome vessel. Museo de San Pedro Sula, Honduras. Photo by Russell N. Sheptak.

Such excavated materials support sixteenth-century documents that describe the lower Ulúa Valley as politically independent. Instead of busying himself with organizing resistance to the Spanish settlement of Santa María de Buena Esperanza, established in 1534 near the *pueblo de indios* (Indian town) of Naco, Çoçumba was most concerned to maintain the integrity of his own territory, what the Spanish called the Río de Ulúa. Rather than an ideal figure of a local indigenous *cacique* (leader) resisting the whole Spanish order, we need to think of Çoçumba as an actor negotiating an already hybrid social landscape.

In his campaign, Çoçumba drew on knowledge gained from a "woman from Sevilla" who spent a decade with him. He also formed an alliance with a renegade Spaniard sent from one of the major Maya towns along the east coast of Yucatán with a fleet of war canoes, perhaps following lines of established trade in cacao, metal, and other luxury goods. Called Gonzalo Aroca in archival documents, this shipwrecked sailor was an ally who understood the tactics of the Spanish invading Çoçumba's land. Fortifications of sites along the river described in sixteenth-century documents appear to be an innovation (Sheptak 2006). The same Spanish writers did not describe fortifications in the contemporary towns of the Naco Valley, and in fact, singled out the Río de Ulúa for these distinctive earthworks. These Ulúa

FIGURE 8.4.
Obsidian dart point recovered in colonial context at Omoa. Photo by Kira Blaisdell-Sloan.

defenses took shape informed by prior experiences of Yucatecan settlements with which there were long-established trade links, and with knowledge of Spanish tactics that Çoçumba's Spanish ally could provide.

Çoçumba's military campaign came to an end with one decisive battle in June 1536. Pedro de Alvarado, then governor of Guatemala, traveled to Honduras in response to an appeal from Cereceda to assist the increasingly restive colony reestablished near Naco, west of Çoçumba's territory. Alvarado was almost certainly motivated by reports of gold obtained from the hills around the colony. Cereceda convinced Alvarado that there was plenty of wealth for both of them in Honduras, if the better armed and more experienced soldier were willing to undertake the "conquest and pacification" of the province of Çoçumba, including the fortified towns along the Río de Ulúa. Alvarado entered into battle with Çoçumba, supported by his own native allies from Guatemala. He traveled to Çoçumba's fortified town, bombarding it from the river with arrows, rifles, and even small cannon, until Çoçumba and his principal supporters surrendered and Gonzalo Aroca was killed.

Blaisdell-Sloan (2006:154) has identified features at Ticamaya dated by stratigraphy and radiocarbon to about the time when this ultimate battle between Alvarado and Çoçumba took place. A catastrophic fire destroyed one structure that yielded obsidian dart points (Figure 8.4), interpreted in other colonial Maya sites as evidence of violent resistance (Oland 2004; Simmons 1995), in frequencies four times higher than in earlier contexts (Blaisdell-Sloan 2006:169, 238).

Whether the final battle in which Çoçumba surrendered occurred at Ticamaya or another of the fortified towns in his domain, as his principal town, Ticamaya was certainly under attack during the Alvarado campaign. What happened there after the battle was lost was not abandonment and discontinuity; it was instead the beginning of a long period of reshaping of social relations from the indigenous territory to the hybrid colony. Çoçumba and his adherents survived and, according to royal documents, accepted Christian baptism. Forty years later, the leader of a colonial town upriver was named Santiago Çoçumba (Gomez 2002), a likely descendant of the military leader who commanded the initial military resistance.

With their surrender to Alvarado, the people of the Río de Ulúa took the first steps in a centuries-long process of colonial transformation. Ticamaya continued to be occupied, and with a small group of neighboring towns entered into a series of less showy, but equally significant, practical engagements through which long-standing patterns of everyday action were reshaped in the new colonial environment. These descendant communities made the Spanish colony their own through a "repertoire of practices" in this new "space designed for someone else," as acts of appropriation that we argue extend significantly beyond a concept of oppositional resistance.

CALCULATED RELATIONSHIPS: *PUEBLOS DE INDIOS*, 1636–1742

The occupied landscape of Honduras was severely altered in the first decades of colonial administration. Conflicts among claimants to Spanish authority continued into the 1540s, and some indigenous communities considered "pacified" either rose up in "rebellion" or never accepted the new colonial yoke and simply continued their own lives when the Spanish troops passed on (Chamberlain 1953). In northern Honduras, local factors produced more Spanish control and massive population reductions. The early colony intensively exploited indigenous labor in pursuit of gold (Newson 1986; Sherman 1979).

The effects are evident in archival documents. Most towns in the Ulúa Valley listed in assignments of labor to Spanish supporters of Alvarado in 1536 vanished from lists of pueblos de indios in the colonial district of San Pedro providing tribute in 1582. Populations reported for remaining towns, including Ticamaya, declined drastically. Described in 1536 as having up to eighty men, in 1582, Ticamaya had only eight tribute-payers, a loss of 90 percent of the population. Francisco de Montejo, who contested the governorship of Honduras with Alvarado, claimed the town had no more than seventeen houses in 1536. But even this more modest beginning point would imply a decline in population at the site of more than 50 percent, paralleled elsewhere in the valley.

Sixteenth-century pueblos de indios paid tribute based on the number of tributaries counted when a labor assignment to a Spanish citizen was confirmed. In the well-documented case of Despoloncal, upriver from Çoçumba's territory, we see a gradual decrease in the amount of tribute allocated and shifts in the goods and services expected during the sixteenth century. We also see points where indigenous people had openings to tactically occupy colonial spaces and shift the relationships being forged.

Despoloncal is the location of an archaeological site where limited excavations in 1983 produced evidence of a Late Postclassic indigenous community (Wonderly 1984b), without recognizable traces of the contact-period village we know from archival documents was here. The rarity of pronounced material changes in early colonial settlements, where everyday life continued without much change (Blaisdell-Sloan 2006; Pendergast 1991), suggests the Despoloncal assemblage could actually extend into the Colonial period. Excavations give us a basis to compare Despoloncal to better-studied contemporary sites, Ticamaya and Naco.

Despoloncal's residents used locally available cherts for a significant proportion of their chipped stone tools, and consumed far less obsidian than either Naco or Ticamaya. The town was either more indirectly connected to routes of obsidian exchange or simply less wealthy. Molds document local production of serving bowls central to pre-Columbian political and social ceremony. Proportions of differently decorated locally produced painted vessels were distinct from those of Ticamaya. The style most common and likely produced at Naco (Nolasco Bichrome, Figure 8.3) formed 4 percent of the pottery assemblage at Despoloncal, far more than at Ticamaya. It is possible Despoloncal enjoyed more significant connections to Naco than to Ticamaya.

Like Ticamaya and Naco, sixteenth-century Despoloncal was a producer of cacao. Early colonial residents were assessed tribute in that valued commodity for at least fifty years. The history of tribute assessment recorded for Despoloncal illustrates how indigenous persistence in producing cacao, which remained important in indigenous ceremonies through the twentieth century, was balanced against labor demands based on a population that declined steadily in the first century of colonial exploitation. Originally allocated in 1536 to a soldier who accompanied

Alvarado, by 1548 Despoloncal was in the hands of Diego Hernandez. Hernandez had received ten small towns and two major places in the 1536 distribution of labor. Six of these towns were never mentioned again, while the two larger were transferred to others in later periods. Hernandez retained two of the small towns in 1548, along with new rights to the products of labor and services of the people of Despoloncal.

Despoloncal was described as led by a village cacique in 1548. The populace was responsible for tribute paid in cacao, and for a variety of personal services. The relationship was formally confirmed by the local justice, speaking through an interpreter and thus dependent on the translation made by this intermediary. Through this translator, the cacique of Despoloncal stated that his town had thirty-five laborers and could pay tribute in cacao and chickens. The actual tribute ordered by the justice was more ambitious: to farm a field of maize for Hernandez; to produce five units of cacao from each of four groves they tended; to supply fifteen chickens per year, and fishermen to provide for Friday, Saturday, and Lenten meals; and two horse-loads of another product, as yet unidentified, that was gathered locally (most likely a plant). In a separate document, two residents of the town were ordered to go to the city of San Pedro for two weeks a year to build or repair the house Hernandez occupied.

While the tally of service and goods expected was much more than offered by the cacique, the justice also recorded expectations that suggest the people of Despoloncal were understood to have some degree of autonomy. The document explicitly ordered that when Hernandez passed by with his herds, the people of the town were to let him pass. The implication is that they had some control over who crossed the Río Ulúa. The justice explicitly noted that "given the said tribute, they will be free to do what they will with their persons." He warned Hernandez not to take "any other thing" from the people of the town. We may think that this was a fairly unilateral contract, but documents like these became the basis for successful legal cases brought by pueblos de indios in the following centuries, discussed below.

In 1571, following Hernandez's death, the husband of his daughter Luciana Adriana received tribute in cacao from only twenty-four tributaries, who were still obliged to farm a maize field for his benefit. All the other tribute listed previously, including personal service, was no longer allowed. This level of tribute continued to the death of Luciana Adriana's first husband in 1583. At this juncture, the colonial government in Santiago de Guatemala stated that "the living do not have to pay tribute for the dead, nor those present for those absent, and when some die or absent themselves, the community may ask for justice," that is, a reduction in tribute. Presumably, it was on such grounds that between 1548 and 1571 the level of cacao tribute had dropped 31 percent.

Counts of tributaries were based on statements by community leaders, whose sworn testimony substantiated how many people obligated to pay tribute lived in pueblos de indios. As the interface for the flow of demographic and economic information out of these towns, community leaders controlled the statistical representation of their populations. That this opportunity was employed tactically is suggested by later efforts to create more accountability for counts of tribute-payers. In population records produced in the early eighteenth century, indigenous leaders are sworn not to conceal anyone present or absent from town, and are asked to bring with them the church registers of births, marriages, and deaths, which by the 1720s included extensive notes on marriages that resulted in the movement of spouses, and on the current status of previously recorded people. Even so, it was ultimately indigenous authorities who identified who lived in each town, and who was subject to or exempt from tribute.

When her second husband filed a petition for confirmation of their grant in 1591, Luciana Adriana held Despoloncal through what was called the "right of second life," as heir to her father, a grant that expired with her. In 1614, Juan Lezcano was confirmed as a new recipient of the income from Despoloncal, a grant the legal guardian for Ana Maria Lezcano, presumably his daughter, requested be reconfirmed in 1649. These later grants show that Despoloncal, a pueblo de indios that struggled with the burdens of Spanish tribute demands in the sixteenth century, found a way to persist while its residents accommodated the demand for surplus production to satisfy the Spanish labor regime. Other archival documents demonstrate that Despoloncal, like other pueblos de indios, was a site of practices through which indigenous people made another central colonial institution, the Roman Catholic Church, thoroughly their own.

TAKING PLACE: CHURCHES AND COFRADIAS, 1583–1796

In 1742 Despoloncal was one of many pueblos de indios included in a survey of cofradias, independent religious societies that provided mutual financial aid, organized charitable works, and fostered shared devotion to specific saints. The Spanish priest responsible for, but not resident in, Despoloncal stated that the origins of the cofradias in the town were not remembered. A note in the statement of tribute expected in 1583 says the "Indians that serve in the church of the town" were required to pay the same tribute as others, but might be given the benefit of community goods, the kind of property later held by cofradias. Whether this note refers to already established cofradias or simply to an indigenous sacristan who cared for the church the majority of the year when no priest was present, it tells us that by 1583 there was a building at Despoloncal dedicated to Catholic religious observances that was controlled by the indigenous people of the town.

The Spanish *cura* (parish priest) of Despoloncal in 1742 cited a lack of documents about cofradias, noting that the indigenous members themselves held this knowledge. The independent practice of Roman Catholic devotions by such lay practitioners was viewed with concern by another of the priests responding to this survey, who asked that in neighboring Petoa an Indian of Christian habits would be appointed to maintain the security of the chapels where he claimed the indigenous people were entering and carrying on "their ancient idolatry," likely a reference to devotions to images of saints, central to cofradias. In the context of a survey of the distribution of an eminently Spanish Catholic set of practices, this comment suggests perceptions that while conforming to Spanish rituals on the surface, the indios were carrying out these practices in ways that were specific to the indigenous society and its history—heterodox, tactical appropriations of the imposed religion.

Services were held in indigenous towns in colonial Honduras in buildings visited at intervals by a priest. Unlike the more familiar Franciscan, Dominican, and Jesuit missions, the Mercedarian missionary order did not create planned communities monitored by resident priests (compare Wernke, Chapter 5, and Voss, Chapter 12, for Franciscan practices, and Quilter, Chapter 6, for the Dominican practice). During the majority of the year, when no priest was present, the chapels in pueblos de indios, and the saints' images and other sacred objects they contained, were under the control and at the service of the community itself. Items in such chapels were made by indigenous craft workers from as early as the mid-sixteenth century. An account of a circuit through the Ulúa Valley by Bishop Jeronimo de Corella in 1554 described a beautifully made cross donated to the church by the indios of the neighboring towns. Statues or paintings of saints were regularly brought out from the central churches in pueblos de indios and taken in procession to partner towns (a practice that continues today, called *guancasco* in the Honduran Lenca language). The significance of such images and the churches where they were housed to indigenous communities is made clear in petitions by the people of Jetegua (in 1679) and Masca (around 1700), two pueblos de indios located on the Río Ulúa Valley near Ticamaya. Both asked permission to relocate to gain security from raiding pirates. Each cited the sacking of the church and the removal of images and sacred vessels as particular losses.

The practices of cofradias were difficult to control, as these societies had their own property by the eighteenth century, including substantial herds of cattle and grazing land and could carry out their own projects. A land title for Yamala, upriver from Despoloncal, identified land parcels held by the cofradias of San Juan (the town's patron saint) and Nuestra Señora de la Encarnación in 1768. In response to the 1742 inquiry, Yamala's cura had identified only one cofradia, dedicated to the Annunciation. Whether the report from 1742 was incomplete, or the number of cofradias grew over the decades, this small town made Roman Catholic observance a centerpiece of community life in the eighteenth century. In addition to its cofradias, Yamala participated in the intervillage visitation of patron saints (guancasco), exchanging visits with Santiago Posta, a pueblo de indios located to the west.

The spatial focus of locally controlled, locally meaningful Roman Catholic rituals in Yamala was the town church (Figure 8.5). In 1778, the community petitioned for relief from taxation to have the resources to complete rebuilding of the church. Documents with this petition described the original church—which would have been the setting for celebrations by three cofradias, and would have hosted the visit of Santiago Posta's saint—as too small and rustic, with a thatched roof. In its place, the people of Yamala had begun construction of a wood, brick, and stone church. They requested relief from tribute to be able to cover the expenses of the roof they hoped to install. Their petition was opposed by civil authorities in Honduras, who would have lost tribute, and ultimately, they were told to use income from their cofradia land and cattle to cover the costs. Nonetheless, in 1796, the indigenous townspeople initiated a new request for relief from the final expenses for completing the roof of the church.

The church that was built in the late eighteenth century was still standing partly intact in 1983, when Joyce and Sheptak visited, mapped nearby late prehispanic mounds, and noted the remains of residences and obsidian tools around the church. What remained of the church was an impressive series of brick and plaster features. Piers supported mostly collapsed adobe walls, with the entry to the west, and the northwest pier supported a small campanile. At the east, an enclosed, complete sanctuary covered by a domed roof was made entirely of brick and plaster. Traces of painting were still discernible on the plaster inside the dome.

Later archaeological surveys in the area around Yamala located nine settlements with seven possible churches in six settlements (Ashmore et al.

FIGURE 8.5.
Ruins of church of the colonial pueblo de indios of Yamala. Photo by Russell N. Sheptak.

1987; Benyo and Melchionne 1987:57–59; Black 1995, 1997; Weeks 1997; Weeks and Black 1991; Weeks et al. 1987). All identified European materials (glazed ceramics, roof tiles, iron nails, and glass beads) were reported as recovered in excavations in possible church buildings. Archival documents say that in 1535, when the first Spanish troops disrupted the town, Yamala contained three hundred houses. Late prehispanic settlement was confirmed throughout the small valley where Yamala's colonial church stood (Weeks 1997:97–98; Weeks et al. 1987:79–80). Lack of published detail does not allow direct comparison of material culture from Yamala and its neighbors with contemporary sites such as Ticamaya and Despoloncal. The excavators of Yamala found very little that they recognized as colonial material culture. Given the abundant historic documentation, not to mention the presence of colonial churches at Yamala and neighboring sites, it seems likely that as in other known colonial sites, most of the products and tools of everyday life continued to be made in ways consistent with preceding practices, and that some features identified by the excavators as late prehispanic actually were created in the Colonial period. Rather than being simply evidence of the presence of Colonial period—or Spanish-identified—people, the distribution of European goods may be related to new kinds of activities taking place in church locations.

At sites like Yamala, churches, the architectural expression of Roman Catholicism, might stand as evidence of the imposition of Spanish customs on unwilling indigenous people, if we did not know, from archival documents, that they were the product of efforts by the townspeople, at Yamala carried out against Spanish opposition. The epitome of a space made by someone else, churches were occupied tactically by residents of pueblos de indios to such a degree that what had been conceived as a tool of conquest became instead a site of anxious concern for Spanish authorities.

DEFENDING THE NEW COLONY: THE COASTAL WATCH AND PUEBLOS DE INDIOS, 1605–1744

The enactment of practices defined by Spanish colonial authorities but given indigenous meaning is recorded in documents and other materials that are traces of various colonial actions. Such tactics were more than simply oppositional "weapons of the weak." In the new colonial society, with its majority indigenous population, everyone's survival was in the hands of the pueblos de indios, literally in the case of one practice with a long Honduran colonial history: the indigenous coastal watch.

Living along the coast of Central America, whether in pueblos de indios or Spanish towns, was dangerous. Shipping routes brought traffic up the Caribbean coast from Panama. Privateers and pirates from England, France, and the Netherlands raided shipping and settlements along the coast and a considerable distance inland in places like the Ulúa Valley.

Starting as early as 1604, people from native towns were engaged in surveillance of shipping along the Honduran coast. At first performed by indigenous workers under supervision of Spanish recruits, whether for pay or else to work off labor obligations, by the late seventeenth century, the coastal watch was entirely in the hands of the indigenous towns. Service in the coastal watch exposed seventeenth- and eighteenth-century people from pueblos de indios to opportunities for contact with European shipping outside the hierarchies of the colony. This included buying and consuming contraband goods such as sugar, alcohol, olive oil, and tobacco.

One remarkable legal case that extended for almost thirty-five years gives insight into how illicit commerce engaged indigenous people, while also illustrating that the lines between those profiting from this trade and those attempting to control it were not drawn between Spanish and non-Spanish. In 1681, the *San Juan de Dios*, owned by Felipe Topete Guevara, a high-ranking Spanish resident from Cuba, was seized by Honduran authorities. The ship stopped briefly in the town of Jetegua and then came to the port at Lemoa on the Ulúa River, serving the larger town of Tehuma (Figure 8.1). Goods from the ship were sold in the community center with the knowledge of Tehuma's alcalde (mayor). Spanish authorities from the capital city of Comayagua, accompanied by the indigenous alcalde of Lemoa, raided Tehuma. Goods seized were moved in a fleet of canoes and securely stored in what was described as the only adobe building at Lemoa, the residence of the *regidor* (city council member). These smuggled goods were stored for almost a year in this pueblo de indios under the guard of a Spanish soldier, whose letter asking a friend to send household possessions he needed to live in the town has survived in the Spanish archives.

The copious inventories of goods seized, and the remaining goods eventually sent to the regional capital, give us a sense of how the life of indigenous people in the valley was enriched by coastal contraband. More important, this episode makes clear that far from being isolated towns where only indigenous actors were at work, pueblos de indios were part of an active economic and social network that brought opportunities of many kinds, even from outside the colony, into the scope of indigenous actors who took many different positions in these networks.

Today, the modern town of San Manuel Tehuma remains archaeologically uninvestigated, and the location of now-abandoned Lemoa, scene of these dramatic events, has never been surveyed. Other towns, including archaeologically investigated Ticamaya, were the sites of other such events. In 1744, a coastal watcher identified as the alcalde of Tehuma sent a note, apparently written in his own hand, to authorities in San Pedro. The alcalde reported the seizure of a British boat entering the river. The indigenous watch was directed to take this boat to Ticamaya. There, Spanish authorities came and inventoried the contents of the boat, while soldiers removed its sailors to the city of San Pedro. As in the incident at Lemoa, the boat and its contents remained in the indigenous community for some time before being removed to the regional capital. The inventory lists personal effects, including firearms, and includes an enslaved African. While not providing opportunities for consumption equal to the Tehuma contraband ship, this event gave residents of Ticamaya close contact with Spanish, British, and Afrocaribbean outsiders.

Handblown glass fragments recovered during research at Ticamaya in 2008 may be a material trace of such historically documented events, which otherwise have left no material evidence. But gaps in archaeological recovery should not prevent us from seeing such contacts as opportunities for the people of places like Ticamaya, whose material culture was effectively "traditional," to benefit from knowledge, products, and social connections extending outside the structures of colonial administration. Within forty years, both documents and excavations suggest that Ticamaya had incorporated African descendants and housed families preferentially using European-tradition foods, pottery, and glass containers (Blaisdell-Sloan 2006:168, 177, 242, 248; Wonderly 1984a).

Tribute lists, churches, and the coastal watch were each intended as strategies by which a colonial "subject with will and power" attempted to "create places in conformity with abstract models" (de Certeau 1984:29, 36). Residents of pueblos de indios were able to "use, manipulate, and divert" these Spanish-introduced cultural practices tactically to "manipulate events in order to turn them into opportunities" within "the space of the other" (de Certeau 1984:xix, 30, 36–37). Nowhere is this tactical occupation clearer than in indigenous uses of the Spanish legal system represented by often-successful petitions.

APPROPRIATING CIVIL DISCOURSE: PUEBLOS DE INDIOS CLAIM THEIR RIGHTS, 1662–1714

Legal petitions are useful as evidence of the kinds of claims indigenous Hondurans understood to be convincing, and of how Spanish authorities weighed and reinterpreted them (Sheptak et al. 2007). Outcomes of indigenous petitions depended, among other things, on preexisting networks of knowledge and repeated histories of tactical engagement with Spanish authorities at the Honduran and Guatemalan capitals. Repeated petitions for financial relief for the construction of the church at Yamala are an example of this kind of persistent tactical engagement, in which the practice of Catholic piety was mobilized against tribute demands.

Masca, another pueblo de indios in the Ulúa Valley, repeatedly cited service in the coastal watch as grounds to be exempt from other labor claims, and in support of requests for land to which they moved from threatened settlements closer to the coast (Sheptak et al. 2007). Account books from 1604 already identified named individuals from Masca, at that point located on the Caribbean shore, paid to serve in the coastal watch. Masca was allocated as an encomienda (a grant of authority over the labor of Indians in exchange for the obligation to educate them in Catholicism) in the early seventeenth century to Diego de Zúñiga, resident in the port city of Trujillo. In encomiendas such as this, with distant beneficiaries of grants, the pueblo was responsible for periodically producing payments against assessed tribute. Such pueblos contained churches built by the residents, where priests would come to say Mass at intervals. Otherwise, the community was left alone.

Officials of Masca traveled to Comayagua, the colonial capital, in 1662 to carry out a ceremony accepting tribute obligations to a new encomendero (the person holding an encomienda), Alonso de Osaguera. Some of these officials had the same surnames as participants in the coastal watch sixty years earlier. Thirteen years after accepting their obligation to Osaguera, the leaders of this town used this relationship to a distant encomendero, and service in the coastal watch, as tactics to resist new labor demands from the residents of nearby cities (Sheptak et al. 2007).

Blas Cuculí, the petitioner representing Masca in 1675, explicitly cited his previous appearance before the court of Guatemala as the reason he was charged with advancing this request. Tactically, he proposed several grounds for exempting the people of his town from additional personal service. He noted that they had a legal relationship to Osaguera, the encomendero, that precluded assignment to anyone in the city of San Pedro. Here, the indigenous residents successfully played off the more distant Spanish in the colonial capital, source of less onerous obligations, against the more local, more demanding, but less politically and economically secure Spanish residents of the backwater that the city of San Pedro had become.

Blas Cuculí did more than this. In his description of the relationship with Alonso de Osaguera, he managed to impute a failure in the latter's duties, his requirement to ensure Christian religious services, without ever precisely accusing the encomendero. In this, he played the interests of the regional capital in Guatemala against those of the Honduran colony as a whole. Religiosity emerged as one of the tactics that demonstrated the worthiness of the pueblo de indios.

The strongest argument Blas Cuculí made was to cite service by community members in the coastal watch and their role in defending San

Pedro from attack. While this argument was essentially ignored by authorities in the Guatemalan capital in 1675, it reemerged as the successful basis for another petition by the community of Masca a generation later, also heard in the court in Guatemala.

Between 1675 and 1711, when the second petition started, the residents of Masca had relocated to a more secure inland location, not far from the pueblo de indios of Ticamaya. Rights to the land on which the community was settled were subject to contestation. To clear their claim to the land they occupied, officials of the town agreed to a contract with a petty officer of San Pedro in which he would drop his claim to the land in return for their paying his tithes to the church. When the pueblo de indios defaulted, the priest in the city of San Pedro who was owed the tithe, and was also responsible for religious services for the pueblo, threatened them with excommunication from the church.

In their petition for the governor to declare the contract void and to block their excommunication, the people of Masca recounted a history of displacement of their town in which the destruction of their church, and the looting of the saint's images it contained, was central. As part of the shift in location inland, the town had adopted a new patron saint, the Virgin of Candelaria, and was beginning to be referred to as Candelaria instead of Masca. Whereas the 1675 petition pointed to the failure to provide religious doctrine as a fault of the Spanish encomendero, the 1711 petition represented Masca as a community centrally united by its relationship to its church. The space of Spanish occupation had become an integral part of the moral basis of the continuity of the community, even when it was displaced by coastal raiders. The residents of Candelaria Masca simultaneously claimed special consideration for their role in defending the city of San Pedro by giving early warning of raids, and represented their community as persisting, not in place but in practice, through the repeated recreation of corn fields, cacao groves, and community church.

The location of Candelaria's final settlement is yet to be identified. But throughout the eighteenth century, the residents of the pueblo de indios—their rights to land reaffirmed, their protection from the kind of contract illegally made by the Spanish officer restated, and the requirement that the local priest not fail to support their religious practice formally confirmed—continued as one of two indigenous communities in the northern Ulúa Valley, crafting connections with its spatially persistent neighbor, Ticamaya. Names recorded for both towns in the late 1700s and early 1800s suggest that families in the two towns were intermarrying. Descendants of indigenous families from Masca that participated in the coastal watch around

1600 ended up resident in Ticamaya in 1800. Documents for the two communities label the residents of each with terms derived from an ultimate form of colonial institution, the racial classification known as *casta*. But even this institution, intended to stratify colonial society racially and maintain boundaries of power and authority, was tactically exploited by the indigenous people of colonial Honduras (Blaisdell-Sloan and Sheptak 2008).

BECOMING OTHER: MARRIAGE, PARENTHOOD, RESIDENCE, AND IDENTITY, 1703–1809

Tribute payment depended on the number of people in an indigenous town. Prior to the eighteenth century, the count of tribute-payers in the town was reported by the town leaders (*principales*) or occupants of specific roles, who testified to the number of those subject to tribute and whose names are the only ones recorded in the documents.

Early in the eighteenth century, however, the civil administration in Comayagua began recording in detail the names, ages, towns of origin, and marital statuses of residents of pueblos de indios. The earliest of these documents, called *padrones* (census or register), while not preserved for most of the communities in the *partido* (jurisdiction) of San Pedro, have survived for the period from 1703 to 1722 from towns upriver. Later in the eighteenth century similar lists, including the towns of Ticamaya and Candelaria, were created for different purposes by the administrators at Fort Omoa. Along with petitions by individuals to be considered as having different statuses in the casta system, these first censuses provide us with ample evidence of the way that the persistence of indigenous communities was based not in resistance to Spanish racial demographic accounts, but through the exploitation of the assumptions on which they were grounded.

The padrones of towns along the middle Ulúa River, close to Despoloncal, recorded in the first twenty-five years of the eighteenth century, document populations with large segments of people identified as members of an indigenous elite. Described as *caciques*, *principales*, or through the use of Spanish honorifics *don* and *doña*, the members of these families tended to intermarry and to monopolize political offices, such as alcalde, in these towns. For members of local indigenous elites, the process of registering the population became an obligatory performance of their power in the town. They were charged to appear with their own books of the town's residents (including the religious registers of the church) and their own copies of tribute documents. They swore to fully account for all the town's residents. The pages filled with the names they provided, including those of widows and widowers, orphans, and community members absent from the town by virtue of marriage or for undefined reasons, suggest they took this charge seriously. Reducing their actions to evidence of assimilation misses the actual dynamics at work, which were less about aligning native elites with Spanish authorities than with affirming their places as the most knowledgeable actors within their own communities.

The lists of population produced through this process are extraordinary for the number of people who belonged to the tributary community but were absent from it. The majorities are explicitly identified as married and residing in the towns of their spouses. Taking these many intermarriages into account, we are presented with an image of indigenous people moving regularly between communities, creating or strengthening ties between pueblos de indios. Nor were all such intercommunity marriages with other Indians: instances of marriages to women or men described as *mestiza* or *mestizo* (mixed race) are found. Such individuals were the offspring of marriages between Spanish and indigenous people. In the strictest interpretation of Spanish policy, they should not have been resident in the pueblos de indios at all.

Occasional cases exist of middle Ulúa people marrying into pueblos de indios in the lower Ulúa Valley, including Candelaria and Jetegua. By the late eighteenth century, when the names of the people of Candelaria and Ticamaya were recorded by the administration of Omoa, both towns had populations with nonlocal people, described as *forasteros* (people from elsewhere). Ties forged between communities through such patterns of intermarriage encouraged or built on the development of indigenous practices like guancasco, the intertown visits of saints' images. Far from being isolated towns dying out over time, the indigenous population in late colonial Honduras might be better thought of as forging local networks through which small communities could survive the rigors of the colonial experience. Population hybridity—a source of great anxiety for the Spanish administration—embodied in the casta classification may well have increased the scope of tactics available to residents in individual towns.

Ticamaya in the late eighteenth century was populated by a mixed group of residents; some were labeled *ladinos*, that is, Spanish-identified and no longer recognizably indigenous. Excavations of this date produced the maximum amount of recognizable European-tradition materials, including majolica serving wares and domesticated animals. But these goods are not distributed uniformly throughout the community. Instead, they are found only in some areas. Such shifts in material practices of everyday life would have contrasted with and been recognizable to practices of others in the town as much as they were to Spanish authorities creating population records.

Yet these shifts in practices, again, cannot simply be interpreted in terms of the acculturation of formerly indigenous people. In addition to the many indigenous and ladino people listed in the community, there were residents at Candelaria Masca identified in the 1780s as *mulato*, that is, of both African and Indian parentage. Africans had been brought enslaved to work in the mines in the sixteenth-century colony, and freed Africans and their descendants were prominent in San Pedro by the mid-seventeenth century. Additional African people were brought as enslaved laborers to construct Fort Omoa in the late eighteenth century. The residents of Ticamaya and Candelaria were literally drawing on multiple roots in their reproduction of the community, and they defined themselves in relation to those source communities in different ways at different times. The most dramatic illustration of this is the redescription in 1809 of one woman of Ticamaya as *mulata* rather than as *india*, as previously recorded. She was simultaneously identified as the mother of a man labeled as *indio*. The strict logic of the Spanish system of casta would not produce such an outcome. But this woman's son had presumably at this later date inherited from his deceased father—now described as *indio tributo*—rights within the community that made his status as indio critical to his family's standing. Meanwhile, as a mulata, his mother would have been exempt from tribute.

Such creative reclassifications were not unique. Numerous petitions during the same period claimed exemption from various labor obligations imposed on indios by virtue of descent from African parents. These petitions go further and reinforce the need to consider identity as something people were actively creating through their everyday material and social practices. Some petitioners identified the status of their parents in arguing their own status. But others argued that they had been treated as ladinos by Spanish authorities, and therefore must be ladinos and not subject to the demands made on Indians for labor, using practice-based definitions in place of the required racial ones.

FROM RESISTANCE TO TACTICAL OCCUPATION OF SPACE

With the declaration of independence from Spain in the early nineteenth century, and the subsequent creation and dissolution of the Central American Republic, many of the pueblos de indios in northern Honduras suffered. In some cases, indigenous towns persisted. Other towns disappeared from archival records—whose production was disrupted with changes in administration—but survived into the twentieth century as rural hamlets whose residents think of themselves as *campesinos* (peasants), not as indios. When new nationalist policies led to the elimination of indigenous identity as a census category in the twentieth century, people whose grandparents might have self-identified as indio could no longer formally register that continued yet changing identity. But material traces of continuity remain as clear testimony of the resistance of these places to disappearance.

Our purpose here has been threefold. First, we have taken a long-term view of indigenous communities over the Colonial period. At some points, we can identify excavated materials, remains of buildings, or simply persistent places as material evidence. At other times, our main or even only evidence of persistence comes from the documentary record. It is only by tacking back and forth between these bodies of evidence that we can arrive at a sufficiently complex understanding of tactics.

Second, we have subordinated the normal site-focus of archaeology to a landscape-based approach. Many of the arguments we make are based on material evidence in the form of mappings, including distributions of occupied and abandoned settlements, circuits of connection across long distances, and networks connecting local places. It does not make any difference if this mapping evidence comes from material analysis of composition, as in the case of obsidian, interpretation of visual style, as in the case of both indigenous and Spanish-tradition pottery, or from itineraries recorded in documents.

Third, our discussion treats excavated materials as the traces of practices, not as evidence of typological uniformities. We are as interested in the presence of a few fragments of handblown bottle glass at Ticamaya, paralleling documentary mention of European bottles inventoried there, as we are in demonstrating that the proportions of obsidian at different early colonial sites vary. On the one hand, we have to push our excavated materials in this way because so little excavated material exists for the Colonial period due to patterns of modern archaeological exploration. But we think this necessity actually draws attention to a challenge shared with other archaeologists interested in the Colonial period. That is, the physical sites identified and excavated simply do not provide as abundant a material register as we would ideally want. What can we make of the presence of small numbers of European-style artifacts? It would clearly be absurd not to talk about the European presence economically, socially, and politically in places in the Americas where indigenous traditions produced the majority of the materials deposited in archaeological sites. Instead, we need to use approaches that treat excavated materials as inspiration for unfolding understandings of broader practices. From this perspective, the story an obsidian point has to tell for Ticamaya echoes the tale written in Spanish reports, allowing us to connect these two forms of evidence.

The combination of archival documentary and excavated material evidence allows us to identify sophisticated and varied tactics used by descendants of the indigenous people who occupied Honduras when the first Spanish adventurers arrived. Through tactical occupations of the spaces opened up by colonial institutions, people survived and reproduced their own meaningful senses of history and identity. That their senses of history and identity are embodied as change, not stasis, does not make the descendant communities less authentic (Hanks 1986). Some of the most important tactics for indigenous persistence used discourses, institutions, spaces, and objects that have long served as evidence that the imposed Spanish colonial order won out over a quickly lost Honduran indigenous heritage. From the perspective of the Honduran colonial documentary and excavated records, resistance can only be usefully modeled as persistence, what de Certeau (1984:29–42) described as "making do": the repeated actions of everyday life through which people make their own place in spaces designed for someone else.

9

The San Pedro Maya and the British Colonial Enterprise in British Honduras

"We may have a perfectly harmless and well affected inhabitant turned into a designing and troublesome neighbor"

Minette C. Church, Jason Yaeger, and Jennifer L. Dornan

It is a strange quirk of history that the Maya once took on the British Empire.
J. Eric Thompson (1963:172), archaeologist camped in San José Yalbac, 1928–1934

Scholars, politicians, and the broader public have tended to dichotomize between accommodation and resistance on the part of colonized peoples, as epitomized in Lieutenant Governor Austin's anxious statement regarding the San Pedro Maya in 1866, which is cited in our title. Archaeologists have been guilty of this oversimplification as well, sometimes imposing these constructs on the archaeological record. Like many of the contributors to this volume, we advocate a more nuanced understanding of the interactions between colonized people and the larger colonial world within which they lived, one that emphasizes agency and strategic ambiguity (e.g., Dornan 2004) and takes into account the uncertainties and miscommunications that often occur in cross-cultural dialogue. We eschew treating either the colonized or the colonizers as monolithic groups with unified intentions. Historians have a long tradition of exploring the different and often conflicting goals and actions of different colonizing groups (e.g., Dumond 1977, 1997; White 1991). While anthropologists have long recognized variation in subaltern groups, we still have had a troubling tendency to refer to colonizers and their institutions in unified terms such as "the Spanish colonial world" or "the British colonial world." In his

173

discussion of the archaeology of colonial encounters, Gil Stein (2005:9) emphasizes "that the interacting complex societies must be seen as heterogeneous entities, composed of different groups whose interests, goals, and social strategies are often in conflict" (see also Sheptak et al., Chapter 8; and Beck et al., Chapter 2). Colonizers were often divided and their positions and goals contradictory. This is clearly the case in nineteenth-century British Honduras, where competing priorities often led to conflicts between British merchants, timber companies, the Foreign Office, the Colonial Office, the lieutenant governor, and the clergy, to name a few interest groups present in the colony (Clegern 1962). These conflicts directly affected the lives of both the British settlers who lived mostly along the colony's coasts and rivers and the San Pedro Maya, the Yucatec Mayan–speaking inhabitants of the colony's northwestern interior (Clegern 1962).

Our study examines these interactions between San Pedro Maya leaders and villagers and other residents of the colony affiliated with various colonial institutions. As Stephen Silliman has noted, "Colonialism, as an analytical framework, ushers in a consideration of social agents—Indigene, colonist—negotiating new, shared social terrain forged in sustained contact (2005a:62)." It was within just such a shifting landscape that Maya villagers made decisions and crafted strategies.[1] Their goals were often ambiguous to the British; in some cases, this ambiguity may have been an intentional strategy to leave various colonizing groups uncertain as to Maya motives and plans. Strategies and tactics both also shift over time. As Stein notes, "[I]t is a mistake to regard inherently unstable, changeable modes of interaction as if they were temporally invariant. Quite often, our perceptions of a given colonial case are skewed by our tendency to project our understanding of the later stages of the sequence onto earlier phases of the encounter" (2005:30).

Such tactics, and the interactions and practices that they engender, are accessible through archaeological, archival, and oral narrative records in our case study. We agree with Sheptak and colleagues (Chapter 8) that all of these data sets are archaeological, and must be integrated into our broader interpretations (Wylie 2000). Coordinating these rich data sets is complex, however (Church 2007; Schuyler 1978). Triangulating independent lines of evidence can create more possible interpretations rather than fewer, particularly of past intentions and goals. Some may seem mutually contradictory, yet all may be valid and defensible as long as we acknowledge the diversity of past perspectives (Thomas 1989). We believe that the tendency of our rich data set to suggest alternative and ambiguous readings of past action rather than a single clear one is a strength rather than a weakness of interpretation. Indeed, ambiguous and less-than-clear interpretations of San Pedro's past may reflect ambiguous and less-than-clear, multivalent realities of the past.

Given this volume's thematic focus, our analysis of a British colonial setting that dates to a period decades after the Spanish Empire had lost most of its New World possessions may seem out of place. Several observations suggest its relevance, however. British Honduras was a small island of British colonial interests surrounded by Spanish colonial and postcolonial societies, and events elsewhere in the region had profound impacts on the colony's history. For example, many people, including the San Pedro Maya we discuss here, immigrated into British Honduras as a result of Mexico's Caste War. We will also see that some British strategies—as well as some Maya strategies—were crafted in part in response to Mexican and Guatemalan policies and actions.

Just as importantly, the effects of colonialism endure for generations. In this case, the culture and institutions of Maya and mestizo peoples who settled in British Honduras in the mid-nineteenth century were influenced by centuries of Spanish colonialism. Both British and Maya leaders sometimes invoked Spanish colonial administrative institutions and constructs in their negotiations with one another, and with Mexico and Guatemala. Thus, this case study offers lessons about the lasting ramifications of Spanish colonialism that this volume seeks to explore.

The San Pedro case study also provides a point of comparison, illustrating important differences between British and Spanish colonial contexts, and also highlighting some similarities. In many ways, the lived experiences of Maya villagers in British Honduras had much in common with those of their counterparts in Mexico or Guatemala. For example, in this chapter we suggest several points of comparison with Joel Palka's work on Lacandon populations in the neighboring Petén (2005). In this respect, this case study serves as a counterpoint to the "Black Legend" tradition of historical scholarship that depicts Spanish colonial oppression as qualitatively different (and worse) than that of other colonial systems (see Liebmann and Murphy, Chapter 1).

In this chapter we seek to understand interactions and engagements between Maya and British agents and institutions during a period of instability and change, comprising the five decades from the founding of San Pedro Sirís as an autonomous Maya village in the late 1850s to its eventual abandonment in the early twentieth century. The inflection points in this history that are most salient in both the documentary and material records consist of two military engagements between San Pedro villagers and

British colonial forces that occurred just over a month apart in late 1866 and early 1867. These battles serve as chronological and political landmarks for our analysis, separating a period of more tentative engagement with British colonial institutions from a later phase that saw a fuller integration of San Pedro Sirís into the colony's political and economic structures.

To elucidate these periods, we employ documents produced by the British and by Maya village leaders, transcribed by secretaries or sympathetic British clergy, and material data collected during four seasons of archaeological work at San Pedro Sirís and brief visits to the satellite village of San José Yalbac. These are contextualized and complemented by oral narratives.

The documents include letters that constituted formal diplomatic negotiations between colonizers and colonized, as well as letters that describe some of the strategies and goals of the negotiations. The material data derive largely from our survey, wide-ranging surface collections, and excavations at San Pedro Sirís. The excavations included long trenches to expose the village's shallow stratigraphy (not more than about 30 cm) and extensive excavation of one house and its associated yard.

The material record complements the documents by providing a window into everyday life, including practices that constituted villagers' "lived ethnicity" (Clark 2005). As Bonnie J. Clark has argued, in contexts of growing power differences, changes and continuities in everyday life—foodways, for example—can be interpreted simultaneously as passive reproductions of tradition by some, and as active and even defiant assertions of that tradition by others, or as Deagan (Chapter 8) notes: "What is resistance in one setting is conformity to cultural mores in another." "Cultural practices often take on new interpretations and meanings in the process of encountering 'others'" (Marshall Sahlins, cited in Lightfoot et al. 1998:201). Similarly, Russell Sheptak and his coauthors (Chapter 9) draw on de Certeau (1984) to frame indigenous actions as tactics, "ways that human subjects occupy the social landscapes that they do not entirely control" (Sheptak et al., Chapter 9). Such tactics can result in an archaeological record marked by continuities in material culture that belie the shifting meanings of those material patterns within changing colonial contexts.

HISTORICAL BACKGROUND

Understanding the ways in which Spanish colonialism influenced Maya people in British Honduras in the second half of the nineteenth century requires a deeper historical context. At the time of its conquest by the Spanish in the 1540s, most of northern Belize was part of the Maya province of Dzuluinicob (Jones 1989). In 1638, the Dzuluinicob Maya threw off the colonial yoke and lived independently for decades. It is important to point out, though, that a century of colonial governance and Catholic evangelization had significantly shaped people's beliefs and practices. At Dzuluinicob villages like Tipu and Lamanai, people practiced rituals inspired by Catholicism while reviving other practices with pre-Columbian roots that had been prohibited under colonial rule (Graham 1991; Pendergast 1991).

The Spanish reconquered Dzuluinicob in the 1690s. They forcibly relocated most of the region's inhabitants to villages around Lake Petén-Itza (Jones 1989), leaving the Caribbean coast of the peninsula sparsely populated. British buccaneers and logwood cutters who had already settled along the coast gradually extended their timber harvesting inland along the major rivers through the eighteenth and nineteenth centuries, resisting Spanish attempts to dislodge them. These settlements—although not a de jure British Crown colony until 1862—were collectively called the Colony of British Honduras and its inhabitants the Baymen (Caiger 1951; Finamore 2006).

Farther north in Yucatán, Spanish colonial rule brought new institutions to Maya society, such as *encomienda, repartimiento,* and *reducción,* that directly or indirectly separated communities from land and the products of their own labor. Maya villagers adapted, however, by finding institutions within the Church and the colonial political administrative structure to maintain some degree of economic, political, and cultural independence at the community level (Farriss 1984; Restall 1997). Furthermore, the Spanish were never able to exert much control over the peoples of the interior jungles of the peninsula, nor along its Caribbean coast. In 1821, Spain recognized the independence of Mexico (which included Guatemala at the time), and Mexico, Guatemala, and the other states of Central America soon emerged as autonomous nation-states. These new states were more assertive of their sovereignty, and they negotiated and disputed the borders with each other and with British Honduras throughout the nineteenth century. The stakes increased as mahogany came to replace logwood as the region's most valuable jungle resource. The logging industry expanded over the course of the nineteenth century, facilitated by new technologies allowing for more wide-ranging timber extraction. By the mid-nineteenth century, the new governments of Mexico and Guatemala, as well as the British, enacted classically liberal economic reforms that again undermined Maya traditions of land use, and encouraged the expansion of commercial ranching, farming, and logging concessions, often accompanied by Catholic (or in the British case, Protestant) missionization (Palka 2005).

Joel W. Palka asserts that these "reforms of 19th-century Mexico and Guatemala can be viewed as the 'Second Conquest' of native peoples in Mesoamerica" (Palka 2005:277). Mexican liberal reforms transformed both land tenure and political administration in ways that undermined the economic, political, and religious institutions that served as the fabric of Maya villages for centuries. The tensions between the centralizing ambitions of the mostly criollo and mestizo leaders of the Mexican state and the Catholic Church on the one hand, and the local autonomy sought by rural Maya and mestizo leaders on the other, gave way to violent conflict in 1847, when the Caste War began (Dumond 1997; Reed 1964; Restall 1997; Rugeley 1996, 2001). The ensuing military campaigns and social upheaval displaced thousands of people.

As Maya armies advanced on Bacalar, a wave of Maya, mestizo, and criollo families sought refuge in British Honduras. The following year, the tide of the Caste War turned. This time, Mexican troops drove the Maya forces into the dense and sparsely inhabited jungles of the southern and eastern margins of Yucatán, accompanied by their entire families and communities. As the war quieted down to a decades-long stalemate, these rebel Maya established networks of hamlets and villages in the disputed territorial interstices between Mexico, Guatemala, and British Honduras.

Factionalism, religious schisms, and policy disagreements split these Maya villages into two opposing groups, defined in terms of their relations with Mexico: the allied Pacíficos to the west and the antagonistic Cruzob to the east (Dumond 1977, 1997). Perhaps to avoid these conflicts, one group of Pacíficos left their parent village of Icaiche and moved south into territory that would later become British Honduras, establishing the villages of San Pedro Sirís, San José Yalbac, and many smaller hamlets (Jones 1977). Grant Jones (1977) has called this group of villages, unified politically under Asunción Ek, the leader of San Pedro Sirís, the San Pedro Maya (Figure 9.1).

Thus San Pedro Sirís was founded sometime around 1857 in a remote jungle region that later would become northwestern Belize. Its inhabitants left an area contested by Pacífico and Cruzob Maya and settled in territory claimed by Great Britain, Guatemala, and Mexico. As negotiations proceeded between those countries and treaties were drafted, international borders shifted around and often across the San Pedro villagers, as did Maya alliances (Jones 1977). One of the strengths of San Pedro Sirís as a case study is its historical situation within landscapes contested by colonial powers, postcolonial nation-states, and other Maya groups.

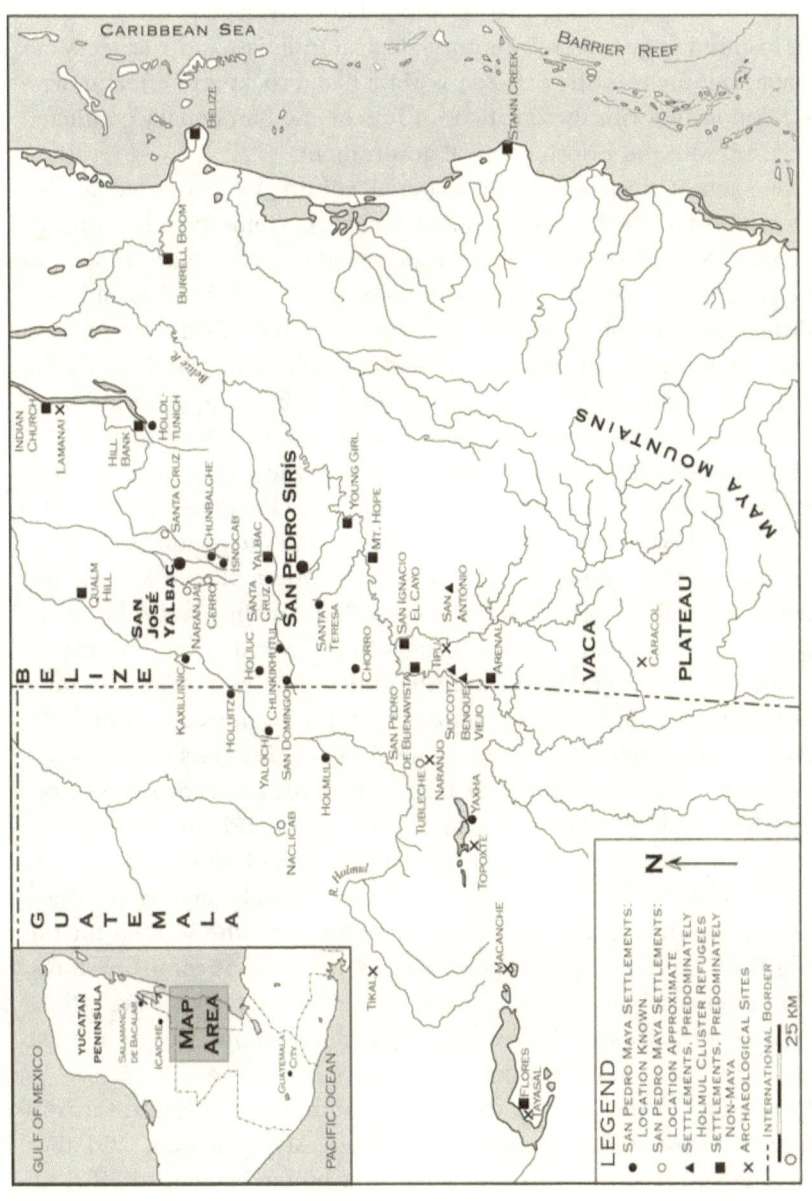

FIGURE 9.1.
Map of region showing San Pedro Sirís and surrounding village clusters described by Grant D. Jones (1977). Map by Jason Yaeger, San Pedro Maya Project.

The San Pedro Maya had much in common with the Pacíficos, shaped by generations of experience of hacienda and encomienda in Spanish and Mexican Yucatán, including their Catholic faith, a village political organization inspired by nineteenth-century Mexican militias, and Yucatec Maya language. Despite this, the San Pedro Maya had a rocky and often antagonistic relationship with the Pacíficos of Icaiche, and an equally conflicted relationship with the British colonial government.

One cannot understand the material culture we excavated at San Pedro—imported British ceramics and French perfume bought with logging money alongside weaponry provided by the British (and sometimes used against them) and indigenous pottery vessels—without considering the diverse agendas of colonizers (logging companies, British merchants, the colonial government, and clergy) and the colonized (the Cruzob, the Pacíficos of Icaiche, and the San Pedro Maya). For example, at the same time some British welcomed Caste War immigrants, whom they hoped would spur agricultural development, others saw these Maya as a threat to the colony because of their perceived reluctance to integrate into the colonial society and economy (Cal 1991). The loggers in the region were beginning to benefit from the land reforms of the new republics of Mexico and Guatemala, as well as England, and direct conflict with the Maya was perhaps inevitable. Pacífico militias from Icaiche, ostensibly acting under Mexican authority, conducted raids on British settlements and logging camps between 1848 and 1872 to collect unpaid rents for logging concessions.

As a result of these raids, labor-hungry logging interests were employing Maya labor but were at the same time leery of the San Pedro Maya, associating them with the Maya of Icaiche. The slash-and-burn subsistence agriculture practiced by the Maya was also a point of tension, as loggers argued that the felling of forests destroyed valuable mahogany trees. Furthermore, farming provided those Maya villagers who worked for the logging firms a buffer against the predatory practices of company stores, which indentured African creole laborers by selling them expensive rations during the long seasons in the isolated logging camps, far from their homes and gardens along the coasts and rivers.

In contrast to the loggers, the colony's authorities in Belize City did distinguish between the interests of different Maya factions, and they hoped the San Pedro Maya could serve as a buffer between the British colony and the more bellicose Pacíficos of Icaiche. Despite differences, the various British interests seem to have agreed on one general goal. Broadly drawn, there was a desire to redefine and renegotiate social identities in line with British imperatives to categorize and place new immigrants into an overarching and hierarchical social order based in large part on nineteenth-century British constructs of race.

SAN PEDRO SIRÍS UNTIL 1867
Diplomatic Encounters

It was not long after the establishment of San Pedro Maya villages that British colonial authorities sought to exert some influence over them and bring them into the British colonial sphere. In 1862, they formally recognized Ek and other San Pedro Maya village leaders as alcaldes, the Spanish term for mayor (Dumond 1997; Bolland 1988). The British recognized Alcalde Ek as having jurisdiction over San Pedro Sirís and the surrounding villages. In this way, the English sought to draw on the Spanish colonial and Mexican institutions of leadership to support leaders they saw as pro-British, and institutionalize the place of the Maya villages within the colony's structures of governance.

Perhaps in part because of these engagements with the British colonial government—which in turn was allied with the Cruzob—tensions grew between the San Pedro Maya and the Pacíficos. In the 1860s, Ek repeatedly requested arms from the British government to defend his towns from Pacífico forces from Icaiche, led by Marcos Canul. Ek would certainly have seen a precedent for such requests in the ongoing sale of British arms that allowed the Cruzob Maya to pursue their ongoing war with Mexico and the Pacíficos. British merchants who traded extensively with the Cruzob and logging firms that held lucrative timber concessions in Cruzob territory encouraged these sales, even though the British Foreign Office often frowned upon them because they complicated England's relationship with Mexico (Dumond 1977; Johnson 1941).

Grant Jones's exploration of the Belize Archives led him to conclude that Lieutenant Governor Seymour provided ammunition in 1863, but it seems the British government was initially reluctant to provide additional munitions. Icaiche aggression led them to reconsider. In 1866, Canul and his soldiers from Icaiche, claiming to be acting under a Mexican government commission to collect rents for logging leases, captured more than sixty residents of Quam Hill, a mahogany camp in territory disputed by Mexico, Guatemala, and England. Canul released the hostages in return for £3,000, ostensibly unpaid rent owed Mexico by a British logging company.

This event reshaped the policy of the British colonial government, if not the attitudes of loggers, and it marked a turning point in the relationships between Icaiche, Mexico, the San Pedro Maya, and the British. British authorities believed that the San Pedro Maya could indeed serve as a buffer between the small, poorly defended colony and the Icaiche Maya. Lieutenant Governor Austin provided more guns and ammunition to San Pedro in 1866 (Jones 1977:148–49).

The government decision to arm the San Pedro Maya undoubtedly caused consternation in the logging camps close to the San Pedro Maya villages. The interests of logging firms and their representatives often ran counter to those of the colonial government, something that is well documented archaeologically as well as through documents (see Finamore 2006). As mentioned above, Maya farming practices destroyed mahogany trees, and their subsistence autonomy made them difficult to draw into the relationship of labor dependency that the logging industry preferred. In short, government support of Ek and San Pedro in the 1860s posed a check to the growing clout of the emerging logging companies.

Military Encounters

In the months after Quam Hill, rumors emerged of a conspiracy to replace Ek with a pro-Icaiche leader at San Pedro Sirís. These rumors may have been spread by the logging firms operating in the area to undermine Ek's authority and fuel distrust of the Maya among colonial authorities (Jones 1977), just as merchants in the adjacent Petén actively created conflicts between indigenous groups and the Guatemalan government (Schwartz 1990:94). Despite his own doubts as to their veracity and origins, these rumors convinced Lieutenant Governor Austin to send the 4th West India Regiment to San Pedro Sirís in December 1866. The Maya sallied forth to engage them, and the resulting rout of the British regiment shocked the colonists and led to widespread fear of a Maya uprising. The lieutenant governor fled offshore and called for reinforcements.

It is likely that the Maya defeated the British with the very weapons they had obtained earlier that year from Austin. We recovered many firearm parts at San Pedro Sirís.[2] Some were flintlock long-arms, which probably predate 1850. These probably were brought with the Maya in their journey south from Yucatán. We also found many fragments of British Enfield rifles, both infantry and artillery types (Figure 9.2). Manufacture of the Enfield rifle began in 1853, and it was a more effective weapon than the older flintlocks. We believe Austin supplied Enfields to Ek in 1866. Villagers may have used these guns for hunting as well, and they were found in surface and subsurface domestic contexts. Of course, the effective use of firearms requires sustained access to ammunition. In this light, it is interesting to note that a letter from one Captain Ainsley to Governor Austin described the forces from San Pedro that fought against him in

FIGURE 9.2.
Muzzle-loading, rifled gun barrels from San Pedro Sirís. Photo by San Pedro Maya Project.

1867 as "half armed" (PRO, CO, 123, 131 – Captain Ainsley to Austin, January 9, 1867). Many of the newer, rifled gun barrels we recovered were flared and split at the firing end, suggesting some may have misfired.

The Maya victory in 1866 speaks to the effectiveness of Maya village militias. By the time of their engagement with the British military, the San Pedro Maya villagers had a long familiarity with European military structures of command, and they had deployed the village militias in their engagements with Mexico during the Caste War and in their later battles with the Cruzob. The basic political structure of San Pedro, Pacífico, and Cruzob villages drew on both European and precontact Maya models (Dornan 2004; Farriss 1984), particularly the hierarchical and military militia structure that was strongly encouraged in the late Spanish colonial and early national periods in Mexico, as a matter of policy (Jones 1977). After breaking with Mexico, village leaders held various ranked military titles influenced by, though not strictly the same, as colonial military ranks (Jones 1977). Asunción Ek, who led the San Pedro Maya into their new territory, was a *comandante*; in 1862, the year he was designated alcalde by the British, he signed himself as "general" (Bolland 1988; Jones 1977).

Just over a month after their defeat by San Pedro Sirís, British troops returned to the village and burned it, as well as San José Yalbac and other nearby settlements. Documents recount the Maya response of village-wide retreat. Entire villages melted into the forest, some people relocating deep into Guatemala (Schwartz 1990:94), leaving frustrated British commanders to destroy buildings using incendiary rockets, casings of which we recovered at San Pedro Sirís (Figure 9.3). This strategy of retreat into the forest is not unlike that described by Palka among the Lacandon of the same

FIGURE 9.3.
Incendiary rocket casings from the burning of San Pedro Sirís in 1867. Photo by San Pedro Maya Project.

period in Petén, as they sought to avoid Guatemalan loggers, Catholic missionaries, and other outsiders (Palka 2005). The Lacandon, however, seem to have adopted a strategy of overall mobility, whereas the villagers of San Pedro Sirís returned to stake more overt claims to territory in the face of various and continuing British colonial inroads, both military and commercial.

Although the British were unable to capture villagers or village leaders during the conflict (PRO, WO, 67, 3202 – Colonel R. W. Harley to Lieutenant Governor Austin, February 9, 1867), the sacking of the San Pedro villages spelled an end to open conflicts between the San Pedro Maya and the British government. Five years later, Canul was killed during an attack on Orange Walk, and Pacífico military activities in British territory declined precipitously (Dumond 1997; Jones 1977).

SAN PEDRO AFTER 1867

The layout of San Pedro Sirís drew upon Spanish colonial conventions of town planning. It was a centralized settlement, with the town's principal institutions materially represented at its heart: a *cabildo* (town hall) and military barracks, and Catholic church and fiesta hall (Jones 1977). During the sack of San Pedro Sirís, Colonel Harvey left a letter for Ek in San Pedro's "fiesta hall." He wrote: "You have however fled with your people and so escaped me for the present. I have now to destroy your town which you will never again be allowed to occupy, unless you make proper submission at Belize and sue for pardon" (PRO, WO, 32, 6202 – Colonel Harley to Asunción Ek). Although there is no direct evidence that Ek complied with

Harley's demands, the San Pedro Maya reoccupied their villages within a few years with Ek as their leader. It is this period, after 1867, that is most clearly represented archaeologically at San Pedro Sirís. The initial manufacture dates (*terminus post quem*) for many artifacts at San Pedro Sirís fall after 1867, demonstrating the San Pedro Maya villagers' decision to return to their homes, despite the events of that year.

Although the San Pedro villagers returned to their old villages, these were now situated within very different political and economic contexts marked by a much greater intrusion of British colonial authority in their lives. Not only had the British destroyed their villages in 1867, but also Governor Austin decreed the same year that "[n]o Indians will be at liberty to reside upon or occupy or cultivate any land without previous payment or engagement to pay rent whether to the Crown or the owner of the land" (cited in Bolland 1977). With this decree, the government delegitimized San Pedro Maya claims to land and undermined their subsistence economy.

In this light, the villagers' decision to return and rebuild is an example of how simple continuity of occupation can be an act of resistance when understood within a context in which virtually all colonizing factions were conspiring against that decision. After resettlement, Pacífico leaders from Icaiche, who continued to collect rents from British loggers through the village of San José Yalbac, claimed jurisdiction over San Pedro Sirís as well, although this may have been simply a claim with no substance (Jones 1977). Furthermore, documents and artifacts alike suggest that villagers once again worked for nearby logging camps run by the Belize Estate and Produce Company, illustrating conflicts of interest within the British logging camps themselves. In sum, the village was claimed by Icaiche, deemed illegal by the British colonial government, and supplied labor and trade to British logging camps who had probably initiated the hostilities in 1867.

Commerce and Subsistence

The San Pedro villagers engaged in the mahogany and chicle sap industries that flourished in northwestern Honduras both directly as laborers and indirectly by selling foodstuffs to the companies and their employees. Besides foodstuffs, evidence for other goods the villagers could trade comes from the site in the form of numerous tobacco pipes and possible pollen evidence of tobacco cultivation (Gust 2006). Palka notes that the Lacandon in Petén traded products like honey and tobacco to *chicleros* and loggers there (Palka 2005). This provided them with cash and kind, which they used to acquire a wide array of goods. At San Pedro we documented items manufactured in England, the United States, Mexico, France, and

FIGURE 9.4.
Example of English hand-painted, polychrome, refined earthenware bowl from San Pedro Sirís. Manufactured 1830–present (Florida Museum of Natural History, Digital Type Collection). Photo by San Pedro Maya Project.

Austria as well as items they manufactured themselves and items imported regionally. The variety of local and imported items we find archaeologically and its diverse relationships to daily practices precludes any simplistic relationships between local or indigenous goods and traditional practices (or resistance) on the one hand, and imported goods and acculturation (and colonial integration) on the other. For example, villagers served and ate foods using bowls and plates manufactured in Britain's pottery districts, but they cooked those foods using ceramic vessels that were either locally manufactured or imported from Maya potters in Yucatán. The villagers apparently preferred the taste of traditional soups and beans simmered in earthenware pots, but liked to serve them in the brightly colored and more impermeable imported bowls (Figure 9.4).

The San Pedro tactic of incorporating particular forms (bowls, for example) of imported wares into existing foodways contrasts with an example from the southern coast of Belize. Charles Cheek (1997) has documented the high frequencies of British imported ceramics, particularly cups and saucers, at British colonial Garifuna (Garinagu) sites. He interprets this data as indicating that the Garifuna adopted the British social ritual of tea. In this way, the Garifuna differentiated themselves from creole and indigenous groups involved in violent uprisings against the French in the Caribbean. Cheek further argues that this tactic assuaged British concerns and led to a higher position of Garifuna within the colonial social hierarchy, providing them better access to British employment (see also Charlton and Fournier [Chapter 7], for a description of locally made wares as social signaling by criollos versus *peninsulares*). Whereas the possibilities of employment and advancement within British colonial institutions may have shaped Garifuna choices to purchase and use certain imported ceramics, San Pedro Maya goals of remaining self-sufficient on the land they claimed seem to have influenced their decision to purchase imported bowls that allowed them to pursue traditional foodways; all groups used wares manufactured in Britain, but the plates, cups, saucers, and flatware common in contemporary British place settings are very rare at San Pedro Sirís.

The contrast with Lacandon tactics farther west in Petén also is striking. Imported painted ceramics are rare on Lacandon sites, while locally produced wares are much more common (Palka 2005). In fact, according to Palka, "even after extensive interaction and influence from missionaries and local settlers they did not typically use Western clothing, guns, food, and other items widely available to them" (Palka 2005:237). All of these items—clothing, guns, imported food, pottery—were relatively abundant at San Pedro, a fact that demonstrates very different decisions as well as deeper engagement with the colonial economy.

We also found a tremendous number of bottles, including condiment and liquor bottles as well as medicine and perfume bottles. The alcohol bottles may not have been acquired for their original contents. When we talked to people willing to guide us to San Pedro and San José sites at the beginning of this project, one guide described the historic villages as "dry" communities. Robert Redfield noted that villagers at Chan Kom, Yucatán, in the early 1930s consumed very little imported alcohol, although it was available, and that locally made *balche* was used only ritually (Redfield and Rojas 1962:38). It is thus unclear whether the abundant alcohol bottles we found at San Pedro represent alcohol consumption by the San Pedro Maya, or whether they obtained the bottles from nearby logging camps. Regardless of their origins, we find it likely that alcohol bottles were reused as containers for other local products, whether for local use or for trade, much as one sees in marketplaces in Belize and Yucatán today. Bottle glass was also used as a raw material to make other tools. We found a number of bottle bases, particularly dark green ones, retouched into cutting or scraping tools using flint-knapping techniques.

The San Pedro Maya likely obtained these imported goods through exchanges with logging camps and the people working with them, and through periodic forays to San Ignacio and Belize City. The latter visits, partially diplomatic in purpose, occurred after Britain negotiated a sort of peace with Icaiche in 1882 (Bolland 1977; Jones 1977). There, in the capital and colonial heart of British Honduras, village leaders demonstrated what political clout they had left and their more considerable economic clout by flaunting their continuing economic and subsistence autonomy in the face of explicit colonial policy. At the same time, these trips maintained the villages' dependence on imported goods. They also reiterated the subordinated place of San Pedro Maya villages within the colony, as village leaders recounted the recent births and deaths that were then inscribed in the colony's records (Belize Archives).

It is worth noting the paradox implied by the material record at San Pedro Sirís. Many of the items purchased from colonial merchants served to perpetuate local practices, such as farming, hunting, and cooking, that contrasted with the practices of other groups in the colony and likely came to have explicit social meanings related to "lived ethnicity" (Clark 2005; see also Horning 2000). Farming and hunting, activities facilitated by imported machetes, firearms, hoes, and axes, were time-honored subsistence practices. These practices had historically been central to the production of tribute and taxes that bound Maya peoples in Spanish colonial labor relations, but at San Pedro Sirís they were central to asserting land use that contravened British law. Clearly the meaning of these practices and their roles in various Maya tactics changed over time.[3] It is also ironic that while these farming and food-making practices provided a degree of independence from the logging economy, they were predicated simultaneously on a deep engagement with the economic networks of the British colonial world.

Religion

Another colonial voice available through both documents and artifacts is that of the clergy. Many documents relevant to the San Pedro Maya derive from their interactions with Protestant and Catholic clerics. There was a Catholic church at San Pedro Sirís, where Mass was officiated by priests who infrequently visited the community. During these periodic visits, the priest would officiate marriages and baptize children who had been born since his last visit. The presence of imported religious icons, specifically crucifixes, in domestic contexts at the site suggests that religious practice was not confined to Mass.

These icons demonstrate long-standing connections to the Catholic institutions of New Spain and Mexico, despite existing within a British (Protestant) colony. However, the exact nature of San Pedro villagers' faith, given their tumultuous Caste War history, is unclear. There is some evidence that the split between Cruzob and Pacífico was in part the rejection by the latter of the prophetic "talking cross," by which the Cruzob were increasingly influenced. Dornan (2004) discusses how anthropologists have tended to view the Catholic syncretic religiosity of indigenous peoples as either accommodation or resistance in colonial settings. She argues they need not be either, or can be both simultaneously (see Wernke, Chapter 5; and Quilter, Chapter 6). In colonial contexts, the converted frequently seized on the multiple possible readings of religious philosophies, often pursuing unorthodox meanings (Bricker 1981; Dumond 1997; Rugeley 2001).

Education

In a colonial role similar to that of state-sponsored religion, we often assume that educational institutions allow colonial powers to indoctrinate the colonized and make them better subjects. However, the data for the San Pedro Maya suggest a more complex dynamic. The role of educational institutions and curricula in the socialization of children in colonial settings is a valuable but understudied avenue for understanding relations between colonizers and colonized. In the Spanish colonial settings, any childhood education would have occurred within the context of the Catholic Church. In San Pedro Sirís and San José Yalbac, however, British colonial authorities oversaw education, and the language of instruction was English.

Before 1867, when relations between the British colonial government and San Pedro Sirís still looked promising, Ek requested a "list of his duties." In addition to munitions for defending British territory, he requested that a school be built at San Pedro Sirís (Dumond 1997:276). The documentary record leaves us uncertain as to whether the government established a school at that time, but archaeologically, the presence of inkwell fragments from excavated domestic contexts at San Pedro Sirís—a sign of literacy and staple of schooling throughout the British Empire—suggests that one was eventually built. Toys were also important in nineteenth-century discourses of education (Beecher 1841; Stork 1859), and we

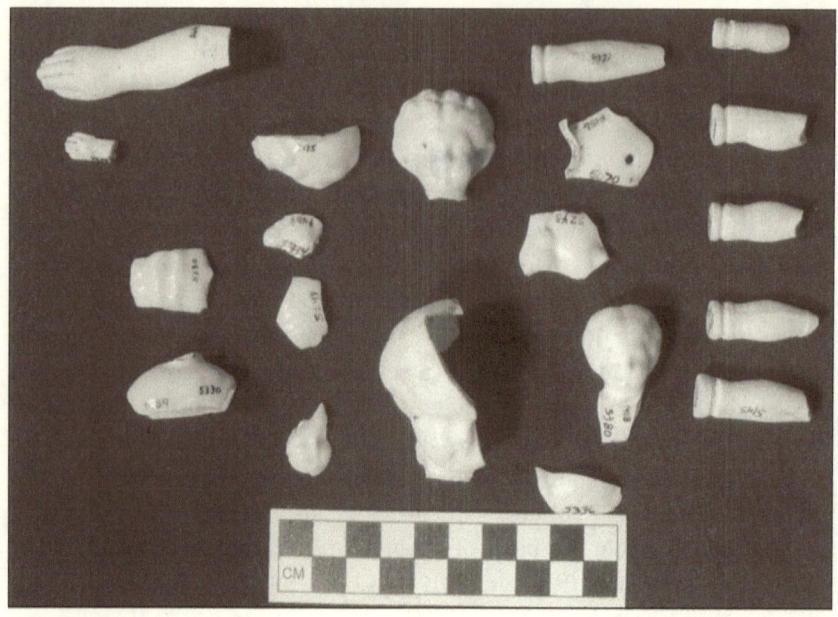

FIGURE 9.5.
Porcelain doll parts recovered from San Pedro Sirís. Photo by San Pedro Maya Project.

find toys throughout San Pedro, including tea sets and doll parts from both surface and excavated domestic contexts (Figure 9.5). Oral narratives tell us that the schoolteacher at the associated village of San José Yalbac school in the early twentieth century taught in English, and this was likely the case at San Pedro, too.

It is striking that Ek placed a school among his first requests. From the standpoint of British authorities in the age of empire, education was seen as an effective vehicle for indoctrination. The toy tea sets and porcelain doll parts also could be interpreted as local acceptance of British notions of edifying play, as well as fundamentally Victorian and Edwardian constructs of childhood, child-rearing, and gender. However, a desire to have one's children understand the language and customs of the colonizers does not imply adoption of colonially imposed values in any simple way. Colonized people sometimes viewed English-language schools as a way for their children to learn the language and customs needed to navigate within the colonial context. At school they could obtain a more sophisticated understanding of the rules of a world increasingly shaped by Victorian and Edwardian values, which they could then use to better negotiate the pressures imposed upon them by colonial institutions.

Abandonment

Several factors weakened the ability of the San Pedro Maya to negotiate their place in the developing colonial system and to maintain lifeways associated with their lived ethnicity. In the years after 1867, the British Crown normalized relations with Mexico and established the international boundary between British Honduras and Mexico, leaving most San Pedro villages squarely within the colony. Without the distraction of unstable relations with Mexico and incursions by its Pacífico allies, the British colonial government was able to turn its attention to claims by the loggers of the Belize Estate and Produce Company over the lands occupied by the San Pedro villages. Although the San Pedro Maya villagers continued to labor in logging camps, they increasingly came into conflict with logging interests. Drought and a drop in the mahogany market in the last decades of the nineteenth century hampered villagers' subsistence activities and curtailed their cash-earning ability, both of which were central to their capacity to stay on the land. Shortly thereafter, San Pedro Sirís was abandoned. We find few diagnostic artifacts with *terminus post quem* dates later than 1900, and the cessation of birth and death records for San Pedro Sirís would suggest that it was abandoned around 1900 (records of births and deaths in the Cayo District, microfilms in Belize Archives, Belmopan), although amateur archaeologist Thomas Gann noted a small settlement there as late as 1924 (Jones 1977:153).

At least one of its satellite villages, San José Yalbac, was occupied until 1936, but conditions there as described by archaeologist J. Eric S. Thompson between 1928 and 1934 provide a strong contrast with earlier times. While the officer in charge of destroying the milpas of San Pedro in 1867 admired their size, richness, and variety (Jones 1977), Thompson noted that sixty years later at San José "practically all the beans and much of the maize were brought in from outside, because so many of the men were away chicle bleeding and could not make milpa" (Thompson 1963:118). The traditional slash-and-burn agriculture and the economic and political freedom it brought had disappeared. In 1936, the Belize Estate and Produce Company relocated the entire population of San José and burned the village in a series of events reminiscent of Spanish colonial reducción.

> The once-pleasant village of San José was no more. The inhabitants had been forced to move to Orange Walk. This was not an isolated phenomenon: Kaxil Uinic had been cleared because it was believed to be a center of chicle smuggling; the inhabitants

> of San José and nearby Yalbac had been uprooted because it was said that in making their milpas they might destroy valuable mahogany trees, whereas at Orange Walk they could enjoy all the amenities of civilization. It was history repeating itself, for the Spanish officials and friars had herded the Maya into new and accessible towns nearly four centuries before with a similar lack of consideration for their real happiness. (Thompson 1963:6)

This action removed the last San Pedro Maya from villages they had occupied for over seventy-five years.

CONCLUSIONS

Over the course of their history, San Pedro Sirís and neighboring villages occupied a variety of political and economic positions vis-à-vis different colonial institutions and assorted national powers. Their experience was shaped in part by their history in Spanish Yucatán. Whereas the early decades of Spanish colonial rule brought policies of encomienda, repartimiento, and reducción, all of which directly or indirectly separated communities from land and the products of labor, nineteenth-century liberal reforms again resulted in alienating Maya from community lands. In the Spanish period, Maya villagers adapted structures of both Church and colonial political administration to maintain some degree of local independence (Farriss 1984; Restall 1997). In the nineteenth century, we see many of the activities of the leaders and inhabitants of San Pedro Sirís as tactics by which they pursued a larger goal of maintaining subsistence autonomy and attachment to place within another cycle of rapidly changing colonial context.

For example, in the arena of government relations and diplomacy evidenced by archival data, we see Ek as pragmatic more than accommodating. He worked within the British colonial system, as did Marcos Canul of Icaiche within the Mexican one, strategically employing tools of colonial systems to his own ends while taking advantage of tensions between Mexico, British Honduras, and the Cruzob. In his letters, Ek used diplomatic language to address the tendency of colonizers not to recognize Maya rights to land and indigenous modes of land use, particularly in the face of pressure from British logging firms.[4]

His requests for and the presence and use of guns at San Pedro belie simplistic dichotomies of accommodation versus resistance. In 1865, Lieutenant Governor Austin and Alcalde Ek were negotiating the place of

San Pedro Maya villages within the British colonial system, and it is within this context that Ek requested the British weapons that we found. Ek's request can be read different ways. Ostensibly, it represents an offer of cooperation with the British, as the weapons were to be used to protect the British Honduran frontier. At the same time, the request can be read in a more nuanced way. Better British arms provided the San Pedro Maya with more options in an unstable and unpredictable colonial setting, allowing them to defend themselves against Canul and his followers, or to turn them against the British (as eventually happened).

As Dornan (2004) notes, we will never know Ek's original intentions. We can, however, acknowledge the ability of Ek, as a historically situated actor, to alter his decisions in light of a changing context (see also Liebmann, Chapter 10), one that ultimately led to military conflict between the San Pedro Maya and the British. As is so often the case in these situations, actions by various colonial actors, including loggers, the colonial magistrate, Canul, and Ek himself led to misunderstanding and bloodshed. It is clear from the documents that none of the actors understood the whole picture at any given time, and all were reacting within the contingencies of the moment in response to letters and word received after days of travel into the interior jungle, at times during the rainy season. Both Maya and British authorities convey a degree of confusion and uncertainty in their written communications. In response to the arrival of British military personnel at San Pedro Sirís, Ek wrote to Lieutenant Governor Austin: "[T]he object of this [letter is] only to enquire of your Excellency what fault [I might] have committed that the Magistrate...should have arranged to come...with 40 soldiers" (Belize Archives 89, 511–13; Dornan 2004). And even before he sent the West India Regiment to raze the village in 1867, Austin expressed his worries in a private letter about turning a "perfectly harmless and well affected" San Pedro into a "designing and troublesome neighbor" (PRO, CO, 123, 126 – Austin to Molesworth, November 5, 1866).

In later letters, Austin more clearly concludes that British actions drove Ek to ally with Canul. He expresses regrets at the time that contrast with the historical narrative related fifty-four years later by Thompson based on his experiences at San José Yalbac in 1931: "In the town were found equipment belonging to the West India Regiment and guns, ammunition and mules looted from Indian Church, clear evidence that San José had fought on Canul's side" (J. E. S. Thompson 1963:172). It may be that during the conflict San José broke from San Pedro and allied with Canul, either by choice or coercion. It may be that the British arms Thomas saw were simply those left behind after the initial route of British troops by the San Pedro Maya.

Of course Thompson's observations were those of a British subject and demonstrate how a narrative of such certainty can become entrenched a mere generation after the events and decisions in question.

While Ek made diplomatic decisions committed to paper, the actions of ordinary villagers are documented in the material record. During the decades of San Pedro Sirís's existence after the 1867 military confrontations, villagers continued to work for and trade with the nearby logging camps, while at the same time those camps opposed the very existence of San Pedro. Unlike the predominately creole labor in those camps, the villagers were not trapped in a debt-driven system of dependency on the camps for subsistence. They were free to use the income they obtained from logging or trading with loggers to buy goods they desired to enhance life in their chosen place: musical instruments, sewing machines, perfume, toys, decorated ceramics, jewelry, and more. In doing so, they openly thwarted both logging interests and British colonial law.

Presumably, the villagers at San Pedro going about their daily lives were not thinking in terms of continuity and change, resistance or accommodation, in any way that we commonly recognize from history texts and some archaeological interpretation. The narrative we construct based on documentary, material, and oral narrative evidence is more nuanced and (we argue) more interesting than one that is artificially or romantically cast as an "archaeology of resistance."

When we explore the archives and analyze patterns in the material culture and we find we cannot outline coherent and consistent strategies in the ways the San Pedro villagers negotiated their status in the colonial world, it may be because their decisions were contingent and at times intentionally obtuse (Dornan 2004). We should be careful not to impose unity of purpose upon past actors and mistake it for clarity of hindsight on our part. No particular outcome was ever inevitable from the perspective of those embedded in those historical moments, and it is easy but wrong for us to bring a subtext of certainty to our analysis.

Even today, the contemporary physical monuments that seem to speak most clearly and publically of resistance—statues of "indigenous" leaders who in every case wield machetes—can be and no doubt have been read in multiple ways by those who erected them and those who have viewed them since. Machetes and machete fragments were among the most common artifacts we found at the village of San Pedro. The machete facilitated the swidden agriculture that allowed the San Pedro villages to continue to live in their villages despite official statements to the contrary, and to work for the loggers without becoming trapped in webs of debt peonage. The machete was (and if one reads Belizean newspapers, clearly still is) also a weapon, and therefore a tool of more direct and violent protest. In light of these contexts, the manner in which the individuals depicted by the statues are holding up the machetes can be read as inspiring, or menacing, depending on the viewer. Machetes tied Maya to British merchants; they were also tools, weapons, and symbols of Maya autonomy (Church et al. 2001).

This variety of possible interpretations surrounding everything from machetes to dolls, from religious syncretism to military organization, leads us to conclude that there can never be a simple mapping of practice onto meaning when attempting to locate historical practices in the context of "colonization" or "resistance." Even with our unique variety of data providing us with multiple lenses through which to view the past, we assert that analyses benefit from an acknowledgment of the complex and often messy relationship between concrete data and interpretive frameworks that rely on dichotomous concepts such as resistance.

That said, ambiguity of intention on the part of past actors and on the part of modern interpreters of the data need not be read as a descent into aimless deconstruction, revisionism, or subjectivity. In fact, the complexities of data and interpretation not only make the archaeology of this period more interesting, but if presented in an accessible way, the resulting narratives are also potentially more meaningful and inclusive for the public and for descendant communities. Descendants who live the complexity of the present might find more nuanced versions of the past more resonant with their own experiences. Oral narratives indicate a variety of different and at times competing perspectives among the descendants of those who were ultimately forcibly relocated from San José to the town of Orange Walk by the Belize Estate and Produce Company in the 1930s. As we pursue this vector of research further, we continue to hope that our work might provide a better understanding of the current situation, as well as a more inclusive narrative of the past.

Acknowledgments

We would like to thank Matt Liebmann and Melissa Murphy for their input and patience in putting this volume together. The Belize Institute of Archaeology (IOA) provided invaluable support to the San Pedro Maya Project, and we have had the pleasure of working with many skilled men and women from across the Cayo District in the course of excavation and laboratory work, as well as undergraduate students from University of Colorado–Colorado Springs. We would particularly like to thank our coinvestigator and friend Richard M. Leventhal, and of course the landowners of the site of San Pedro Sirís and surrounding areas, Mr. Carlos Montalban, Mrs. Pitts, and Mr. Alwin Smith.

Financial support for archival research came to Jennifer L. Dornan from the Mellon Foundation via the University of London, Institute of Historical Research. The archivists at the Public Records Office in Kew, the School of Oriental and African Studies at University of London, and the Belize Archives Department were all extremely helpful. Funding for field and laboratory work came from the Vilas Fund of the University of Wisconsin, the UCLA Friends of Archaeology, the Ivor Noël Hume Historical Archaeology Research Fund, the School of American Research, the Fulbright-Hays Foundation, and a University of Colorado–Colorado Springs Creative Research Creative Works grant.

We also owe a special debt of gratitude to those people born in San José Yalbac who continue to share so generously with us their memories and stories of what it was like to live in a San Pedro Maya village.

Archives

Belize Archives
CO = Colonial Office
PRO = Public Records Office
WO = War Office

Notes

1. We refer to these groups as Maya, but with two caveats. First, this broad cultural and linguistic connotation of the term *Maya* is a construct of nineteenth- and twentieth-century Western scholarship (Borgstede and Yaeger 2008; Dornan 2004; Schackt 2001). The people we are discussing likely referred to their language as *Maya t'aan* and themselves as *masewal* (Gabbert 2001, 2004; Tzul 1993); the British called them Indians. Second, although most villagers were Maya, a few were from mestizo and creole heritage groups (Jones 1977; see also Deagan, Chapter 3). The ethnic composition of San Pedro Sirís and related villages was complex; however, in this paper we will use the term *Maya* to refer to them in recognition of that group's demographic predominance. We use the equally problematic term *mestizo* to refer to people of mixed Spanish and Maya heritage, the term *criollo* (Spanish for creole) to refer to people of Spanish heritage, and follow contemporary Belizean usage of the term *creole* to refer to people of African heritage.

2. The presence of high frequencies of gun parts at San Pedro Sirís contrasts with findings at contemporary Lacandon sites in Petén. Palka (2005:217) notes that guns and many other imported items were "shunned," and that the Lacandon preferred bows and arrows for hunting animals. They occasionally used arrows against

human intruders, but they never engaged in more formal military conflict with the Guatemalan state.

3. We would note here the parallels with the early colonial village of Ticamaya, Honduras. After surrendering to Alvarado, "a small group of neighboring towns entered into a series of less showy, but equally significant practical engagements through which long-standing patterns of everyday action were reshaped in the new colonial environment" (Sheptak et al., Chapter 8).

4. Of course, the tensions between subsistence agrarian and commercial extractive uses of land are not exclusively "indigenous" versus "non-indigenous" ones (Dornan 2004). Melissa A. Johnson (2003) notes that in early colonial British Honduras, the ethnic/racial mix of the laboring class—including both black creole and poor white—was less important than their structural opposition to wealthy mahogany cutters who were expropriating what had been effectively commons for generations (see also Deagan, Chapter 3). By the nineteenth century, however, British colonial authorities expressed these class tensions in the language of race.

10

The Best of Times, the Worst of Times
Pueblo Resistance and Accommodation during the Spanish Reconquista *of New Mexico*

Matthew Liebmann

Why did indigenous peoples throughout the Americas resist Spanish attempts at conquest and colonization between the fifteenth and nineteenth centuries? The answer seems at first obvious: in addition to the vicious uses of military force common to Spanish colonial endeavors, exploitive policies including conscripted labor (encomienda and repartimiento), mandatory resettlement (*congregación* and *reducción*), extortionate taxation, and forced conversion typically worked against Native American interests, while the ravages of disease, demographic collapse, and the exploitation of prized resources provided further impetus to oppose the foreigners. Considering these factors, resistance seems the logical, natural response. Yet if this is the case, it begs the opposite question: why then did many other indigenous groups, subjected to the very same circumstances, sometimes choose to accommodate and collaborate with the Spaniards?

Ironically, the oft-cited rationale for indigenous responses (whether addressing anticolonial resistance or procolonizer collaboration) is frequently one and the same:

Q_1: Why did Tribe X resist Spanish control?
A_1: It was a strategy of survival to mitigate the brutalities of colonial occupation.

Q_2: And why did Tribe Y acquiesce to Spanish control?
A_2: It was a strategy of survival to mitigate the brutalities of colonial occupation.

"Survival," it seems, has become the catchall explanation for Native American actions in the post-Columbian world. This is not to imply that threats to native existence during the colonial period were either uncommon or trivial. But clearly survival is more descriptive than explanatory in the interpretation of these actions, and problematic for a host of reasons. Such a simplistic interpretation risks "flattening" the past, producing accounts of the past five hundred years of native history that are superficial at best, inaccurate at worst. They overlook indigenous agency, characterizing Native Americans as passive responders, rather than as dynamic actors who negotiated and shaped the colonial encounter (although clearly their options were often limited [Silliman 2005b:281; Voss, Chapter 12]). Defaulting exclusively to "survival" in an attempt to account for indigenous actions during the colonial era revives elements of the familiar myth of the Native American as Noble Savage (Ellingson 2001:47): with no options, no agency, and no strategies but to stay alive, Indians are cast as stoic one-dimensional characters who do not develop or change, but merely subsist. Furthermore, the suggestion that any decision made by Native Americans during this period was done merely to mitigate colonial oppression is inherently Eurocentric. It prioritizes the colonizer–colonized relationship above all else and neglects to account for the importance of politics within and among indigenous groups in the formation of native tactics and strategies (Beck et al., Chapter 2; Sheptak et al., Chapter 8).

Indigenous experiences under colonialism were, of course, sufficiently more complicated than just a choice between resistance or accommodation, and cannot be summed up through simple monocausal explanations (see Quilter, Chapter 6; Deagan, Chapter 3). Postcolonial scholars such as Homi Bhabha (1994) and Partha Chatterjee (1993) have challenged such clear-cut oppositions in recent decades, noting that the relationship between colonizer and colonized is always more complex than one of straightforward control or defiance. Rather than conceiving of resistance in binary opposition to colonial dominance, these scholars note the profound *ambivalence* inherent in the colonial system (see also Wernke, Chapter 5). Ambivalence, or the simultaneous desire for and repulsion from an object, person, or action (Young 1995:161), describes the continuous fluctuations between appeal and aversion that typify relationships among participants on all sides of the colonial encounter. If we are to develop improved understandings of the Spanish Conquest in the Americas, archaeologists need to pay attention to the whole range of responses to colonialism employed by indigenous peoples. We need to investigate reciprocity, accommodation, complicity, and ambivalence in colonial situations in addition to resistance in its many forms. The acknowledgment of these factors as key structuring components of colonial relations forces a reconsideration of standard binary classifications of colonial dominance versus colonized resistance (Schurr 2010:44–45) and can ultimately help to avoid the ethnographic flattening of the past that results from a myopic focus on opposition alone (Ortner 1995:174–76).

What follows, then, is an attempt to parse the phenomena of anticolonial resistance and procolonizer complicity through an examination of the archaeology and ethnohistory of the Pueblo of Zia in the late seventeenth century. The Zia case is particularly interesting, as it involves one ethnic group who adopted two seemingly opposed strategies toward Spanish colonization at various times during the Pueblo–Spanish battles of the 1680s–90s (see also Preucel, Chapter 11). At first, the Zias allied with their Pueblo brethren in bitter opposition to Spanish control, manifested most famously in the Pueblo Revolt of 1680. A dozen years later they swapped allegiances, siding with colonial forces and even marching with the Spaniards in battle against their Pueblo neighbors. These contrasting strategies coincided with sequential settlements at two different villages: armed resistance to their would-be colonizers was employed at Zia Pueblo (also known as the mission of Nuestra Señora de la Asunción de Zia) throughout the 1680s, while their alliance with the Spaniards corresponded with the construction of a new village in the early 1690s, known as Cerro Colorado. The question of why the Zias adopted such seemingly antipodal stances during the Pueblo Revolt and the ensuing Spanish Reconquest of New Mexico has puzzled historians and anthropologists alike. The following analysis attempts to shed new light on this historical mystery through the use of archaeological data, providing insights into the resistance, complicity, and ambivalence that seem to have characterized Zia peoples during the late seventeenth century. The investigation of native accommodation and ambivalence is crucial for improving our understandings not only of the Zia case, but of the colonization of the Americas more generally. Moreover, the insights gained from the study of their alliance and ambivalence stand to improve our understandings of indigenous resistance as well.

A TALE OF TWO PUEBLOS

On the Feast of San Lorenzo (August 10) in 1689, a Spanish militia under the command of Don Domingo Jironza Petrís de Cruzate left the colonial settlement of El Paso del Norte, following the Rio Grande north with the intent of reconquering the Pueblo Indians. The date was carefully chosen to coincide with the anniversary of the native rebellion nine years prior, when the Indians of New Mexico rose up in the famous Pueblo Revolt of 1680. That insurrection had forced the Spaniards to flee the Pueblo world, inaugurating a new era of native independence in New Mexico after eighty-two years of colonial control. Nearly three weeks after leaving the colonial capital-in-exile of El Paso, Jironza's forces arrived at Zia Pueblo to find its inhabitants fortified in anticipation of the impending attack (Figure 10.1). At dawn on the Feast of the Martyrdom of San Juan Bautista (August 29), the Spaniards laid siege to the village. The battle raged throughout the day and into the evening, with more than seventy Indians captured alive and many more choosing death over surrender as they perished in the flames of the burning pueblo. According to a laudatory certification awarded a year later, six hundred Zias lost their lives that day. As the fighting ceased, four of the Pueblo's religious leaders were marched into the main plaza of the village and executed before a firing squad. Jironza's force ultimately prevailed, but it proved a pyrrhic victory, as more than half of the Spanish soldiers were wounded in the fighting. Recognizing that his army could ill afford another victory of that sort, Jironza and his tattered militia limped back to El Paso del Norte, leaving the still-smoldering remains of Zia at their backs (Kessell and Hendricks 1992:25–26; Kessell et al. 1995:217).

Three years later, again on the Feast of San Lorenzo, Governor Diego de Vargas followed in Jironza's footsteps by leading another recolonizing expedition up the Rio Grande. He found the burned-out shell of Zia Pueblo deserted and in ruin, its former residents now living eight miles upstream on a mesa he dubbed Cerro Colorado (where they had been joined by their allies from the pueblos of Santa Ana and Santo Domingo). This time, instead of meeting the Spaniards with armed resistance, the Zias greeted them with crosses in their hands as a sign of their vassalage, pledging to "obey and serve" both majesties, King Carlos II and Christ. Vargas sealed the bond of friendship between colonizer and colonized by creating fictive kin with the Zias, establishing ties of *compadrazgo* with one of the leaders of the pueblo by serving as godfather at the baptism of his youngest son (Kessell and Hendricks 1992:518–20). Over the course of the next two years, the residents of Cerro Colorado would fight side by side with their newfound *compadres* against their former Pueblo allies, proving to be a crucial asset in the Spaniards' reconquest of the northern Rio Grande.

BEST OF TIMES, WORST OF TIMES IN NEW MEXICO

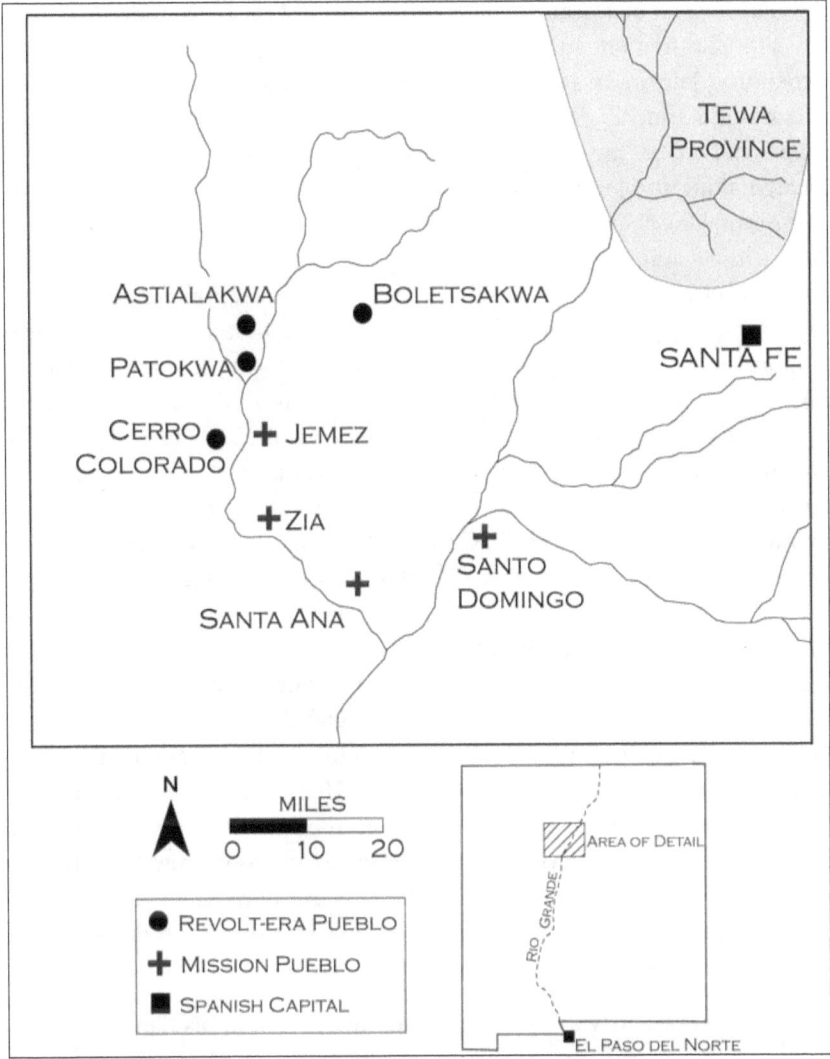

FIGURE 10.1.

Pueblo villages of the Revolt and Reconquest eras (1680–1694) mentioned in this chapter.

So why did the Zias choose such radically different courses of action during the various stages of the New Mexican reconquista? What led them to initially resist colonial efforts at virtually all costs, only to form an alliance with the Spaniards just three years later? While there are no simple answers to these questions, the roots of those fateful decisions stretch back to the origins of Spanish–Pueblo interactions in the sixteenth century.

Matthew Liebmann

The Season of Darkness: The Early Mission Era, 1598–1680

The Zias first encountered the Spaniards in 1541 when the Coronado expedition laid waste to some of their unfortunate neighboring pueblos (Hammond and Rey 1940:233). Over the next six decades, the Spaniards noted Zia to be the paramount pueblo of five Keres-speaking villages located along the Jemez River, known as "Los Punames" (White 1962:20). But significant changes to Pueblo life as a result of European influences began in earnest only after 1598, when the first missions and permanent colonial settlements were established in New Mexico. For the next eighty-two years, Spanish policies of taxation, forced labor, and evangelization combined with demographic collapse to provide fertile ground for Pueblo resistance. The Zias quickly fell under the burden of tribute obligations to the colonial governor. Adding insult to injury was the awarding of grants of encomienda during the first half of the seventeenth century, whereby favored subjects of the Spanish Crown were extended the privilege of extracting tribute from the Zias, theoretically in exchange for educating them in the ways of Christianity (Hordes 2005:145; Anderson 1985).

This exorbitant taxation had ramifications beyond the depletion of stores of maize, causing changes in Pueblo social organization that are reflected in the architecture of seventeenth-century pueblos (Liebmann 2006:392). Zia pueblos constructed after 1600 display rooms with larger floor areas and considerably more variation in size than rooms constructed at Zia villages in the precolonial era (Figure 10.2), a fact that seems to stem from the Zias' resistance to Spanish colonization. In the early seventeenth century, the Spaniards levied taxes on Pueblo Indians in New Mexico on a household-by-household basis, regardless of the number of family members living under one roof. Fray Alonso Benavides described the situation in 1630:

> Each house pay[s] a tribute consisting of a cotton blanket, the best of which are about a yard and a half square, and a fanega of corn. This is understood to be for each house and not for each Indian, even though many Indian families live in such houses. It often happens that the pueblos increase or decrease in houses, or, if one tumbles down, its dwellers move to that of their relatives, and none of these pay tribute, except for the house in which they live. (Hodge et al. 1945:169–70)

In an attempt to subvert the colonial system of taxation, Pueblo families consolidated their households in the early seventeenth century, combining more members under fewer roofs (Anderson 1985:365). Over time, this

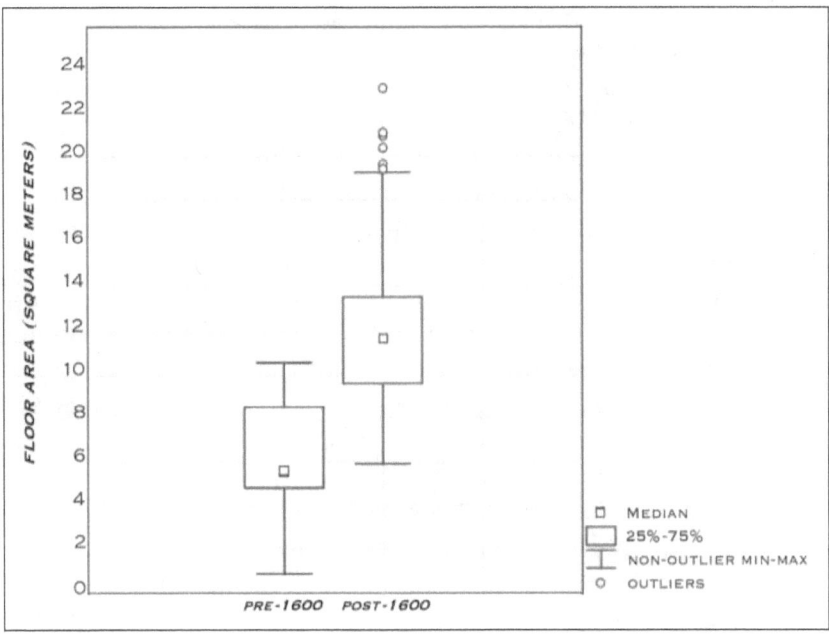

FIGURE 10.2.
Box-and-whisker plot comparison of room sizes at pre- and post-1600 Zia settlements. Pre-1600 data from Barnett 1973:17; post-1600 data from Liebmann 2006:434–37.

appears to have resulted in the construction of larger rooms in order to accommodate the increased numbers of persons living in each structure. Tribute regulations were reassessed in 1643 as a result of declining Pueblo populations, and the burden of encomienda shifted from households to individuals (Forbes 1960:139). But the impact on Pueblo social organization was lasting, and the Zias continued to utilize these larger rooms into the late seventeenth century.

Starting in 1610, the Zias began to suffer the attendant blessings of Christianity with the establishment of Franciscan missions and *visitas* (unstaffed mission facilities) among the Puname pueblos (White 1962:22). Besides the corporeal punishments regularly meted out by the friars (Liebmann 2006:87–89), the priests disrupted Pueblo ritual life throughout New Mexico by filling kivas (Montgomery et al. 1949:157; Smith et al. 1966:42–44; Riley 1999:124), burning kachina masks (Spicer 1962:160–61), destroying "idols" and fetishes (Kessell 1979:110; Kidder 1932:86–88, 96), and prohibiting masked dances. The establishment of *congregación* missions in the region seems to have triggered the spread of Old World diseases among both the Zias and their neighbors in the seventeenth century as well.

Franciscan correspondence notes multiple waves of epidemic disease sweeping though nearby villages between 1620 and 1680 (Scholes 1938:95; Milich 1966:26; Morrow 1996:29). By midcentury, the majority of the Zia population was congregated in a single pueblo, reduced from the five villages they had reportedly inhabited on the eve of colonization, with a concomitant population decrease of 80 percent or more (White 1962:20; Schroeder 1979:244).

Given the generally dire circumstances that accompanied Spanish colonization for the indigenous residents of New Mexico, it would seem reasonable to expect resistance among the Pueblos during the early colonial period. And although the historical records pertaining to these years are poor, there is evidence of organized rebellions in many of the pueblos prior to the famous Revolt of 1680. Beginning with a rebellion among the Zias' northern neighbors, the Jemez, in 1623, a series of indigenous insurrections erupted among the Pueblos throughout the seventeenth century: at Zuni in 1632, at Taos in 1639, and twice more at Jemez in the 1640s and 1650s. Keres warriors were implicated in the last of these uprisings, although the spotty records do not specify whether this included the Zias or not. The Zias may also have participated in another abortive uprising planned in 1675, for which forty-seven accused Pueblo *hechiceros* (sorcerers) were arrested, flogged, and imprisoned—including the eventual leader of the 1680 rebellion, a native of Ohkay Owingeh (San Juan Pueblo) named Po'pay (Scholes 1938:95–96; Hackett and Shelby 1942, 2:291–303; Kessell and Hendricks 1992:42n9; Riley 1999:214–15).

The Season of Light: The Pueblo Revolt of 1680

Following his release from prison, Po'pay formulated a plot to purge the Pueblo world of Spanish influences and return to traditional, prehispanic ways of life. The plan hinged on the coordination of a rebellion among more than thirty different Pueblo villages (speaking six different languages) throughout the northern Rio Grande. Word of this plan spread through the pueblos during the summer of 1680, and on the Feast of San Lorenzo they rose up together in unison, attacking the Spaniards in their midst. Pueblo warriors burned mission churches, sacked haciendas, and executed more than four hundred colonial settlers and Franciscan priests throughout the Kingdom of New Mexico that day. Over the next two weeks, the Pueblos laid siege to the colonial capital of Santa Fe, eventually driving the colonists and their sympathizers out of Pueblo lands and ushering in a twelve-year period of native independence.

The Spanish colonists who survived this initial uprising fled the northern Rio Grande, following the river south for three hundred miles to El

Paso del Norte, where they established a colonial refuge-in-exile. Along the route of their exodus they noted a curious pattern: while many of the mission churches had been pillaged in the revolt, Pueblo warriors left others virtually untouched. Maybe the most powerful display of nativistic fervor was found at Sandia Pueblo, where the church doors were ripped from their hinges; the mission bells were smashed; a crucifix had been whipped with such ferocity that all the paint was removed; and in the ultimate act of desecration, someone had defecated on the main altar of the church (Hackett and Shelby 1942, 1:177–78). Yet just upriver, the people of Santo Domingo Pueblo left their church intact, careful not to disturb any of the Christian icons, altars, or sacred contents of the sacristy. In fact, the only signs that the revolt had taken place at all were the bodies of three dead friars they had placed at the base of the altar before carefully closing the door of the church and leaving their mission village (Hackett and Shelby 1942, 1:21).

Pueblo responses to Po'pay's nativistic prophecy were clearly complex; while some Pueblo people attempted to purge their world of Spanish influences, others were content to retain colonial innovations. Just upriver from Zia at the Jemez mission of San Diego de la Congregación, Pueblo warriors reportedly killed the resident friar, burying his corpse next to a kiva (Espinosa 1988:35; Kessell et al. 1998:342–43). The Jemez then removed the effigies of Santa Maria, Christ, and the saints from the sacristy, along with the church bells, smashing them all before setting fire to the chapel and the rest of the mission village, burning their own homes in the process (Bloom and Mitchell 1938:108; Kessell et al. 1998:237). In contrast, Zia participation in the Revolt of 1680 was more measured. There they did not kill their priest, burn their village, or pillage their church; instead they focused their efforts on the estancias of nearby colonial settlers, seizing livestock and other valuables. Indeed, the Zias, whom the Spaniards called their "Christian enemy," allowed the Franciscan minister to flee, ringing the mission bells and mocking him in derision as he made his escape (Hackett and Shelby 1942, 1:66–67). Following the expulsion of the friar, Zia warriors went on to participate in the siege on Santa Fe, side by side with their Jemez neighbors (Kessell et al. 1995:145).

THE SPRING OF HOPE, THE WINTER OF DESPAIR: PUEBLO INDEPENDENCE, 1681–91

In the months following the successful expulsion of the Spanish colonists and their sympathizers, Po'pay toured the newly freed pueblos to encourage them to complete the nativistic purgation by ridding their world of all Spanish influence and constructing new villages in the manner of their ancestors (De Marco 2000:416; Liebmann 2008a). Many of the Pueblos who had not destroyed their churches in the initial uprising heeded Po'pay's call, sacking mission facilities throughout the northern Rio Grande in the months following the revolt and migrating to new, mesa-top pueblos (Liebmann et al. 2005). Such was the case with the Jemez, who left their mission village and built two new pueblos between 1680 and 1683, Patokwa and Boletsakwa (Liebmann 2006:107–9, 158; see Figure 10.1). The Zias, however, chose not to destroy the mission of Nuestra Señora de la Asunción or tear down their village even after Po'pay's visit, leaving the church walls standing and carrying on living at the pueblo for most of the 1680s.

The motives behind the destruction of the Jemez village and the continued occupation of Zia were likely rooted in the differing histories of the two villages. In the Spanish colony of New Mexico, missions and visitas were commonly constructed at Pueblo villages that had been founded prior to the Spaniards' arrival. This was certainly the case at Zia, where the excavation of midden areas indicates that the village was continuously occupied from its founding in the fourteenth century through the 1680s (Ellis 1966a: 810). The Jemez mission of San Diego de la Congregación was a notable exception, however. Spanish records state that this village was founded by a Franciscan priest in the 1620s (Morrow 1996:29), and excavations at the site of the mission have failed to produce any evidence of occupation prior to the seventeenth century (Dodge 1982; Liebmann 2008b). As its name suggests, the Jemez mission pueblo was intended to facilitate congregación, inducing the inhabitants that had been living in various villages scattered across the rugged landscape to settle at this centralized, more accessible location (which the Franciscans could more easily monitor, if not control). It seems likely that the Jemez would have associated their mission village with their recent colonial history of dislocation and forced removal from their ancestral lands, while the Zia village may have evoked notions of rootedness and a continuation of prehispanic tradition for its residents. Thus it makes sense that the two tribes reacted as they did when Po'pay called for the elimination of Spanish influences and a return to traditional Pueblo life, with the razing of a relatively new, Spanish-founded village by the Jemez and the continued occupation of Zia, which had been inhabited for more than two hundred years prior to the arrival of the Spaniards.

While the Jemez moved north to construct the new villages of Patokwa and Boletsakwa, the people of Zia remained at their mission pueblo throughout the 1680s. Ceramics from Patokwa and Boletsakwa document the strong ties that were forged through trade between Jemez and Zia

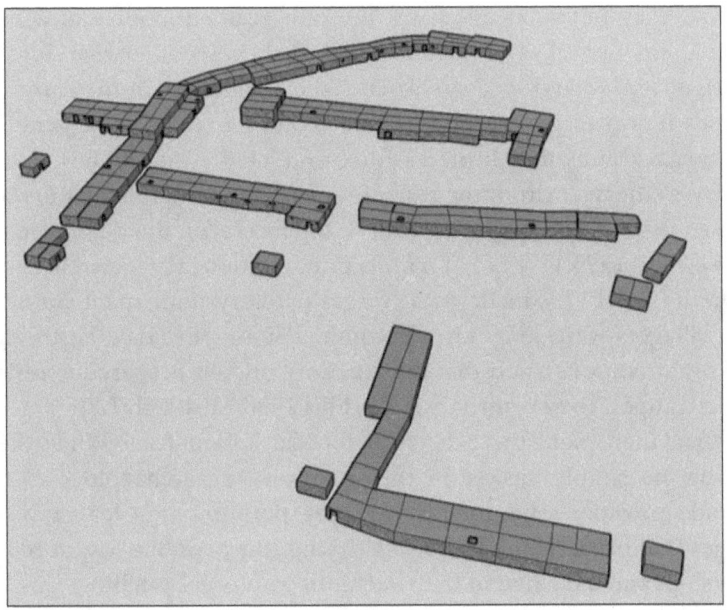

FIGURE 10.3.
Cerro Colorado, 1689–94 (reconstruction by Anna Hayden).

peoples during this period, indicating relatively amiable relations during the Spanish interregnum (Liebmann 2006:352; 2007). These relations were disrupted in 1689, when Zia Pueblo was attacked in the aforementioned battle.

The Epoch of Belief, the Epoch of Incredulity: The Archaeology of Cerro Colorado

Following the 1689 battle, the people of Zia left their ruined pueblo, seeking refuge in the Jemez Province (Kessell et al. 1995:117). They migrated approximately 7.5 miles upstream, settling on a mesa just west of Jemez Pueblo overlooking the crumbling remains of the San Diego de la Congregación mission. There the Zias constructed a new village between 1689 and 1692, known today as Cerro Colorado, where they were joined by their Keres-speaking allies from the pueblos of Santa Ana and Santo Domingo (Figure 10.3). It was at Cerro Colorado in 1692 that the Zias met the Spaniards returning under the command of Diego de Vargas with crosses in their hands, declaring their allegiance to the pope over Po'pay.

What happened between 1689 and 1692 to effect the Zias' reversal of opinion? Was it simply that their losses in the 1689 battle so weakened the

Zias that they felt submission was the only prudent course of action to ensure their survival? The historical record suggests otherwise. According to Vargas, who interviewed survivors of the 1689 battle in the early 1690s, Jironza's report of his crushing victory at Zia was greatly exaggerated. In fact, Vargas claims that Jironza's forces inflicted relatively few casualties that day, as the majority of the residents of Zia "were away from the pueblo, hunting, fishing, and gathering fruit in the forest" on the day of the battle (Kessell et al. 1995:117, 145, 201). Zia oral traditions (collected in the mid-twentieth century) concur with Vargas's observation, maintaining that many villagers were away on a communal hunt that day. Furthermore, these oral traditions assert that the Zias were initially prepared to resist the Spaniards upon their return in 1692 (Ellis 1956:32; 1966b:100).

What, then, were the causes for the Zias' about-face? While there is probably no simple answer to this question, the archaeology of Cerro Colorado provides some interesting clues, pointing to at least two major changes that occurred in Zia society during this period: a loss of religious leadership, and a change in their relations with other pueblos.

A comparison of the archaeology of Cerro Colorado with that of the Jemez pueblos of Patokwa and Boletsakwa sheds light on some of these changes (Figure 10.4). All three villages are similar in size, with 168 ground-floor rooms at both Cerro Colorado and Boletsakwa, and an estimated 217 rooms on the first floor at Patokwa. (Both Patokwa and Boletsakwa had more second- and third-story rooms than Cerro Colorado, however.) All three pueblos consist of long, narrow room blocks defining proportionally large plazas, a layout identified in the American Southwest as the "linear plaza" form (Cameron 1999:207). Linear plaza plans are frequently utilized in construction resulting from large-scale, well-organized communal migrations, such as those that occurred among the Jemez and Zias in the 1680s. Yet there is a conspicuous absence in the architectural plan of the Zia pueblo that is present at the two postrevolt Jemez villages: Cerro Colorado contains no circular, subterranean kivas (the ritual chambers in which much of Pueblo ceremonial activity takes place).

This lack of subterranean kivas is not surprising, as the pueblo of Cerro Colorado sits on exposed sandstone bedrock, and the excavation of an underground chamber would prove difficult, if not impossible, in this location. Kivas were, however, sometimes constructed above ground and included within room blocks, particularly during the Spanish colonial period in the northern Rio Grande (in order to hide these "houses of idolatry" from the watchful eyes of disapproving Franciscans). So while there are no circular, subterranean chambers at Cerro Colorado, this does not necessarily mean

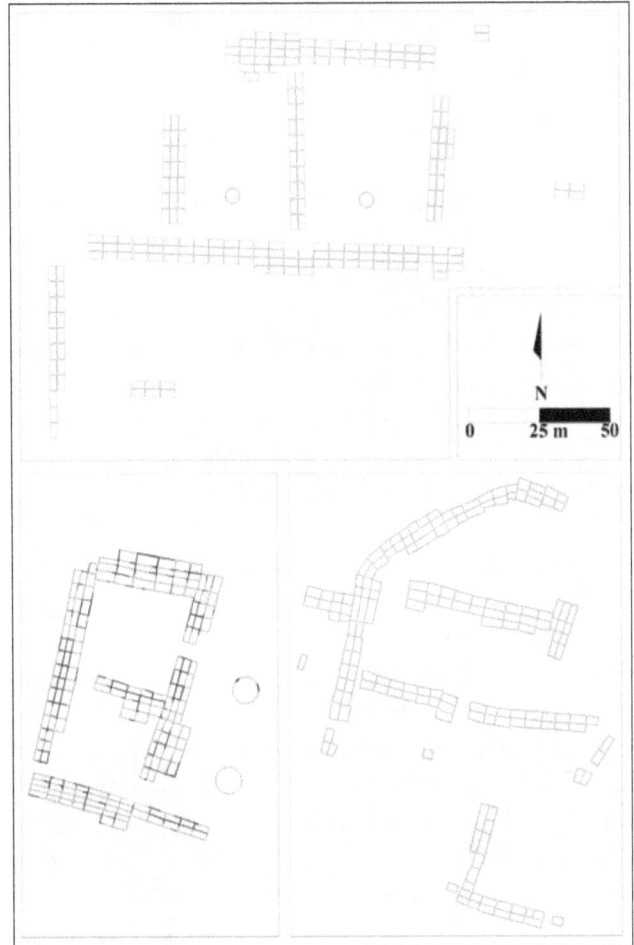

FIGURE 10.4.
1689–94 architectural layouts of: Patokwa (top), *Boletsakwa* (bottom left), *Cerro Colorado* (bottom right).

that there were no kivas; a particularly large rectangular room might have served as such a communal gathering place. (At other Revolt-era pueblos, kivas typically exhibit floor areas nearly three times the size of the largest residential rooms [Liebmann 2006:245–57; Preucel 1998:58].) Yet Cerro Colorado exhibits a relatively even distribution of room sizes with no extreme outliers (Figure 10.5), suggesting that none of the extant rooms served a unique or specialized function. Furthermore, no rooms at Cerro Colorado exhibit a floor area large enough to have served as a kiva or more

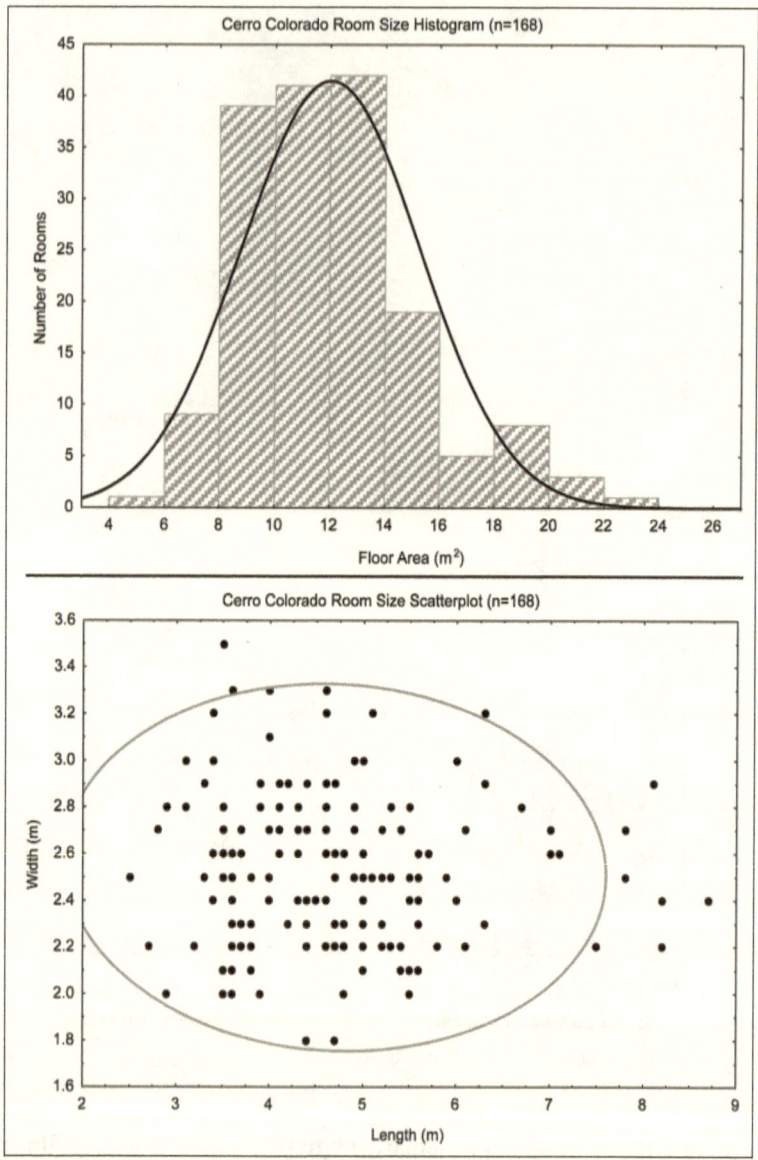

FIGURE 10.5.

Histogram (top) *and scatterplot* (bottom) *of room sizes at Cerro Colorado.*

general communal gathering space.[1] Based on these data, it is safe to conclude that the Zias constructed no kivas at their post-1689 refuge, either subterranean or aboveground, circular or square. Any suprahousehold gatherings that did take place at Cerro Colorado were likely extramural, occurring in the plazas.

The lack of kivas at Cerro Colorado points to a disparity in the ritual activities that occurred there between 1689 and 1694 in comparison with those that took place among the Jemez at Patokwa and Boletsakwa. Without an enclosed space in which to carry out the secretive ceremonies commonly performed in kivas (rites that are today directed by high-ranking religious specialists who are commonly the elites of Pueblo society), the ritual leaders of Cerro Colorado would have faced significant obstacles in the maintenance of their social positions within the Zia community.

Why, then, did Cerro Colorado lack kivas? One possibility is that the Zias (along with their Santa Ana and Santo Domingo allies) truly were the committed Christians the Spaniards asserted them to be in 1680. Yet given their participation in the revolt that year, as well as their armed resistance to the Spaniards in 1689, this seems an unlikely scenario. Rather, the Zias appear to have been profoundly ambivalent regarding Christianity in the late 1600s, fluctuating between acceptance and aversion in a manner typical of colonized persons the world over (Young 1995:161). And while this ambivalence may have tipped to the side of traditional Pueblo religion in the early 1680s (at Po'pay's nativistic behest), the tide seems to have turned by 1692, likely as a result of the execution of the four Zia hechiceros in 1689. With those keepers of sacred knowledge dead, gone too was the leadership that might have guided the construction and consecration of new kivas at Cerro Colorado. Their voices silenced, the Zias' ambivalence toward the colonizers tipped back in support of the Spaniards.

The lack of kivas at Cerro Colorado does not index a wholesale dearth of leadership, however—merely the absence of one specific kind of religious authority, which was apparently crucial to Zia resistance. The architecture of Cerro Colorado attests to a degree of centralized leadership in the planning and construction of the pueblo. Linear plaza pueblos such as Cerro Colorado result from preconstruction planning, developing as a result of work activities in which many rooms are built at the same time by erecting two or more parallel axial (long) walls first, then subdividing the space between them with multiple (shorter) cross-walls to form individual rooms. This technique, termed "ladder-type" construction (Creamer et al. 1993:16; Cameron 1999:207), was used to erect the room blocks surrounding the south plaza at Cerro Colorado, resulting in rooms of similar size and walls with shared azimuths (Liebmann 2006:277). Ladder construction typically requires coordination of labor above the household level (Cordell 1998:27; Kidder 1958:63) because it is usually undertaken by large communal work groups rather than individual family units (Hill 1982:73). Communal work groups such as these require a modicum of centralized leadership to function effectively, usually with a single individual or a small group of leaders coordinating site planning and construction. At Cerro Colorado, one of those leaders was a man named Antonio Malacate (Kessell and Hendricks 1992:431, 513, 518–19, 557, 608).

AMBIVALENCE AND ALLIANCE DURING THE RECONQUISTA OF NEW MEXICO

If ever a figure embodied colonial ambivalence it was Antonio Malacate, who continually vacillated between anticolonial resistance and pro-Spanish complicity throughout the reconquista. Even his name, derived from the Nahuatl term *malacatl* (meaning spindle or winch), suggests a man in constant motion, spinning from one position to another (Kessell and Hendricks 1992:488). A war captain who was active in planning the 1680 Revolt (Riley 1999:218), Malacate was referred to as the "leader whom they obey" when he met Vargas in 1692 (Kessell and Hendricks 1992:518–19). At that meeting, Malacate forged ties of compadrazgo with Vargas, assuring the Spaniards that the Zias were now their allies. Yet in the course of the next year, Malacate left Cerro Colorado, reportedly advising his former followers "neither to make peace nor be friends with the Spaniards." (The Zias responded by telling him, "If you go, you will be our enemy, because we made peace last year and must keep it" [Kessell et al. 1995:404].) In 1693 Malacate had yet another change of heart, seemingly returning to the Spanish fold (Kessell et al. 1995:427); six weeks later, Vargas ordered his arrest for secretly fomenting another rebellion with the help of the Jemez and their Navajo allies (Kessell et al. 1995:540).

The combination of Malacate's ambivalence and the 1689 execution of Zia's ritual leaders set the stage for another man, Bartolome de Ojeda, to assume a primary position of leadership at Cerro Colorado upon the Spaniards' return. Although the 1689 incursion had not succeeded in its goal of reconquering the Pueblo world, the Spaniards did not return to El Paso empty-handed, either. Among the spoils gathered from the battlefield was Ojeda, a Keres warrior taken hostage by the Spaniards, who would eventually become a crucial asset in the reconquest campaigns of the 1690s.

Born of Pueblo and Hispano parentage, the Spanish-speaking Ojeda was educated by the Franciscans as a child and could read and write—skills rare among the residents of the seventeenth-century pueblos. A supporter of the Revolt of 1680, Ojeda went on to fight valiantly against the Spaniards in their assault on Zia nine years later but was critically injured in the battle. Bleeding and near death, Ojeda surrendered to the Spaniards and begged for a priest to administer last rites (Kessell and Hendricks 1992:26). To his surprise, he did not die, however, and he was transported to El Paso where he was nursed back to health. As his wounds healed over the following months, Ojeda transformed himself from a fierce enemy of the Spaniards into one of their strongest native allies. While in El Paso, he revealed shocking details to his captors regarding life in the pueblos during the 1680s, including gruesome descriptions of the deaths of Franciscans after the Pueblo Revolt as well as an account of his own grandmother, a Christian mestiza, being stripped naked and executed for her faith (Kessell 1994:34). These fantastic reports served to stoke the desires of the exiled El Paso colonists to restore Christian order to the Pueblos (Flint and Flint 2008).

When the Spaniards returned to the northern Rio Grande in 1692, Ojeda proved to be a significant factor in the Zias' strategic swapping of allegiances: before his return, they stood in opposition to the Spaniards; after his homecoming, they sided with the colonizers (Kessell 1994:25). Following Malacate's departure from Cerro Colorado, Ojeda assumed the mantle of a war captain, formalizing his position of leadership within the community (Kessell et al. 1995:398, 538). Thus the influence of individual leaders—especially that of Ojeda, Malacate, and the tetrarchs executed in 1689—was a crucial factor in shaping Zia attitudes of resistance, ambivalence, and complicity during the revolt and reconquista years. In other words, the choice of the Zias to confront or cooperate with the Spaniards depended largely upon the influence of individual leaders, and was not wholly determined by their previous treatment at the hands of the Spaniards or a simple will to survive.

The Importance of Inter-Pueblo Politics in the Reconquista

It would be a mistake, however, to assume that any one person was single-handedly responsible for inducing the Zias to resist or collaborate with the Spaniards in the 1680s and 1690s. The community of Cerro Colorado was receptive to Ojeda's strategy of accommodation during the reconquista largely because of conditions that existed prior to the Spaniards' return—specifically, the complex web of inter-Pueblo alliances and animosities that developed in the wake of the Pueblo Revolt. Although Po'pay succeeded in unifying the disparate Pueblos in 1680, that solidarity all but disintegrated over the course of the subsequent decade. When Ojeda was taken into captivity in El Paso, he reported to the Spaniards that the Pueblo world was in chaos, having fragmented into multiple blocs of warring factions. He claimed that the Jemez, Keres (including the Zias at Cerro Colorado), Pecos, and Taos were at war with Picuris and the Tewa Pueblos (Kessell and Hendricks 1992:26). This state of affairs worked in the Spaniards' favor when they returned to the northern Rio Grande in 1692.

The ceramic assemblages of Cerro Colorado and the Jemez Revolt-era pueblos serve as useful gauges of inter-Pueblo interactions in the wake of the Pueblo Revolt. As mentioned above, the pottery of Cerro Colorado, Patokwa, and Boletsakwa indicates that significant trade and interaction took place between the Zias and the Jemez in the wake of the revolt, with both groups embracing the same new pottery types during this period (Liebmann 2008a). In fact, some Jemez potters adopted Zia methods of ceramic production after 1680, favoring the Zia tradition of basalt temper over volcanic tuff, the customarily preferred tempering material in pre-revolt Jemez decorated wares (Liebmann 2006:361–64).

Coterminous with the adoption of shared ceramic types and technologies among the Zia and Jemez Pueblos was a dramatic shift in trade with neighboring Tewa-speaking Pueblos, located northeast of the Jemez and Puname provinces (see Figure 10.1). The Tewas were staunch in their resistance to the Spaniards in the late seventeenth century; in addition to the abortive 1675 rebellion mentioned previously, Po'pay was himself a Tewa, and much of the Revolt-era resistance to the Spaniards emanated from the Tewa homeland. Judging from the ceramic assemblage, Jemez Pueblos apparently had very little contact with the Tewas prior to the 1680 Revolt (Figure 10.6); Tewa wares account for just 0.1 percent of prerevolt Jemez ceramic assemblages (Reiter 1938:189–92; Elliott 1991:80), and stylistic studies of design elements on precontact Jemez and Tewa ceramics support the notion that interaction between these regions was infrequent before 1680 (Futrell 1998; Graves and Eckert 1998; Morley 2002:38). At Zia, the pattern was different, however. The Zias seem to have maintained steady, if not voluminous, trade relations with the Tewas before the revolt, with Tewa wares composing between 2 and 4 percent of prerevolt Zia ceramic assemblages (Ellis 1966a:807–10). After 1680, however, these patterns reversed. Tewa wares increased dramatically in the assemblages of the Jemez pueblos, rising to 5.3 percent overall. Conversely, at Cerro Colorado, Tewa ceramics were virtually nonexistent, accounting for just 0.1 percent of the total assemblage.

These patterns suggest that the Jemez forged new relations with the Tewas in the wake of the revolt, presumably developing as a result of Po'pay's fleeting unification of the Pueblos in 1680. The Tewa Pueblos were uncompromising in their resistance throughout the Revolt and Reconquest eras, maintaining stalwart ties with other like-minded Pueblos during the

BEST OF TIMES, WORST OF TIMES IN NEW MEXICO

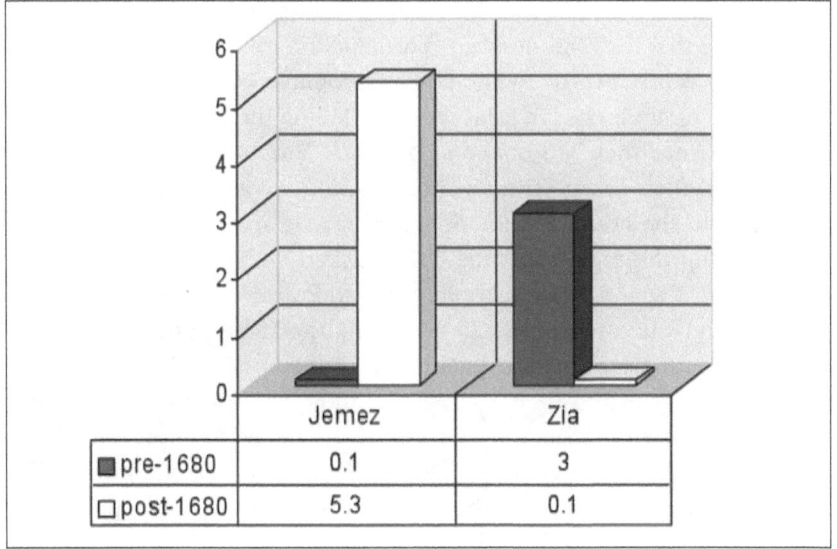

FIGURE 10.6.
Tewa wares as a percentage of the total ceramic assemblages of Jemez and Zia Pueblos. Pre-1680 data from Reiter 1938, Ellis 1966, Lambert 1981, and Elliott 1991. Post-1680 data from Liebmann 2006, 2007.

Spanish interregnum (including the Jemez and the Keres of the nearby redoubt of Kotyiti); thus the Tewa Province became a linchpin of anticolonial resistance in late seventeenth-century New Mexico. The Jemez appear to have fostered an alliance with the Tewas throughout the 1680s and 1690s, and in fact, interaction between these two regions was stronger in the sixteen years following the revolt than it had been for three centuries prior to 1680. Thus the ceramic record calls into question Ojeda's statement that the Jemez were at war with the Tewas during the Spanish interregnum. In fact, in 1694 the Zias were attacked by a coalition of Jemez and Tewa warriors, demonstrating that the strength of their partnership endured nearly fourteen years after Po'pay's initial uprising (Kessell et al. 1998:320, 798).

By contrast, all the available evidence—from both documentary and archaeological sources—suggests that the Zias had become alienated from the Tewas by the late 1680s. Although we do not have ceramic data to assess the relationship between these two groups during the early years of the Revolt period, it appears that by the time the Zias were living at Cerro Colorado (1689–94), they were no longer in regular contact with the Tewas, as evidenced by the nearly complete lack of Tewa pottery found at

Cerro Colorado. The cause of this rift is unknown, although it is tempting to speculate that the Zias' desultory participation in the 1680 uprising and subsequent reluctance to follow Po'pay's commands in the wake of the revolt (leaving their church intact and not killing the priest, for example) may have earned their reprobation from the Tewas. In fact, the Zias reportedly offered their prospective obedience to the Spaniards just a year after the revolt, in the event that the Spaniards would have been successful in reconquering the region in late 1681 (Hackett and Shelby 1942, 2:387). This course of action almost certainly earned Po'pay's reproach.

Whatever the cause of the Zia–Tewa rift, the fact that the residents of Cerro Colorado were the odd Pueblo out of the anti-Spanish coalition of resistance likely played a central role in their decision to side with the Spaniards during the reconquista, a choice calculated to improve their lot in relation to the rest of the Pueblo world. Thus the decisions of individual Pueblos to oppose or support the Spaniards during the Reconquest were sometimes shaped by their desires to settle grudges with other native villages (Kessell 1994:39), and not, as modern assumptions would often have it, merely to survive. The turnabout of the Zias in 1692 was a strategy developed largely independently of their relationship with the Spaniards, with the internal politics of native New Mexico playing a major role. Indeed, inter-Pueblo politics was likely a major factor (if not the decisive one) in the Zia's swapping of allegiances.

CONCLUSION: DE-CENTERING RESISTANCE AND ALLIANCE

The complex history of the Zias' seemingly antipodal stances of opposition and alliance during the reconquista of New Mexico underscores the value of reexamining contemporary assumptions about indigenous resistance. Resistance is never the only rational strategy available to colonized peoples. As the Zia case illustrates, colonizer–colonized interactions are commonly structured by alliances and ambivalence as well (see Wernke, Chapter 5). Furthermore, although many institutions, policies, and practices of seventeenth-century Spanish colonialism were undoubtedly brutal (according to twenty-first-century Western sensibilities), we should question the assumption that there is anything "natural" about resistance to these circumstances. The brutality of the colonial system was not the sole motivating factor behind indigenous resistance or alliance. After all, the Zias who assisted the Spaniards in 1692 were one and the same as those who resisted in 1689, suffering identical trials and tribulations under the colonial systems of missionization and encomienda.

Clearly there is a need to look to additional causes, outside of the colonizer–colonized relationship, to develop better understandings of indigenous resistance and alliance during the Spanish Conquest. In other words, we need to "de-center" resistance studies by shifting the focus away from the traditional Indian versus European dichotomy, affording a central role to the internal politics of native communities in the reconstruction of colonial pasts (Beck et al., Chapter 2). By conceiving of resistance and complicity as merely responses to the actions of colonizers—that is, as uncomplicated examples of either straightforward opposition or the pervasive hegemony of colonial power—we risk "flattening" the archaeology of colonial encounters and promoting the myopia, homogeneity, and romance of resistance studies that have been critiqued of late (Abu-Lughod 1990; Ortner 1995; Brown 1996; Given 2004:11).

This is, of course, not an entirely novel argument, as historians have long recognized the centrality of indigenous politics in the aid of or resistance to Spanish colonialism (Restall 2003:44–51), dating back at least to the nineteenth-century studies of William H. Prescott (1843, 1847). Throughout the Americas, native disputes aided the Spanish advance: Cortés benefited from the Tlaxcalans' disdain for the Aztecs; Cakchiquel–Quiché discord helped Alvarado to colonize the Maya highlands; and the civil war between Atahualpa and Huascar proved central to Pizarro's conquest of the Inca Empire. In much the same way, the Zias' alienation from other Pueblos, most conspicuously the Tewas, contributed directly to Vargas's ultimate success in the reconquest of New Mexico.

De-centering resistance studies also focuses attention on the important roles played by individual leaders in fomenting rebellion, cooperation, and ambivalence. These are not the famous aforementioned conquistadores whose names are so well known to us today, but native leaders like Po'pay, Bartolome de Ojeda, and the quartet of Zia sacerdotalists executed in 1689. Removing any of these actors from the equation of the reconquest would likely have brought about a different outcome for the Zias. The significance of these individuals becomes especially apparent when we break down the colonizer–colonized binary that structures so much of our analysis of the Spanish colonial period in the Americas. Like a grainy picture coming into focus, indigenous actors emerge from the blurry background of the historical and archaeological records when we direct our attention specifically to native politics.

Indigenous agency is further brought into focus when we consider archaeological evidence alongside texts in the analysis of colonial encounters.

Because the documentary record was penned primarily by the colonizers, indigenous actors tend to be marginalized in the historical record. Attention to the material culture produced by native peoples thus helps to de-center studies of resistance by wresting its creators from the blurry backdrop of the documentary record. In the Zia case, the archaeology of Cerro Colorado draws attention to the significance that the loss of ritual leadership likely played in their decision to ally with the Spaniards (a loss manifested archaeologically in the lack of kivas at Cerro Colorado). Material culture also highlights the role of internecine warfare among the Pueblos in the wake of the revolt, and serves to correct some of the inaccuracies in the documentary record (such as the report that the Jemez were at war with the Tewas during this period). At the same time, artifacts help to elucidate some of the enduring inter-Pueblo relationships that were ignored by historical texts (again, the Jemez-Tewa alliance being a prime example).

The addition of this information is not trivial. Without archaeology, accounts of Zia history tend to emphasize the influence of Ojeda in explaining the Zias' changing allegiances during the reconquista. This is understandable, as Ojeda is the primary Zia actor described in the documentary record and the only literate Zia voice able to represent himself. But the addition of archaeological evidence suggests that the situation was much more complicated; the Zias did not alter their loyalties simply because of Ojeda, but due to a host of inter- and intra-Pueblo political factors, including the death of some leaders, the ambivalence of others, and the Zias' alienation from and alliances with neighboring pueblos.

De-centering resistance is vital to improving our understanding of why some native groups chose to oppose Spanish rule while others opted to side with the colonizers. Archaeology has a central role to play in this process. Attention to the internal politics of indigenous groups and the role of native agency helps to develop more nuanced understandings of colonial resistance and accommodation. Because indigenous peoples often did not record their versions of colonial encounters in writing, the study of their material remains can act as a corrective to some of the biases of the historical record, uncovering details of native life not documented in official histories. Material culture can also counter the biases of written histories, giving voice to the subalterns of the past and contributing to new histories. Through the study of these materials, archaeologists stand to make an essential contribution to the history of the Spanish Conquest, as well as to the anthropological study of colonial resistance, alliance, and ambivalence.

Acknowledgments

This research was made possible through the generous support of the National Science Foundation, the Wenner-Gren Foundation for Anthropo-logical Research, the Pueblo of Jemez Department of Resource Protection, the College of William and Mary, the University of Pennsylvania Museum of Archaeology and Anthropology, the Louis J. Kolb Foundation, and Harvard University.

Note

1. The largest room at Cerro Colorado has a floor area of 23.2 m^2; by comparison, the northern kiva at Boletsakwa exhibits a floor area of 60.4 m^2.

11

Becoming Navajo

Refugees, Pueblitos, and Identity in the Dinétah

Robert W. Preucel

In his Revised Memorial of 1634, fray Alonso de Benavides portrayed the state of Apache-Pueblo relations in unambiguous terms, asserting that the Apache nation was always at war with the Pueblo Indian people. He wrote, "[T]he Apaches surround the above-mentioned [Pueblo Indian] nations on all sides and have continuous wars with them" (Hodge et al. 1945:81). Since he had successfully "converted" the Pueblo nations, it only remained for him to convert the belligerent Apache groups. He then summarized his conversion efforts among the five provinces of the Apache nation, which he identified as the Xila Apache, the Perrillo Apache, the Navajo Apache, the Quina Apache, and the Vaqueros Apache.

Benavides, the custodian of New Mexico from 1623 to 1629, prepared his Revised Memorial at the request of Pope Urban VIII. It is clear that he wished to present his missionizing agenda in the most positive light in order to secure desperately needed financial support for the fledgling New Mexican missions. For this reason, he quickly glossed over his failures, particularly the revolts and martyrdom of priests at Jemez in 1623 and at Zuni in 1632. Similarly, Benavides emphasized the warlike nature of the Apache people and their constant attacks on the Pueblo missions to justify additional military aid. He neglected to mention that these attacks were, in many cases, due to the Spanish disruption of traditional trade relations between native peoples. Indeed, the Apache and Pueblos were not always antagonistic, and there were long-standing political and economic alliances between different subgroups.

In my chapter, I consider the social and cultural effects of Spanish colonialism on indigenous Southwestern peoples. In particular, I examine the ethnogenesis of the Navajo (Diné) people as part of a cultural survival strategy. The Navajo Apache of the seventeenth century became the modern Navajo Nation through a complex series of political, social, and economic interactions involving Apache, Ute, Pueblo, Spanish, Mexican, and American peoples. I restrict my discussion here, however, to the early Navajo-Pueblo relations in the post-Revolt period (1680–1775). Traditionally, this period has been interpreted as a time of rapid acculturation due to Pueblo peoples taking refuge from the Spaniards among the Navajo (Kidder 1913, 1920; Hester 1962). This is the time when it is thought that the Navajo Apache adopted many Pueblo traits such as architecture, pottery making, weaving, clans, matrilineal descent, and matrilocal residence (Hester 1962:89). However, this period is by no means fully understood by historians and archaeologists, and my analysis must therefore be considered preliminary.

Of special interest in this discussion have been the pueblitos, or pueblo-like sites, perched on the isolated pinnacles in the Gobernador and Largo districts of northwestern New Mexico. These sites consist of small coursed masonry buildings and often include forked-stick hogans in their plazas.[1] Recently, some scholars have challenged the refugee hypothesis largely on the grounds of new dendrochronological dates and proposed that they are better explained as an indigenous Navajo response to Ute warfare (Hogan 1991; Towner 1992, 1996, 2003; Towner and Dean 1992, 1996; Towner and Johnson 1998). I disagree and suggest that the refugee hypothesis has been discarded prematurely. Part of the problem in this debate is that it has unfortunately been haunted by an outmoded trait-list approach that assumes an essentialist ethnic identity for both Navajo and Pueblo peoples. I then provide an alternative practice-based approach emphasizing the variability and dynamism of early Navajo culture and, in particular, its hybrid qualities and invented traditions.

ETHNOHISTORICAL ACCOUNTS OF EARLY NAVAJO-PUEBLO RELATIONS

The starting place for the investigation of early Navajo Apache–Pueblo relations is the ethnohistorical accounts produced by the Spanish authorities. These documents are of two broad kinds: reports prepared by ecclesiastical representatives implementing the Catholic missionizing program, and reports by secular officials overseeing the colony. Because the Church and state were in competition for the control of New Mexico, they sometimes provided sharp critiques of each other's practices (Scholes 1936, 1937, 1942). For example, in 1750, fray Carlos Delgado wrote a scathing indictment of the governors, *alcaldes mayores*, and judges of *residencia* and identified a range of abuses such as inadequate payment, forced labor, sexual violence, and onerous taxation (Hackett 1937:426–28).

The standard Borderlands histories characterize the Spanish colonization of New Mexico as a period of unprecedented political interaction and ethnic transformation among Pueblo Indian communities (Bolton 1921; Bannon 1970). In response to the Spanish programs of missionization, *encomienda*, *repartimiento*, and *reducción*, some Pueblo people established military alliances with different Indian groups and forcibly resisted. This resistance culminated in the infamous revolts of 1680 and 1696 (Liebmann, Chapter 10). Others fled their mission villages and took refuge with Indian peoples (Pueblo and non-Pueblo alike) living at the edges of the Spanish Empire. Some stayed for only short durations and returned to their homes. Others intermarried and became permanent members of their host communities. These population shifts were frequent enough that they posed a continual threat to the Spaniards. For this reason, the Spanish governors generally adopted a strategy of pursuing the refugees and resettling them in their original mission village homes.

There is considerable historical evidence for Pueblo people collaborating with and seeking refuge among both Pueblo and non-Pueblo peoples during the Colonial period (Schaafsma 2002:208–304). In 1609, don Luis de Velasco informed the governor of New Mexico that "the few natives in the land are scattered everywhere so that not only are they poorly grouped for proper administration, only a few living in each place and these far apart, but also for support and protection, and as some of the pueblos and nations are on the frontiers of the Apaches, who are usually a refuge and shelter for our enemies." Velasco continued to say that on these frontiers, "they hold meetings and consultations, hatch their plots against the whole land, and set out to plunder and make war" (Hammond and Rey 1953:1089). In 1638, fray Juan de Prada sent a petition to the king of Spain stating that "they have not yet entirely lost the habits of heathen nor their love of a life of liberty, without subjection to any lord or king. And experience has shown the force of this truth, namely, that upon the slightest occasion of annoyance with the soldiers some of the baptized Indians, fleeing from their pueblo, have gone over to the heathen, believing that they enjoy greater happiness with them, since they live according to their whims, and in complete freedom" (Hackett 1937:111). Here the word *heathen* probably includes the Navajo Apache as well as the Western Pueblos since, as of 1629, the Hopi, Zuni, and Acoma were still unconverted (Schaafsma 2002:249).

During the first half of the seventeenth century, there was considerable unrest among the pueblos due to their "ruthless exploitation" by the Spaniards (Scholes 1937:105). During the administration of Governor Fernando de Argüelo (1644–47), the Jemez joined with the Apache and killed a Spaniard. The Spaniards immediately retaliated and hung twenty-nine Jemez leaders. The Apache mentioned here are probably the Navajo Apache, since they had well-established trade relations with the Jemez people. In 1650 the pueblos of Isleta, Alameda, San Felipe, Cochiti, and Jemez established a military alliance with some Apache groups to plan a revolt against the Spaniards (Scholes 1937:105–6). The plan, however, was discovered and the ringleaders were hung as traitors (Hackett and Shelby 1942, 2:266). In 1679, fray Francisco de Ayeta wrote that some of the southern Pueblos "were in danger of ruin through the constant attacks made upon them by the Chichimecos of the Apache nation, with whom the rest of the heathen Indians were confederated" (Hackett 1937:296).

There is good evidence that Pueblo people conspired with the Apache in carrying out the Pueblo Revolt of 1680. When Governor Otermín first learned of an imminent revolt on August 9, 1680, he was told that "all the nations of this kingdom were now implicated in it, forming a confederation with the heathen Apaches" (Hackett and Shelby 1942, 1:3–4). There is clear evidence of Apache participation in the uprising at Taos Pueblo. The lieutenant governor recorded the arrival of two Spaniards in Santa Fe "who were retreating from the pueblo of Taos, leaving their wives and children in the said pueblo, dead at the hands of the Christian Taos and the heathen Apaches" (Hackett and Shelby 1942:71–72). Otermín identified these Apaches as members of the Achos nation (Hackett and Shelby 1942, 1:98). There is also evidence of Apache and Pueblo alliances during the uprising of 1696. Diego Xenome (Dieguillo), the cacique of Nambe, testified that the "Apaches...had agreed to advise them what they decided and determine about what they must do and carry out" (Kessell et al. 1998:754).

THE PUEBLO REFUGEE HYPOTHESIS

The Pueblo refugee hypothesis was originally proposed by Adolph Bandelier and later elaborated by Alfred V. Kidder. Bandelier first mentioned the idea in his historical account of a battle between the Spaniards

FIGURE 11.1.
Three Corn Pueblito (LA 1871). Courtesy of Curtis F. Schaafsma.

and Jemez people at Jemez Pueblo on June 29, 1696. He suggested that the Spanish victory "broke up the confederacy with Acoma and Zuni, and caused the Jemez to flee to the Navajo country. When [Captain Miguel de] Lara reconnoitered the mesas [in the Jemez District] in August following they were deserted. For several years the Jemez remained among the Navajo, until they finally returned to their old range, establishing themselves at or near the site of their present village" (Bandelier 1892:215–16). It is not clear, however, what Bandelier's historical sources are for these statements, and this has caused a certain degree of confusion (Schaafsma 2002:283–87).

In 1912, Kidder refined the hypothesis to explain three small sites in the upper San Juan region of New Mexico: Three Corn Pueblito (Figure 11.1), Old Fort Pueblito, and an unnamed pueblito in Largo Canyon. In his published report, he commented upon their defensive locations and the co-occurrence of pueblo-type masonry rooms and wooden structures closely resembling modern Navajo hogans (Kidder 1913, 1920). He also observed a hooded corner fireplace, wood cut with metal axes, and cow and sheep bones, which he interpreted as clear evidence of Spanish contact. He described three new pottery types: a blackware (now known as

Dinétah grey), a thin-walled painted ware (now known as Gobernador Polychrome), and a thick-walled bichrome and polychrome pottery, "not distinguishable...from the modern painted ware of the Pecos and Tano countries in central New Mexico" (these are historic Pueblo Indian wares) (Kidder 1920:325).

Kidder concluded that these small sites, or "pueblitos," were built during the historic period and offered two alternative interpretations. The first was that they were constructed by indigenous peoples in contact with the Navajo or some other people who made circular earth-covered lodges of wood. The second was that they were built by Jemez refugees who joined the Navajo following the Revolt of 1696. Because he could find no ethnohistorical evidence in support of his first thesis, he favored the refugee hypothesis. He then cited Bandelier's (1892) statement that Jemez people fled to Navajo country following the battle on June 29, 1696 as the most likely explanation.

A number of pueblitos were excavated in the 1940s and 1950s. Most scholars adopted Kidder's view that they were evidence for Pueblo refugees living among the Navajo Apache. For example, Dorothy Keur (1944:86) concluded that the mixture of Pueblo and Navajo traits at these sites indicated that they were built by "uprooted Puebloans [who] joined the erstwhile hostile Navajos to hide out against a common foe." Al Dittert (1958) defined the Gobernador phase (1700–1775) in the Navajo Reservoir District as a period of intensive "acculturation" between the Navajo and Pueblo refugees. The only cautionary note to this picture was Roy Carlson's (1965:98) observation that the tree ring dates and ceramic types indicated an occupation in the first quarter of the eighteenth century, some twenty years after the 1696 revolt!

In the last twenty years, the refugee hypothesis has been called into question and challenged on two distinct fronts. First, old tree ring dates from the pueblitos have been reexamined and new ones have been obtained. These studies unambiguously support Carlson's thesis and demonstrate that most pueblitos are too late to have been occupied immediately following the 1696 revolt. Second, the Spanish ethnohistorical data have been reviewed and reinterpreted. Little unambiguous historical evidence has been found to support the idea that large numbers of Pueblo people were living with the Navajo during the first half of the eighteenth century.

In 1990, Ronald Towner began a dissertation project to explicate the role of pueblitos in Navajo culture. Central to his project was the redating of the pueblitos using modern dendrochronological methods and procedures. He compiled a database of 808 tree ring specimens (Towner 1992,

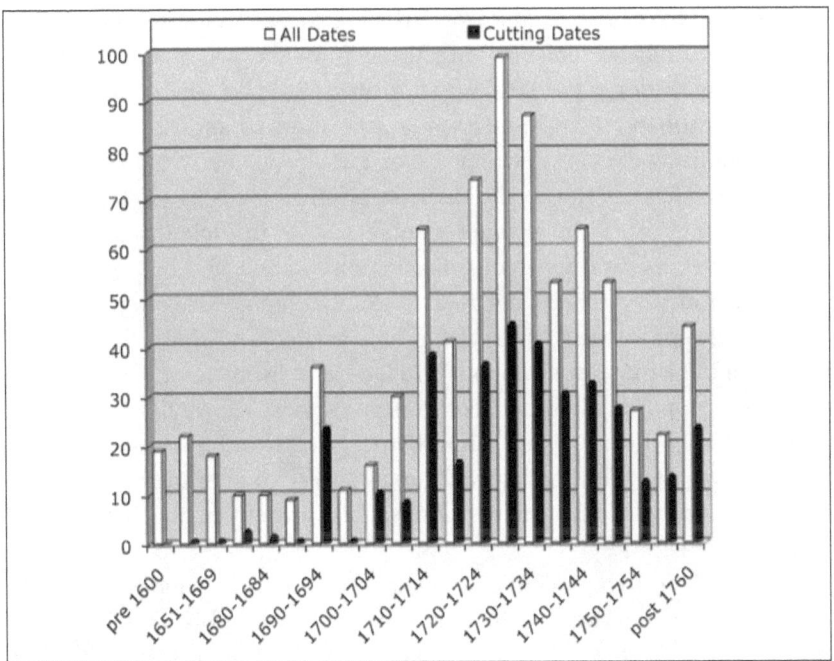

FIGURE 11.2.
Pueblito tree ring dates (from Towner 1996, Figures 7.2 and 7.3).

1996, 2003). These dates include both cutting and noncutting dates and reveal a relatively normal distribution. The greatest amount of building activity is indicated for the period between 1720 and 1760 (Figure 11.2). Citing Frank Reeve (1959), he suggested that this activity corresponds to a period of relative peace between the Navajo and Spaniards. Because the pueblitos postdate the supposed refugee influx by at least fifteen years and there is historical evidence of Ute raiding, Towner (1996:164) concluded that the majority of sites were built by Navajo people for protection against the Ute.

Only a single site, Tapacito Pueblito, has cutting dates that fall between 1690 and 1694 and thus could have been constructed by Pueblo refugees immediately after Diego de Vargas's reconquest of 1692. For this reason, Towner and Dean (1992:327) have characterized Tapacito as "the only genuine Pueblo refugee structure in the Dinétah." Towner (1996:166) sees it as unrelated to the later pueblitos and a separate entity unto itself. He has further speculated that it may have been the original home of the Coyote Pass clan, a Navajo clan that is traced to an original Jemez matriarch (Towner 1996:168).

Patrick Hogan has conducted a critical review of the ethnohistoric literature. He finds evidence for only three Tewa and two Jemez communities seeking refuge in the Dinétah after the 1696 rebellion and concludes that they probably comprised only a few hundred individuals (Hogan 1991). He finds even less evidence that Pueblo people remained among the Navajo. He cites Roque de Madrid's punitive expedition of 1705 that restored some captive or refugee Pueblo people to their former homes. The mission records refer to only five Pueblo women who had come from Navajo country and were married to Navajo men. He concluded that "although archaeologists have chosen to interpret this evidence as indicating that a large number of Pueblo refugees were living among the Navajos after the Reconquest, it is equally consistent with an alternative hypothesis: that the Navajo incorporated a number of Pueblo and Spanish traits into their culture as a result of more than a century of alternatively peaceful and hostile contact with Pueblo and Spanish groups in the Rio Grande area" (Hogan 1991:8).

Towner's and Hogan's critiques, while persuasive to many archaeologists, have not been universally accepted among ethnohistorians and cultural anthropologists. David Brugge (1996:261) writes that Towner "suggests a radical revision of our view of Navajo culture history on the basis of this more detailed chronological picture, one that is challenging and stimulating, but one that I feel fails to take full advantage of ethnographic and ethnohistorical knowledge." He agrees with Towner's thesis that the pueblitos were built by Navajo people (even if they were of Pueblo origin or part-Pueblo ancestry) and regards them as defensive structures for protection against Indian raiders (probably, but not exclusively, the Ute and Comanche). But he disagrees with the position that Pueblo refugees played only a limited role in Navajo culture. Citing Gladys Reichard (1928:11–19), he draws attention to seventeen clans as originating among the Pueblo plus two others of probable Pueblo origin. Fully one-third of all Navajo clans claim Pueblo origins (Reichard 1928:22–25).

Rick Hendricks and John Wilson (1996:92) have evaluated Hogan's analysis of the ethnohistorical evidence for Pueblo refugees among the Navajo and concluded that it is incomplete. They write that "a number of documents that may not have been available to Hogan clearly state that 'many' Pueblo Indians who had been living among the Navajos, some since as early as 1680, were returned to their respective missions and pueblos following the Navajo campaigns of 1705" (Hendricks and Wilson 1996:92). For example, they cite Blas Martin who estimated that when he was in Navajo country (sometime between 1712 and 1715) more than two hundred

Christian Indians were living among the Navajo (Hendricks and Wilson 1996:92). They also observe that these documents obviously mention the people who returned to their homes and not those who chose to stay behind with the Navajo.

Similarly, I have argued that Towner's important confirmation that the majority of the pueblitos were constructed in the mid-eighteenth century does not, by itself, contradict the refugee hypothesis (Preucel 2002:16); that is, it does not demonstrate that Pueblo people did not take refuge with the Navajo Apache. This is because some Pueblo families may have joined the Navajo Apache after the Pueblo Revolts of 1680 and 1696 and not built pueblitos. As Brugge (1996:262) explains, concealment and flight would have been the first option. Later, after the warfare had subsided, "the presence of naturalized Navajos who still remembered something of pueblo building practices or of their descendants who felt some kin ties to Pueblo ways, could, and probably did, lead to construction of fortresses to defend against Indian enemies." Moreover, Towner does not consider the possibility that some Pueblo people may have left their traditional villages due to the return of Spanish persecution in the first half of the eighteenth century. The famous Navajo-Spanish peace dating from 1720 to 1770 does not necessarily imply that Pueblo-Spanish relations during this same period were unproblematic.

There is, in fact, considerable historical evidence for Tewa and Tano refugees fleeing to the Navajo Apache following the 1696 revolt. In particular, don Diego de Vargas's statement of July 23, 1696, indicates that the people of the pueblos of Jacona, San Cristóbal, and San Lázaro all took refuge with the Navajo (Kessell et al. 1998:842). It seems likely that they joined with the Navajo who were living in the Piedre Lumbre area of the Chama Valley (Schaafsma 2002). On August 27, 1696, Vargas took testimony from the governor of San Juan Pueblo who told him that the people of Santa Clara "had all gone away, some to Moqui [Hopi] and others to live with the Navajo Apaches" (Kessell et al. 1998:1003). In November of that year, Roque de Madrid learned that Pueblo people from San Ildefonso "had gone to the provinces of Zuni and Moqui and to the Navajo Apaches" (Kessell et al. 1998:1059). While these statements do not document a wholesale movement of Pueblo people to the Navajo Apache, Towner's (1996:168) estimate of a few families almost certainly underrepresents the number of people involved.

More to the point, there is also evidence for religious persecution by the Spaniards in the first half of the eighteenth century. In January 1714, Governor Juan Ignacio Flores Mogollón initiated a punitive campaign against the use of kivas. He regarded kivas and *cois* as associated with "great abuses, superstitions and idolatries" (Kessell 1992:409).[2] Mogollón, therefore, ordered the alcalde mayores of each pueblo to identify and destroy all kivas and cois. Regarding the situation at Pecos Pueblo, he wrote:

> Inasmuch as I have been informed that in the pueblo of Pecos a partially subterranean room in the form of a kiva or coi has been built apart from the pueblo under the pretext of the women getting together to spin; inasmuch as it should have a door opening onto the street, and the king our lord (may God keep him) has ordered all his ministers to see most diligently that such rooms are not built because of the great abuses, superstitions, and idolatries that have been committed therein, as is proven; and inasmuch as there are, besides this one, others in that pueblo, I order the alcalde mayor of that district to go immediately and ascertain if this is true. If it is, he will make them destroy and level it immediately, ordering these Indians that, if they wish to build a room where the women may get together to work, it must be inside the pueblo in a public place adjoining the convento or casas reales with its door onto the street so those who come and go and what they do inside may be known. (Kessell 1992:409)

This order was also carried out at the pueblos of San Juan, Nambé, Tesuque, Jemez, Laguna, Acoma, and Halona (Kessell 1992). It is possible that some Pueblo people saw this persecution as the return of a repressive regime and, regarding it as the last straw, fled their Rio Grande homes to take refuge among the Navajo Apache (and other Indian peoples).

The abuses perpetrated by the governors and alcaldes mayores are described in some detail in a letter written by the Franciscan friar Carlos Delgado dated March 27, 1750 (Hackett 1937:424). He listed four kinds of abuses: (1) the governors required the pueblos to supply large amounts of corn with little recompense; (2) the governors compelled them to work on buildings and drive cattle at low pay; (3) the alcaldes mayores forced them to weave four hundred blankets per year and seized groups of thirty or forty Indians to cultivate their fields; and (4) the alcaldes and some of the governors raped Indian women.[3] Fray Delgado wrote "that losing patience and possessed by fear, they turn their backs to our holy mother, the Church, abandon their pueblos and missions, and flee to the heathen, there to worship the devil, and, most lamentable of all, to confirm in idolatries those who have never been illuminated by the light of our holy faith" (Hackett 1937:429).

In 1744, fray Delgado made a trip to the Navajo District to petition them to convert to Christianity (Brugge 1985:45). A year later, he returned and performed baptisms at a "Navajo pueblo" called "los Collotes" (Reeve 1959:15). Brugge (1985:45) regards this village as "undoubtedly one of the pueblos of the Dinétah." He further suggests that the name means "the coyotes" or "the halfbreeds," which implies it was occupied by people of mixed Pueblo and Navajo descent. Fray Delgado wrote that when he was "among the heathen (Navajo) to reduce the apostates there were among them some (Pueblos) who, with an aggrieved air, showed me their scars, thus giving me to understand that the reason why they fled and did not return to the pale of the church was their fear of these cruel punishments" (Hackett 1937:428).

There is additional evidence of close interaction between the Pueblos and Navajo Apache during this period. Fray Juan Sanz de Lezaún wrote that "the Christian Indians are so intermingled with the many heathen that they are almost indistinguishable," and "the heathen Navajos are continually coming into and going out of the pueblos, and they see iniquities and hear the clamors of the Christian Indians" (Hackett 1937:474). Given the political implications of admitting failure in the conversion of the Pueblos, it seems entirely likely that the number of Pueblo refugees would be underreported by the Spaniards.

NAVAJO AND PUEBLO DEMOGRAPHY

There is limited demographic information regarding Navajo Apache and Pueblo Indian populations during this period. What few data exists were compiled mainly by government administrators and mission priests and are of uncertain accuracy. In 1744, Governor don Joachin Codallos y Rabal reported on the conversion of the Indians in the province of Navajo. This report was based upon the testimony of a dozen Spaniards with military experience in the Navajo campaigns. The Rabal witnesses estimated that there were between two to four thousand Navajo people (Hill 1940:396). In 1744, fray Carlos Delgado and fray José Yrigoyen claimed that they "converted" five thousand Navajo to the faith in Cebollita and Encinal (Hackett 1937:421). This claim is generally regarded as a gross exaggeration, since it is unlikely that there were this many Navajo in the entire Dinétah District during this period (Hester 1962:22).

The best available census data for the Pueblos are those compiled by the mission priests in 1701, 1744, 1765, 1779, and 1782. These data, however, are of variable quality and do not cover all the Pueblos. Moreover, the recording methods are inconsistent. In some cases, the priests reported the number of families while, in others, they reported the number of people (souls). In addition, reporting practices varied both within and across years. Finally, there are likely biases in the data. The mission priests may have underreported people in some cases or overreported them in others for specific political reasons.

Many of these demographic data are summarized in fray Juan Agustín de Morfi's letter of 1782, which was presumably sent to the provincial minister of the convent of Nuestro Padre de San Francisco de Mexico (Thomas 1932). Morfi was one of the most prolific authors on New Spain's northern frontier during this period. In 1777, he served as chaplain for Teodoro de Croix's inspection tour of the Provincias Internas. His letter is a geographical account of New Mexico with a description of the eight *alcaldías mayores*—Santa Fe, Santa Cruz de la Cañada, Taos, Queres, San Carlos de la Alameda or Zandia, Albuquerque, Laguna, and Zuni, in addition to the pueblo and mission of El Paso and the province of Moqui. It reports population figures for the following years: 1707 (souls), 1744 (families), 1765 (souls and families), 1779 (families), and 1782 (souls) (Table 11.1).

One way to estimate Pueblo mobility strategies is to analyze these demographic data, notwithstanding their limitations with respect to recording methods and reporter bias. A comparison of individuals (souls) from 1707 and 1765 shows that seven pueblos suffered substantial losses, while only three made substantial gains.[4] The losses were reported at Tesuque (–267), Pecos (–656), Nambe (–96), San Juan (–84), Taos (–195), Cochiti (–50), and Zuni (–816). Pueblos exhibiting gains for the same period included San Ildefonso (+184), Laguna (+270), and Acoma (+392). The total losses for all pueblos (2,180 people) is nearly twice the total gains (1,121 people). An unknown portion of this demographic decline may be due to death from disease and drought (Ramenofsky 1988; Reff 1995). However, some of the missing Pueblo people likely left their communities and took refuge with other Indian communities, including the Navajo.

It is also possible to compare changes in the number of Pueblo *families* between 1744 and 1765, a period in which four Pueblos exhibited substantial losses while seven made significant gains.[5] Tesuque (–19), San Juan (–20), Picuris (–25), and Taos (–11) all showed declines, while Galisteo (+30), San Felipe (+18), Santa Ana (+48), Santo Domingo (+36), Cochiti (+74), Laguna (+114), and Zuni (+31) all reported increases in the number of families. The total gains for all pueblos (361 families) outnumber the total losses (75 families), a nearly fivefold increase. Combined with the

TABLE 11.1
Pueblo demographic data reported by fray Juan Agustín de Morfi in 1782 (from Thomas 1932)

Pueblo	1707 Families	1707 Souls	1744 Families	1744 Souls	1765 Families	1765 Souls	Avg. Fam. Size	Families Loss/Gain 1744/1765	Souls Loss/Gain 1707/1765
Tesuque	—	500	50		31	233	7.52	-19	-267
Galisteo	—		50		80	225	2.81	30	
Pecos	—	1000			178	344	1.93		-656
Pojoaque	—		30		31	99	3.19	1	
Nambe	—	300		212	49	204	4.16		-96
San Ildefonso	—	300			90	484	5.38		184
Santa Clara	—	210		272	70	257	3.67		47
San Juan	—	400	70		50	316	6.32	-20	-84
Picuris	—	300	80		55	328	5.96	-25	28
Taos	—	700	170		159	505	3.18	-11	-195
San Felipe	—	330	80		98	458	4.67	18	128
Santa Ana	—	340	50		98	404	4.12	48	64
Santo Domingo	—	240	40		76	224	2.95	36	-16
Cochiti	—	500	80		154	450	2.92	74	-50
Sia	—	500			150	508	3.39		8
Jemez	—	500	100		109			9	
Alameda	—	50	100						
Sandia	—				67	291	4.34		
Isleta	—		80						
Laguna	—	330	60		174	600	3.45	114	270
Acoma	—	660		110	308	1052	3.42		392
Zuni	—	1500	150		181	684	3.78	31	-816
Totals	—	8110	960		2141	6917		286	-1059

235

reported decline in population demonstrated above, this suggests that the increase in the number of families is accompanied by a reduction in family size. Because both families and souls are reported for 1765, it is possible to calculate the mean Pueblo family size at 4.06 people (with a standard deviation of 1.38). Tesuque has the largest family size at 7.5 people per family, while Pecos has the smallest at 1.9 people per family.

While it is obviously difficult to draw firm conclusions from this preliminary analysis, it is nonetheless evident that there was considerable population mobility among Pueblo peoples during this period. It is suggestive that the time when the pueblitos experienced their greatest florescence, 1720 to 1760, was also the time when some pueblos, especially Pecos, Taos, Tesuque, and Zuni, experienced sharp population losses. These losses are not necessarily due to disease. As Ann Palkovitch (1985:420) notes, the known epidemic outbreaks are not consistently associated with population declines, and it seems that they exacerbated, rather than initiated, settlement shifts. This finding is consistent with the interpretation that some portion of the Pueblo population took refuge among the Navajo Apache.

NAVAJO APACHE–PUEBLO HYBRID IDENTITIES

Perhaps the most interesting question is not the refugee issue. Clearly the archaeological and ethnohistorical evidence suggests that some Pueblo people took refuge in the Gobernador District (Carlson 1965), in the Chaco District (Brugge 1986), and in the Piedre Lumbre District (Schaafsma 2002). Rather, the pertinent question is how the different admixtures of Pueblo and Navajo Apache people in these areas contributed to the emergence of a range of new identities that came to be known as Navajo.

Part of the difficulty in addressing this question is the "essentialist" or "typological" bias shared by many scholars. For example, it is popularly assumed that Navajo people lived in hogans and made black utility wares, while Pueblo people lived in pueblos and made polychrome wares. We need to question the either/or-ness of this characterization and focus on contextually specific variation in social practices (cf. Brugge 1996:262). We can take our cue from anthropologists who have recognized the hybrid nature of early Navajo (and, to a lesser degree, Pueblo) cultures. For example, Bailey and Bailey (1986:15) have observed that "[t]he Navajos consisted of two culturally distinct populations in the first decade or so after 1700—Athapaskans and Puebloans—that were rapidly fusing. Although scholars have tended to view the Navajos as Athapaskans whose culture had absorbed Puebloan cultural traits, we prefer to see them as biological and cultural hybrids, neither Athapaskan nor Puebloan, but a product of both."

This is a valuable insight, but what remains unarticulated are the kinds of social practices associated with asserting collective identity while maintaining continuity in the face of dramatic social change.

Eric Hobsbawm (1983:1–2) has defined invented traditions as "a set of practices, normally governed by overtly or tacitly accepted rules and of a ritual or symbolic nature, which seek to inculcate certain values and norms of behaviour by repetition, which automatically implies continuity with the past." For him, "the peculiarity of 'invented' traditions is that the continuity with [the past] is largely fictitious" and "they are responses to novel situations which take the form of reference to old situations, or which establish their own past by quasi-obligatory repetition" (see also Liebmann 2006:395; 2008a:364). It is useful to examine the Pueblito phenomenon with respect to two kinds of social practices: those that are unconscious and the outcome of enculturation, and those that are conscious and designed to publically assert social identity. The former, what Pierre Bourdieu (1977) calls "habitus," are useful in identifying recent migrants within a community. The basic premise is that the new arrivals will tend to replicate certain habitual aspects of their own culture in their new environment. The latter speaks to the creation of community solidarity by means of strategic material practices designed to minimize social conflict. This is the invention of tradition in Hobsbawm's sense.

One particularly revealing social practice is how people discard trash. This is largely unconscious and intimately related to received notions of purity and pollution (Douglas 1966; Hodder 1987). Brugge (1986) has used the distribution of ash deposits to distinguish changes in Navajo refuse disposal practices over time. He observes that Pueblo practices typically involve the creation of heterogeneous middens where ash is mixed with daily refuse, while Navajo practices tend to be associated with homogeneous deposits associated with only ash. He then identifies a temporal trend at pueblito sites in the Chaco District. He finds that in the later sites, "ash heaps seem to conform to modern Navajo practice and to have been used for purposeful disposition only of ashes" (Brugge 1986:19). The average distance of ash heaps from architectural remains at the later sites is only 12.5 feet. In the dwellings believed to date during the early part of the eighteenth century, there is greater variation, with a range from 8 to 35 feet (and an average of 11.9 feet). He concludes that some of the earlier people were "conforming somewhat more to Puebloan standards for ash disposal" (Brugge 1986:19). This important analysis needs to be extended to pueblito sites in other areas.

There is considerable evidence for the invention of new traditions in the pueblito context. Indeed, this is what originally defined the Gobernador phase. Here it is useful to look at ritual architecture. As Brugge (1986:156) writes, "the ideology of the Pueblo Revolt had to accommodate to the defeat of the Pueblos in their home territory and the success of the Navajo in remaining free." The Revolt-period discourse associated with "living in accord with the laws of the ancestors" was no longer viable (Preucel 2006; Liebmann and Preucel 2007). New discourses were needed to accommodate the different ethnicities represented by the various Navajo and Pueblo groups living in close proximity. The perceived success of Navajo ceremonial practices in ensuring Navajo freedom may explain why there is no unambiguous evidence for kivas at Gobernador-phase pueblitos and may account for why kachina ceremonialism becomes absorbed into Yé'i ceremonialism.

One discourse that was likely emphasized in this context was the origins narrative. The accounts of the emergence of the first peoples from the underworld, which was part of preexisting Pueblo and Apache ideologies, could have been deployed to emphasize common origins and shared life experiences. This discourse may have been made material by the use of special hogans. It seems significant that prior to this period, hogans were either of the forked-stick variety or, more rarely, of stone construction, while following this period, cribbed-roof hogans become more common. Brugge (1986:20) has reported an early eighteenth-century cribbed-roof hogan in the Chaco District. Given its contemporaneity with four forked-stick hogans, it is possible that this hogan was a special-purpose structure and used to house new ritual practices, such as the Yé'i bi chei ceremony (Keur 1941:39). Other early examples of possible cribbed-roof hogans have been reported from the Gobernador District (Farmer 1942:67) and the Canyon de Chelly District (Hurt 1942:91).[6]

This argument is lent further support by the pottery evidence. The dominant painted pottery at the pueblito sites is Gobernador Polychrome. This is a high-fired ware with a yellow surface color (Carlson 1965:51–57). Both bowls and jars are divided into registers by the application of a thin red slip paint, and design elements are composed from the red slip and flat black paint. Bowls are often carinated and have similar forms to both Tewa Polychrome and Kotyiti glazeware bowls, while jars have long necks and bulbous bodies similar to contemporaneous Tewa Polychrome and Kotyiti glazeware jars. Significantly, the applied designs show the influence of several different Puebloan styles (Brugge 1963:19). Some scholars have identified similarities with Hopi and Tewa ceramics (Dittert 1958). Curtis Schaafsma (personal communication, 2008) has remarked on similarities to Keres ceramics, particularly Puname Polychrome. Frank Harlow et al.

FIGURE 11.3.
Largo Canyon rock art panel (LA 102399) showing a group of female Yé'i figures wearing Plains-style headdresses. Note the fringed kilts with Pueblo-style tassels.

(2005) have recently defined two new types, San Diego Polychrome, a glazeware, and Jemez River Polychrome, a matte paint ware, which bear strong stylistic similarities to Gobernador Polychrome. Both of these types may have been made by Jemez potters (Liebmann 2006). Significantly, Jemez River Polychrome has been found at pueblito sites in the Gobernador District (Harlow et al. 2005). Although additional studies are needed, Gobernador Polychrome's hybrid nature seems to reference the emergence of a new collective identity that integrates technological practices and design elements from several different Pueblo sources.[7]

The strongest evidence for the invention of new traditions, however, is found in the rock art from the Upper San Juan and Gobernador districts. Polly Schaafsma (1963, 1966, 1975) has conducted the most important analysis of this material. She identifies Yé'i figures as the diagnostic features of this rock art. Male Yé'i are generally depicted with round heads, straight bodies, decorative kilts, and a variety of headgear including feathered, pointed caps, and horns, while female figures are shown with rectangular heads, mantas, and feathered headgear (Figure 11.3). Both genders are represented holding staffs, dance wands, and corn stalks. These religious subjects were likely inspired by the Pueblo tradition of wall and altar painting as well as by ceremonial rock art representations (Schaafsma 1975:32). Significantly, Schaafsma attributes some of these rock paintings to the hand of actual Pueblo refugees (Schaafsma 1975:40). She posits that Navajo rock art may have served mnemonic purposes in recording prayers and memorizing ritual procedure (Schaafsma 1963:65). The practices of inscribing these images on the canyon walls would have helped reinforce new hybrid identities.

CONCLUSION

Navajo ethnogenesis can be interpreted as a cultural survival strategy associated with a complex series of social and political interactions implicating several different Indian groups that was heightened in the context of Spanish colonialism. The relationships of the Navajo Apache and Pueblo Indian peoples during the first half of the eighteenth century are of particular significance, since they gave rise to new identities and traditions that persist in various forms to this very day. While there is no doubt that the Navajo Apache raided Pueblo missions and villages, it is also clear that they aided the Pueblo people in resisting Spanish authority. In addition, there was a long-standing practice of Pueblo people taking refuge among the Navajo Apache during times of stress. While many of these Pueblo refugees returned to their mission villages, others intermarried with Navajo people and introduced the Pueblo clans still present among the Navajo.

The Pueblito phenomenon debate has quite properly dominated the archaeological interpretations of Navajo ethnogenesis. It shapes how we understand the origins of the modern Navajo people. For this reason, it is crucial to make careful use of the existing data. As Brugge (1996: 263) notes in his response to Towner, we need to be wary of "disciplinocentrism," the assumption that one's own field is somehow superior to others. Rather, we need to incorporate data from multiple fields, including archaeology, ethnohistory, and oral history, paying special attention to the areas where they contradict one another. The recent arguments for interpreting the Pueblito phenomenon as a Navajo response to Ute raiding in the mid-eighteenth century are not compelling, given the ethnohistorical documentation of the flagrant abuses of the Pueblo people by the Spanish authorities in the eighteenth century. The return of a repressive regime of religious persecution likely caused many Pueblo families, once again, to take refuge with the Navajo Apache, as well as with other Indian peoples.

A focus on social practices offers a valuable means of reconstructing salient discourses of identity within these hybrid communities. One useful approach is to differentiate conscious and unconscious practices. In the Chaco District, there is evidence of distinct Pueblo and Navajo practices of ash disposal that lessen over time. There is also evidence for the conscious invention of tradition. Special hogans, which unite kiva-style cribbed-roof construction with Navajo domestic architecture, may have physically embodied discourses about common origins. The pottery data from the Gobernador District also support this idea. Gobernador Polychrome has often been interpreted as a hybrid ware with influences from Tewa, Keres, and Hopi pottery. This characteristic likely allowed pottery to mediate new Navajo identities. Rock art, however, is one of the strongest lines of evidence for the influence of Pueblo refugees, particularly in the transition from kachina to Yé'i ceremonialism. It is significant that there is regional variation in the rendering of Yé'i figures during this period, indicating that they were not yet standardized (Schaafsma 1963:66). It seems highly unlikely that these ideas could have been conveyed to the Navajo Apache without direct and sustained Pueblo involvement (Polly Schaafsma, personal communication, 2009). The result of this practice-based approach is the recognition that there is not one monolithic Navajo identity, but rather many different locally based Navajo identities each expressed in specific ways, which over time became the modern Navajo Nation.

Acknowledgments

I thank Matt Liebmann and Melissa Murphy for soliciting my contribution to their SAR seminar. This chapter has greatly benefited from their feedback as well as the comments by the other invited scholars, especially Rus Sheptak and Rosemary Joyce. I am especially grateful to Curtis and Polly Schaafsma for their ongoing advice on Navajo ethnohistory, ceramics, and rock art. They introduced me and my wife, Leslie Atik, to the remarkable rock art of Largo Canyon.

Notes

1. Although pueblitos have received the most archaeological attention, they typically exist within a settlement system that includes a variety of residential sites and features (Towner and Johnson 1998).

2. A cois is a rectangular ceremonial room with a roof entrance contained within a residential room-block, that is, a room-block kiva.

3. Similar accusations were made by don Juan Antonio de Ornedal, but summarily discounted by the provincial father of Mexico (Hackett 1937:438).

4. Substantial losses are here defined as losses of greater than fifty people.

5. Substantial losses are here defined as losses of greater than ten families (not people).

6. Cribbed roofs were also sometimes incorporated into pueblito architecture. Roy Carlson (1965:8) reports a cribbed roof for Room 7 at Old Fort Ruin.

7. Paul and Lori Reed (1996), however, claim that Gobernador Polychrome predates the Pueblito phenomenon. Unfortunately, their evidence is not entirely convincing, based as it is on radiocarbon and archaeomagnetic dates from only six sites.

12

The Archaeology of Indigenous Heritage at Spanish-Colonial Military Settlements

Barbara L. Voss

As a discipline that seeks to produce meaningful information about the past, archaeology articulates with heritage in multiple ways. *Heritage* is a broad and unwieldy term that defies strict definition. The diverse uses of this term all share an emphasis on the profound interconnections between past and present. Much of the research presented in this volume uses archaeological research to trace the complex ways that indigenous people in the past responded to Spanish colonization. This chapter similarly uses archaeological evidence to recover indigenous history, but I focus more directly on the relationship between archaeological research and the heritage practices of present-day indigenous peoples.

I approach the relationship between archaeology and indigenous heritage through an unconventional vantage point: the archaeology of Spanish-colonial military settlements. Military settlements institutionalized the violent and forceful components of Spanish colonization of the Americas. Although some military outposts functioned to guard Spain's colonial territories against incursions by other European powers, most were established to suppress indigenous resistance to colonization (see also Beck et al., Chapter 2, and Murphy et al., Chapter 4). They provided the military "muscle" behind colonial appropriation of indigenous territory, labor, and goods and enforced missionization programs. Consequently, Spanish-colonial

Barbara L. Voss

military settlements are conventionally studied to investigate the military tactics the colonizers used to secure Spain's territorial claims. Additionally, Spanish-colonial military settlements were often the demographic center of the colonial population, especially in frontier regions. Thus, military settlements are also studied to understand Spanish-colonial culture, particularly settlers' adaptations to life in the Americas. For these reasons, military settlements are often interpreted as sites that stand as material reminders of colonial military strategy and colonial social history.

I contend that Spanish-colonial military settlements are sites of indigenous as well as colonial heritage. Drawing on archaeological and documentary research at El Presidio de San Francisco, Spain's northernmost military outpost in the Americas, I examine the labor relations that produced architecture and artifacts that have been conventionally interpreted as colonial material culture. Attention to labor relations brings visibility to hidden or overlooked indigenous populations at colonial settlements, and prompts a reevaluation of the cultural attribution of the material traces of Spanish colonization. Taking labor relations seriously as an aspect of heritage complicates current anthropological interest in indigenous resistance in the past by bringing coercion and subjugation to the forefront of archaeological analysis (see also Deagan, Chapter 3, and Liebmann, Chapter 10). However, this approach also generates new conceptual tools and historical perspectives that can be used in present-day struggles over indigenous participation in the management and interpretation of Spanish-colonial heritage sites.

CENTER AND PERIPHERY IN COLONIAL-INDIGENOUS HERITAGE

Although colonial settlements in the Americas were first investigated as sites of European heritage, since the mid-twentieth century researchers have increasingly emphasized the multiethnic demographics of these communities. This interest in colonial–indigenous interaction initially developed from acculturation research in anthropology (Foster 1960; Herskovits 1938; Quimby and Spoehr 1951). It expanded dramatically during the public and academic debates surrounding the 1992 Columbian Quincentenary, leading to a paradigm shift that emphasized indigenous agency, resistance, and survival in the face of European imperialism. The 1990 passage of the Native American Graves Protection and Repatriation Act (NAGPRA) amplified public and scholarly attention to indigenous heritage in the Americas.

Archaeologists developed new research methodologies to investigate indigenous and multiethnic heritage at colonial settlements. Prior investigations had generally focused on the central compound of Spanish-colonial settlements—the fortifications and quadrangles of presidios (frontier military outposts) and the churches and *conventos* (central building complexes) of missions, along with public buildings and residences of high-ranking colonial officials in civilian pueblos (towns). In the early 1970s, Charles Fairbanks and Kathleen Deagan pioneered "backyard archaeology" research at St. Augustine, Florida, which investigated commoners' residences in the colonial town with the explicit objective of understanding the multiethnic character of the settlement and the dynamics of mixed-race households (Deagan 1983). Investigations of St. Augustine also reached beyond the colonial town walls to include investigations of two adjacent Native American villages (Merritt 1983; Milanich 1999) and a free black militia settlement (Deagan and MacMahon 1995). Similarly, Kent Lightfoot's (1998) research at Colony Ross, a nineteenth-century Russian settlement in northern California, surveyed and excavated areas outside the colonial stockade to investigate colonial-era neighborhoods occupied by Native Alaskans and Native Californians. Also in California, Stephen Silliman (2004) located and excavated a Native Californian village located just across the creek from Rancho Petaluma's central compound. At El Presidio de Los Adaes in present-day Louisiana, Diana Loren (2001) researched colonial identity negotiation through analysis of artifacts recovered from multiethnic residential neighborhoods that lay outside the settlement's enclosed fort. My own research at El Presidio de San Francisco has also embraced this extramural approach, using historical research and archaeological surveys to identify the locations of pluralistic agricultural settlements located in a valley outside the presidio quadrangle (Voss 1999, 2008:161–70). In addition to this extramural approach, there is increasing attention to autonomous historic Native American communities that were not directly connected with particular colonial settlements (e.g., Frink 2007; Hull 2005; Jordan 2008; Silliman 2009) along with investigations of fugitive multiethnic communities, such as maroon settlements (e.g., Funari 1999), that formed in the hinterlands of colonized territories (see Preucel, Chapter 11).

Extramural and hinterlands investigations of indigenous and pluralistic communities have substantially transformed archaeological understandings of the dynamics and outcomes of colonization. Through these studies, archaeologists have literally redrawn the boundaries of colonial sites to encompass broad social landscapes that extended far beyond the walls of formal colonial compounds. However, extramural and hinterlands research may unwittingly reinforce the original presumption that the central compounds of colonial sites are strongholds of European heritage. Unless the colonial core is reexamined, indigenous heritage claims will continue to remain peripheral.

INDIGENOUS HERITAGE AT THE CORE: THE CASE OF EL PRESIDIO DE SAN FRANCISCO

El Presidio de San Francisco was founded in 1776, during Spain's final territorial expansion in North America (see Figure 1.1). Although the western coast of North America had been explored by Spanish ships since 1542, Spain did little but nominally claim California until 1767, at the end of the Seven Years' War. With increased British, Dutch, and Russian maritime activity in the Pacific Ocean, Spain moved to settle California to prevent other European empires from occupying this strategic coastline. Four presidios were established during 1767–82 at key locations along the coast, along with a string of missions that aggregated and converted Native Californians. El Presidio de San Francisco, the northernmost of these, was situated to guard the entry point to San Francisco Bay. It was the military, administrative, and economic headquarters of a colonial district that stretched along the Pacific Coast from present-day Sonoma County to Santa Cruz County.

The settlement itself was occupied by about twenty to thirty colonial families, most of whom had been recruited from agricultural towns and mining districts in Sinaloa and Sonora, in present-day northwest Mexico. After Mexican Independence in 1821, El Presidio de San Francisco was maintained as a military fortification by the Mexican Army and the California *diputación*. However, it declined in strategic importance as defense concerns shifted from maritime threats to the growing land-based incursions resulting from the United States' westward expansion. In 1834 and 1835, most of El Presidio de San Francisco's troops were relocated to a new military installation in Sonoma, California, leaving only a small caretaking population in San Francisco. Upon U.S. annexation of California in 1847, El Presidio de San Francisco was appropriated as a U.S. Army post, which remained in continuous operation until the property was transferred to the National Park Service in 1994.

El Presidio de San Francisco's Quadrangle

The nucleus of El Presidio de San Francisco was its quadrangle. Archaeological studies have found that the quadrangle was produced through a

FIGURE 12.1.
Artist's conception of El Presidio de San Francisco as it may have appeared in 1792. National Park Service, Golden Gate National Recreation Area.

dynamic articulation between local practices and colonial regulations. The 1772 Reglamento (executive order) specified that each presidio settlement should take the form of a quadrangle, with buildings constructed of adobe surrounded by a defensive wall and two bastions at opposing corners (Brinkerhoff and Faulk 1965). In San Francisco, the quadrangle conformed in the rectangular alignment of buildings around a central plaza. However, it consistently lacked the defensive attributes—bastions, defensive walls, and fortified gates—required in the 1772 Reglamento. Further, until the 1810s, San Francisco's quadrangle was constructed using heterogeneous materials and techniques, including wattle-and-daub, thatch, rammed earth, and palisade, in addition to regulation adobe.

Archaeological research has also revealed that the architectural production of San Francisco's presidio quadrangle changed markedly over the life of the settlement. The first quadrangle, which has not yet been discovered archaeologically, was described in 1777 by Governor Felipe de Neve as "mere huts"; it appears to have been a small quadrangle measuring 92 *varas* (77 m) on each side, partially enclosed by an adobe wall with small adobe, stone, palisade, and wattle-and-daub shelters located inside.[1] By all accounts, this quadrangle had substantially collapsed by 1780. The second quadrangle (Figure 12.1) is known primarily from a 1792 plan map and accompanying letter penned by Acting Commander Hermenegildo Sal (1792a, b), written descriptions by other colonial officials and foreign visitors (e.g., Vancouver 1984), and archaeological evidence of the quadrangle's south and north sides (Blind and Bartoy 2006; Simpson-Smith and

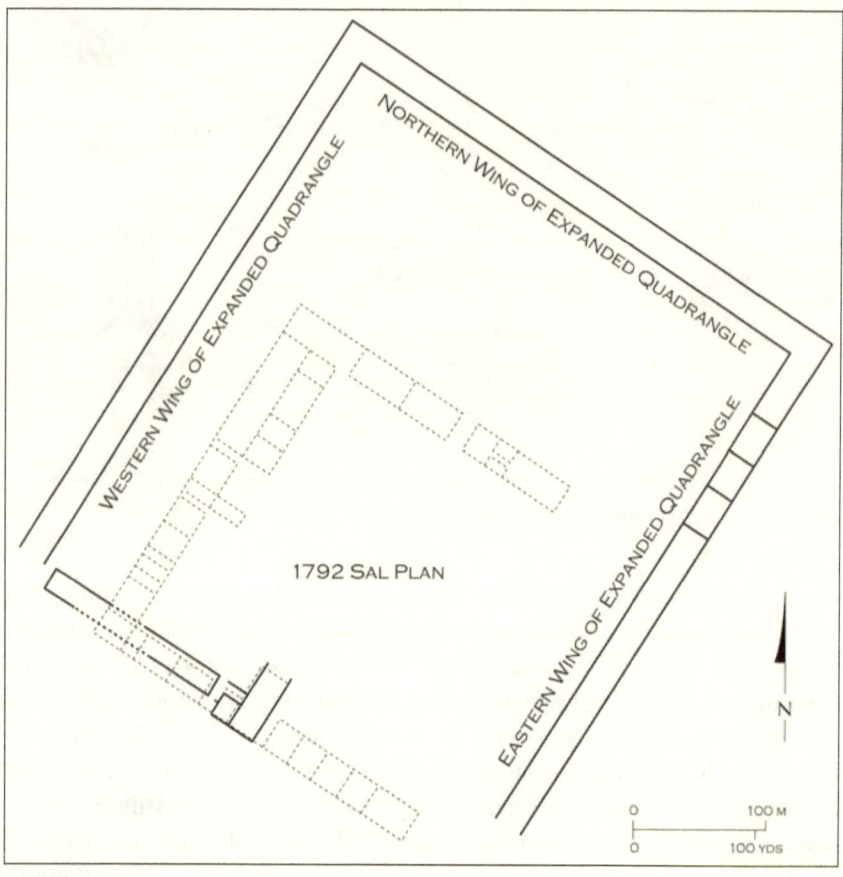

Figure 12.2.
Relative locations of the 1792 quadrangle and the expanded 1815 quadrangle.

Edwards 2000; URS Greiner Woodward Clyde 1999). This quadrangle was slightly larger than the first (116 × 120 varas [27 × 101 m]). Like the first quadrangle, it appears to have been only partially enclosed, and contained a mixture of adobe, stone, wattle-and-daub, and palisade buildings, with a gradual increase in the use of adobe. Additionally, the colonial settlers increasingly used *tejas* (clay roof tile) rather than thatch for roofing material. During the late 1790s, new architectural projects in the quadrangle were often organized by the military command, including the construction of a block of nine adobe apartments for military families and a communal barracks for unmarried men (Langellier and Rosen 1996:89).

In 1815, El Presidio de San Francisco began a massive construction project that replaced the second quadrangle with a greatly expanded third

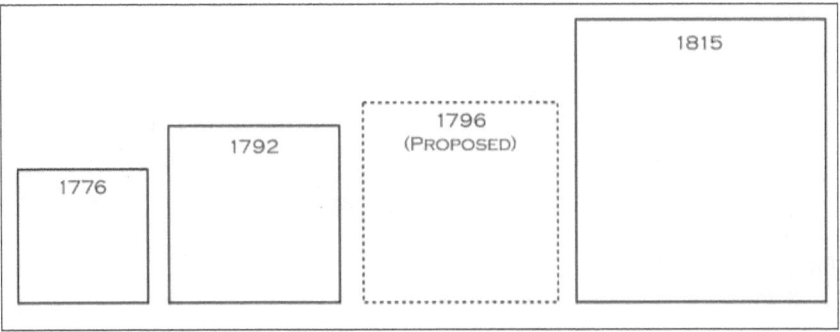

FIGURE 12.3.
Size-based comparison of El Presidio de San Francisco's quadrangles.

quadrangle, measuring 172 × 192 varas (144 × 161 m) (Figure 12.2). Our knowledge of this third quadrangle comes almost entirely from archaeological evidence (Ramsay and Voss 2002; Voss and Benté 1996; Voss et al. 2000). This construction signaled a turning point in architectural practices at the settlement. The west, north, and east wings of the quadrangle were continuous rows of adobe rooms constructed all-of-a-piece, using uniform materials and methods. (The remodeled south wing, which contained the settlement chapel and possibly the *comandancia* [headquarters], appears to have incorporated a mix of older and new buildings.) Each new wing consisted of two parallel adobe walls set 6 varas (5.0 m) apart, with the interior (plaza-facing) wall measuring about 1.3 varas (1.1 m) thick. The exterior wall was slightly thicker, about 1.5 varas (1.3 m). These load-bearing walls rested on stone foundations that had been set into U- or V-shaped trenches extending about 0.60 m below the historic grade and projecting 0.10–0.20 m above the same grade. The space formed by the two parallel adobe walls was subdivided by partition walls measuring 1 vara (0.84 m) thick. The partition walls created rooms of identical size measuring 6 varas (5.0 m) × 12 varas (10.1 m). The entire quadrangle was roofed with tejas. Both documentary and archaeological evidence indicate that this new quadrangle was under construction from 1815 to 1819.

The sequence of quadrangle construction at El Presidio de San Francisco highlights both continuity and change in colonial architectural practices at this remote frontier settlement. The general configuration of the quadrangle—a single row of structures lining the edges of a rectangular plaza—was particularly consistent. However, the footprint of the quadrangle expanded with each reconstruction (Figure 12.3), although the population of El Presidio de San Francisco remained remarkably constant, even declining

Barbara L. Voss

Table 12.1
Architectural trends at El Presidio de San Francisco

	Early Attributes	Later Attributes
Wall construction	Adobe, stone, palisade, wattle-and-daub	Adobe only
Roofing	Thatch	Clay tile
Building size and shape	Variable	Uniform
Organization	Household-level	Military command
Plaza	Smaller	Larger
Enclosure	No enclosure	Partially or fully enclosed

during the final expansion in the 1810s. Additionally, over time there was a gradual homogenization of architectural materials, techniques, and form (Table 12.1). Finally, architectural production shifted from being the responsibility of colonial households to being directed by the military command.

The architectural transformations described above have been interpreted primarily within the framework of Spanish-colonial military history. The 1790s, which saw the first centrally coordinated residential building projects and the growing use of adobe and clay tile, was a period of increased military concern about British, French, and Russian incursions into Spain's North American territories. In addition to new construction in El Presidio de San Francisco's quadrangle, two coastal batteries were built during this decade. The 1815 expansion of the quadrangle also coincided with a period of heightened international tension: the Russian American Company had expanded its fur hunting and mercantile operations south from Alaska into California's waters, and in 1812 established Colony Ross only 60 km north of El Presidio de San Francisco. In this light, the reconstruction of the quadrangle is often interpreted as a direct response to Russian territorial incursions.

The quadrangle has also been interpreted as a site of colonial social history. The majority of colonial settlers in the San Francisco Bay region lived in the quadrangle when not assigned to military expeditions or guard duty at nearby missions. Accordingly, interpretations of the quadrangle's architecture and associated archaeological deposits have focused on how these materials can illuminate colonial community life and identity formation (Voss 2008). This focus is congruent with the archaeological evidence: as of 2006, excavations in the quadrangle had yielded approximately 465,000 artifacts, but only ten of these are objects traditionally associated with Native Californian material culture. In contrast, Native Californian material culture is ubiquitous in deposits outside the quadrangle. Excavations of a colonial-era midden located north of the quadrangle and of three colonial-era residential deposits located in a valley west of the quadrangle have yielded rolled clay pipes; shell and fish vertebrae beads; flaked obsidian, chert, and glass tools and debitage; steatite groundstone; carved bird bone tubes; and bone awl tips. In addition, these extramural deposits contain dense pockets of shell, primarily *Macoma nasuta* (bent-nosed clam) and *Mytilus* sp. (mussel). These dietary by-products are common at late prehistoric and colonial-era Native Californian sites throughout the region, but they are not found in any meaningful quantities within the quadrangle itself. So both historic residential patterns and the archaeological record point to the quadrangle's association with the colonial population.

Given the archaeological evidence and residential patterns noted above, is it possible to reconsider El Presidio de San Francisco's quadrangle as a site of indigenous heritage? One approach might be to highlight the indigenous ancestry of the colonists themselves. In 1776, when El Presidio de San Francisco was founded, 12 percent of the colonial settlers were listed as *indios* (Indians) from Mexico and 31 percent as mestizos (people of mixed European and Native American ancestry). *Mulatos* (people of mixed heritage that included African ancestry), who accounted for 18 percent of the settler population, often had Mexican Indian as well as African ancestors. However, as I have documented elsewhere (Voss 2005, 2008), within a few decades the colonial settlers repudiated these racial categories in favor of a shared Californio identity. The degree to which the military settlers should be conceptualized as "indigenous" is thus a complicated question. They did not identify themselves as such and maintained firm legal and social distinctions from local Native Californians.

Another approach would be to interpret El Presidio de San Francisco's quadrangle as a hybrid European-American architectural form that emerged through centuries of indigenous–colonial interaction along the frontiers of Spanish settlement in the Americas (Moorhead 1975; Navarro Garcia 1964). In a recent review of archaeological studies of presidio sites throughout northern New Spain (presently, the U.S. Southwest and northwest Mexico), I found that the physical remains of presidio architecture revealed even greater variation and hybridization of architectural form than historic records had documented (Voss 2007). However, in San Francisco itself, there is little evidence that Native Californian architectural methods and forms were incorporated into the quadrangle's design. In fact, the architectural trends described above trace a movement away from construction techniques that were used in local Native Californian communities. So, while colonial demography and architectural history suggest that El Presidio de San Francisco was shaped by substantial interplay between European, Mexican Indian, and African populations and architectural traditions, these approaches fall short of illuminating Native Californian heritage.

A third approach would be to return to the vantage point of military history, but from an indigenous, rather than colonial, perspective. Presidios were frontier military institutions that were specifically established to secure newly colonized territory. When a region had been pacified, the presidios were usually converted to civilian pueblos—a process that occurred in San Francisco in 1835 with the establishment of the Pueblo of Yerba Buena and the concurrent transfer of most presidio troops to Sonoma. In this sense, presidio sites can be interpreted as an inverted trace of indigenous resistance: the establishment and movement of colonial military settlements trace the shifting contours of territories that were in contest between colonial and indigenous populations. At times, the relocation of presidios signaled indigenous success and colonial retreat, as in the 1772 reorganization of frontier defenses in northwest New Spain (Brinkerhoff and Faulk 1965). Additionally, documentary records from El Presidio de San Francisco provide further insights into the way that the quadrangle itself was an important site for these military contests: not only did colonial soldiers reside and train in the quadrangle, but Native Californian prisoners of war were held captive in a small jail and publically flogged in the quadrangle's plaza. Simultaneously, Indian auxiliary troops, recruited from missionized Native Californian populations, were trained and drilled in the plaza to prepare them to fight alongside colonial troops (Bancroft 1886a:175; Langellier and Rosen 1996:105–6, 128, 131; Milliken 1995; Phillips 1993:72).

In this respect, indigenous and colonial heritage are inseparable. El Presidio de San Francisco was never directly attacked by Native Californians; battles and skirmishes between colonial troops and Native Californian villages primarily occurred in missions and in California's inland Central Valley and mountain ranges. Yet daily life in the quadrangle must have included constant reminders of the routine violence that underpinned colonization. Colonial soldiers met violent deaths in combat; others returned home wounded and maimed. Every monthly troop roster included a list of invalid soldiers on temporary or permanent leave from active duty. Colonial residents witnessed corporal punishment of Native Californian prisoners of war and heard their cries from the jail where they were incarcerated.

These documentary sources are helpful in bringing indigenous heritage to the fore but provide few resources for forging a direct connection between indigenous history and colonial archaeological remains. A fourth approach, explored below, traces indigenous heritage through analysis of architectural production of colonial settlements. This methodology is drawn from Ruth Tringham's investigations of earthen architecture in Neolithic Central Europe and Anatolia. There, Tringham has analyzed earthen architectural remains to investigate how episodes and cycles of construction, repair, maintenance, remodeling, and demolition were intertwined with the production and reproduction of prehistoric social relationships (e.g., Tringham 1991, 1994; Tringham and Stevanovic 2000). This turns attention away from architectural form to architectural process. In other words, construction labor builds more than physical structures; it also builds social relations. The materiality of archaeological remains and the diachronic perspective afforded by the archaeological record provide a unique set of evidence that can be directly used to reconstruct the social relations of architectural production.

Colonial Buildings, Indigenous Labor

At El Presidio de San Francisco, architectural production of the quadrangle began to shift from the household to the military command in the 1790s. The documentary record leaves no question that with this shift, architectural production relied increasingly on centrally organized groups of indigenous laborers, predominantly adult men (Figure 12.4). Colonial documents, although sparse, suggest that recruitment and retention of these Native Californian laborers became more violent and coercive with the increasing centralization of architectural production. During the first decade of colonization, individual households hired Native Californian servants to assist with construction projects or other laborious tasks. In 1782, Commander José Joaquín Moraga issued a directive outlining procedures to be used to recruit Native Californian workers. Expressing concern about local indigenous uprisings, Moraga cautioned that "in no case are they to be brought in by force. Those who want to come are to be paid according to the work that they have done, so that they will return to their villages content" (Moraga, as quoted in Milliken 1995:75). That such a directive was necessary suggests that coercive and abusive labor relationships were already present, and indicates a general attitude that Native Californians should be compensated for their work.

This attitude appears to have continued into the early 1790s, when the military command first began directing large construction projects. Acting

Barbara L. Voss

FIGURE 12.4.
Detail of View of the Presidio of San Francisco, *by Louis Choris, 1816. Color engraving. Courtesy of the Bancroft Library, University of California, Berkeley.*

Commander Hermenegildo Sal and Sergeant Pedro Amador negotiated labor agreements between native villages in the southern San Francisco Bay region and El Presidio de San Francisco, in which villages were offered military protection, rations, and clothing in exchange for providing gangs of twenty to forty adult male laborers for periods of one to three months. However, these agreements were rarely fulfilled: fugitivism was rampant, with laborers rarely staying at El Presidio de San Francisco for more than a few days. Although Sal eventually offered to pay for travel time to and from San Francisco, and promised bonus gifts for tribal leaders who could provide laborers, wage labor agreements were not sufficient to recruit the increased labor force necessary to accomplish the proposed construction (Bancroft 1886a:614; Langellier and Rosen 1996:61, 70–71; Milliken 1995: 122–23, 150).

From the mid-1790s, El Presidio de San Francisco's commanders turned to captive labor from the missions and the battlefield. Mission laborers were provided through contracts between priests and presidio officers in which the military paid the Church for supplying baptized Native Californian workers. There are some indications that mission priests used labor assignments at the presidio as punishment "for stubbornness or other infractions against the padres" (Langellier and Rosen 1996:71).

Alongside mission laborers, El Presidio de San Francisco increasingly captured its own labor force in raids and battles with inland Native Californian villages. These military excursions were launched to recapture mission runaways, to suppress indigenous insurgent movements, and to punish villages that resisted missionization. In general, unbaptized Native Californian women and children captured during these battles were sent to a mission for Christian instruction, but Native Californian men were brought to the presidio for trial and sentence. Sentences included combinations of imprisonment, short rations, corporal punishment, and hard labor; upon completion of their sentence, captives were remanded to a nearby mission (Voss 2008:80–81).

In the 1780s and early 1790s, most captive laborers were individuals charged with specific crimes against the colonial order, with only two to ten captives being arrested in any given expedition. In the late 1790s, this pattern shifted to mass arrests in which captives were sentenced as a group. A 1797 battle with a fugitive community near Mission San José yielded four baptized and nine unbaptized captives (Milliken 1995:159–60). A subsequent raid on the Apalmes village resulted in the capture of "more or less" than fifty Native Californians (Mora-Torres 2005:35). Another 1804 punitive expedition brought thirty-two captives to El Presidio de San Francisco. In 1805, the presidio commander boasted to the Alta California governor that all construction activity at the settlement was being accomplished "by the labor of Indian captives without cost to the King" (Bancroft 1886b:127).

The archaeological evidence of the 1815 expansion of the quadrangle helps us understand, in concrete terms, exactly how much Native Californian labor was involved in these construction projects. Laying foundations for the west, north, and east wings required quarrying, transporting, and laying a minimum of 590 m^3 of serpentinite stone. Constructing the walls and roofs involved quarrying, mixing, and forming clay to produce no less than 2,800 m^3 of adobe brick and enough tejas to cover an area of over 4,800 m^2. In addition to these archaeologically recoverable materials, timber was harvested and prepared for roofing beams, supporting pillars, and door and window lintels. Applying historic descriptions of construction practices to the archaeologically determined dimensions of the expanded quadrangle indicates that approximately four thousand timber beams would have been required. Finishing the buildings required mud mortar and plaster for wall finishes and additional clay for packed earthen floors, materials that are not easily quantifiable with available data.

These archaeologically based quantities can be used in conjunction with historic accounts of labor productivity on other presidio construction projects (Schuetz-Miller 1994:45) to estimate the labor effort involved in the 1815 quadrangle. Using the most conservative assumptions, these calculations yield a total of fifty thousand person-days. If the workforce were consistent, there would have been a steady force of fifty-four Native Californian laborers present at the settlement during the four-year duration of the project. To put this in perspective, there were approximately only twenty colonial troops on active duty at El Presidio de San Francisco. Even considering the soldiers' wives and a few civilian employees, Native Californian workers likely outnumbered the entire adult colonial population of El Presidio de San Francisco during this period.

This labor force analysis shows that Native Californians were working at El Presidio de San Francisco in far greater numbers than historical sources alone would suggest. However, the documentary record does provide some indications that this workforce was neither stable nor constant. Commander Luis Antonio Argüello wrote in 1816 that construction work had halted because eighteen of the captive workers had escaped; in September of the same year, fourteen additional prisoners escaped and could not be recaptured. In 1819, it was recorded that the quadrangle could not be completed until sixteen new captives had been obtained, as the rest had fled the settlement (Bancroft 1886b:372; Langellier and Rosen 1996:131, 193). Thus while Native Californian resistance to this labor regime is not archaeologically visible, it is clear from these few accounts that the workers who constructed El Presidio de San Francisco's expanded quadrangle did not passively accept their situation.

This analysis of archaeological and documentary traces of Native Californian labor demonstrates that Native Californians were not only present in the presidio quadrangle but also that they were prominent "authors" of the archaeological site. The dependence of the colonists on captive Native Californian labor reveals the weak economic and demographic position of the Spanish-colonial project in California: earlier attempts at architectural self-sufficiency failed, and the initial practice of recruiting paid workers collapsed under indigenous dissatisfaction with wages and working conditions and administrative pressures to reduce costs. From the mid-1790s, violence and architectural production became tightly linked.

In this light, the 1815 expansion of El Presidio de San Francisco's quadrangle needs to be reexamined. I argue that this massive architectural undertaking was simultaneously a product of escalating colonial violence and a process through which such violence was enacted and naturalized.

The 1815 expansion of the quadrangle was not functionally necessary. It occurred during a period when El Presidio de San Francisco's colonial population was at best stable and possibly declining. Even when population pressure or changing standards of living led to new construction at other presidios in Alta California, the residential capacity of these settlements was increased not by tearing down existing buildings or enlarging the quadrangle but by constructing new structures in the plaza or adding extra rows of rooms along the quadrangle's exterior. As noted above, a common

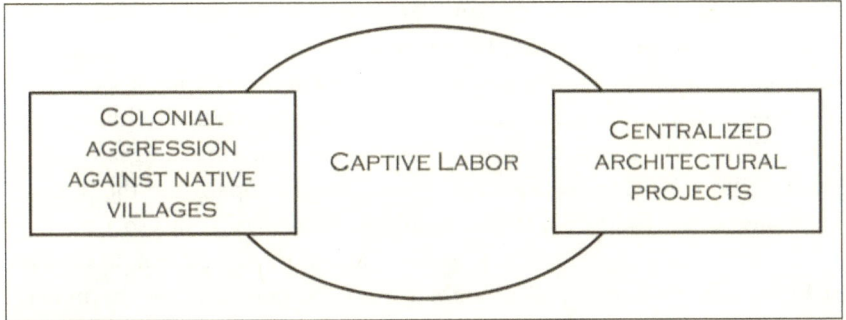

FIGURE 12.5.
Diagram of the recursive relationship between colonial military aggression and colonial architectural expansion.

interpretation of the 1815 reconstruction of San Francisco's quadrangle is that this was a military response to Russian territorial expansion in California. If so, this was a symbolic, not tactical, response: the expanded quadrangle does not appear to have had the defensive walls or bastions required of presidio settlements.

Without denying the importance of the quadrangle's changing architecture to El Presidio de San Francisco's colonial residents (Voss 2008:196–201), I want to suggest here that the architectural history of the quadrangle can be interpreted as a product of a recursive relationship between colonial military aggression and the social relations of architectural production (Figure 12.5). The appearance and intensification of centralized architectural production, including the homogenization of architectural materials and forms, is chronologically coincident with the intensification of military campaigns against inland Native Californian communities. Battles and raids produced prisoners of war who under colonial logic required punishment for their resistance to colonization. Centrally organized construction projects required laborers. With no substantial civilian colonial population, and the failure of the military command's earlier attempts to obtain Native Californian workers through contractual agreements with independent villages, the war captives provided a solution to this labor supply "problem." But once started, new construction projects gave added incentive to do battle to acquire new captives, especially given high rates of fugitivism. And the arrival of each convoy of new captives that were sentenced to punitive labor created a social "need" for such construction projects. I should be clear that I am not suggesting that this cycle was a deliberate outcome of colonial policies or that colonial settlers living at El Presidio de San Francisco were themselves aware of the relationship between battlefield violence and home-front architectural production. In the language of systems theory, we might describe this as a "positive feedback loop" in which each aspect of colonial practice reinforced the other. This cycle seems to have escalated over time, into the late 1810s, shortly before Mexico obtained independence from Spain and the political economy of Alta California began to shift to an agro-capitalist society.

I have already described how responsibility for architectural production at El Presidio de San Francisco shifted from the household to the military command, a shift that was only possible with the growing use of captive Native Californian labor. As a result, architectural production increasingly became a venue in which differences among men were materially enacted through a rigid chain of command. Presidio officers designed and directed architectural projects that were implemented by rank-and-file soldiers who supervised captive Native Californians. Through these labor projects, colonial men of all ranks experienced authority over Native Californians, not only in military conflict, where outcomes were uncertain, but also in the context of structured daily routines involving little risk to the colonists themselves. While materially transforming the place they called home, colonial officers and soldiers simultaneously consolidated their status in the social order and put Native Californians "in their place" as subordinate manual laborers.

With the end of Spanish-colonial rule and the rise of the Mexican-era ranching economy, many officers and soldiers became landowners and ranchers. As Silliman (2004) has powerfully documented, ranches in Mexican-era California were labor-intensive operations, with most commanding forty to one hundred Native Californian workers and some marshaling seasonal labor forces that may have numbered in the low thousands. One of the largest was Rancho Petaluma, which was owned by Mariano Vallejo, a former commander of El Presidio de San Francisco. While Silliman (2001b; 2004:24) has argued that ranch labor practices mirrored those used in Spanish-colonial missions, the history of architectural labor at El Presidio de San Francisco suggests that military labor regimes may have also been precedents that supported the later intensification of labor hierarchies between colonists and Native Californians during California's Mexican-era entry into the global capitalist trade system.

IMPLICATIONS: HERITAGE, MULTICULTURALISM, AND ETHICAL CLIENTS

My primary objective has been to trouble the conventional practice of interpreting the "core" of imperial settlements as places of colonial heritage. Clearly, El Presidio de San Francisco's quadrangle must also be understood as an indigenous heritage site as well as a colonial one. That a Spanish-colonial military fortification can be reconceptualized as an "indigenous" artifact illustrates that scholars interested in Native American experiences under colonization must be willing to consider "indigeneity without indigenisms" (Kurt Jordan, personal communication 2008; see also Sheptak et al., Chapter 8 and Wernke, Chapter 5). By tracing the history of production as well as the history of the use of buildings and artifacts, archaeologists may be able to identify connections between indigenous life and objects that are otherwise entirely "colonial" in material, technology, appearance, or use. Doing so upsets conventions that privilege design over craft and consumption over production. When the interconnectedness between these aspects of social life is made apparent, it becomes clear that archaeological sites such as El Presidio de San Francisco's quadrangle need to be understood as the product of power-laden social relationships among people who occupied different positions in colonial hierarchies.

Positing a relationship between labor and heritage complicates current archaeological interest in indigenous resistance and agency. Without question, Native Californians actively resisted Spanish imperial appropriation of their homelands and the colonizing institutions that were used to accomplish that project. Indeed, Native Californians were largely successful in confining colonial territorial control to a narrow strip of coastal lands. Escapism, sabotage, and active revolts challenged missionization programs (see Preucel, Chapter 11), and autonomous indigenous communities fought fiercely against colonial encroachments (Castillo 1989; Milliken 1995; Phillips 1993; see Liebmann, Chapter 10). However, those who resisted colonial rule often paid a high price—death or injury on the battlefield, and captivity and forced labor in colonial institutions.

The focus on labor used in this analysis emphasizes these power relations and challenges the trends toward multiculturalism in research and interpretation of colonial heritage sites. As an interpretive modality, multiculturalism celebrates the important contributions of the diverse cultures associated with a given historic site. But the Native Californian "contribution" to El Presidio de San Francisco's quadrangle was largely coerced and involuntary. For Native Californian war captives, the quadrangle was a place of confinement, punishment, suffering, and forced separation from family and community. Heritage management and public interpretation of Spanish-colonial sites often center on architectural preservation and reconstruction of colonial buildings. Even when the historic presence of Native Californians is acknowledged, their suffering is rarely discussed.

Considering labor as an aspect of heritage challenges us to rethink these management and heritage strategies.

Native Californian Heritage Practices at the Presidio of San Francisco

Today, the Spanish-colonial site of El Presidio de San Francisco is located within the Presidio of San Francisco National Historic Landmark (NHL), a 1,491-acre segment of the 75,500-acre Golden Gate National Recreation Area. At present, Native Californian heritage issues at the Presidio of San Francisco NHL are managed in contradictory and confusing ways.

The situation is complicated by three factors. First, the Ohlone, whose ancestral lands include the park, are not federally recognized. This is related to the profound disruption caused to their ancestral communities by Spanish colonization (Lightfoot 2005). Second, the Spanish-colonial use of war captives brought from inland areas means that indigenous heritage of the historic presidio is traced not only to the Ohlone, but also to Coast Miwok, Bay Miwok, Eastern Miwok, Pomo, Wappo, Patwin, and Yokuts.

Third, by act of Congress, the Presidio of San Francisco NHL is jointly managed by two distinct federal agencies: the Presidio Trust and the National Park Service (NPS). The NPS is the lead agency for 381 acres of coastal lands that border San Francisco Bay and the Pacific Ocean, while the Presidio Trust is the lead agency for 1,110 inland acres. Most known prehistoric archaeological sites are located within the coastal lands, and nearly all Spanish-colonial archaeological sites are located in the inland area administered primarily by the Presidio Trust. Some Presidio Trust staff have developed informal relationships with some Native Californians and have invited Native Californian involvement in some public interpretation and educational initiatives. However, the Presidio Trust as a federal agency has not conducted formal consultations with any Native Californian groups on the grounds that the Ohlone are not federally recognized and that other federally recognized tribes in the region do not have ancestral territory in the park. The result is that, at best, Ohlones and other Native Californians are considered to be "interested parties" with no special relationship to the historic-period cultural resources in the park. As part of its management of cultural resources throughout the Golden Gate National Recreation Area, the NPS conducts formal consultations with both federally recognized and non–federally recognized tribes throughout the San Francisco Bay region. This program includes an information-sharing program that alerts Native Californians about federal projects in the Golden

Gate National Recreation Area, including the Presidio of San Francisco NHL. However, this valuable service does not alter the legal status of Native Californians' heritage claims within the inland area administered by the Presidio Trust.

Present-day Native Californian communities, particularly Ohlones, began to make public heritage claims on the Presidio of San Francisco NHL beginning in the late 1980s, with the passage of the Base Realignment and Closure Act that selected the Presidio of San Francisco Army Post for closure and conversion into a national park. The earliest of these claims was a campaign led by the Muwekma Ohlone to claim the Presidio of San Francisco as tribal property under federal provisions that give tribal groups the "right of first refusal" to excess government property within their ancestral territory. The Muwekma Ohlone claim was never seriously considered by the Secretary of the Interior because they are not a federally recognized tribe. However, the land claim generated considerable media attention for several years (Field et al. 1992; Russell 2008; Sarkar 2001; Smith 1998) and raised public awareness of Ohlone history and of the presence of living Ohlone communities in the area. Over the past two decades, the Muwekma Ohlone have publically criticized many of the heritage policies and practices of both the NPS and the Presidio Trust.

Other Ohlones have partnered with the Presidio Trust and the NPS in public interpretation programs at the park. These efforts have included consulting on educational programs and native plants revegetation programs as well as designing exhibits and participating in public events and festivals. One prominent example of this is the relatively new Ohlone involvement in an annual event, Presidio Pasados, which commemorates the founding of El Presidio de San Francisco. Since at least the 1980s, Los Californianos, a pedigreed heritage organization of colonial descendants, has organized an anniversary event that reenacts Juan Bautista de Anza's historic arrival in San Francisco. In a ceremony at the site of El Presidio de San Francisco's quadrangle, descendants of the presidio's colonial population place red and yellow (Spain's national colors) carnations into a wreath as their ancestors' names are read.

In 2003, the NPS and the Presidio Trust developed "Presidio Pasados," a daylong cultural festival that coincides with the Los Californianos ceremony honoring the anniversary of the presidio's founding. Several Ohlone artists and educators participate in Presidio Pasados every year, demonstrating Native Californian arts such as basketry, tule house manufacture, and traditional singing. This festival is typical of the multicultural approach to heritage interpretation, in that the negative effects of colonization on local indigenous peoples are not explicitly discussed. However, Ohlone participation in Presidio Pasados has generated subtle changes in the rhetoric of the anniversary ceremony, which is now referred to as a commemoration, rather than a celebration, of San Francisco's colonization. Speakers, who often include local politicians as well as delegates from the Spanish and Mexican consulates, increasingly acknowledge that El Presidio de San Francisco was established on Ohlone territory.

Another key Ohlone heritage initiative was a photography exhibit, "Ohlone Portraits: Our Faces, Our Families, Our Stories," which was displayed at a visitor center in the NPS-managed coastal zone of the Presidio of San Francisco NHL. The exhibit was jointly organized and curated by NPS historian and American Indian liaison Paul Scolari, NPS outreach specialist Naomi Torres, and Ohlone artist and educator Linda Yamane. The installation paired life-size portraits of present-day Ohlone with historic photographs of their ancestral relatives. The photographs were accompanied by captions written by present-day Ohlone and traced the historical connections between themselves and their ancestors.

A key theme of this exhibit was the multigenerational persistence of Ohlone culture through Spanish colonization, the Mexican republic, the U.S. gold rush and annexation, and industrialization during the late nineteenth and twentieth centuries. The introductory panel to the exhibit read, "The individuals portrayed in this exhibit represent generations of Ohlone Indians from the late-19th and early-20th century period, survivors of successive waves of colonialism.... As evidenced by the testimony of their descendants, the legacy of these Ohlones touches us in the Bay Area today." The interpretive power of this exhibit comes from its quiet disruption of the master narratives that usually dominate the interpretation of colonial-era historic sites. By focusing on indigenous cultural continuity in a place that is usually interpreted as a site of European conquest and indigenous cultural disruption, the exhibit simultaneously traces the violence of colonization while foregrounding indigenous survival. The exhibit was so well received that it has since been installed at two other historic sites in San Francisco.

Whether through territorial claims or public interpretation, Ohlone heritage practices are slowly influencing both public perception and federal management of the Presidio of San Francisco NHL. However, Native Californian populations affected by colonization still have no direct input into the Presidio Trust's management or interpretation of Spanish-colonial archaeological sites. At best, they have been considered interested parties among many other public stakeholders who are allowed to comment on federal undertakings at the Presidio of San Francisco NHL.

From Interested Parties to Ethical Clients

Archaeologists and heritage site managers need to consider the special impacts that colonization continues to have on Native American communities when studying and interpreting Spanish-colonial military sites. My own thinking on this question has been inspired by the approach used by Michael Blakey and the Howard University team in their research on the African Burial Ground in New York City. Like El Presidio de San Francisco, the African Burial Ground is an urban archaeological site located on federal land. In 1989, the African Burial Ground was rediscovered during exploratory excavations for construction of a thirty-four-story government office building. Excavation of the African Burial Ground in preparation for building construction generated widespread public controversy and academic concern, ultimately leading to congressional actions that stopped further disturbance of the burial ground and provided for research and memorialization of New York's historic African and African American residents.

The Howard University team approached the African Burial Ground project through an "ethical epistemology" in which a plurality of perspectives is used to generate "useful and exciting paths of inquiry" and provide "elevated scrutiny of evidential proof" (Blakey 2008:21). A core element of this approach is the concept of the "ethical client": those populations to whom scholars should be accountable and who have a right to participate in research decisions, including the right to refuse research entirely (Blakey 2008:20).

The concept of the ethical client acknowledges that there are groups of people today—both direct living descendants and culturally affiliated groups—whose historiography puts them at risk for economic, social, and psychological harm. These communities "have an ethical right to be protected from harm resulting from the conduct of research" (Blakey 2008:20). While Blakey developed this concept to address the legacies of slavery in the contemporary United States, the legacies of Spanish colonization also continue to place certain communities at risk, both through the long-term effects of colonization and through the legal and social effects of scholarship about colonialism. In the case of San Francisco's Ohlone communities, the present-day effects of Spanish colonization are multitude, including complete loss of tribal lands and devastating historic population losses. Sometimes, the anthropology and historiography of the Ohlones have made a bad situation worse. For example, Alfred Kroeber's (1925) assertion that the Ohlones were "extinct" contributed to the legal disempowerment and termination of federal recognition of the tribe in

BARBARA L. VOSS

1927. Moreover, as Ohlone heritage practices at the Presidio of San Francisco attest, the relative invisibility of the Ohlones and public misperceptions of their history are a central concern to many Ohlones.

The focus on architectural labor presented in this chapter provides empirical grounds for considering the Ohlone and other Native Californian communities as ethical clients of archaeological research and public interpretation of the site of El Presidio de San Francisco. For the Ohlones, the first and direct impact of the founding of El Presidio de San Francisco was the forcible alienation of their lands by a foreign colonizing power. The troops housed at El Presidio de San Francisco provided the military muscle behind further appropriations of tribal lands and relocations of Native Californian populations to the missions. The use of captive Native Californian labor at El Presidio de San Francisco caused widespread disruptions to Native Californian society, not only among Ohlones but also among other tribal communities throughout central California. As noted above, these disruptions continue to have present-day effects on contemporary Native Californians who are struggling to establish their legal standing in the face of public amnesia about California's rich indigenous history.

Given the ways that anthropological scholarship has been used in the past to disenfranchise indigenous communities, it is particularly important to use caution in studying indigenous heritage at Spanish-colonial military settlements. In their work on the African Burial Ground, Blakey and his colleagues have particularly cautioned that the historiography of captive labor is rife with epistemological and ethical hazards. In Euro-American history, captive Africans and African Americans are often described as "slaves" who "are not recognizable as people. They become instead a category of labor...that are therefore not readily identified with as subjects of human rights abuses" (Blakey 2008:19). Captive laborers, Blakey notes, are complex human beings who are not defined by their captivity and who resist captivity psychologically, politically, and militarily (Blakey 2008:22). In turning attention to labor in investigating indigenous heritage at colonial sites, archaeologists must be cautious not to define captive laborers in the terms of their captivity. This is one of the reasons why it is particularly important to identify and involve ethical clients in all stages of archaeological research and interpretation.

In this vein, the importance of investigating resistance becomes even more important. Native Californians entangled with El Presidio de San Francisco resisted colonial rule along multiple registers and multiple time scales. It is, in fact, in the history of Native Californian resistance that we can clearly see the cultural continuity and persistence that has been made invisible by anthropological scholarship that prioritized static markers of cultural conservatism rather than the flexibility and innovations that were necessary to community survival in the face of colonization (Castillo 1989; Field et al. 1992; Yamane 2002). Today, heritage practices are central in fostering a counter-amnesia (Pearce 2005) to institutionalized denials of indigenous history. Analyzing Spanish-colonial architecture with respect to the labor relations that were deployed to produce colonial buildings provides one tangible, material link that can be used to establish a heritage relationship between contemporary indigenous populations and the physical remains of Spanish-colonial settlements.

Acknowledgments

My research at the Presidio of San Francisco NHL is conducted in partnership with the Presidio Trust and the NPS. This chapter presents my views as an independent researcher and does not represent the policies of either agency.

I would like to particularly thank the many Ohlones who have generously shared their perspectives on these issues with me throughout my research at the Presidio of San Francisco. Much of the archaeological data and documentary analyses discussed here were first presented in chapter 7 of *The Archaeology of Ethnogenesis: Race and Sexuality in Colonial San Francisco* (University of California Press, 2008), which analyzed El Presidio de San Francisco's architecture in relation to social identity changes in the colonial population. I am grateful to Matt Liebmann and Melissa Murphy for encouraging me to rethink these bodies of evidence from a very different vantage point, and to the participants of the SAR seminar, who all helped me situate this study within the broader context of indigenous heritage throughout the Spanish Americas. Kurt Jordan and his students in the fall 2008 "Political Economy in Archaeology" seminar at Cornell University offered valuable feedback on an earlier version of this chapter. Paul Scolari provided key information about the history of heritage events and exhibits at the Presidio of San Francisco. Figures 12.2, 12.3, and 12.5 were drafted by Landis Bennett and Kat Bennett of 360 Geographics.

Note

1. A *vara* is a Spanish unit of measurement generally equivalent to the British yard. Its precise length varied in different regions. In Alta California, a vara measured 33 in. or 0.84 m.

References

Abercrombie, Thomas A.
1998   Pathways of Memory and Power. Madison: University of Wisconsin Press.

Abu-Lughod, Lila
1990   The Romance of Resistance: Tracing Transformations of Power through Bedouin Women. American Ethnologist 17(1):41–55.

Altamirano, Alfredo José, Edinilsa Ramos de Souza, and Marlie de Albuquerque Navarro
2006   Political Violence in the Inca Empire: Skeletal Data from the 15th–16th Century in the Rimac Valley, Peru. Paleopathology Newsletter, June(134):27–28.

Altman, Ida
2007   The Revolt of Enriquillo and the Historiography of Early Spanish America. Americas 63:587–614.

Anderson, H. Allen
1985   The Encomienda in New Mexico, 1598–1680. New Mexico Historical Review 60(4):353–77.

Andrushko, Valerie
2007   The Bioarchaeology of Inca Imperialism in the Heartland: An Analysis of Prehistoric Burials from the Cuzco Region of Peru. PhD dissertation, Department of Anthropology, University of California, Santa Barbara.

Appadurai, Arjun, ed.
1986   The Social Life of Things: Commodities in Cultural Perspective. Cambridge: Cambridge University Press.

Archive of the Archbishopric of Lima (AAL)
        IV-18 (II-20)
1656   Causa seguida contra varios indios de Cajamarquilla por idolatras y hechiceros. 30 folios.

References

VI-10 (II-32)
1656 Causa hecha contra los camachicos del pueblo de Santo Domingo de Guangri de Pariac, por auer sacado los cuerpos cristianos de la iglesia y ileuado a los machayes y otras idolatrias. 24 folios.

Archive of the Convent of Saint Francis, Lima (AFSL), registro 15, parte 5
1585 Parecer acerca de las doctrinas de los Collaguas. 6 folios.

Arranz Marquéz, Luis
1991 Repartimiento y encomienda en la isla Española. Santo Domingo: Fundación García Arévalo.

Arriaga, Pablo Joseph de
1920[1621] La extirpación de la idolatría en el Perú. Coleccion de libros y documentos referentes a la historia del Perú. Lima: Imprenta y Librería Sanmartí y Cia.

Arrom, Juan José, and Manuel García Arévalo
1986 Cimarrón. Santo Domingo: Fundación García Arévalo.

Ashmore, Wendy, Edward M. Schortman, Patricia A. Urban, Julie C. Benyo, John M. Weeks, and S. M. Smith
1987 Ancient Society in Santa Barbara, Honduras. National Geographic Research 3:232–54.

Baart, Jan M.
1992 *Terra Sigillata* from Estremoz, Portugal. *In* Everyday and Exotic Pottery from Europe, c. 650–1900. Studies in Honour of John G. Hurst. D. Gaimster and M. Redknap, eds. Pp. 273–78. Oxford: Oxbow Books.

Bailey, G. A., and R. G. Bailey
1986 A History of the Navajos: The Reservation Years. Santa Fe: School of American Research Press.

Bancroft, Hubert Howe
1886a History of California, vol. I: 1542–1800. The Works of Hubert Howe Bancroft, vol. XVIII. Santa Barbara: Wallace Hebberd.
1886b History of California, vol. II: 1801–1824. The Works of Hubert Howe Bancroft, vol. XIX. Santa Barbara: Wallace Hebberd.

Bandelier, Adolph F.
1892 Final Report of Investigations among the Indians of the Southwestern United States, Carried on Mainly in the Years from 1880–1885. Part II. Papers of the Archaeological Institute of America, American Series, IV. Cambridge, MA: Cambridge University Press.

Bandera, Juan de la
1990a Proceedings for the Account Which Captain Juan Pardo Gave of the Entrance Which He Made into the Land of the Floridas. Paul Hoffman, trans. *In* The Juan Pardo Expeditions: Explorations of the Carolinas and Tennessee, 1566–1568, by Charles Hudson. Washington, D.C.: Smithsonian Institution Press.

References

1990b   Relation. Paul Hoffman, trans. *In* The Juan Pardo Expeditions: Explorations of the Carolinas and Tennessee, 1566–1568, by Charles Hudson. Washington, D.C.: Smithsonian Institution Press.

Bannon, John Francis
1970   The Spanish Borderlands Frontier, 1513–1821. New York: Holt, Rinehart, and Winston.

Barlow, Robert
1951   El códice de los alfareros de Cuauhtitlán. Revista mexicana de estudios antropológicos 12:5–13.

Barnett, Franklin
1973   San Ysidro Pueblos: Two Prehistoric Pueblo IV Indian Ruins in New Mexico. Albuquerque: Albuquerque Archaeological Society.

Beck, Robin A. Jr.
1997   From Joara to Chiaha: Spanish Exploration of the Appalachian Summit Area, 1540–1568. Southeastern Archaeology 16(2):162–68.

Beck, Robin A. Jr., Douglas J. Bolender, James A. Brown, and Timothy K. Earle
2007   Eventful Archaeology: The Place of Space in Structural Transformation. Current Anthropology 48(6):833–60.

Beck, Robin A. Jr., and David G. Moore
2002   The Burke Phase: A Mississippian Frontier in the North Carolina Foothills. Southeastern Archaeology 21(2):192–205.

Beck, Robin A. Jr., David G. Moore, and Christopher B. Rodning
2006   Identifying Fort San Juan: A 16th-Century Spanish Occupation at the Berry Site, North Carolina. Southeastern Archaeology 25(1):65–77.

Beecher, Catherine
1841   A Treatise on Domestic Economy, for the Use of Young Ladies at Home. Boston: Source Book Press.

Benito, José Antonio
2006   Libro de visitas de Santo Toribio Mogrovejo (1593–1605). Lima: Fondo Editorial Pontificia Universidad Católica del Perú.

Benyo, Julie C., and Thomas L. Melchionne
1987   Settlement Patterns in the Tencoa Valley, Honduras: An Application of the Co-Evolutionary Systems Model. *In* Interaction on the Southeast Mesoamerican Frontier, part 1. E. J. Robinson, ed. Pp. 49–64. Oxford: BAR International Series, 327 (i).

Berkhofer, Robert F. Jr.
1978   The White Man's Indian: Images of the American Indian from Columbus to the Present. New York: Alfred A. Knopf.

Berryman, Hugh, and Susan Haun
1996   Applying Forensic Techniues to Interpret Cranial Fracture Patterns in an Archaeological Specimen. International Journal of Osteoarchaeology 6:2–9.

References

Berryman, Hugh, and Steven Symes
1998   Recognizing Gunshot and Blunt Cranial Trauma through Fracture Interpretation. *In* Forensic Osteology. K. Reichs, ed. Pp. 333–52. Springfield: Charles Thomas.

Bhabha, Homi K.
1994   The Location of Culture. New York: Routledge.

Bird, Junius B., John Hyslop, and Milica D. Skinner
1985   The Preceramic Excavations at the Huaca Prieta Chicama Valley, Peru. Anthropological Papers of the American Museum of Natural History, 62, part 1. New York: American Museum of Natural History.

Black, Nancy Johnson
1995   The Frontier Mission and Social Transformation in Western Honduras: The Order of Our Lady of Mercy, 1525–1773. Leiden: E. J. Brill.
1997   The Mercedarians and Missionization of the Lenca in Santa Barbara de Tencoa, Honduras. *In* Approaches to the Historical Archaeology of Mexico, Central and South America. J. Gasco, G. Smith and P. Fournier-Garcia, eds. Pp. 83–89. Los Angeles: Institute of Archaeology, UCLA.

Blaisdell-Sloan, Kira
2006   The *pueblo de indios* of Ticamaya, Honduras. PhD dissertation, Department of Anthropology, University of California, Berkeley. Ann Arbor: University Microfilms.

Blaisdell-Sloan, Kira, and Russell Sheptak
2008   Casta, Sexuality, and Reproduction: Negotiating Mixed Race Identity in 18th Century Honduras. Paper presented at the World Archaeological Congress, Dublin.

Blakey, Michael L.
2008   An Ethical Epistemology of Publicly Engaged Biocultural Research. *In* Evaluating Multiple Narratives: Beyond Colonialist, Imperialist Archaeologies. Junko Habu, Clare Fawcett, and John M. Matsunaga, eds. Pp. 17–28. New York: Springer.

Blind, Heather, and Kevin Bartoy
2006   Archaeological Investigations of the Mesa Room, Building 50 of the Officers' Club, El Presidio de San Francisco, San Francisco, California. Berkeley: Pacific Legacy Inc., submitted to the Presidio Trust, San Francisco.

Bloom, Lansing B., and Lynn Mitchell
1938   The Chapter Elections in 1672. New Mexico Historical Review 13:85–119.

Bolland, O. Nigel
1977   The Maya and the Colonization of Belize in the Nineteenth Century. *In* Archaeology and History in the Yucatán. G. D. Jones, ed. Austin: University of Texas Press.

1988   Colonialism and Resistance in Belize: Essays in Historical Sociology. Belize City: Cubola.

Bolton, Herbert E.
1921   The Spanish Borderlands. New Haven: Yale University Press.

Borah, Woodrow
1983   Justice by Insurance: The General Indian Court of Colonial Mexico and the Legal Aides of the Half-Real. Berkeley: University of California Press.

Borgstede, Greg, and Jason Yaeger
2008   Notions of Cultural Continuity and Disjunction in Maya Social Movements and Maya Archaeology. In Archaeology and the Postcolonial Critique. Matthew Liebmann and Uzma Z. Rizvi, eds. Pp. 91–107. Walnut Creek: AltaMira Press.

Bourdieu, Pierre
1977   Outline of a Theory of Practice. R. Nice, trans. Cambridge: Cambridge University Press.

Boyd-Bowman, Peter
1972   Two Country Stores in XVIIth Century Mexico. The Americas 18(3):237–51.

Boylston, Althea
2000   Evidence for Weapon-Related Trauma in British Archaeological Samples. In Human Osteology in Archaeology and Forensic Science. M. Cox and S. Mays, eds. Pp. 357–80. Cambridge: Cambridge University Press.

Bray, Tamara
2003   Inca Pottery as Culinary Equipment: Food, Feasting, and Gender in Imperial State Design. Latin American Antiquity 14(1):1–22.

Brezine, Carrie
2008   Preliminary Report on the Textiles from the Colonial Site of El Brujo, Summer 2008. Document on file at the Peabody Museum of Archaeology and Ethnology, Harvard University, Cambridge.

Bricker, Victoria R.
1981   The Indian Christ, The Indian King: The Historical Substrate of Maya Myth and Ritual. Austin: University of Texas Press.

Brickley, Megan
2006   Rib Fractures in the Archaeological Record: A Useful Source of Sociocultural Information? International Journal of Osteoarchaeology 16:61–75.

Brinkerhoff, Sidney B., and Odie B. Faulk
1965   Lancers for the King: A Study of the Frontier Military System of Northern New Spain, with a Translation of the Royal Regulations of 1772. Phoenix: Arizona Historical Foundation.

Brown, Michael
1996   Resisting Resistance. American Anthropologist 98(4):729–35.

References

Brown, R. B., Patricia Fournier, John A. Peterson, David V. Hill, and Mark Willis
2004   Settlement and Ceramics in Northern New Spain: A Case Study of Brownware Pottery and Historical Change. *In* Surveying the Archaeology of Northwest Mexico. G. Newell and E. Gallaga, eds. Pp. 265–88. Salt Lake City: University of Utah Press.

Brugge, David M.
1963   Navajo Pottery and Ethnohistory. Navajoland Publication Series, 2. Window Rock: Navajo Tribal Museum.
1985   Navajos in the Catholic Church Records of New Mexico, 1694–1875. Tsaile: Navajo Community College Press.
1986   Tsegai: An Archaeological Ethnohistory of the Chaco Region. Washington, D.C.: U.S. Department of the Interior, National Park Service.
1996   Navajo Archaeology: A Promising Past. *In* The Archaeology of Navajo Origins. Ronald H. Towner, ed. Pp. 255–74. Salt Lake City: University of Utah Press.

Burkhart, Louise M.
1998   Pious Performances: Christian Pageantry and Native Identity in Early Colonial Mexico. *In* Native Traditions in the Postconquest World. Elizabeth H. Boone and Tom Cummins, eds. Pp. 361–81. Washington, D.C.: Dumbarton Oaks.

Bushnell, Amy
1978   "That Demonic Game": The Campaign to Stop Indian Pelota Playing in Spanish Florida, 1675–1684. Americas 35(1):1–19.
1979   Patricio de Hinachuba: Defender of the Word of God, the Crown of the King and the Little Children of Ivitachuco. American Indian Cultural Research Journal 3(3):1–21.
1989   Ruling the "Republic of Indians" in Seventeenth Century Florida. *In* Powhatan's Mantle: Indians in the Colonial Southeast. Peter Wood, Gregory Waselkov, and M. Thomas Hatley, eds. Pp. 134–50. Lincoln: University of Nebraska Press.
1994   Situado and Sabana: Spain's Support System for the Presidio and Mission Provinces of Florida. New York: American Museum of Natural History, Anthropological Papers, 74.
1996   Republic of Spaniards, Republic of Indians. *In* The New History of Florida. M. Gannon, ed. Pp. 62–77. Gainesville: University Press of Florida.

Caiger, Stephen L.
1951   British Honduras, Past and Present. London: Allen and Unwin.

Cal, Angel E.
1991   Rural Society and Economic Development: British Mercantile Capital in 19th-Century Belize. PhD dissertation, Department of Anthropology, University of Arizona. Ann Arbor: University Microfilms.

References

Cameron, Catherine M.
1999 Room Size, Organization of Construction, and Archaeological Interpretation in the Puebloan Southwest. Journal of Anthropological Archaeology 18:201–39.

Cañizares-Esguerra, Jorge
2005 Racial, Religious, and Civic Creole Identity in Colonial Spanish America. American Literary History 17(3):420–37.

Carlson, Roy
1965 Eighteenth Century Navajo Fortresses of the Gobernador District. Boulder: University of Colorado Museum Series in Anthropology, 10.

Casanovas, María Antonia
2001 En torno a la mesa. Tres siglos de formas y objetos en los palacios y monasterios reales. CeramicAntica 3:32–47.

Castañeda M., Juan
2006 Etnohistória de Magdalena de Cao, informe de investigación. Document on file at the Peabody Museum of Archaeology and Ethnology, Harvard University, Cambridge, MA.
2007 Eventos de historia ambiertal en el valle de Chicama, siglos XVI–XIX. Document on file at the Peabody Museum of Archaeology and Ethnology, Harvard University, Cambridge, MA.

Castillo, Edward D.
1989 The Native Response to the Colonization of Alta California. *In* Columbian Consequences: Archaeological and Historical Perspectives on the Spanish-Colonial Borderlands West, vol. 1. D. H. Thomas, ed. Pp. 377–93. Washington, D.C.: Smithsonian Institution Press.

Cervantes de Salazar, Francisco
2000[1560] México en 1554 y Túmulo Imperial. México: Porrúa.

Chamberlain, Richard S.
1953 The Conquest and Colonization of Honduras, 1502–1550. Washington, D.C.: Carnegie Institution of Washington.

Charlton, Thomas H.
1995 Patterns of Continuity and Change in the Aztec Ceramic Complex after the Conquest: Urban, Rural and Ethnic Contrasts. Paper presented at the 28th Annual Meeting of the Society for Historical Archaeology, Washington, D.C.
1996 Early Colonial Period Ceramics: Decorated Red Ware and Orange Ware Types of the Rural Otumba Aztec Ceramic Complex. *In* Arqueología Mesoamericana, Homenaje a William T. Sanders, vol. 1. A. G. Mastache, J. R. Parsons, R. S. Santley, and M. C. Serra Puche, eds. Pp. 461–79. México: Instituto Nacional de Antropología e Historia.

References

Charlton, Thomas H., Patricia Fournier, and Juan Cervantes
1995   La cerámica del período Colonial Temprano en Tlatelolco: El caso de la loza roja bruñida. *In* Presencias y encuentros, Investigaciones arqueológicas de Salvamento. Pp. 135–55. México: Dirección de Salvamento Arqueológico del Instituto Nacional de Antropología e Historia.

Charlton, Thomas H., Patricia Fournier, and Cynthia Otis Charlton
2007   La cerámica del periodo Colonial Temprano en la cuenca de México: Permanencia y cambio. *In* La producción alfarera en el México antiguo, vol. 5. B. L. Merino and A. García Cook, eds. Pp. 429–96. México: Instituto Nacional de Antropología e Historia.

Charlton, Thomas H., Hector Neff, Deborah L. Nichols, Cynthia Otis Charlton, and Michael D. Glascock
1999   Household, City State, and Regional Production, Distribution, and Consumption. Paper presented at the 64th Annual Meeting of the Society for American Archaeology, Chicago.

Charlton, Thomas H., and Cynthia L. Otis Charlton
1998   Continuidad y cambio después de la conquista: Hallazgos recientes en la ciudad-estado azteca de Otumba, Estado de México. *In* Primer Congreso Nacional de Arqueología Histórica. Memoria. E. Fernández y and S. Gómez, coords. Pp. 458–67. México: Instituto Nacional de Antropología e Historia.

Chaterjee, Partha
1993   The Nation and Its Fragments: Colonial and Postcolonial Histories. Princeton: Princeton University Press.

Cheek, Charles D.
1997   Setting an English Table: Black Carib Archaeology on the Caribbean Coast of Honduras. *In* Approaches to the Historical Archaeology of Mexico, Central & South America. Janine Gasco, Greg C. Smith, and Patricia Fournier-García, eds. Pp. 101–9. Monograph 38. Los Angeles: Institute of Archaeology, UCLA.

Church, Minette C.
2007   Introduction. *In* Colorado Historical Archaeology Context. Denver: Colorado Council of Professional Archaeologists.

Church, Minette C., Jason Yaeger, and Richard M. Leventhal
2001   Foodways and Firearms: The Archaeology of Maya Caste War Refugees. Paper presented at the 34th Annual Meeting of the Society for Historical Archaeology, Long Beach, CA.

Clark, Bonnie J.
2005   Lived Ethnicity: Archaeology and Identity in Mexicano America. World Archaeology 37(3):440–52.

Clegern, Wayne M.
1962   British Honduras and the Pacification of Yucatan. The Americas 18:243–55.

References

Clendinnen, Inga
1987 Ambivalent Conquests. Maya and Spaniard in Yucatan, 1517–1570. Cambridge: Cambridge University Press.
2003 Ambivalent Conquests: Maya and Spaniard in Yucatan, 1517–1570. 2nd edition. Cambridge: Cambridge University Press.

Cieza de León, Pedro
1985[1553] Crónica de Perú. Segunda Parte. F. Cantu, ed. Lima: Pontificia Universidad Católica del Perú and Academia Nacional de la Historia.

Coben, Lawrence S.
2006 Other Cuzcos: Replicated Theaters of Inka Power. *In* Archaeology of Performance: Theaters of Power, Community, and Politics. Takeshi Inomata and Lawrence S. Coben, eds. Pp. 223–60. Berkeley: AltaMira Press.

Cobo, Bernabé
1979[1653] History of the Inca Empire. An Account of the Indians' Customs and Their Origin Together with a Treatise on Inca Legends, History and Social Institutions. Austin: University of Texas Press.
1990[1653] Inca Religion and Customs. R. Hamilton, trans. Austin: University of Texas Press.

Cock, Guillermo A.
2006 Proyecto de recuperación de contextos funerarios en el Cementerio 57AS03–Zona Arqueológica Puruchuco-Huaquerones. Lima: Emape S. A./ConsultPatCu EIRL. MS on file, Instituto Nacional de Cultura.

Cock, Guillermo A., and C. Elena Goycochea
2004 Puruchuco y el cementerio Inca de la quebrada de Huaquerones. *In* Puruchuco y la sociedad de Lima: Un homenaje a Arturo Jiménez Borj. L. F. Villacorta Ostolaza, L. Vetter Parodi, and C. Ausejo Castillo, eds. Pp. 179–97. Lima: Concytec.

Cohen, J. M.
1969 The Four Voyages of Christopher Columbus. London: Penguin Books.

Cook, Noble David
1982 The People of the Colca Valley: A Population Study. Boulder: Westview Press.
1998 Born to Die: Disease and New World Conquest, 1492–1650. Cambridge: Cambridge University Press.
2002 "Tomando Posesión": Luis Gerónimo de Oré y el retorno de los franciscanos a las doctrinas del valle del Colca. *In* El hombre y los Andes: Homenaje a Franklin Pease G.Y., vol. 2. Javier Flores Espinoza and Rafael Varón Gabai, eds. Pp. 889–903. Lima: Pontificia Universidad Católica del Perú.
2007 People of the Volcano: Andean Counterpoint in the Colca Valley of Peru. Durham, NC: Duke University Press.

References

Cordell, Linda S.
1998   Before Pecos: Settlement Aggregation at Rowe, New Mexico. Maxwell Museum of Anthropology Anthropologica Papers, 6. Albuquerque: University of New Mexico Press.

Creamer, Winifred, with Catherine M. Cameron and John D. Beal
1993   The Architecture of Arroyo Hondo Pueblo, New Mexico. Arroyo Hondo Archaeological Series 7. Santa Fe: School of American Research Press.

Cummins, Tom
2002   Forms of Andean Colonial Towns, Free Will, and Marriage. *In* The Archaeology of Colonialism. Claire L. Lyons and John K. Papadopoulos, eds. Pp. 199–240. Los Angeles: Getty Research Institute.

D'Altroy, Terence
2005a   The Incas. Malden, MA: Blackwell Publishers.
2005b   Remaking the Social Landscape: Colonization in the Inka Empire. *In* Archaeology of Colonial Encounters. G. Stein ed. Pp. 263–96. Santa Fe: School of Advanced Research Press.

Deagan, Kathleen
1983   Spanish St. Augustine: The Archaeology of a Colonial Creole Community. New York: Academic Press.
1987   Columbus's Lost Colony. National Geographic, November: 672–76.
2004   Reconsidering Taíno Social Dynamics after Spanish Conquest: Gender and Class in Culture Contact Studies. American Antiquity 69(4):597–626.
2007   Eliciting Contraband through Archaeology: Illicit Trade in Eighteenth-Century St. Augustine. Historical Archaeology 41(4):96–114.
2008   Thirty Years of Archaeology at the Fountain of Youth Park, St. Augustine, 8SJ31. Final Report to the Florida Department of State, Special Category Grant Project No. SC 616 (493 pp.). Gainesville: Florida Museum of Natural History Miscellaneous Project Reports in Archaeology, 59.

Deagan, Kathleen, and José M. Cruxent
2002   Columbus's Outpost among the Taínos: Spain and America at La Isabela, 1493–1498. New Haven: Yale University Press.

Deagan, Kathleen, and Darcie MacMahon
1995   Fort Mose: Colonial America's Black Fortress of Freedom. Gainesville: University Press of Florida/Florida Museum of Natural History.

de Certeau, Michel
1984   The Practice of Everyday Life. Steven Rendail, trans. Berkeley: University of California Press.

deFrance, Susan D.
2003   Diet and Provisioning in the High Andes: A Spanish Colonial Settlement on the Outskirts of Potosí, Bolivia. International Journal of Historical Archaeology 7(2):99–125.

Deive, Carlos
1989   Los guerrilleros negros. Esclavos fugitives y cimarrones en Santo Domingo. Santo Domingo: Fundación Cultural Dominicana.

Del Busto Duthurburu, Jose Antonio
1966   Francisco Pizarro. El Marques Gobernador. Madrid: Ediciones RIALP, S.A.
1978   Historia general del Peru. Descubrimiento y conquista. Lima: Librería Studium.

De Marco, Barbara
2000   Voices from the Archives, Part 1: Testimony of the Pueblo Indians in the 1680 Pueblo Revolt. Romance Philology 53:375–448.

DeMarrais, Elizabeth, Timothy K. Earle, and Luis Jaime Castillo
1996   Ideology, Materialization, and Power Strategies. Current Anthropology 37(1):15–31.

DeMarrais, Elizabeth, Chris Gosden, and Colin Renfrew, eds.
2004   Rethinking Materiality: The Engagement of Mind with the Material World. Cambridge: McDonald Institute for Archaeological Research.

DePratter, Chester B.
1994   The Chiefdom of Cofitachequi. *In* The Forgotten Centuries: Indians and Europeans in the American South, 1521–1704. Charles Hudson and Carmen Chaves Tesser, eds. Pp. 197–226. Athens: University of Georgia Press.

DePratter, Chester B., Charles Hudson, and Marvin T. Smith
1983   Juan Pardo's Explorations in the Interior Southeast, 1566–1568. The Florida Historical Quarterly 62:125–58.

Dias Diogo, A. M., and Laura Trindade
2002   Cerâmicas de barro vermelho, encontradas em entulhos do terramoto de 1531, na intervenção arqueológica da Rua dos Correeiros, Lisboa. Revista Portuguesa de Arqueologia 3(2):201–35.

Dillehay, Tom D.
2007   Monuments, Empires, and Resistance: The Araucanian Polity and Ritual Narratives. Cambridge: Cambridge University Press.

DiMaio, Vincent
1999   Gunshot wounds. Boca Raton, FL: CRC Press.

Dittert, Alfred E. Jr.
1958   Preliminary Archaeological Investigations in the Navajo Project Area of Northwestern New Mexico. Museum of New Mexico Papers in Anthropology, 1; Navajo Project Studies, 1. Santa Fe: Museum of New Mexico and School of American Research.

Dobyns, Henry
1983   Their Numbers Become Thinned: Native American Population Dynamics in Eastern North America. Knoxville: University of Tennessee Press.

References

Dodge, William A.
1982   Archaeological Investigations at Jemez Pueblo, New Mexico: The Monitoring of Indian Health Service Waterline Trenches. Albuquerque: University of New Mexico, Office of Contract Archaeology.

Dornan, Jennifer Lynn
2004   "Even by night we only become aware they are killing us": Agency, Identity, and Intentionality at San Pedro Belize (1857–1930). PhD dissertation, Department of Anthropology, University of California, Berkeley. Ann Arbor: University Microfilms.

Douglas, Mary
1966   Purity and Danger: An Analysis of Concepts of Pollution and Taboo. London: Routledge and Kegan Paul.

Doutriaux, Miriam
2002   Relaciones étnicas y económicas de poder: La conquista incaica en el valle del Colca, Arequipa. Boletín de arqueología PUCP 6:411–32.
2004   Imperial Conquest in a Multiethnic Setting: The Inka Occupation of the Colca Valley, Peru. PhD dissertation, Department of Anthropology, University of California, Berkeley. Ann Arbor: University Microfilms.

Doyle, Mary
1988   The Ancestor Cult and Burial Ritual in Seventeenth and Eighteenth Century Central Peru. PhD dissertation, Department of Anthropology, University of California, Los Angeles. Ann Arbor: University Microfilms.

Drake, James David
2004   Appropriating a Continent: Geographical Categories, Scientific Metaphors, and the Construction of Nationalism in British North America and Mexico. Journal of World History 15(3):323–57.

Dumond, Don E.
1977   Independent Maya of the Late 19th Century: Chiefdoms and Power Politics. *In* Anthropology and History in the Yucatán. G. D. Jones, ed. Austin: University of Texas Press.
1997   The Machete and the Cross: Campesino Rebellion in Yucatan. Lincoln: University of Nebraska Press.

Durán, Fray Diego de
1967[1581]   Historia de las Indias de Nueva España e islas de la Tierra Firme. 3 vols. México: Porrúa.

Durston, Alan
1999   El proceso reduccional en el sur andino: confrontación y síntesis de sistemas espaciales. Revista de Historia Indigena 4:75–101.
2004   Pastoral Quechua: The History of Christian Translation in Peru, 1550–1650. PhD dissertation, Department of Anthropology, University of Chicago. Ann Arbor: University Microfilms.

2007 Pastoral Quechua: The History of Christian Translation in Colonial Peru, 1550–1650. Notre Dame, IN: University of Notre Dame Press.

Duviols, Pierre
1986 Cultural andina y represion. Procesos y visitas de isolatrías y hechicerías Cajatambo, siglo XVII. Cuzco: Archivos de Historia Andina, Centro de Estudios Rurales Andinos Bartolomé de Las Casas.
2002 Procesos y visitas de idolatrías. Cajatambo, siglo XVII. Lima: Pontificia Universidad Católica del Perú.

Earle, Timothy
1994 Wealth Finance in the Inca Empire: Evidence from the Calchaqui Valley, Argentina. American Antiquity 59(3):443–60.

Edgerton, Samuel Y., and Jorge Pérez de Lara
2001 Theaters of Conversion: Religious Architecture and Indian Artisans in Colonial Mexico. Albuquerque: University of New Mexico Press.

Ellingson, Ter
2001 The Myth of the Noble Savage. Berkeley: University of California Press.

Elliott, J. H.
2006 Empires of the Atlantic World: Britain and Spain in America, 1492–1830. New Haven: Yale University Press.

Elliott, Michael L.
1991 Pueblo at the Hot Place: Archaeological Excavations at Giusewa Pueblo and San Jose de los Jemez Mission, Jemez State Monument, Jemez Springs, New Mexico. Santa Fe: New Mexico State Monuments.

Ellis, Florence Hawley
1956 Anthropological Evidence Supporting the Claims of the Pueblos of Zia, Santa Ana, and Jemez. MS on file at Archaeological Records Management Service, Laboratory of Anthropology, Museum of New Mexico, Santa Fe.
1966a The Immediate History of Zia Pueblo as Derived from Excavation in Refuse Deposits. American Antiquity 31:806–11.
1966b Pueblo Boundaries and Their Markers. Plateau 38(4):97–105.

Elson, Christina M.
2006 Aztec Elites and the Post Classic Economy: Instrumental Neutron Activation Analysis (INAA) of Museum Collections from Chiconautla, México. Report presented to FAMSI. http://www.famsi.org/reports/03019/index.html, accessed October 31, 2010.

Espinosa, J. Manuel, ed.
1988 The Pueblo Revolt of 1696 and the Franciscan Missions in New Mexico: Letters of the Missionaries and Related Documents. Chicago: Institute of Jesuit History.

References

Estenssoro, Juan Carlos
2001   El simio de Díos: Los indígenas y la iglesia frente a la evangelización del Perú, siglos XVI–XVII. Bulletin de l'Institut Français d'Études Andines 30(3):455–74.

2003   Del paganismo a la santidad: La incorporación de los indios del Perú al Catolicismo, 1532–1750. Lima: IFEA, Pontificia Universidad Católica del Perú, Instituto Riva-Agüero.

Farmer, M.
1942   Navajo Archaeology of the Upper Blanco and Largo Canyons, Northern New Mexico. American Antiquity 8:65–79.

Farriss, Nancy M.
1984   Maya Society under Colonial Rule: The Collective Enterprise of Survival. Princeton: Princeton University Press.

Feijoó de Sosa, Miguel
1984[1763]   Relación descriptiva de la ciudad y provincia de Truxillo del Perú. Lima: Edición facsimilar, Banco Industrial del Perú.

Field, Les, Alan Leventhal, Dolores Sanchez, and Rosemary Cambra
1992   A Contemporary Ohlone Tribal Revitalization Movement: A Perspective from the Muwekma Costanoan/Ohlone Indians of the San Francisco Bay Area. California History 71(3):412–32.

Finamore, Daniel
2006   A Mariner's Utopia: Pirates and Logwood in the Bay of Honduras. *In* X Marks the Spot: The Archaeology of Piracy. R. K. Skowronek and C. R. Ewen, eds. Gainesville: University of Florida Press.

Flint, Richard, and Shirley Cushing Flint
2003   The Coronado Expedition: From the Distance of 460 Years. Albuquerque: University of New Mexico Press.

2008   Bartolome de Ojeda. http://www.newmexicohistory.org/filedetails.php?fileID=481, accessed March 26, 2010.

Forbes, Jack D.
1960   Apache, Navajo, and Spaniard. Norman: University of Oklahoma Press.

Foster, George M.
1960   Culture and Conquest: America's Spanish Heritage. Viking Fund Publications in Anthropology, 27. Chicago: Quadrangle Books.

Foucault, Michel
1975   Discipline and Punish: The Birth of the Prison. New York: Pantheon.

1978   The History of Sexuality: An Introduction. New York: Pantheon.

1980   Power/Knowledge: Selected Interviews and Other Writings, 1972–77. New York: Pantheon.

Fournier, Patricia
1989 Cultura material en el Real de Parral en el siglo XVIII. *In* Actas del Primer Congreso de Historia Regional Comparada. Pp. 63–76. Chihuahua: Universidad Autónoma de Ciudad Juárez.

1997 Símbolos de la conquista hispana: Hacia una interpretación de significados de artefactos cerámicos del periodo Colonial Temprano en la cuenca de México. *In* Simbológicas. M. O. Marion, coord. Pp. 125–38. México: Plaza y Valdés, Consejo Nacional para la Ciencia y la Technología, and Instituto Nacional de Antropología e Historia.

Fournier, Patricia, M. James Blackman, and Ronald L. Bishop
2007 Los alfareros purépecha de la cuenca de Pátzcuaro: Producción, intercambio y consumo de cerámica vidriada durante la época virreinal. *In* Arqueología y complejidad social. P. Fournier, W. Wiesheu, and T. H. Charlton, coords. Pp. 195–221. México: PROMEP-CONACULTA-ENAH.

Fournier, Patricia, Margarita Carballal, and María Flores
1995 Las "copas" de la tradición Rojo Texcoco de las ofrendas tlatelolcas: Interpretaciones funcionales alternas. *In* Presencias y encuentros, Investigaciones arqueológicas de Salvamento. Pp. 111–33. México: Dirección de Salvamento Arqueológico del Instituto Nacional de Antropología e Historia.

Fournier, Patricia, and Thomas H. Charlton
1996–97 Patrones arqueológicos de diferencias socioétnicas en Nueva España: Contrastes urbanos y rurales. Revista colombiana de antropología XXX–II:55–83. Bogotá: Instituto Colombiano de Antropología.

Fournier, Patricia, and Joel Santos
2007 Arqueología histórica de Sinaloa: Producción y comercialización de cerámicas vidriadas en el periodo Colonial. Paper presented at the Seminario la Religión y los Jesuitas en el Noroeste Colonial. El Colegio de Sinaloa, Culiacán, Sinaloa.

Fowler, Don D., and David R. Wilcox
1999 From Thomas Jefferson to the Pecos Conference: Changing Anthropological Agendas in the North American Southwest. *In* Surveying the Record: North American Scientific Exploration to 1930. E. C. Carter II, ed. Pp. 197–223. Philadelphia: American Philosophical Society Memoir, 231.

Fraser, Valerie
1990 The Architecture of Conquest: Building in the Viceroyalty of Peru, 1535–1636. New York: Cambridge University Press.

Frink, Lisa
2007 Storage and Status in Precolonial and Colonial Coastal Western Alaska. Current Anthropology 48(3):349–74.

References

Funari, Pedro Paulo A.
1999   Maroon, Race, and Gender: Palmares Material Culture and Social Relations in a Runaway Settlement. *In* Historical Archaeology: Back from the Edge. Pedro Paulo A. Funari, Sian Jones, and Martin Hall, eds. Pp. 308–28. London: Routledge.

Futrell, Mary E.
1998   Social Boundaries and Interaction: Ceramic Zones in the Northern Rio Grande Pueblo IV Period. *In* Migration and Reorganization: The Pueblo IV Period in the American Southwest. A. S. Katherine, ed. Pp. 285–92. Tempe: Arizona State University Anthropological Research Papers, 51.

Gabbert, Wolfgang
2001   On the Term Maya. *In* Maya Survivalism, vol. 12. Ueli Hostettler and Matthew Restall, eds. Pp. 25–34. Acta Mesoamericana, 12. Markt Schwaben: Verlag Anton Saurwein.

2004   Becoming Maya: Ethnicity and Social Inequality in Yucatan since 1500. Tucson: University of Arizona Press.

Gaither, Catherine, Melissa Murphy, Elena Goycochea, and Guillermo Cock
2007   Consequences of Conquest? Interpretation of Subadult Trauma at Puruchuco-Huaquerones, Peru. Poster presented at the Annual Meeting of the Paleopathology Association, Philadelphia.

Galindo, Mary Jo
2003   Con un pie en cada lado: Ethnicities and the Archaeology of Spanish Colonial Ranching Communities along the Lower Río Grande Valley. PhD dissertation, Anthropology, University of Texas, Austin.

Gannon, Michael
1965   The Cross in the Sand: The Early Catholic Church in Florida, 1513–1870. Gainesville: University Press of Florida.

García Arévalo, Manuel
1990   Transculturation in Contact Period and Contemporary Hispaniola. *In* Columbian Consequences, vol. 2: Archaeological and Historical Perspectives in the Spanish Borderlands East. D. Thomas, ed. Pp. 269–80. Washington, D.C.: Smithsonian Institution Press.

García Sáiz, María Concepción
1989   Las castas mexicanas: Un género pictórico americano. Milán: Olivetti.

Gasco, Janine, Greg Charles Smith, and Patricia Fournier-Garcia, eds.
1997   Approaches to the Historical Archaeology of Mexico, Central, and South America. Los Angeles: Institute of Archaeology, UCLA.

Gaulton, Barry, and Cathy Mathias
1998   Portuguese *Terra Sigillata* Earthenware Discovered at the 17th-Century Colonial Site in Ferryland, Newfoundland. Avalon Chronicles 3:1–17.

Geller, Pamela L., and Miranda K. Stockett, eds.
2006   Feminist Anthropology: Past, Present, and Future. Philadelphia: University of Pennsylvania Press.

References

Gerhard, Peter
1972   A Guide to the Historical Geography of New Spain. Cambridge: Cambridge University Press.
1986   Geografía histórica de la Nueva España. 1519–1821. México: Universidad Nacional Autónoma de México.

Gibson, Charles
1964   The Aztecs under Spanish Rule. Stanford: Stanford University Press.
1980   Los Aztecas bajo el dominio español. 1519–1810. México: Siglo Veintiuno.

Giddens, Anthony
1979   Central Problems in Social Theory. London: Macmillan.
1984   The Constitution of Society: Outline of the Theory of Structuration. Berkeley: University of California Press.

Gieryn, Thomas F.
2002   What Buildings Do. Theory and Society 31:35–74.

Given, Michael
2004   The Archaeology of the Colonized. London: Routledge.

Goldberg, Rita
1971   Más datos sobre don Pedro Cortés, IV Marqués del Valle de Oaxaca. Boletín del Archivo General de la Nación 12:477–568.

Gomez, Pastor Rodolfo
2002   Evolución demografica del cacicazgo de Çoçumba, Honduras durante el siglo XVI. Paper presented to the Congreso Centroamericano de Historia VI, Panama.

Gose, Peter
2003   Converting the Ancestors: Indirect Rule, Settlement Consolidation, and the Struggle over Burial in Colonial Peru, 1532–1614. *In* Conversion: Old Worlds and New. Kenneth Mills and Anthony Grafton, eds. Pp. 140–74. Rochester, NY: University of Rochester Press.

Graham, Elizabeth
1991   Archaeological Insights into Colonial Period Maya Life at Tipú, Belize. *In* Columbian Consequences, vol. 3: The Spanish Borderlands in Pan-American Perspective. D. H. Thomas, ed. Pp. 319–35. Washington, D.C.: Smithsonian Institution Press.
1998   Mission Archaeology. Annual Review of Anthropology 27:25–62.

Graves, William M., and Suzanne L. Eckert
1998   Decorated Ceramic Distributions and Ideological Developments in the Northern and Central Rio Grande Valley, New Mexico. *In* Migration and Reorganization: The Pueblo IV Period in the American Southwest. K. A. Spielmann, ed. Pp. 263–84. Tempe: Arizona State University Anthropological Research Papers, 51.

References

Greenhouse, Carol J.
2005   Hegemony and Hidden Transcripts: The Discursive Arts of Neoliberal Legitimation. American Anthropologist 107(3):356–68.

Gross, Samuel
1861   A Manual of Military Surgery; or Hints on the Emergencies of Field, Camp and Hospital Practice. Philadelphia: J. B. Lippincott & Co.

Guaman Poma, Felipe
1980[1615]   Nueva corónica y buen gobierno. Caracas: Biblioteca Ayacucho.

Guilmartin John F.
1991   The Cutting Edge: An Analysis of the Spanish Invasion and Overthrow of the Inca Empire, 1532–1539. *In* Transatlantic Encounters: Europeans and Andeans in the Sixteenth Century. K. Andrien and R. Adorno, eds. Pp. 40–69. Berkeley: University of California Press.

Guitar, Lynne
1998   Cultural Genesis: Relationships among Indians, Africans and Spaniards in Rural Hispaniola, First Half of the Sixteenth Century. PhD dissertation, Vanderbilt University. Ann Arbor: University Microfilms.

Gust, John
2006   An Investigation of the Catchment and Resource Base of the Historic Period Village of San Pedro Sirís, Belize. MA thesis, Department of Geography, University of Colorado, Colorado Springs.

Gutiérrez, Alejandra
2000   Mediterranean Pottery in Wessex Households (13th to 17th Centuries). Oxford: BAR British Series, 306.

Gutiérrez, Alejandra, David Williams, and M. J. Hughes
2003   A Shipwreck Cargo of Sevillian Pottery from the Studland Bay Wreck, Dorset, UK. International Journal of Nautical Archaeology 32(1):24–41.

Gutiérrez, Ramón
1991   When Jesus Came the Corn Mothers Went Away. Palo Alto, CA: Stanford University Press.

Hackett, Charles W., ed.
1937   Historical Documents Relating to New Mexico, Nueva Vizcaya, and Approaches Thereto, to 1773. Adolph F. A. and Fanny R. Bandelier, comps. and trans. Washington, D.C.: Carnegie Institute of Washington Publication No. 330, vol. 3.

Hackett, Charles W., and Charmion C. Shelby
1942   Revolt of the Pueblo Indians of New Mexico and Otermin's Attempted Reconquest, 1680–1682. Coronado Cuarto Centennial Publications, 1540–1940. 2 vols. Albuquerque: University of New Mexico Press.

References

Hammond, George P., and Agapito Rey
1953   Don Juan de Oñate, Colonizer of New Mexico, 1596–1628. Albuquerque: University of New Mexico Press.

Hammond, George P., and Agapito Rey, eds.
1940   Narratives of the Coronado Expedition. Albuquerque: University of New Mexico Press.

Hanke, Lewis
1949   The Spanish Struggle for Justice in the Conquest of America. Boston: Little, Brown and Co..

Hanks, William F.
1986   Authenticity and Ambivalence in the Text: A Colonial Maya Case. American Ethnologist 13:721–44.

Hann, John
1988   Apalache: The Land between the Rivers. Gainesville: University Press of Florida.
1993   Visitations and Revolts in Florida, 1656–1695. Florida Archaeology, 7. Tallahassee: Florida Bureau of Historic Preservation.
2003   The Indians of Central and South Florida, 1565–1763. Gainesville: University Press of Florida.

Hanson, Craig A.
1995   Hispanic Horizon in Yucatan: A Model of Franciscan Missionization. Ancient Mesoamerica 6(1):15–28.

Harlow, Francis H., Duane Anderson, and Dwight P. Lanmon
2005   The Pottery of Santa Ana Pueblo. Santa Fe: Museum of New Mexico Press.

Hemming, John
1983   The Conquest of the Incas. New York: Penguin Books.

Henderson, John S.
1977   The Valley of Naco: Ethnohistory and Archaeology in Northwestern Honduras. Ethnohistory 24:367–77.

Henderson, John S., Ilene Sterns, Anthony Wonderly, and Patricia Urban
1979   Archaeological Investigations in the Valley of Naco, Northwestern Honduras. Journal of Field Archaeology 6:169–92.

Hendricks, Rick, and John R. Wilson, eds.
1996   The Navajos in 1705: Roque Madrid's Campaign Journal. Albuquerque: University of New Mexico Press.

Herskovits, Melville J.
1938   Acculturation: The Study of Culture Contact. New York: J. J. Augustin Publisher.

REFERENCES

Hester, James J.
1962 Early Navajo Migrations and Acculturation in the Southwest. Santa Fe: Museum of New Mexico Papers in Anthropology, 6.

Hill, W. W.
1940 Some Navajo Culture Changes during Two Centuries. *In* Essays in Historical Anthropology of North America, Published in Honor of John R. Swanton. Pp. 395–416. Washington, D.C.: Smithsonian Miscellaneous Collections, 100.
1982 An Ethnography of Santa Clara Pueblo, New Mexico. Charles H. Lange, ed. Albuquerque: University of New Mexico Press.

Hobsbawm, Eric
1983 Introduction: Inventing Tradition. *In* The Invention of Tradition. E. Hobsbawm and T. Ranger, eds. Pp. 1–14. Cambridge: Cambridge University Press.

Hodder, Ian
1987 The Meaning of Discard: Ash and Domestic Space in Baringo. *In* Method and Theory in Activity Area Research. Susan Kent, ed. New York: Columbia University Press.
2004 The "Social" in Archaeological Theory: An Historical and Contemporary Perspective. *In* A Companion to Social Archaeology. L. Meskell and R. W. Preucel, eds. Pp. 23–42. London: Blackwell.

Hodge, Frederick W., George P. Hammond, and Agapito Rey
1945 Fray Alonso de Benavides' Revised Memorial of 1634. Albuquerque: University of New Mexico Press.

Hodge, Mary G., Hector Neff, M. James Blackman, and Leah D. Minc
1993 Black-on-Orange Ceramic Production in the Aztec Empire's Heartland. Latin American Antiquity 4(2):130–57.

Hordes, Stanley J.
2005 To the End of the Earth: A History of the Crypto-Jews of New Mexico. New York: Columbia University Press.

Hoffman, Diane
1999 Turning Power Inside Out: Reflections on Resistance from the (Anthropological) Field. Qualitative Studies in Education 12(6):671–87.

Hoffman, Paul
1990 A New Andalucia and a Way to the Orient: The American Southeast during the Sixteenth Century. Baton Rouge: Louisiana State University Press.

Hogan, Patrick
1991 Navajo-Pueblo Interaction during the Governador Phase: A Reassessment of the Evidence. Cultural Resources Series, 8. Albuquerque: Bureau of Land Management.

Holland, Dorothy C., and Margaret A. Eisenhart
1990 Educated in Romance: Women, Achievement, and College Culture. Chicago: University of Chicago Press.

References

Hollander, Jocelyn A., and Rachel L. Einwohner
2004   Conceptualizing Resistance. Sociological Forum 19(4):533–54.

Horning, Audrey J.
2000   Archaeological Considerations of "Appalachian" Identity. *In* The Archaeology of Communities: A New World Perspective. J. Yaeger and M. A. Canuto, eds. New York: Routledge.

Hudson, Charles
1990   The Juan Pardo Expeditions. Washington, D.C.: Smithsonian Institution Press.
1997   Knights of Spain, Warriors of the Sun: Hernando de Soto and the South's Ancient Chiefdoms. Tuscaloosa: University of Alabama Press.

Hudson, Charles, Robin A. Beck Jr., Chester B. DePratter, Robbie Ethridge, and John Worth
2008   On Interpreting Cofitachequi. Ethnohistory 55:465–90.

Hudson, Charles, Marvin T. Smith, and Chester B. DePratter
1984   The Hernando de Soto Expedition: From Apalachee to Chiaha. Southeastern Archaeology 3:65–77.

Hull, Kathleen L.
2005   Process, Perception, and Practice: Time Perspectivism in Yosemite Native Demography. Journal of Anthropological Archaeology 24:354–77.

Huertas Vallejos, Lorenzo, ed.
1987[1578]   Ecología e Historia: Probanzas de indios y españoles referentes a las catastróficas lluvias de 1578, en los corregimietios de Trujillo y Saña. CED Solidaridad, Chiclayo, Peru.

Hurt, Wesley R.
1942   Eighteenth Century Navaho Hogans from Canyon de Chelly National Monument. American Antiquity 8:89–99.

Hussey, Raymond
1932   Text of the Laws of Burgos Concerning the Treatment of the Indians. Hispanic American Historical Review 12(3):301–26.

Ingold, Timothy
1993   The Temporality of the Landscape. World Archaeology 25(2):152–74.

Isbell, William
1997   Mummies and Mortuary Monuments. Austin: University of Texas Press.

Ivey, James E., and David Hurst Thomas
2005   "The Feeling of Working Completely in the Dark": The Uncertain Foundations of Southwestern Mission Archaeology. *In* Southwest Archaeology in the Twentieth Century. L. S. Cordell and D. D. Fowler, eds. Pp. 204–19. Salt Lake City: University of Utah Press.

Jamieson, Ross W.
2005   Colonialism, Social Archaeology and Lo Andino: Historical Archaeology in the Andes. World Archaeology 37(3):353–72.

REFERENCES

Jiménez Borja, Arturo
1973   Puruchuco. Lima: Editorial Jurídica.

Johnson, Melissa A.
2003   The Making of Race and Place in Nineteenth-Century British Honduras. Environmental History 8(4):598–617.

Johnson, Richard A.
1941   Spanish-Mexican Diplomatic Relations, 1853–1855. The Hispanic American Historical Review 21(4):559–76.

Jones, Grant D.
1977   Levels of Settlement Alliance among the San Pedro Maya of Western Belize and Eastern Petén, 1857–1936. *In* Anthropology and History in Yucatán. G. D. Jones, ed. Pp. 139–89. Austin: University of Texas Press.

1989   Maya Resistance to Spanish Rule: Time and History on a Colonial Frontier. Albuquerque: University of New Mexico Press.

Jordan, Kurt A.
2008   The Seneca Restoration, 1715–1754: An Iroquois Local Political Economy. Gainesville: University Press of Florida.

Kagan, Richard L.
2000   Urban Images of the Hispanic World, 1493–1793. New Haven: Yale University Press.

Katzew, Ilona
2004   Casta Painting. Images of Race in Eighteenth-Century Mexico. New Haven: Yale University Press.

Keane, Webb
2003   Semiotics and the Social Analysis of Material Things. Language and Communication 23:409–25.

2007   Christian Moderns: Freedom and Fetish in the Mission Encounter. Berkeley: University of California Press.

Keen, Benjamin
1985   Main Currents in United States Writings on Colonial Spanish America, 1884–1984. Hispanic American Historical Review 65(4):657–82.

Kellner, Corinna
2002   Coping with Environmental and Social Challenges in Prehistoric Peru: Bioarchaeological Analyses of Nasca Populations. PhD dissertation, Department of Anthropology, University of California, Santa Barbara. Ann Arbor: University Microfilms.

Kepecs, Susan, and Rani T. Alexander, eds.
2005   The Postclassic to Spanish-Era Transition in Mesoamerica. Albuquerque: University of New Mexico Press.

Kessell, John
1979   Kiva, Cross, and Crown: The Pecos Indians and New Mexico, 1540–1840. Albuquerque: University of New Mexico Press.

References

1992   Return to a Previous Century: Gov. Juan Ignacio Flores Mogollón's Campaign against Pueblo Indian Kivas, 1719. *In* The Native American and Spanish Colonial Experience in the Greater Southwest I: Introduction to the Documentary Records. D. H. Snow, ed. Pp. 409–14. New York: Garland Press.

1994   The Ways and Words of the Other: Diego de Vargas and Cultural Brokers in Late Seventeenth-Century New Mexico. *In* Between Indian and White Worlds: The Cultural Broker. M. C. Szasz, ed. Pp. 25–43. Norman: University of Oklahoma Press.

1997   Restoring 17th Century New Mexico, Then and Now. Historical Archaeology 31(1):46–54.

Kessell, John L., and Rick Hendricks, eds.

1992   By Force of Arms: The Journals of Don Diego de Vargas, New Mexico, 1691–1693. Albuquerque: University of New Mexico Press.

Kessell, John L., Rick Hendricks, and Meredith Dodge, eds.

1995   To the Royal Crown Restored: The Journals of Don Diego de Vargas, New Mexico, 1692–1694. Albuquerque: University of New Mexico Press.

1998   Blood on the Boulders: The Journals of Don Diego de Vargas, New Mexico, 1694–1697. 2 vols. Albuquerque: University of New Mexico Press.

Keur, Dorothy L.

1941   Big Bead Mesa: An Archaeological Study of Navajo Acculturation, 1745–1812. Menasha, WI: Memoirs of the Society for American Archaeology, 1.

1944   A Chapter in Navajo-Pueblo Relations. American Antiquity 10:75–86.

Kidder, A. V.

1913   Some Undescribed Ruins of the Historic Period from the Upper San Juan. American Journal of Archaeology 2(17):88–90.

1920   Ruins of the Historic Period in the Upper San Juan Valley, New Mexico. American Anthropologist 22:322–29.

1932   The Artifacts of Pecos. New Haven: Papers of the Phillips Academy Southwest Expedition, 6.

1958   Pecos, New Mexico: Archaeological Notes. Papers of the Peabody Foundation for Archaeology, 5. Andover: Phillips Academy.

Kirkpatrick, F. A.

1939   Repartimiento-Encomienda. Hispanic American Historical Review 19(3):372–79.

Klaus, Haagen D.

2008   Out of Light Came Darkness: Bioarchaeology of Mortuary Ritual, Health, and Ethnogenesis in the Lambayeque Valley Complex, North Coast of Peru (AD 900–1750). PhD dissertation, Department of Anthropology, Ohio State University, Columbus. Ann Arbor: University Microfilms.

Klaus, Haagen D., J. Centurión, and M. Curo

N.d.   Bioarchaeology of Human Sacrifice: An Integrated Study of Health, Identity, and Ritual Violence at Cerro Cerrillos, Peru. Unpublished MS.

References

Klaus, Haagen D., Manuel Tam, and Cesar Maguiña
2005   Requiem Aeternum Dona Eis, Domine: The Physical and Social Manipulation of the Dead at the Colonial Chapel of San Pedro, Mórrope, Peru. Paper presented at the 70th Annual Meeting of the Society for American Archaeology, Salt Lake City, Utah.

Knight, Alan
2002   Mexico: The Colonial Era. Cambridge: Cambridge University Press.

Kroeber, Alfred L.
1925   Handbook of the Indians of California. Washington, D.C.: Government Printing Office.

Kubler, George
1961   On the Colonial Extinction of the Motifs of Pre-Columbian Art. *In* Essays in Pre-Columbian Art and Archaeology. Samuel K. Lothrop, ed. Pp. 14–34. Cambridge, MA: Harvard University Press.

Lambert, Marjorie F.
1981   Spanish Influences on the Pottery of San Jose de los Jemez and Giusewa. *In* Collected Papers in Honor of Erik Kellerman Reed. A. H. Schroeder, ed. Albuquerque: Papers of the Archaeological Society of New Mexico, 6.

Landers, Jane G.
1990   African Presence in Early Spanish Colonization of the Caribbean and Southeastern Borderlands. *In* Columbian Consequences, vol. 2: Archaeological and Historical Perspectives on the Spanish Borderlands East. D. H. Thomas, ed. Pp. 315–28. Washington, D.C.: Smithsonian Institution Press.
1999   Black Society in Spanish Florida. Urbana: University of Illinois Press.
2006   Cimarrón and Citizen: African Ethnicity, Corporate Identity, and the Evolution of Free Black Towns in the Spanish Circum-Caribbean. *In* Slaves, Subjects, and Subversives: Blacks in Colonial Latin America. Jane G. Landers and Barry Robinson, eds. Pp. 111–46. Albuquerque: University of New Mexico Press.

Langellier, John P., and Daniel B. Rosen
1996   El Presidio de San Francisco: A History under Spain and Mexico, 1776–1846. Spokane: Arthur H. Clark Company.

Lara, Jaime
2004   City, Temple, Stage: Eschatological Architecture and Liturgical Theatrics in New Spain. Notre Dame, IN: University of Notre Dame.

Larsen, Clark
1993   On the Frontier of Contact: Mission Bioarchaeology in La Florida. *In* The Spanish Missions of La Florida. B. G. McEwan, ed. Pp. 322–56. Gainesville: University Press of Florida.

Larsen, Clark, Mark C. Griffin, Dale L. Hutchinson, Vivan E. Noble, Lynette Norr, Robert F. Pastor, Christopher B. Ruff, Katherine T. Russell, Margaret Schoeninger, Michael Schultz, Scott W. Simpson, and Mark Teaford
2001   Frontiers of Contact: Bioarchaeology of Spanish Florida. Journal of World Prehistory 15(1):69–123.

Las Casas, Bartolomé de
1951   Historia de las Indias, vol. 2. Edición de Agustín Millares Carlo. 3 vols. Mexico City: Fondo de Cultura Económica.

Levillier, Roberto
1935   Don Francisco de Toledo, supremo organizador del Perú. Buenos Aires: Biblioteca del Congreso Argentino.

Libro de las Tasaciones de los Pueblos de la Nueva España
1952   Prólogo de Francisco González de Cossío. México: Archivo General de la Nación.

Liebmann, Matthew
2006   "Burn the Churches, Break Up the Bells": An Archaeological Study of Pueblo Revolt–Era Revitalization in New Mexico, AD 1680–1696. PhD dissertation, Department of Anthropology, University of Pennsylvania, Philadelphia. Ann Arbor: University Microfilms.
2007   Ceramic Investigations of the Historic Occupation at Boletsakwa (LA 136), A Pueblo Revolt–Era Jemez Village on the Santa Fe National Forest. Santa Fe National Forest and Pueblo of Jemez Department of Resource Protection.
2008a   The Innovative Materiality of Revitalization Movements: Lessons from the Pueblo Revolt of 1680. American Anthropologist 110(3):360–72.
2008b   Historic Ceramics from Jemez Pueblo (LA 8860): An Inventory of the Ellis Excavations of 1955 at Walatowa. Report on file, Maxwell Museum of Anthropology, Albuquerque.

Liebmann, Matthew J., T. J. Ferguson, and Robert W. Preucel
2005   Pueblo Settlement, Architecture, and Social Change in the Pueblo Revolt Era, A.D. 1680 to 1696. Journal of Field Archaeology 30(1):45–60.

Liebmann, Matthew, and Robert W. Preucel
2007   The Archaeology of the Pueblo Revolt and the Formation of the Modern Pueblo World. Kiva 73(2):195–218.

Lightfoot, Kent G.
2005   Indians, Missionaries, and Merchants: The Legacy of Colonial Encounters on the California Frontiers. Berkeley: University of California Press.

Lightfoot, Kent G., Antoinette Martinez, and Ann M. Schiff
1998   Daily Practice and Material Culture in Pluralistic Social Settings: An Archaeological Study of Culture Change and Persistence from Ft. Ross, California. American Antiquity 63(2):199–222.

References

Lister, Florence C., and Robert H. Lister
1987   Andalusian Ceramics in Spain and New Spain: A Cultural Register from the Third Century B.C. to 1700. Tucson: University of Arizona Press.

Lockhart, James
1968   Spanish Peru, 1532–1560: A Colonial Society. Madison: University of Wisconsin Press.
1972   The Men of Cajamarca. Austin: University of Texas Press.

Longmore, Thomas
2006   Gunshot Wounds. In A Manual of Military Surgery, Confederate States Army, 1863. Philadelphia; Thomas Jefferson University. Available from Jefferson Digital Commons, http://jdc.jefferson.edu/milsurgcsa/4, accessed October 31, 2010.

Loren, Diana DiPaolo
2001   Manipulating Bodies and Emerging Traditions at the Los Adaes Presidio. In The Archaeology of Traditions: Agency and History Before and After Columbus. Timothy R. Pauketat, ed. Pp. 58–76. Gainesville: University Press of Florida.

Loucks, J. Lana
1993   Spanish-Indian Interaction in the Florida Missions: The Archaeology of Baptizing Springs. In The Spanish Missions of La Florida. B. G. McEwan, ed. Pp. 193–216. Gainesville: University Press of Florida.

Lovell, Nancy. C.
2008   Analysis and Interpretation of Skeletal Trauma. In Biological Anthropology of the Human Skeleton. M. A. Katzenberg and S. R. Saunders, eds. Pp. 341–86. New York: Wiley-Liss.

Lyon, Eugene
1976   The Enterprise of Florida: Pedro Menéndez de Avilés and the Spanish Conquest of 1565–1568. Gainesville: University Press of Florida.

MacAlister, Lyle N.
1984   Spain and Portugal in the New World, 1492–1700. Minneapolis: University of Minnesota Press.

MacCormack, Sabine
1991   Religion in the Andes. Vision and Imagination in Early Colonial Peru. Princeton: Princeton University Press.

Magee, Reginald
1995   Muskets, Musket Balls, and the Wounds They Made. Australia New Zealand Journal of Surgery 65:890–95.

Málaga Medina, Alejandro
1977   Los Collagua en la historia de Arequipa en el siglo XVI. In Collaguas I. Franklin Pease, ed. Pp. 93–130. Lima: Pontificia Universidad Católica del Perú.

References

Mallios, Seth
2006   The Deadly Politics of Giving: Exchange and Violence at Ajacan, Roanoke, and Jamestown. Tuscaloosa: University of Alabama Press.

Manchester, William
1993   A World Lit Only by Fire: The Medieval Mind and the Renaissance: Portrait of an Age. Boston: Back Bay Books.

Martinez, Juan
1990   Relation. P. Hoffman, trans. *In* The Juan Pardo Expeditions: Explorations of the Carolinas and Tennessee, 1566–1568, by Charles Hudson. Washington, D.C.: Smithsonian Institution Press.

Matienzo, Juan de
1910[1567]   Gobierno del Perú. Buenos Aires: Compañía Sud-americana de Billetes de Banco.

Mazzotti, José Antonio
2005   Epic, Creoles, and Nation in Spanish America. *In* A Companion to the Literatures of Colonial America. S. Castillo and I. Schweitzer, eds. Pp. 480–98. Oxford: Blackwell.

McEwan, Bonnie G.
2001   The Spiritual Conquest of Florida. American Anthropologist 103(3):633–44.

McEwan, Bonnie G., ed.
1993   The Spanish Missions of La Florida. Gainesville: University Press of Florida.

Mendieta, Gerónimo de
1945[1596]   Historia eclesiástica indiana. Mexico: Editorial Salvador Chavez Hayhoe.

Merritt, J. Daniel
1983   Beyond the Town Walls: The Indian Element in Colonial St. Augustine. In Spanish St. Augustine: The Archaeology of a Colonial Creole Community. Kathleen Deagan, ed. Pp. 125–47. New York: Academic Press.

Meskell, Lynn
1999   Archaeologies of Social Life. Oxford: Blackwell.

Milanich, Jerald T.
1999   Laboring in the Fields of the Lord: Spanish Missions and Southeastern Indians. Washington, D.C.: Smithsonian Institution Press.

Milich, Alicia Ronstadt
1966   Relaciones: An Account of Things Seen and Heard by Father Jeronimo de Zarate Salmeron from the Year 1538 to Year 1626. Albuquerque: Horn and Wallace.

Milliken, Randall
1995   A Time of Little Choice. Ballena Press Anthropological Papers. Menlo Park, CA: Ballena Press.

References

Millones, Luis, Sara Castro-Klarén, and Cristóbal de Albornoz
1990 El retorno de las huacas: Estudios y documentos sobre el Taki Onqoy, siglo XVI. Lima: Instituto de Estudios Peruanos.

Mills, Kenneth
1994 An Evil Lost to View: An Investigation of Post-Evangelisation Andean Religion in Mid-Colonial Peru. Liverpool: Institute of Latin American Studies, University of Liverpool.
1997 Idolatry and Its Enemies: Colonial Andean Religion and Extirpation, 1640–1750. Princeton: Princeton University Press.

Milner, George R.
2005 Nineteenth-Century Arrow Wounds and Perceptions of Prehistoric Warfare. American Antiquity 70(1):144–57.

Milner G., E. Anderson, and V. Smith
1991 Warfare in Late Prehistoric West-Central Illinois. American Antiquity 56(4):581–603.

Mira Caballos, Esteban
1997 El indio antillano: Repartimiento, encomienda y esclavitud (1492–1542). Seville: Muñoz Moya Editora.

Mohar, Luz M., and Rita Fernández
2006 El estudio de los códices. Desacatos 22:9–36.

Montgomery, Ross Gordon, Watson Smith, and John Otis Brew, eds.
1949 Franciscan Awatovi: The Excavation and Conjectural Reconstruction of a 17th Century Spanish Mission Establishment at a Hopi Indian Town in Northeastern Arizona. Cambridge, MA: Papers of the Peabody Museum of American Archaeology and Ethnology, 36, Harvard University.

Moore, David G.
2002 Catawba Valley Mississippian. Tuscaloosa: University of Alabama Press.

Moore, Jerry D.
1996 The Archaeology of Plazas and the Proxemics of Ritual. American Anthropologist 98(4):789–802.

Moorhead, Max L.
1975 The Presidio: Bastion of the Spanish Borderlands. Norman: University of Oklahoma Press.

Mora-Torres, Gregorio, ed. and trans.
2005 California Voices: The Oral Memoirs of José María Amador and Lorenzo Asisara. Denton: University of North Texas Press.

Morley, Selma E.
2002 Stylistic Variation and Group Self-Identity: Evidence from the Rio Grande Pueblos. Los Angeles: University of California Press.

Morris, Craig, and Donald E. Thompson
1985 Huánuco Pampa: An Inca City and Its Hinterland. London: Thames and Hudson.

Morrow, Baker H., ed.
1996 A Harvest of Reluctant Souls: The Memorial of Fray Alonso de Benavides, 1630. Niwot: University Press of Colorado.

Moya Pons, Frank
1992 The Politics of Forced Indian Labor in La Española, 1492–1520. Antiquity 66(250):130–39.

Mujica Barreda, Elías, ed.
2007 El Brujo, Huaca Cao: centro ceremonial Moche en el valle de Chicama/ Huaca Cao: A Moche Ceremonial Center in the Chicama Valley. Lima: Fundación Wiese.

Mumford, Jeremy R.
1998 The Taki Onqoy and the Andean Nation: Sources and Interpretations. Latin American Research Review 33(1):150–65.
2005 Vertical Empire: The Struggle for Andean Space in the Sixteenth Century. PhD dissertation, Department of History, Yale University. Ann Arbor: University Microfilms.

Muriel, Josefina
1978 En torno a una vieja polémica. Erección de los dos primeros conventos de San Francisco en la ciudad de México, siglo XVI. Estudios de historia novohispana 6:7–38.

Muriel, Josefina, and Teresa Lozano
1995 Las instituciones educativas novohispanas: Fuentes para el estudio de los precios. Ejemplos de los siglos XVI–XIX. *In* Los precios de alimentos y manufacturas novohispanos. V. García Acosta, coord. Pp. 37–71. México: CIESAS.

Murphy, Melissa S.
2004 From Bare Bones to Mummified: Understanding Health and Disease in an Inca Community. PhD dissertation, Department of Anthropology, University of Pennsylvania. Ann Arbor: University Microfilms.

Murphy, Melissa S., Maria Fernanda Boza, Andrew Scherer, Elena Goycochea, and Guillermo Cock
2008 Identity, Violence, and Spanish Conquest at Puruchuco-Huaquerones, Peru. Poster presented at the Society for American Archaeology, Vancouver, B.C., March 27–31.

Murphy, Melissa S., Catherine Gaither, Elena Goycochea, John Verano, and Guillermo Cock
2010 Violence and Weapon-Related Trauma at Puruchuco-Huaquerones, Peru. American Journal of Physical Anthropology 142(4):636–50.

Murra, John V.
1980 The Economic Organization of the Inca State. Greenwich, CT: JAI Press.
1986 The Expansion of the Inka State: Armies, War, and Rebellions. *In* Anthropological History of Andean Polities. J. Murra, N. Wachtel, and J. Revel, eds. Pp. 49–58. Cambridge: Cambridge University Press.

References

Navarro Garcia, Luis
1964   Don José de Gálvez y la comandancia general de las provincias internas del norte de Nueva España. Seville: Escuela de Estudios Hispano-Americanos.

Neff, Theodore, Patricia A. Urban, and Edward M. Schortman
1990   Late Prehistoric Developments in Northwestern Honduras: Preliminary Report on the 1990 Investigations at Viejo Brisas del Valle. Report in the archives of the Instituto Hondureño de Antropología e Historia, Tegucigalpa, Honduras.

Newson, Linda A.
1986   The Cost of Conquest: Indian Decline in Honduras under Spanish Rule. Dellplain Latin American Studies, 20. Boulder: Westview Press.

Novak, Shannon
2000   Battle-Related Trauma. *In* Blood Red Roses. The Archaeology of a Mass Grave from the Battle of Towton, AD 1461. V. Fiorato, A. Boylston, and C. Knusel, eds. Pp. 90–103. London: Oxbow Books Limited.

Oland, Maxine
2004   Maya Resistance and Spanish Authority at Chanlacan, Northern Belize. Paper presented at the 69th Annual Meeting of the Society for American Archaeology, Montreal.

Orozco y Berra, Manuel
1853a   Conjuración del Marqués del Valle. M. Orozco y Berra. Noticia histórica de la conjuración del Marqués del Valle. Años de 1565–1568. Formada en vista de nuevos documentos originales y seguida de un extracto de los mismos documentos. Pp 1–72. México: Tipografía de R. Rafael.
1853b   Documentos. M. Orozco y Berra. Noticia histórica de la conjuración del Marqués del Valle. Años de 1565–1568. Formada en vista de nuevos documentos originales y seguida de un extracto de los mismos documentos. Pp. 1–502. Mexico: Tipografía de R. Rafael.

Ortíz, Alfonso
1969   The Tewa World: Space, Time, Being, and Becoming in a Pueblo Society. Chicago: University of Chicago Press.

Ortiz Sotelo, Jorge, ed.
1993   Derrotero general del Mar del Sur del Capitán Pedro Hurtado de Mendoza, hecho por Capitan Manuel Joseph Hertado en el Puerto del Callao—Año de 1730. Lima: Dirección de Intereses Maritimos.

Ortner, Sherry B.
1984   Theory in Anthropology since the Sixties. Comparative Studies in Society and History 26(1):126–66.
1995   Resistance and the Problem of Ethnographic Refusal. Comparative Studies in Society and History 37(1):173–93.

Otis-Charlton, Cynthia
1994   Plebeians and Patricians. Contrasting Patterns of Production and

Distribution in the Aztec Figurine and Lapidary Industries. *In* Economies and Polities in the Aztec Realm. M. G. Hodge and M. E. Smith, eds. Pp. 195–219. Albany: Institute of Mesoamerican Studies, State University of New York, and Austin: University of Texas Press.

Paar, Karen
1999   "To settle is to conquer": Spaniards, Native Americans and the Colonization of Santa Elena in Sixteenth Century Florida. PhD dissertation, Department of History, University of North Carolina, Chapel Hill.

Paiva, Fray Juan de
1676   Origen y principio del juego del pelota que los Indios Apalachinos y Yustacanos an estado jugando desde su infielidad asta 1676. Archivo de Indias, Escribanía de Cámara, leg. 156C, folios 569–583. Microfilm copy, Stetson Collection, P. K. Yonge Library of Florida History, University of Florida, Gainesville.

Palka, Joel
2005   Unconquered Lacandon Maya: Ethnohistory and Archaeology of Indigenous Culture Change. Gainesville: University Press of Florida.

Palkovitch, Ann M.
1985   Historic Population of the Eastern Pueblos: 1540–1910. Journal of Anthropological Research 41(4):401–26.

Pardo, Juan
1990   Relation. P. Hoffman, trans. *In* The Juan Pardo Expeditions: Explorations of the Carolinas and Tennessee, 1566–1568, by Charles Hudson. Washington, D.C.: Smithsonian Institution Press.

Parsons, Jeffrey R.
1966   The Aztec Ceramic Sequence in the Teotihuacan Valley, Mexico. PhD dissertation, Department of Anthropology, University of Michigan. Ann Arbor: University Microfilms.

Paso y Troncoso, Francisco del, ed.
1905   Papeles de la Nueva España. Vols. 1 and 3. Establecimiento Tipografía "Sucesores de Rivadeneyra." Madrid: Impresores de la Real Casa.
1940   Epistolario de Nueva España. 1505–1818. Vols. 14 and 15. México: Antigua Librería Robredo, de José Porrúa e Hijos.

Pauketat, Timothy
2001   A New Tradition in Archaeology. *In* The Archaeology of Traditions. T. Pauketat, ed. Pp. 1–16. Gainesville: University Press of Florida.

Pearce, Susan C.
2005   Contesting "Nation" through the "Local": The New York African Burial Ground in 2005. General Anthropology: Bulletin of the General Anthropology Division of the American Anthropological Association 12(1&2):1–6.

REFERENCES

Pease, Franklin
1977 Collaguas: Una etnía del siglo XVI. *In* Collaguas I. Franklin Pease, ed. Pp. 131–68. Lima: Pontificia Universidad Católica del Perú.

Pendergast, David M.
1991 The Southern Maya Lowlands Contact Experience: The View from Lamanai, Belize. *In* Columbian Consequences, vol. 3: The Spanish Borderlands in Pan-American Perspective. David Hurst Thomas, ed. Pp. 337–54. Washington, D.C.: Smithsonian Institution Press.

Phillips, George Harwood
1993 Indians and Intruders in Central California, 1769–1849. Norman: University of Oklahoma Press.

Porras Muñoz, Guillermo
1968 Diego de Ibarra y la Nueva España. Estudios de historia novohispana 2:49–78.

Poster, Mark
1992 The Question of Agency: Michel de Certeau and the History of Consumerism. Diacritics 22:94–107.

Prescott, William H.
2000[1843] History of the Conquest of Mexico. London: Cooper Square Press.

Preucel, Robert W.
1998 The Kotyiti Archaeological Project: Report of the 1996 Field Season. Report on file, Pueblo de Cochiti and USDA Forest Service, Santa Fe.
2002 Writing the Pueblo Revolt. *In* Archaeologies of the Pueblo Revolt: Identity, Meaning and Renewal in the Pueblo World. R. W. Preucel, ed. Pp. 3–29. Albuquerque: University of New Mexico Press.
2006 Archaeological Semiotics. London: Blackwell.

Preucel, Robert W., ed.
2002 Archaeologies of the Pueblo Revolt. Albuquerque: University of New Mexico Press.

Queirós, José
1987[1907] Cerâmica portuguesa e outros estudos. José Manuel Garcia and Orlando da Rocha Pinto, eds. Lisbon: Presenta.

Quilter, Jeffrey
1996 Continuity and Disjunction in Pre-Columbian Art and Culture. RES 29/30. The Pre-Columbian (Spring/Autumn):303–17.
2007 El Brujo a inicios de la Colonía/El Brujo at the Beginning of the Colonial Period]. *In* El Brujo, Huaca Cao: centro ceremonial Moche en el valle de Chicama/Huaca Cao: A Moche Ceremonial Center in the Chicama Valley. Elías Mujica Barreda, ed. Pp. 287–308. Lima: Fundación Wiese.

References

Quilter, Jeffrey, William R. Doonan, Hal Starratt, and Regulo Franco Jordan
2005   Magdalena de Cao Viejo: A Late Sixteenth Century Church in Northern Peru. Paper presented at the 70th Annual Meeting of the Society for American Archaeology, Salt Lake City, Utah.

Quimby, George I., and Alexander Spoehr
1951   Acculturation and Material Culture—I. Fieldiana: Anthropology 36(6):107–47.

Ramenofsky, Ann F.
1988   Vectors of Death: The Archaeology of European Contact. Albuquerque: University of New Mexico Press.

Ramírez, Susan E.
1996   The World Upside Down. Cross-Cultural Contact in Sixteenth Century Peru. Stanford: Stanford University Press.
2005   To Feed and Be Fed: The Cosmological Bases of Authority and Identity in the Andes. Stanford: Stanford University Press.

Ramos Gómez, Luis Javier
1993   Cristóbal Colón y los indios taínos Valladolid. Casa-Museo de Colón. Cuadernos Colombinos 18. Valladolid, Spain: Seminario Americanista de la Universidad de Valladolid.

Ramsay, Amy, and Barbara L. Voss
2002   Final Report, Funston Avenue Archaeological Research Project, Presidio of San Francisco, 2000. Archaeological Research Facility, University of California, Berkeley. Submitted to the Presidio Trust and the National Park Service, Golden Gate National Recreation Area, San Francisco.

Redfield, Robert, and Alfonso Villa Rojas
1962   Chan Kom: A Maya Village. Chicago: University of Chicago Press.

Reed, Nelson A.
1964   The Caste War of the Yucatan. Palo Alto: Stanford University Press.

Reed, Paul F., and Lori S. Reed
1996   Reexamining Gobernador Polychrome: Toward a New Understanding of Early Navajo Chronological Sequence in Northwestern New Mexico. In The Archaeology of Navajo Origins. R. H. Towner, ed. Pp. 83–108. Salt Lake City: University of Utah Press.

Reeve, F. D.
1959   The Navajo-Spanish Peace: 1720s–1770s. New Mexico Historical Review 34:9–40.

Reff, Daniel T.
1995   The Predicament of Culture and Spanish Missionary Accounts of the Tepehuan and Pueblo Revolts. Ethnohistory 42:63–90.

Reichard, Gladys A.
1928   Social Life of the Navajo Indians. New York: Columbia University Contributions to Anthropology No. 7.

References

Reiter, Paul
1938   The Jemez Pueblo of Unshagi, New Mexico, with Notes on the Earlier Excavations at "Amoxiumqua" and Giusewa. Monographs of the School of American Research, 6. Santa Fe: University of New Mexico and the School of American Research.

Renfrew, Colin, and Ezra B. W. Zubrow, eds.
1994   The Ancient Mind: Elements of Cognitive Archaeology. Cambridge: Cambridge University Press.

Restall, Matthew
1997   The Maya World: Yucatec Culture and Society, 1550–1850. Palo Alto: Stanford University Press.
2003   Seven Myths of the Spanish Conquest. Oxford: Oxford University Press.
2008   Spanish Creation of the Conquest of Mexico. In Invasion and Transformation: Interdisciplinary Perspectives on the Conquest of Mexico. R. P. Brienen and M. A. Jackson, eds. Pp. 93–102. Boulder: University Press of Colorado.

Ricard, Robert
1966   The Spiritual Conquest of Mexico: An Essay on the Apostolate and the Evangelizing Methods of the Mendicant Orders in New Spain, 1523–1572. Lesley Byrd Simpson, trans. Berkeley: University of California Press.

Rice, Prudence
1996a   Archaeology of Wine: The Wine and Brandy Haciendas of Moquegua, Peru. Journal of Field Archaeology 23(2):187–204.
1996b   Peru's Colonial Wine Industry and Its European Background. Antiquity 70(270):785–800.

Riley, Carroll L.
1999   The Kachina and the Cross: Indians and Spaniards in the Early Southwest. Salt Lake City: University of Utah Press.

Rodríguez-Alegría, Enrique
2002   Food, Eating, and Objects of Power: Class Stratification and Ceramic Production and Consumption in Colonial Mexico. PhD dissertation, Department of Anthropology, University of Chicago.
2005a   Eating Like an Indian: Negotiating Social Relations in the Spanish Colonies. Current Anthropology 46(4):551–65.
2005b   Consumption and the Varied Ideologies of Domination in Colonial Mexico City. In The Postclassic to Spanish-Era Transition in Mesoamerica. Susan Kepecs and Rani T. Alexander, eds. Pp. 35–48. Albuquerque: University of New Mexico Press.
2008   Narratives of Conquest, Colonialism, and Cutting-Edge Technology. American Anthropologist 110(1):33–43.

Rostworowski, Maria
1977   Etnía y sociedad. Costa peruana prehispánica. Lima: Instituto de Estudios Peruanos.

1978   Señoríos indígenas de Lima y Canta. Lima: Instituto de Estudios Peruanos.
2002   Pachacamac. Obras Completas II. Lima: Instituto de Estudios Peruanos.

Rowe, John H.
1946   Inca Culture at the Time of the Spanish Conquest. *In* Handbook of South American Indians. J. Steward, ed. Pp. 183–330. Washington, D.C.: Smithsonian Institution, Bureau of American Ethnology.
1957   The Incas under Spanish Colonial Institutions. The Hispanic American Historical Review 37(2):155–99.
1996   Inca. *In* Andean Art at Dumbarton Oaks. Elizabeth Hill Boone, ed. Pp. 301–20. Washington, D.C.: Dumbarton Oaks Research Library and Collection.

Rugeley, Terry
1996   Yucatan's Maya Peasantry and the Origins of the Caste War. Austin: University of Texas Press.
2001   Of Wonders and Wise Men: Religion and Popular Cultures in Southeast Mexico, 1800–1876. Austin: University of Texas Press.

Russell, R.
2008   The Little Tribe that Could. SF Weekly, March 28, 2007. San Francisco, CA.

Sahagún, Fr. Bernardino de
1989[1577]   Historia general de las cosas de Nueva España. México: Dirección General de Publicaciones del CONACULTA.

Sal, Hermenegildo
1792a   Escala que demuestra las habitaciones que tiene el Presidio de San Francisco. California Archives 6, Provincial State Papers, Tomo XI: 234. Bancroft Library, University of California, Berkeley.
1792b   Hermenegildo Sal to Romero—Information about the Presidio of San Francisco. Mother Dolores Sarre, trans. *In* The Presidio of San Francisco 1776–1976: A Collection of Historical Source Materials (Compiled in 1976) Pp. 47–49. San Francisco: National Park Service, Western Regional Office.

Salas, A. Mario
1950   Las armas de la Conquista. Buenos Aires: Emecé Editores.

Salomon, Frank
1991   Introductory Essay: The Huarochirí Manuscript. *In* The Huarochiri Manuscript. F. Salomon and G. Urioste, eds. Pp. 1–40. Austin: University of Texas Press.
1995   "The Beautiful Grandparents": Andean Ancestor Shrines and Mortuary Ritual as Seen Through Colonial Records. *In* Tombs for the Living. T. Dillehay, ed. Pp. 315–53. Washington, D.C.: Dumbarton Oaks.

Salomon, Frank, and Gary Urioste
1991   The Huarochiri Manuscript. Austin: University of Texas Press.

References

Sandstrom, Alan R., and Pamela Effrein Sandstrom
1986   Traditional Papermaking and Paper Cult Figures of Mexico. Norman: University of Oklahoma Press.

Sarkar, Pia
2001   The Urban Gamble. San Francisco Chronicle, May 28, 2001.

Sassaman, Kenneth E.
2001   Hunter-Gatherers and Traditions of Resistance. *In* The Archaeology of Traditions: Agency and History Before and After Columbus. T. R. Pauketat, ed. Gainesville: University Press of Florida.

Sauer, Carl O.
1966   The Early Spanish Main. Berkeley: University of California Press.

Scarry, John
2001   Resistance and Accommodation in Apalachee Province. *In* The Archaeology of Traditions. T. Pauketat, ed. Pp. 34–57. Gainesville: University Press of Florida.

Schaafsma, Curtis F.
2002   Apaches de Navajo: Seventeenth-Century Navajos in the Chama Valley of New Mexico. Salt Lake City: University of Utah Press.

Schaafsma, Polly
1963   Rock Art in the Navajo Reservoir District. Santa Fe: Museum of New Mexico Papers in Anthropology, 7.
1966   Early Navaho Rock Paintings and Carvings. Santa Fe: Museum of Navaho Ceremonial Art.
1975   Rock Art in New Mexico. Albuquerque: University of New Mexico Press.

Schackt, Jon
2001   The Emerging Maya: A Case of Ethnogenesis. *In* Maya Survivalism. Ueli Hostettler and Matthew Restall, eds. Pp. 3–14. Acta Mesoamericana, 12. Markt Schwaben: Verlag Anton Saurwein.

Schaffer, Scott E.
1995   Hegemony and the Habitus: Gramsci, Bourdieu, and James Scott on the Problem of Resistance. Research and Society 8:29–53.

Scholes, France V.
1936   Church and State in New Mexico, 1610–1650. New Mexico Historical Review 11:9–76, 145–78, 283–94, 297–349.
1937   Church and State in New Mexico, 1610–1650. New Mexico Historical Review 12:78–106.
1938   Notes on the Jemez Missions in the Seventeenth Century. El Palacio 44:61–71, 93–102.
1942   Troublous Times in New Mexico, 1659–1670. Albuquerque: University of New Mexico Press.

Schoneboom, Abigail
2007 Diary of a Working Boy: Creative Resistance among Anonymous Workbloggers. Ethnography 8(4):403–23.

Schroeder, Albert H.
1979 Pueblos Abandoned in Historic Times. *In* Handbook of North American Indians, vol. 9. A. Ortiz, ed. Pp. 236–54. Washington, D.C.: Smithsonian Institution Press.

Schuetz-Miller, Mardith K.
1994 Buildings and Builders in Hispanic California. Santa Barbara: Santa Barbara Trust for Historic Preservation.

Schurr, Mark
2010 Archaeological Indices of Resistance: Diversity in the Removal Period Potawatomi of the Western Great Lakes. American Antiquity 75(1):44–60.

Schuyler, Robert L.
1978 The Spoken Word, the Written Word, Observed Behavior and Preserved Behavior: The Contexts Available to the Archaeologist. *In* Historical Archaeology: A Guide to Substantive and Theoretical Contributions. R. L. Schuyler, ed. Amityville, NY: Baywood Publishing.

Schwartz, Norman B.
1990 Forest Society: A Social History of Peten, Guatemala. Philadelphia: University of Pennsylvania Press.

Scott, James C.
1985 Weapons of the Weak: Everyday Forms of Peasant Resistance. New Haven: Yale University Press.
1990 Domination and the Arts of Resistance: Hidden Transcripts. New Haven: Yale University Press.
1998 Seeing Like a State: How Certain Schemes to Improve the Human Condition Have Failed. New Haven: Yale University Press.

Sewell, William H. Jr.
2005 The Logics of History: Social Theory and Social Transformation. Chicago: University of Chicago Press.

Shapiro, Gary, and Bonnie McEwan
1992 Archaeology at San Luis Part One: The Apalachee Council House. Florida Archaeology 6:1–170. Tallahassee: Florida Bureau of Archaeological Research.

Sheptak, Russell N.
2004 Noticias de un cacique indígena de la época colonial: Una contribución a la historia colonial de Honduras. Paper presented at the VII Congreso Centroamericano de Historia, Tegucigalpa, Honduras.
2005 The Continuity of Social Practices in the Colonial Period Ulua Valley, North Honduras. Paper presented at the 70th Annual Meeting of the Society for American Archaeology, Salt Lake City, Utah.

References

2006   Rereading Çoçumba's Documentary Record. Paper presented at the 71st Annual Meeting of the Society for American Archaeology.

2008   Çoçumba Contested: Documentary and Material Traces of Early Colonial Indigenous Practice. Paper presented at the 73rd Annual Meeting of the Society for American Archaeology, Vancouver, B.C.

Sheptak, Russell N., and Rosemary A. Joyce

2008   The Circulation of Sacred Images in the Archives of Colonial Honduras. Paper presented at the Annual Meeting of the Theoretical Archaeology Group–United States in New York, New York.

Sheptak, Russell N., Rosemary A. Joyce, and Kira Blaisdell-Sloan

2007   Echoes of Native Voices: Reading Archival Documents with Discourse in Mind. Paper presented at the Annual Meeting of the Society for Historical Archaeology, Williamsburg, VA.

Sherman, William

1979   Forced Native Labor in Sixteenth Century Central America. Lincoln: University of Nebraska Press.

Silliman, Stephen W.

2001a   Agency, Practical Politics and the Archaeology of Culture Contact. Journal of Social Archaeology 1:190–209.

2001b   Theoretical Perspectives on Labor and Colonialism: Reconsidering the California Missions. Journal of Anthropological Archaeology 20:379–407.

2004   Lost Laborers in Colonial California: Native Americans and the Archaeology of Rancho Petaluma. Tucson: University of Arizona Press.

2005a   Culture Contact or Colonialism? Challenges in the Archaeology of North America. American Antiquity 70(1):55–74.

2005b   Social and Physical Landscapes of Contact. In North American Archaeology. T. R. Pauketat and D. D. Loren, eds. Pp. 273–97. Malden, MA: Blackwell.

2009   Change and Continuity, Practice, and Memory: Native American Persistence in Colonial North America. American Antiquity 74(2):211–30.

Silva Tena, Teresa

1990   Estudio preliminar. Tratado del descubrimiento de las yndias y su conquista. Pp. 13–40. México: CONACULTA.

Silverman, Helaine

2002   Introduction. The Space and Place of Death. In The Space and Place of Death. H. Silverman and D. Small, eds. Pp. 1–11. Arlington, VA: Archeological Papers of the American Anthropological Association.

Simmons, Scott

1995   Maya Resistance, Maya Resolve: The Tools of Autonomy from Tipu, Belize. Ancient Mesoamerica 6:135–46.

Simpson-Smith, Charr, and Rob Edwards

2000   San Francisco Spanish Colonial Presidio: Field and Laboratory Report for 1996, 1997, 1998, and 1999, with Stratigraphic Discussion. Cabrillo College

Archaeological Technology Program, Aptos, California. Submitted to the Presidio Trust and National Park Service, Golden Gate Recreation Area, San Francisco.

Singleton, Theresa A.
1998   Cultural Interaction and African American Identity in Plantation Archaeology. *In* Studies in Culture Contact: Interaction, Culture Change, and Archaeology. J. G. Cusick, ed. Carbondale, IL: Center for Archaeological Investigations.

Sivaramakrishnan, K.
2005   Some Intellectual Genealogies for the Concept of Everyday Resistance. American Anthropologist 107(3):346–55.

Smith, Marvin
1989   Aboriginal Population Movement in the Early Historic Period. *In* Powhatan's Mantle: Indians in the Colonial Southeast. Peter Wood, Gregory Waselkov, and M. Thomas Hatley, eds. Pp. 21–24. Lincoln: University of Nebraska Press.

Smith, Marvin T., and Mary E. Good
1982   Early Sixteenth Century Glass Beads in the Spanish Colonial Trade. Greenwood, MS: Cottonlandia Museum Publications.

Smith, Mary O.
2003   Beyond Palisades: The Nature of Frequency of Late Prehistoric Deliberate Violent Trauma in the Chickamauga Reservoir of East Tennessee. American Journal of Physical Anthropology 121:303–18.

Smith, Matt
1998   Presidio Originals. SF Weekly, May 13, 1998. San Francisco, CA.

Smith, Roger C.
1999   Pensacola's Colonial Maritime Resources. *In* Archaeology of Colonial Pensacola. J. A. Bense, ed. Pp. 91–120. Gainesville: University Press of Florida.

Smith, Watson, Richard B. Woodbury, and Nathalie F. S. Woodbury
1966   The Excavation of Hawikuh by Frederick Webb Hodge: Report of the Hendricks-Hodge Expedition, 1917–1923. New York: Museum of the American Indian, Heye Foundation.

Soja, Edward W.
1989   Postmodern Geographies: The Reassertion of Space in Critical Social Theory. New York: Verso.

Spalding, Karen
1984   Huarochirí: A Colonial Province under Inca and Spanish Rule. Stanford: Stanford University Press.
1999   The Crises and Transformations of Invaded Societies: Andean Area (1500–1580). *In* The Cambridge History of the Native Peoples of the Americas, vol. 3. F. Salomon and S. B. Schawrtz, eds. Pp. 904–72. Cambridge: Cambridge University Press.

References

Spicer, Edward H.
1962 Cycles of Conquest: The Impact of Spain, Mexico, and the United States on the Indians of the Southwest, 1533–1960. Tucson: University of Arizona Press.

Spielmann, Katherine A., Tiffany Clark, Diane Hawkey, Katharine Rainey, and Suzanne K. Fish
2009 "...being weary, they had rebelled": Pueblo Subsistence and Labor under Spanish Colonialism. Journal of Anthropological Archaeology 28:102–25.

Spielmann, Katherine A., Jeannette L. Mobley-Tanaka, and James M. Potter
2006 Style and Resistance in the Seventeenth-Century Salinas Province. American Antiquity 71(4):621–49.

Steadman, Dawnie W.
2008 Warfare Related Trauma at Orendorf, a Middle Mississippian Site in West-Central Illinois. American Journal of Physical Anthropology 136(1):51–65.

Stein, Gil J.
2005 Introduction: The Comparative Archaeology of Colonial Encounters. *In* The Archaeology of Colonial Encounters. G. J. Stein, ed. Santa Fe: School of American Research Press.

Stern, Steve J.
1982 Peru's Indian Peoples and the Challenge of Conquest: Huamanga to 1640. Madison: University of Wisconsin Press.

Stork, Theophilus, D. D.
1859 The Home-Scenes of the New Testament; or Christ in the Family. London: Lindsay and Blakiston.

Strong, William Duncan, Alfred Kidder II, and A. J. Drexel Paul
1938 Preliminary Report on the Smithsonian Institution–Harvard University Archaeological Expedition to Northwestern Honduras 1936. Washington, D.C.: Smithsonian Institution.

Suárez de Peralta, Juan
1990[1589] Tratado del descubrimiento de las yndias y su conquista. Edition, preliminary study, and notes by Giorgio Perissinotto. Madrid: Alianza.

Tabio, Ernesto
1965 Una tumba tardía de Puruchuco, Lima. Excavaciones en la costa central del Perú, 1955–58:91–101.

Tedlock, Dennis, and Bruce Mannheim
1995 The Dialogic Emergence of Culture. Champaign: University of Illinois Press.

Thomas, Alfred B., ed. and trans.
1932 Forgotten Frontiers: A Study of the Spanish Indian Policy of Don Juan Bautista de Anza, Governor of New Mexico, 1777–1787. Norman: University of Oklahoma Press.

Thomas, Cyrus
1891   Catalog of Prehistoric Works East of the Rocky Mountains. Washington, D.C.: Bulletin 12, Bureau of American Ethnology, Smithsonian Institution.
1894   Report on the Mound Explorations of the Bureau of American Ethnology. Pp. 3–730. Washington, D.C: Twelfth Annual Report of the Bureau of American Ethnology, 1890–1891.

Thomas, David Hurst
1988   Saints and Soldiers at Santa Catalina: Hispanic Designs for Colonial America. *In* The Recovery of Meaning. Mark Leone and Parker Potter, eds. Pp. 73–140. Washington, D.C.: Smithsonian Institution Press.
1989   Columbian Consequences: The Spanish Borderlands in Cubist Perspective. *In* Columbian Consequences, vol. 1: Archaeological and Historical Perspectives on the Spanish Borderlands West. D. H. Thomas, ed. Pp. 1–16. Washington, D.C.: Smithsonian Institution Press.
1990   The Spanish Missions of La Florida: An Overview. *In* Columbian Consequences, vol. 2: Archaeological and Historical Perspectives in the Spanish Borderlands East. D. H. Thomas, ed. Pp. 357–98. Washington, D.C.: Smithsonian Institution Press.

Thomas, David Hurst, ed.
1989   Columbian Consequences, vol. 1: Archaeological and Historical Perspectives on the Spanish Borderlands West. Washington, D.C.: Smithsonian Institution Press.
1990   Columbian Consequences, vol. 2: Archaeological and Historical Perspectives on the Spanish Borderlands East. Washington, D.C.: Smithsonian Institution Press.
1991   Columbian Consequences, vol. 3: The Spanish Borderlands in Pan-American Perspective. Washington, D.C.: Smithsonian Institution Press.

Thomas, Hugh
2000   Who's Who of the Conquistadors. London: Cassell.

Thompson, Edward Palmer
1963   The Making of the English Working Class. New York: Pantheon Books.

Thompson, J. Eric S.
1963   Maya Archaeologist. London: Robert Hale Limited.

Tibesar, Antonine
1953   Franciscan Beginnings in Early Colonial Peru. Washington, D.C.: Academy of American Franciscan History.

Torres-Rouff, Christina, and Maria Antonietta Costa Junqueira
2006   Interpersonal Violence in Prehistoric San Pedro de Atacama, Chile: Behavioral Implications of Environmental Stress. American Journal of Physical Anthropology 130:60–70.

References

Torquemada, Fray Juan
1969[1615] Monarquía indiana, vol. 3. México: Porrúa.

Towner, Ronald H.
1992 Dating the Dinétah Pueblitos: The Tree-Ring Data. *In* Interpreting the Past: Research with Public Participation. L. Jacobson and J. Piper, eds. Pp. 55–72. Cultural Resource Series, 10. Albuquerque: New Mexico Bureau of Land Management.
1996 The Pueblito Phenomenon: A New Perspective on Post-Revolt Navajo Culture. *In* The Archaeology of Navajo Origins. R. H. Towner, ed. Pp. 149–70. Salt Lake City: University of Utah Press.
2003 Defending the Dinétah: Pueblitos in the Ancestral Navajo Homeland. Salt Lake City: University of Utah Press.

Towner, Ronald H., and Jeffrey S. Dean
1992 LA 2298: The Oldest Pueblito Revisited. Kiva 59:315–31.
1996 Questions and Problems in Pre-Fort Sumner Navajo Archaeology. *In* The Archaeology of Navajo Origins. Ronald H. Towner, ed. Pp. 3–18. Salt Lake City: University of Utah Press.

Towner, Ronald H., and Bryon P. Johnson, eds.
1998 The San Rafael Survey: Reconstructing Eighteenth Century Navajo Population Dynamics in the Dinétah using Archaeological and Dendrochronological Data. Arizona State Museum Archaeology Series, 190. Tempe: University of Arizona Press.

Tringham, Ruth E.
1991 Households with Faces: The Challenge of Gender in Prehistoric Architectural Remains. *In* Engendering Archaeology: Women and Prehistory. Joan M. Gero and Margaret W. Conkey, eds. Pp. 92–131. Cambridge, MA: Basil Blackwell, Inc.
1994 Engendered Places in Prehistory. Gender, Place, and Culture 1(2):169–203.

Tringham, Ruth E., and Mirjana Stevanovic
2000 Different Excavation Styles Create Different Windows into Çatalhöyük. *In* Towards Reflexive Method in Archaeology: The Example at Çatalhöyük. Ian Hodder, ed. Pp. 111–18. Ankara, Turkey: British Institute of Archaeology.

Trusted, Marjorie
2007 The Arts of Spain: Iberia and Latin America, 1450–1700. University Park: Pennsylvania State University Press.

Tung, Tiffiny
2007 Trauma and Violence in the Wari Empire of the Peruvian Andes: Warfare, Raids, and Ritual Fights. American Journal of Physical Anthropology 133(3):941–56.

References

Tzul, A. A.
1993　After 100 Years: The Oral History and Traditions of San Antonio, Cayo District, Belize. Belize: U Kuxtal Masewal Maya Institute of Belize.

URS Greiner Woodward Clyde
1999　Archaeological Ground Truthing of a Ground Penetration Radar Study at the Presidio de San Francisco. URS Greiner Woodward Clyde, Oakland. Submitted to Sacramento District U.S. Army Corps of Engineers and the National Park Service, Golden Gate National Recreation Area, San Francisco.

Valero de García de Lascuráin, Ana R.
1991　Solares y conquistadores. Orígenes de la propiedad en la ciudad de México. México: Colección Divulgación, Instituto Nacional de Antropología e Historia.

Valle, Perla
1993　Memorial de los indios de Tepetlaóztoc o Códice Kingsborough. México: Colección Científica 263, Instituto Nacional de Antropología e Historia.

Van Buren, Mary
1999　Tarapaya: An Elite Spanish Residence near Colonial Potosí in Comparative Perspective. Historical Archaeology 33(2):108–22.
2005　Huayrachinas and Tocochimbos: Traditional Smelting Technology of the Southern Andes. Latin American Antiquity 16(1):3–25.
2010　The Archaeological Study of Spanish Colonialism in the Americas. Journal of Archaeological Research 18:151–201.

Vancouver, George
1984　A Voyage of Discovery to the North Pacific and Round the World, 1791–1795. Cambridge: The Hakluyt Society.

van Dommelen, Peter
2002　Ambiguous Matters: Colonialism and Local Identities in Punic Sardinia. *In* The Archaeology of Colonialism. C. L. Lyons and J. K. Papadopoulos, eds. Pp. 121–47. Los Angeles: The Getty Research Institute.
2005　Colonial Interactions and Hybrid Practices. Phoenician and Carthaginian Settlements in the Ancient Mediterranean. *In* The Archaeology of Colonial Encounters. G. J. Stein, ed. Pp. 109–41. Santa Fe: School of American Research Press.

VanderVeen, James
2007　A New Look at Old Food: Reconstructing Subsistence Patterns at La Isabela, Dominican Republic. Proceedings of the Twenty-First Congress of the International Association for Caribbean Archaeology (July 2007):41–47.

Van Valkenburgh, Nathaniel
2007　Informe de excavaciones en la Unidad 2, Sector—Pueblo, Sitio—Colonial, Complejo Arqueológico El Brujo, Julio-Agosto 2007. Internal project report on file at the Peabody Museum of Archaeology and Ethnology, Harvard University, Cambridge, MA.

References

Vasconcellos, Carolina Michaëlis de
1921   Algumas palavras a respeito de Púcaros de Portugal. Coimbra, Portugal: Imprensa da Universidade.

Vásquez Sánchez, Víctor and Teresa E. Rosales Tham
2008   Análisis de restos de fauna y vegetales de la igesia y pueblo–Complejo Arqueológico el Brujo. Internal project report on file at the Peabody Museum of Archaeology and Ethnology, Harvard University, Cambridge, MA.

Veeckman, J.
1994   Iberian Unglazed Pottery from Antwerp (Belgium). Medieval Ceramics 18:9–18.

Vega, Bernardo
1979a   Los metales y los aborigines de la Hispaniola. Santo Domingo: Museo del Hombre Dominicano.
1979b   Arqueología de los cimarrones del maniel del Bahoruco. Boletín del Museo del Hombre Dominicano 12:11–48. Santo Domingo.

Vega, Juan José
1980   Incas contra Españoles. Lima: Pacific Press.

Verano, John W.
2003   Human Skeletal Remains from Machu Picchu: A Reexamination of the Yale Peabody Museum's Collections. *In* The 1912 Yale Peruvian Scientific Expedition Collections from Machu Picchu, Human and Animal Remains. R. L. Burger and L. C. Salazar, eds. Pp. 65–118. New Haven: Yale University Publications in Anthropology.
2007   Conflict and Conquest in Pre-Hispanic Andean South America. *In* Latin American Indigenous Warfare and Ritual Violence. R. J. Chacon and R. G. Mondoza, eds. Pp. 105–15. Tucson: University of Arizona Press.
2008   Communality and Diversity in Moche Human Sacrifice. *In* The Art and Archaeology of the Moche. S. Bourget and K. L. Jones, eds. Pp. 195–213. Austin: University of Texas Press.

Villacorta O., Luis Felipe
2001   Arquitectura monumental: Forma, función y poder en los asentamientos del valle medio bajo del Rímac (Períodos Intermedio Tardío y Horizonte Tardío). Tesis de Licenciatura presentada a la Pontificia Universidad Católica del Perú. Lima.
2004   Los palacios en la costa central durante los periodos tardíos: De Pachacamac al Inca. Bulletin de l'Institut Français d'Etudes Andines 33(3):539–70.

Vincent, Victoria Anne
1993   The Avila-Cortes Conspiracy: Creole Aspirations and Royal Interests. PhD dissertation, Department of History, University of Nebraska, Lincoln.

References

Voss, Barbara L.
1999 Report on Archaeological Shovel Probe Survey at the Presidio of San Francisco, 1997–1998. Archaeological Research Facility, University of California, Berkeley. Submitted to the National Park Service, Golden Gate National Recreation Area, San Francisco.
2005 From *Casta* to *California*: Social Identity and the Archaeology of Culture Contact. American Anthropologist 107(3):461–74.
2007 Image, Text, Object: Interpreting Documents and Artifacts as "Labors of Representation." Historical Archaeology 41(4):144–68.
2008 The Archaeology of Ethnogenesis: Race and Sexuality in Colonial San Francisco. Berkeley: University of California Press.

Voss, Barbara L., and Vance G. Benté
1996 Archaeological Discovery and Investigation of the Historic Presidio de San Francisco. Woodward-Clyde Consultants, Oakland, CA. Submitted to the Sacramento District, U.S. Army Corps of Engineers.

Voss, Barbara L., Amy Ramsay, and Anna Naruta
2000 Final Report, Funston Avenue Archaeological Research Project, Presidio of San Francisco, 1999. Archaeological Research Facility, University of California, Berkeley. Submitted to the Presidio Trust and the National Park Service, Golden Gate National Recreation Area, San Francisco.

Wachtel, Nathan
1977 The Vision of the Vanquished: The Spanish Conquest of Peru through Indian Eyes, 1530–1570. B. Reynolds and S. Reynolds, trans. New York: Harper and Row.

Walker, Philip
2001 A Bioarchaeological Perspective on the History of Violence. Annual Review of Anthropology 30:573–96.

Weber, David
1992 The Spanish Frontier in North America. New Haven: Yale University Press.
2005 Barbaros: Spaniards and Their Savages in the Age of Enlightenment. New Haven: Yale University Press.

Weeks, John
1997 The Mercedarian Mission System in Santa Barbara de Tencoa, Honduras. *In* Approaches to the Historical Archaeology of Mexico, Central and South America. J. Gasco, G. Smith, and P. Fournier-Garcia, eds. Pp. 91–100. Los Angeles: Institute of Archaeology, UCLA.

Weeks, John, and Nancy Black
1991 Mercederian Missionaries and the Transformation of Lenca Society in Western Honduras, 1550–1700. *In* Columbian Consequences, vol. 3: The Spanish Borderlands in Pan American Perspective. D. H. Thomas, ed. Pp. 245–61. Washington, D.C.: The Smithsonian Institution Press.

References

Weeks, John, Nancy Black, and J. Stuart Speaker
1987   From Prehistory to History in Western Honduras: The Care Lenca in the Colonial Province of Tencoa. *In* Interaction on the Southeast Mesoamerican Frontier, part 1. E. J. Robinson, ed. Pp. 65–94. Oxford: BAR International Series, 327 (i).

Weik, Terrance
2004   Archaeology of the African Diaspora in Latin America. Historical Archaeology 38(1):32–49.

Wernke, Steven A.
2003   An Archaeo-History of Andean Community and Landscape: The Late Prehispanic and Early Colonial Colca Valley, Peru. PhD dissertation, Department of Anthropology, University of Wisconsin-Madison. Ann Arbor: University Microfilms.
2006   The Politics of Community and Inka Statecraft in the Colca Valley, Peru. Latin American Antiquity 17(2):177–208.
2007a   Analogy or Erasure? Dialectics of Religious Transformation in the Early Doctrinas of the Colca Valley, Peru. International Journal of Historical Archaeology 11(2):152–82.
2007b   Negotiating Community and Landscape in the Peruvian Andes: A Trans-Conquest View. American Anthropologist 109(1):130–52.
2009   La interfaz política-ecológica en el valle del Colca durante la época inkaica. *In* Arqueología del Área Centro Sur Andina, Actas del Simposio Internacional 30 de junio–2 de julio de 2005, Arequipa, Perú. Mariusz S. Ziólkowski, Justin Jennings, Luis A. Belan Franco, and Andrea Drusini, eds. Pp. 587–614. ANDES (Boletín del Centro de Estudios Precolombinos de la Universidad de Varsovia), 7. Warsaw: Centro de Estudios Precolombinos de la Universidad de Varsovia, and Warsaw University Press; Lima: Instituto Francés de Estudios Andinos.
N.d.   Andean Households in Transition: The Politics of Domestic Space at an Early Doctrina in the Peruvian Highlands. Chapter in review for Lost in Transition: Decolonizing Indigenous Histories at the "Prehistoric/Colonial" Intersection in Archaeology. Maxine Oland and Siobhan Hart, eds. Tucson: University of Arizona Press; Lima: Instituto Francés de Estudios Andinos.

White, Christine Pelzer
1986   Everyday Resistance, Socialist Revolution and Rural Development: The Vietnamese Case. Journal of Peasant Studies 13(2):49–63.

White, Leslie A.
1962   The Pueblo of Sia, New Mexico. Smithsonian Institution Bureau of American Ethnology Bulletin 184. Washington, D.C.: United States Government Printing Office.

White, Richard

1991   The Middle Ground: Indians, Empires, and Republics in the Great Lakes Region, 1650–1815. Cambridge: Cambridge University Press.

Willey, P., and Thomas E. Emerson

1993   The Osteology and Archaeology of the Crow Creek Massacre. Plains Anthropologist 38(145):227–69.

Willey, P., and Douglas D. Scott

1996   "The Bullets Buzzed Like Bees": Gunshot Wounds in Skeletons from the Battle of Little Bighorn. International Journal of Osteoarchaeology 6:15–27.

Wilson, Samuel

1990   Hispaniola: Caribbean Chiefdoms in the Age of Columbus. University of Alabama Press, Tuscaloosa.

Wonderly, Anthony

1981   Late Postclassic Excavations at Naco, Honduras. Latin American Studies Program, Dissertation Series, 86. Ithaca: Cornell University.

1984a   Rancho Ires Phase (Colonial) Test Excavations. *In* Archaeology in Northwestern Honduras: Interim Reports of the Proyecto Arqueológico Sula, vol. 1. J. Henderson, ed. Pp. 4–26. Ithaca: Cornell University Archaeology Program–Latin American Studies Program.

1984b   Test Excavations of the Naco (Late Postclassic) Phase. *In* Archaeology in Northwestern Honduras: Interim Reports of the Proyecto Arqueológico Sula, vol. 1. J. S. Henderson, ed. Pp. 27–66. Ithaca: Cornell University Archaeology Program–Latin American Studies Program.

1985   The Land of Ulua: Postclassic Research in the Naco and Sula Valleys, Honduras. *In* The Lowland Maya Postclassic. Arlen Chase and Prudence Rice, eds. Pp. 254–69. Austin: University of Texas Press.

1986a   Material Symbolics in Pre-Columbian Households: The Painted Pottery of Naco, Honduras. Journal of Anthropological Research 42:497–534.

1986b   Naco, Honduras—Some Aspects of a Late Precolumbian Community on the Eastern Maya Frontier. *In* The Southeast Maya Periphery. Patricia Urban and Edward Schortman, eds. Pp. 313–23. Austin: University of Texas Press.

Worth, John

1995   The Struggle for the Georgia Coast: An Eighteenth Century Spanish Retrospective on Guale and Mocama. New York: American Museum of Natural History, Anthropological Papers, 75.

1998   The Timucua Chiefdoms of Spanish Florida, vol. 2: Resistance and Destruction. Gainesville: University Press of Florida.

Wylie, Alison

2000   Questions of Evidence, Legitimacy, and the (Dis)Unity of Science. American Antiquity 65(2):227–37.

References

2002   Thinking from Things: Essays in the Philosophy of Archaeology. Berkeley: University of California Press.

Yamane, Linda, ed.
2002   A Gathering of Voices: The Native Peoples of the Central California Coast. Santa Cruz, CA: The Museum of Art and History.

Yaremko, Jason M.
2006   Gente Bárbara: Indigenous Rebellion, Resistance and Persistence in Colonial Cuba, 1500–1800. Kacike: Journal of Caribbean Amerindian History and Anthropology 7(3):157–84.

Young, Robert J. C.
1995   Colonial Desire: Hybridity in Theory, Culture, and Race. London: Routledge.

Zimmerman, Arthur Franklin
1938   Francisco de Toldeo: Fifth Viceroy of Peru, 1569–1581. Caldwell, ID: Caxton Printers.

Index

57AS03 cemetery (Peru), 59–61, 63–68

Accommodation, 14–15, 18, 199, 220; and evangelical encounters, 78; in Hispaniola and La Florida, 41; identification of, 103; and Native Americans (US Southeast), 41, 45, 48, 54–55; and religious practices, 73, 80, 110–11; and resistance, 44–45, 56, 192, 200; as strategy, 7, 9, 58, 215; study of, 200–201
acculturation, 6, 16–17, 186, 228, 230, 244
Acoma Pueblo (New Mexico), 226–27, 232, 234–35
Adriana, Luciana, 159
African: Americans, 245, 263–64; descendants, 165, 170, 251; free, 13–14, 43–44, 170, 245; heritage of *creoles*, 196n1; resistance, 56; slaves, 13–14, 43–44, 47–48, 52, 54, 170. See also *mulato/mulata*
African Burial Ground (New York City), 263–64
agency, 149, 173; and Basin of Mexico pottery, 144–45; indigenous, 18, 39, 78, 108, 200, 219–20, 244; and material culture, 79; Sewell's approach to, 20, 27–28, 33; and social life, 7–10
agriculture, 57, 109, 167, 177, 180, 182, 185, 188, 191, 194, 197n4, 244–46, 258
Aguilar, Pedro de, 143
Ahuízotl, King, 131
Ainsley, Captain, 182–83
Alameda Pueblo (New Mexico), 226, 234–35
Alaska, 245, 250

alcades, 138, 164, 168, 181, 183, 192, 225, 232, 234
Alta California, 255, 258, 265n1
Alvarado, Pedro de, 155–58, 197n3, 219
Amador, Pedro, 254
ambiguity, 17–18, 173–74, 195, 200–201
ambivalence, 14–16, 18, 103, 201, 213, 215, 218, 220
Ambivalent Conquests (Clendinnen), 77
American Southeast, 13, 19–21, 38, 41, 48–49, 52, 145
Andeans: clothing practices of, 115; evangelization of, 100; and "nativeness" appreciated, 124; polities of, 62; religious practices of, 57–58, 70–71, 100, 116–19; and resistance, 111; textiles of, 111–15; use Spanish for own purposes, 119. See also burials; Peru
Anza, Juan Bautista de, 261
Apache nation, 223–26
Apalache Indians, 53–54
architecture: adobe, 107, 118, 161, 164, 247–50, 255; at Berry site (North Carolina), 34–36; brick/plaster, 161; built by Native Americans for Spanish, 24–25, 28–31, 34–36; church/plaza centered, 80; of "conquest," 100; council houses, 53; defensive, 229–31, 243, 245–50, 252; domestic, 89, 93–98, 100, 106–7, 115–16, 245; earthen, 253; for elites, 51, 98–99, 245; great hall/plaza complexes (Peru), 85–86, 89–91; and labor relations, 265; Late Horizon, 94; masonry, 91–94, 224, 227, 247–48, 250, 255; palisade, 247–48;

Index

rammed earth, 247; and refuse disposal, 237; and religion/ritual, 79–80, 82, 87, 99, 238, 241n2; and social relations, 253, 257; of Spanish influence, 105–6; study of, 150, 245, 253, 257, 259, 264–65; and violence, 256, 258; wattle-and-daub, 106–7, 247–48, 250. *See also* El Presidio de San Francisco; kivas; Malata *doctrina*; specific types; specific places

Archivo General de Indias (AGI), 143

Argüello, Luis Antonio, 256

Argüelo, Fernando de, 226

Aroca, Gonzalo, 154–55

artifacts. *See* individual types; specific sites

Atahualpa (Inca monarch), 61, 119, 124, 219

Austin, Governor, 173, 182–85, 192–93

Austria, 186

Avila, Alonso de (the elder), 136, 138, 140

Avila, Alonso de (the younger), 136, 139–43, 146–47

Avila, Gil González de, 136, 138

Ayeta, Francisco de, 226

ayllus, 57, 76n1, 87, 97

Aztec Red Ware, 147

Aztecs, 122–23, 131, 219

Bahoruco War, 47–48

Bandelier, Adolph, 226–28

Bandera, Juan de la, 22, 24–26, 29–31, 37

Basin of Mexico, 15, 127–31, 135, 140, 146. *See also* Red Ware

beads, 31–32, 87, 89, 95, 97, 117, 162, 251

Belize, 152, 176, 178, 184, 187–88

Belize Estate and Produce Company, 185, 191, 195

Benavides, Alonso de, 204, 223–24

Berry site (North Carolina), 20, 23, 29, 32–36, 38

Bhabha, Homi, 200

bioarchaeology, 14, 58, 63, 74

Bird, Junius, 105

Black-on-Orange ware, 131, 133–34, 144, 147

Blakey, Michael, 263–64

Boletsakwa village (Jemez Pueblo, NM), 203, 208, 210–11, 213, 216, 221n1

bottles. *See* glass containers

Bourdieu, Pierre, 237

Brezine, Carrie, 112

British colonial: economic networks, 188; Empire/Crown, 177, 185, 189–91; forces, 175–76, 193; government, 180–82, 184–85, 189–91, 197n4; institutions, 174, 176, 187; law, 188, 194; merchants, 16, 174, 180–81, 188, 195; policies, 16; system, 193

British Foreign Office, 174, 181

British Honduras, 16; and abandonment of San Pedro Sirís, 191–92; archaeological sites of, 176, 182, 185–90; Britain's goals/strategies in, 175, 180–81, 192; and education, 189–90; historical background of, 176–81, 191; and logging, 16, 174, 177, 180–82, 185, 188, 191–92, 194, 197n4; military encounters in, 182–85, 193–94; peace negotiations and, 188; and religion, 188–89; and San Pedro Sirís, 180–82, 184–92; Spanish influence on, 175–76; study of, 174–76. *See also* Maya people; San José Yalbac; San Pedro Maya; San Pedro Sirís

Brugge, David, 230–31, 233, 237–38, 240

built environment, 15, 75, 79–80, 82, 98–99. *See also* architecture

burials: and Andean coprse removal, 71–75; Andean sacred, 57–58, 75, 76n1; atypical (Peru), 58, 60–61, 63–64, 67–69, 75; and bundles, 60, 73; in churches, 14, 45, 70–71, 73–74; Early Colonial, 14, 60, 71–75; for elites, 47, 49; Late Horizon (Peru), 58–61, 63, 69, 71–73; and Malata tombs, 87; and mummies, 85; of Native Americans, 45, 52; and offerings, 60, 69, 73, 76n2, 115–17; at Puruchuco-Huaquerones (Peru), 58–61, 63–69, 71–75; at Taíno sites, 47, 49; and textiles, 113–15; in upper Yadkin River, 31–32. *See also* cemeteries

Burke County, North Carolina, 20

Burke phase sites (North Carolina), 23, 25, 31–32

Cacao, 152, 154, 157–59, 167

caciques, 24–26, 29, 46–48, 51, 54–56, 154, 158, 168, 226

Cajatambo, Peru, 70

California: and agro-capitalist society, 258; history of, 261; and labor agreements, 254, 257; and Mexican-era ranching, 258; and Presidio Pasados, 261–62; rich indigenous history of, 264; Russian settlements in, 245, 250, 257; Spanish-colonial project in, 246, 256; US annexation of, 246. *See also* El Presidio de San Francisco; Native Californians; Ohlone people

Callalli (Peru), 86–87

Candelaria (Honduras), 167–70. *See also* Masca

Canos (South Carolina), 19, 21–26, 29–31

Canul, Marcos, 181, 184, 192–93

Caribbean, 3–4, 13, 41–43, 45–49, 52, 152, 163, 166, 177, 187

Carlos II, King, 202

Carlson, Roy, 228, 242n6

castas, 130, 133, 168–70

Catawba River (North Carolina), 23, 25

Catawba Valley (North Carolina), 23, 32, 38

Index

Catholicism, 68, 78, 80, 161, 163, 165–66, 177, 180, 188–89, 224–25. *See also* Christianity; missions; religious conversion
Cauchi (North Carolina), 19, 25
cemeteries, 14, 58–61, 63–75, 106, 109–10
Central America, 163, 170, 177
Ceramics: British, 180, 186–87; colonial, 71–73, 87, 95, 98, 132; effigy vessels, 138–39; figurines, 116–17; funerary, 60; glazed, 87, 95, 130, 132, 162; of Honduras, 153–54, 157, 165, 194; Hopi, 238, 241; Incan, 98; by the Keres, 238, 241; Late Horizon style, 87; of Late Intermediate period, 101n1; materials/techniques of, 15, 97, 131–34, 216; native, 15, 171, 180, 186–87; of the Navajo, 112, 224, 236, 241; of NM Pueblos, 208–9, 216–18, 227–28, 236, 238–39, 241; pipes, 185, 251; polychrome, 98, 228, 236, 238–39, 241, 242n7; sale of, 133; service wares, 89, 131–32, 134, 144, 157, 169; Spanish, 48, 132, 135, 148, 171; study of, 59, 123; Taíno, 49; Tewa, 238, 241; upper Yadkin River, 32, 38; utilitarian, 97–98, 131. *See also* specific types
Cereceda, Andres de, 152–53, 155
Cerro Colorado village (Zia Pueblo, NM), 201–3, 209–18, 220, 221n1
Chaco District (New Mexico), 236–38, 241
chapels, 79, 85–86, 89–94, 98–99, 160, 249
Chatterjee, Partha, 200
Cheek, Charles, 187
cherts, 157, 251
Chiaha (eastern Tennessee), 19, 24–25
Chicama River (Peru), 106
Chicama Valley (Peru), 15, 103–5
chiefs, 23–26, 30–33, 47–48
children, 64, 71–73, 189–90
Christianity, 43; acceptance of, 51, 156; ambivalence towards, 213; artifacts relating to, 113–14, 117–18; and built environment, 82, 99; and daily life (Peru), 80–82, 99; and education, 204; and Franciscan missions, 77–78, 81; icons of, 73, 207; and indigeneity, 124; and Native Americans (New Mexico), 231; and Native Americans (US Southeast), 45; rejection of, 51–52, 80; strict tenets of, 115; as tactic, 166; triumph of, 110–11. *See also* burials; Catholicism; religious conversion
chullpas (burial towers), 87
churches, 150, 184, 245; appropriated by indigenous people, 15, 110, 159–60; built by Franciscan friars, 85; and cofradias, 160–61; destroyed during Pueblo Revolt, 206–8; in Honduras, 160–63, 165–67; at Magdalena de Cao Viejo (Peru), 105–11; registers of, 159, 168; and Spanish urban planning, 80
Cieza de León, Pedro, 70
cimarrón communities, 47, 52
Ciudad de los Reyes (Peru). *See* Lima, Peru
"civilizing," of Native Americans, 46, 48–49, 56, 81
Clapera, Francisco, 136
Clark, Bonnie J., 176
class divisions, 14, 43–44, 47, 55, 119, 197n4
Clemente II, Pope, 140
Clendinnen, Inga, 77–78, 99
clergy, 80, 82, 86, 174, 176, 180, 188–89. *See also* Franciscan friars; priests
clothing, 51, 108, 111–13, 122
Cochiti Pueblo (New Mexico), 226, 234–35
Çoçumba (Honduran leader), 152–56
Codallos y Rabal, Joachin, 233
Codex of Chimalpopoca, 136
Códice de los Alfareros (Codex of the Potters), 15, 137–38, 144, 148, 148n1
Cofitachequi (South Carolina), 22–23, 25–26. *See also* Canos (South Carolina)
cofradias (Honduras), 159–61
Colca Valley (Peru), 14, 79, 83–87, 123
Collaguas (Peru), 83–85, 95
Colombia, 48
Colón, Cristóbal, 3
Colony Ross settlement (northern California), 245, 250
Columbian Quincentenary, 7, 244
Columbus, Christopher, 46, 48–49
Comanche, 230
Comayagua (Honduras), 164, 166, 168
compadrazgo, 202, 214
Compañón, Martínez, 108
conflict-related trauma. *See* perimortem traumatic injuries
congregación system, 199, 205, 207–8
conventos, 84–87, 234, 245
Cook, Guillermo, 60
cooperation, 4, 9, 16, 20, 35–36
copas, 131
Corella, Jeronimo de, 160
Coronado expedition, 204
Cortés de Zúñiga, Martín, 140–41, 143, 147
Cortés, Hernando, 135–36, 140–41, 145–46, 153, 219
Cortés, Pedro, 141
Councils of Lima, Ecclesiastical, 83, 86, 123
Counterreformation, 86
creoles, 43–44, 150, 180, 187, 194, 196n1, 197n4
criollos, 5, 18, 196n1; American, 55–56; elite, 127, 130, 135, 140–41, 144–45, 147; leaders of, 178; and patriotism, 147; and resistance, 147; white, 13, 56

317

Index

Croix, Teodoro de, 234
crosses, 99, 110–11, 113–14, 117, 160, 189, 202, 207, 209
Cuauhtitlán (Mexico), 129, 136–43, 147
Cuculí, Blas, 166
cultural: practices, 69, 176; schemas, 27–28; survival, 224; traditions, 45
Cuzco, Peru, 61–62, 70, 83, 85

De Certeau, Michel, 15, 149–50, 172, 176
Deagan, Kathleen, 245
Delgado, Carlos, 225, 232–33
demographics, 16, 52, 204, 233–36, 244, 252, 256
dendrochronology, 228–29
Despoloncal (Honduras), 151, 157–60, 163
disease, 41, 46, 49, 52, 58, 136, 199, 205–6, 236
Dittert, Al, 228
doctrinas, 14, 79–80, 84, 87, 97, 136. *See also* Malata *doctrina*
Dominican friars, 106–8, 110, 115, 119, 160
Dominican Republic, 46, 49. *See also* Hispaniola; La Isabela
Dzuluinicob Maya (British Honduras), 176–77

Ecclesiastical memorials, 16, 78, 83–85, 100
economic: divisions, 130; networks, 164; opportunity, 15; reforms, 177; subsistence, 185, 188
Ecuador, 48
education, 166, 189–90, 204
Einwohner, Rachel, 45
Ek, Asunción, 178, 181–85, 189–90, 192–94
El Brujo Archaeological Complex (El Brujo terrace), 104–6, 108–9, 124
El Paso del Norte, 202–3, 206–7, 214–15, 234
El Presidio de Los Adaes (Louisiana), 245
El Presidio de San Francisco: architectural practices/production at, 249–51, 253–55, 257–58; excavations at, 250–51; history of, 246, 251; and indigenous labor, 17, 253–58; and Native Californian heritage, 251–53; Ohlone heritage practices at, 261–64; population of, 249–50, 256; and Presidio Pasados, 261–62; as product of power-laden relationships, 259; public interpretation of, 17, 259–62, 264; quadrangles of, 246–53, 255–57, 259, 261; study of, 245; and violence, 256
elites: cacique, 54; colonial, 6; homes of, 51, 98–99; indigenous, 4, 85, 168–69; of NM Pueblos, 213; in Peru, 68; Spanish, 130, 138; Taíno, 47. *See also criollos*
En Bas Saline (Haiti), 46, 48–49
encomenderos, 46–47, 61, 133, 138–41, 143, 166–67

encomienda system: in Basin of Mexico, 133, 136, 139–40, 146–47; description of, 46–47; in Masca (Honduras), 166; and Native Americans (New Mexico), 199, 204–5, 218, 225; outlawed, 46, 50; in Peru, 61, 83; and Taínos (Hispaniola), 46–49, 51; in Yucatán, 177, 180, 192
Enriquillo (Taíno leader), 47–48
"ethical client," 263–64
ethnogenesis, 11; Navajo, 16–18, 240
ethnography, 44, 150, 201
ethnohistorical accounts, 6, 224–26, 228, 230, 236, 240
European: artifacts, 171; clothing, 111–13; colonies, earliest, 23; domination, 17; foods, 165; goods, 162–63, 169, 180, 185–88; grave goods, 52; heritage, 246; imperialism, 244; incursions in New Spain, 250; influences Andeans, 122–23; in La Traza, 127; military structures, 183; powers, 243; shipping, 163–64; textiles, 108; villages, 80. *See also* trade goods; weapons
evangelization (Peru), 14, 70–71, 73–74, 77–83, 85, 91, 94, 99–100, 123

Fairbanks, Charles, 245
famine, 46, 54
Feast of San Lorenzo, 201–2, 206
Feijoó de Sosa, Miguel, 108
fishhook, 152–53
Florida, 38, 48–50, 135, 146. *See also* La Florida
foodways, 176, 185–87
Fort San Juan de Joara (North Carolina), 12, 19–20, 23–26, 29, 32–38
Fort San Pedro/San Pablo (North Carolina), 25
forts. *See* military: settlements (Spanish); specific fort names
Foucault, Michel, 7
France, 24, 163, 185, 187
Franciscan friars, 47; and built environment, 99–100; killed by Puebloans, 215, 223; in La Florida, 50–54; and Native Americans (New Mexico), 205–8, 210, 214, 232–33; in Peru, 14, 79–80, 83–87, 94–95, 97. *See also* specific names
Franciscan missions. *See* missions
Fundación Wiese, 105

Galisteo Pueblo (New Mexico), 234–35
Gallegos, Baltasar de, 25
Gann, Thomas, 191, 193
Garifuna sites (Belize), 187
Giddens, Anthony, 27
Ginés, Juan de, 84
glass containers, 165, 171, 187–88

Index

Gobernador district/phase (New Mexico), 224, 228, 236–39, 241
Gobernador Polychrome, 238–39, 241, 242n7
gold, 155–56
Golden Gate National Recreation Area, 260–61
Gonzalo, Don, 68, 83
gourds, 60, 116–17
Goycochea, Elena, 60
Guacanagarí (La Navidad) (Caribbean), 46, 48
Guale people (La Florida), 4, 49–50
Guale Revolt of 1576, 54
guancasco. *See* processions, religious
Guatari Mico, 24–26, 31
Guatari (North Carolina), 19, 23–24, 26, 31, 37
Guatemala, 62, 155, 165–67, 175, 177–84, 197n2
Guevara, Felipe Topete, 164

Haciendas, 138, 180, 206
Haiti, 46
Harlow, Frank, 238–39
hegemony, 8–9, 44, 219
Hendricks, Rick, 230
Hernandez, Diego, 158
hide processing, 107–8
"Hispanicization," of Native Americans, 43, 56
Hispaniola, 41–43, 46–49, 51–52, 54
historical documents: for British Honduras, 174, 176, 185, 193; for Honduras, 150, 152–54, 156–57, 159, 162–66, 171. *See also* Spanish historical documents
Hobsbawm, Eric, 237
Hogan, Patrick, 230
hogans, 224, 227–28, 236, 238, 241
Hollander, Jocelyn, 45
Honduras: archaeological sites of, 150, 152–57, 165, 171; and coastal surveillance, 163–65; cofradias and churches of, 159–63; indigenous residents of, 168–71; and military campaigns, 152–56; and *pueblos de indios*, 154, 156–70; tactics used in, 15, 150–51, 153, 163, 165–66, 168–69, 171–72; towns of, 151. *See also* British Honduras
Hopi people (Moqui), 226, 231, 234, 238, 241
Howard University, 263
Huaca Cao Viejo (Peru), 105–6, 109–10
Huaca Cortada (Peru), 109
Huaca Prieta (Peru), 105, 108
huacas, 86, 105–6, 109–10, 124. *See also* specific huacas
Huaquerones cemetery (Peru), 59, 63–68, 71–75

Iberian ceramic tradition, 132, 145–46
Icaiche (Mayan village, British Honduras), 178, 180–82, 185, 188, 192

identity, 241; collective, 237, 239; formation, 170, 250; indigenous, 171–72; social, 237
ideology: and church placement, 109; and NM Pueblos, 238; patriotic, 147; semiotic, 14, 80–82, 99–100; of space, 80; of state magnanimity, 85
idolaters/idolatries: New Mexico, 205, 210, 232; Peru, 70–71, 75, 78
immigrant Spanish (nonelite), 55–56
Incas, 60, 87, 98; architecture of, 14, 58, 80, 85–86, 89–91, 95; and religious practices, 14, 57–58, 86, 116; rulers of, 61, 70, 119, 124, 219; under the Spanish, 61–62, 74–75, 79–80, 219; and state-subject relations, 85–86; and warfare, 61–62, 65–66, 68
indigeneity, 11, 43–44, 124, 259
indigenous heritage, study of, 4–6, 17, 244–46, 253, 259, 262, 265
indios peones (Indian laborers), 43, 51–52
infieles/indios bárbaros, 51–52
Instituto Nacional de Antropología e Historia (INAH), 133
instrumental neutron activation analyses (INAA), 131, 136
invented traditions, 237–41
ironwork, 31–32, 34, 36, 95
Isleta Pueblo (New Mexico), 226, 235

Jacona Pueblo (New Mexico), 231
Jemez Pueblo (New Mexico), 203, 206–11, 214, 216–17, 220, 223, 226–30, 232, 235, 239
Jesuits, 50, 146, 160
Jetegua (Honduras), 160, 164, 169
Jironza Petris de Cruzate, Domingo, 201–2, 210
Joara Mico, 24–26, 28, 31, 33, 38
Joara (North Carolina), 19, 23, 25, 28, 31–38
Johnson, Melissa A., 197n4
Jones, Grant, 178–79, 181
Juan Pardo expeditions, 13, 144–45; forts of, 33, 35, 37–39; and gift exchange, 12, 20, 26, 31–32; history/description of, 19–26; and labor mobilization, 12, 20, 28–31; and military support, 12, 20; natives' perspective of, 27–28

Kachina ceremonialism, 205, 238
kallankas (Inca great halls), 85–86, 89
Keane, Webb, 81
Keres-speaking Puebloans (New Mexico), 206, 209, 216–17, 238, 241
Kessell, John, 43
Keur, Dorothy, 228
Kidder, Alfred V., 226–28
kivas, 205, 207, 210–13, 220, 221n1, 232, 238, 241, 241n2
Kroeber, Alfred, 263–64

319

Index

Kubler, George, 123–24
kurakas (local lords, Peru), 61, 68

La Florida, 4, 21, 26, 38, 41, 43, 45, 47, 49–55
La Isabela (Caribbean), 46, 49
La Navidad (Caribbean), 3–4, 46
La Traza (Mexico), 127–30, 134, 136, 138–40, 145, 147
labor, 86, 91, 170; analysis of, 7, 255–56; captive, 254–60, 264; and colonial heritage sites, 259–60, 264; in Despoloncal (Honduras), 157–59; drafts, 48–49, 51–52, 54; exploitation of, 46–50, 139, 156, 180, 199, 232; forced, 204, 225, 243, 253–55, 259; indigenous, 51, 253–58, 264; and logging, 180, 182, 185, 191, 194; and the missions, 254–55; relations, 188, 244, 265; resistance to, 47, 166. See also *encomienda* system; slavery
Lacandon people (Petén), 175, 183–85, 187, 196n2
ladinos, 169–70
Laguna Pueblo (New Mexico), 232, 234–35
Lambayeque culture (Peru), 105, 109
land: appropriation of, 243, 259, 264; extractive uses of, 197n4; forced removal from, 105, 192, 208; grants, 46, 48, 139, 167; of the Ohlone, 263–64; reforms, 180; of Spanish-speaking America, 56; tenure, 178. See also *encomienda* system; *reducciónes*
Lara, Jaime, 80, 123
Lara, Miguel de, 227
Largo district (New Mexico), 224, 239
Late Horizon period (Peru), 58–61, 63, 73, 87, 89, 94
Late Intermediate period, 89, 101n1
Late Mississippian societies, 32, 34–35
Lezaún, Juan Sanz de, 233
Lezcano, Juan and Ana Maria, 159
Libro de las Tasaciones, 136
Lightfoot, Kent, 245
Lima, Peru, 61, 70, 83–84, 86, 107, 119, 123
Lima, Siege of, 14, 58, 61–65, 68–69, 74–75, 83
logging industry, 16, 174, 177, 180–82, 184–85, 188, 191–92, 194, 197n4
Loren, Diana, 245
Los Californianos, 261
Luna y Arellano, Tristán de, 21, 139

Madrid, Roque de, 230–31
Magdalena de Cao Viejo (Peru), 124; architecture/landscape of, 15, 108–11; buildings of, 106–7; church of, 105–11, 118–20; history of, 103–8; and hybridity/syncretism of site, 112; location of, 103–4, 108–9; and paper documents, 15, 107–9, 119–22; plaza of, 106, 110–11; religious material culture/practices of, 108, 115–19; rich material record of, 122; and signs of resistance, 118; Spanish policies in, 108; textiles/crafts of, 15, 108, 111–16
maize, 20, 22, 24–25, 29–30, 37, 60, 118–19, 158, 191, 204, 232
majolica, 130, 132, 169
Malacate, Antonio, 214–15
Malata *doctrina*, 14; atrium of, 89, 91–94, 98–99; buildings of, 87–89, 93–98, 100; chapel of, 89–94, 98–99; craft production at, 97; history of, 89, 94; location of, 87; movement through (paths), 97–99; plaza of, 89–95, 98–100; processions at, 98–100; and semiotic ideologies, 99–100; Spanish attributes of, 93–94
Malata (Peru), 79–80, 87–100
Manco Inca (emperor, Peru), 61–62, 68
marriage, 56, 167–69, 189, 225, 230, 240
Martin, Blas, 230–31
Martín de Badajoz, Juan, 26, 37
Martín, Teresa, 37
Martinez, Francisco, 24, 32–33
Martínez, Pedro, 108
Masca (Honduras), 160, 165–68, 170
material culture: of Basin of Mexico, 130; at Berry site (North Carolina), 38; of British Honduras, 176, 180, 182–83, 185–90; and built environment, 79–80; of En Bas Saline site (Haiti), 48–49; in Honduras, 150–51, 153, 162–63, 165, 169, 171–72; importance of, 220; of NM Pueblos, 220, 227–28; and Pardo expeditions, 31–32; pre-conquest, 115; precontact, 122; religious, 15; study of, 5–7, 10–11, 44, 171–72, 194, 220, 244, 259; at Yadkin River, 38. *See also* specific items; specific sites
material world, 79–80, 82–83
Matienzo, Juan de, 81
Maya people (British Honduras), 16, 219; autonomy of, 175, 178, 182, 188, 192, 195; Cruzobs, 178, 180–81, 183, 189, 192; definition of, 196n1; and logging, 180; military victories of, 182–83; Pacificos, 178, 180–81, 183–85, 189, 191; and Spanish colonial rule, 177; Spanish influence on, 175–76; strategies of, 174–75, 190, 192
Menéndez de Avilés, Pedro, 21, 23–24
Mercedarian missionaries, 160
Mesoamerica, 79, 85, 178
mestizos, 5, 13–14, 18, 43, 48, 108, 130, 169, 175, 178, 196n1, 245, 251
Mexican Independence, 139, 177, 246, 258

Mexico, 4, 23, 28, 48, 123–24, 175, 177–78, 180–81, 185, 191–92. *See also* Basin of Mexico
Mexico Caste War, 4, 16, 175, 178, 180, 183, 189
Mexico City, Mexico, 127
mico, 24–26, 31. *See also* specific names of micos
military, 32–33, 183; campaigns, 152–56, 175–76, 178, 182–84, 193–94, 250; command and architecture, 250, 253, 257–58; excursions, 254; resistance, earliest, 41–42, 46; settlements (Spanish), 17, 19, 243–44, 246, 250–52, 259, 263–64; soldiers (Spanish), 4, 252, 256, 258; tactics (Spanish), 199, 201–2, 243–44. *See also* El Presidio de San Francisco; Juan Pardo expeditions
miscegenation, 11, 130
mission buildings, 51, 53, 79, 82, 208, 245. See also *conventos*
missionaries, 4–7. *See also* Dominican friars; Franciscan friars; Jesuits; missions; specific names
missions, 14; in California, 246, 250, 252, 259, 264; Church instructions for, 78, 83, 86, 91, 110; failure of, 38, 49–50; first within interior, 24; growth/formalization of, 94; in La Florida, 49–54; and military settlements, 243; and Native Californian labor, 254–55, 258; in New Mexico, 203–9, 218, 230, 232, 240; at NM Pueblos, 208, 223–25; in Peru, 14, 77–81; and refugees, 52; violent resistance to, 54; in Yucatán, 77. See also *doctrinas*; Franciscan friars
Moche culture (Peru), 105–6, 109–11, 118
Moctezuma, Emperor, 145–46
Mogollón, Juan Ignacio Flores, 231–32
Monarquía Indiana (Torquemada), 141
Montejo, Francisco de, 157
Montero, Sebastian, 24
Monzón, Juan de, 84–85
Moore, David, 32, 38
Moqui. *See* Hopi people
Moraga, José Joaquín, 253
Morfi, Juan Agustín de, 234–35
Morisco Green-style ceramics, 87, 95
mortuary practices, 57–58, 69–75, 87. *See also* burials
Moyano, Hernando, 23–25, 32–33
mulato/mulata, 170, 251

Naco (Honduras), 151, 153–54, 157
nails, 89, 95, 162
Nambé Pueblo (New Mexico), 226, 232, 234–35
Narváez, Pánfilo de, 21
National Park Service (NPS), 246, 260–62
National Science Foundation, 34
Native American Graves Protection and Repatriation Act (NAGPRA), 244
Native Americans, New Mexico. *See* individual Pueblos; New Mexico; Pueblo revolts; Pueblos of New Mexico
Native Americans, North Carolina Piedmont: build houses for Spanish, 20, 22, 24–25, 28–31; destroy forts, 19, 26, 33–34, 36–38; express autonomy, 30–31; and gift exchange, 31–32, 37–38; leaders of, 20, 23–26, 28, 31–33; powerful polities of, 22, 24, 39; provide maize for Spanish, 20, 22, 24–25, 29–30; reject Spanish colonialism, 33; religious conversion of, 23–24; and sexual politics, 37–38; and Spanish military support, 32–33; used Spanish for own purposes, 20, 27, 31–33, 38–39
Native Californians: architectural methods of, 251–52; arts and crafts of, 261; and battles with Spanish military, 252, 254–55, 257; communities of, 245; different tribes of, 260, 264; as laborers at El Presidio, 17, 253–60, 264; lands of, 263–64; and material culture, 250–51; and population losses, 263; present-day communities of, 261; prisoners of war, 252, 257, 259; and public interpretation of El Presidio, 259–62, 264; religious conversion of, 246, 252, 254–55; resistance of, 252, 256–57, 259, 264; survival of, 262
Navajo Apaches: and acculturation, 16–17, 228, 230; architecture of, 230–31, 236, 241; ceremonial practices of, 238–41; clans of, 224, 229–30, 240; demographics of, 233; early culture of, 224; hybrid nature of, 17, 236–41; influenced by Puebloans, 236, 238–41; and inter-tribal relationships, 224; and inter-tribal trade, 226; and peace with Spanish, 229–31; and Pueblo refugees, 224, 226–33, 236, 240; and refuse disposal, 237, 241; and relationship with Puebloans, 224–26, 240; religious conversion of, 223, 226, 233; rock art of, 239–41
Navajo Nation (modern), 224, 236, 240–41
Neve, Felipe de, 247
New Laws of 1542, 139
New Mexico, 16, 135, 146, 201–4, 224–25, 234. *See also* pueblitos; Pueblos of New Mexico; specific Pueblos
New Spain, 127, 132, 135, 138–41, 143, 145–47, 189, 234, 251–52
Nicaragua, 62

321

Index

Niza, Marcos de, 84
Nolasco Bichrome ceramics, 153–54, 157
North Carolina Piedmont, 19–26, 31–32, 35, 37, 39. *See also* Native Americans, North Carolina Piedmont
Nuestra Señora de la Asunción de Zia mission (New Mexico), 201, 203. *See also* Zia Pueblo
Nueva Cádiz beads, 87

Obsidian, 152, 155–57, 161, 171–72, 251
Ohkay Owingeh Pueblo, 206. *See also* San Juan Pueblo
Ohlone people (California), 260–64
Ojeda, Bartolome de, 214–17, 219–20
Olamico (eastern Tennessee), 24–25
Olivera, Luis de, 124
Omoa (Honduras), 168–70
oral narratives, 16, 176, 190, 194–95, 210, 240
orata, 24–26, 30. *See also* specific names
Ornedal, Juan Antonio de, 241n3
Orozco y Berra, Manuel, 140–41, 143
Osaguera, Alonso de, 166
Otermín, Governor, 226
Otumba (Mexico), 131, 139

Paiva, Juan de, 53
Palka, Joel W., 175, 178, 183, 185, 187, 196n2
Palkovitch, Ann, 236
Panama, 48, 62, 163
Pardo, Juan, 19, 21–26, 28–33, 35, 37–39. *See also* Juan Pardo expeditions
Parsons, Jeffrey R., 131
Patokwa village (Jemez Pueblo, NM), 203, 208, 210–11, 213, 216
Pecos Pueblo (New Mexico), 216, 228, 232, 234–36
Peirce, Charles Sanders, 81
peninsulares, 127, 130, 135, 145, 147
Peralta, Gastón de, 139
perimortem traumatic injuries, 63–68, 75, 76n3, 76n4
Peru, 99; Andean polities; Andean religious practices; burials; evangelization; Huaquerones cemetery; Magdalena de Cao Viejo; Puruchuco-Huaquerones; and ancestor cult, 57, 70–71, 73–75, 76n1; and campaign against idolaters/idolatries, 70–71; and corpse removal practice, 71–75; extirpation of native practices in, 69–70, 78, 85; indigenous resistance and, 74–75; precontact, 123; prehispanic violence in, 65–67; resists religious conversion, 80, 118; Spanish invasion of, 58, 61, 68–70, 74, 80, 119; traditional mortuary rituals of, 57–58, 69–75. *See also* 57AS03 cemetery

Peruvian National Institute of Culture, 105
Philip II, King, 21
Picuris Pueblo (New Mexico), 216, 234–35
Piedre Lumbre District (New Mexico), 231, 236
Pizzarro, Francisco, 61–62, 65, 83, 119, 219
plazas: and the Incas, 85–86; at Magdalena de Cao Viejo (Peru), 106; at Malata (Peru), 89–95, 98–100; in presidios, 247, 249, 252; of pueblitos, 224; of pueblos, 210–11, 213; and Spanish urban planning, 80
politics, indigenous, 13, 17, 145, 200, 215–20
polities, native, 12, 19–20, 24–25, 31, 39, 50
Poma de Ayala, Guaman, 70
Ponce de León, Juan, 21, 49
Po'pay (Pueblo leader), 206–9, 213, 215–19
population, 156–57, 169, 199, 204–6. *See also* demographics
Portugal, 145–46
post-Columbian Taíno sites, 14, 47, 49
Postclassic period, 131, 135–36, 157
pottery. *See* ceramics; specific types
Prada, Juan de, 225
Prescott, William H., 6, 219
Presidio of San Francisco National Historic Landmark, 260–62
Presidio Pasados (California), 261–62
Presidio Trust, 260–62
presidios, 17, 50, 245–47, 251–52, 255–57. *See also* El Presidio de San Francisco
priests: mission, 233–34, 254; and NM Pueblos, 205–7; parish, 69–71, 74, 85, 159–60; visiting, 166, 188–89, 205
processions, religious, 98–100, 160–61, 169
Protestants, 188–89
Pueblito phenomenon, 16, 237, 240, 242n7
pueblitos (New Mexico), 16–17, 224, 227–31, 236–39, 241n1, 242n6
Pueblo Revolt of 1680, 4, 16, 26, 36, 144, 201–3, 213–18, 220, 225–26, 231, 238
Pueblo Revolt of 1696, 16, 225–26, 228, 230–31
pueblos, civilian, 245, 252
pueblos de indios (Honduras), 154, 156–70
Pueblos of New Mexico: and acculturation, 228; and the Apaches, 223–24, 226; architecture of, 204–5, 207–8, 210–14, 221n1, 224, 227–28, 236, 242n6; ceramics of, 144, 208–9, 216–18; demographics of, 16, 225, 233–36; European influence on, 204; exploitation/abuse of, 226, 240; influences Navajo, 238–41; and inter-Pueblo politics, 215–20, 223, 225; and material culture, 220; military alliances of, 225–26; mobility of, 234–36; refugees of, 224–33, 236, 240–41; and refuse disposal, 237, 241; and

322

relationships with Navajo Apaches, 224–26, 240; religious persecution of, 231–33, 240; resist Spanish colonialism, 204, 207–8, 225–26; ritual life of, 205, 210, 213, 232, 238–40; social organization of, 204–5; taxation of, 204–5; trade between, 223–24. *See also* individual Pueblos; Pueblo revolts

Punames pueblos (New Mexico), 204–5, 216, 238

Puruchuco-Huaquerones (Peru), 14; burials of, 58–61, 63–69, 71–75; cemeteries of, 58–61, 63, 67–69, 71–75; location of, 58–59, 63, 68; and Siege of Lima, 62–63, 68; Spanish invasion of, 61

Quincha (wattle-and-daub) walls, 106–7, 247–48, 250

Rancho Petaluma (California), 258

Red Ware (Basin of Mexico): aesthetic preference for, 135–36, 144; archaeological record of, 130; background of, 131–32; burnished/polished in colonial period, 133–34; created for royal celebrations, 131, 140, 142–43, 147; different forms of, 15, 131–35, 138–39, 142–44; and early colonial ceramics, 132–33; and economic motivation, 144–45, 147–48; materials/techniques of, 131–34, 144; as memories of home, 145–46, 148; and pottery of Cuauhtitlán, 136–43; and resistance, 15, 146–48; as tools of negotiation, 145; used by elites, 140–45, 147–48; used by natives, 144–45, 147–48

Redfield, Robert, 187

reducciónes, 74, 191–92; daily life in, 4; description of, 47; of Magdalena de Cao Viejo, 15; and NM Pueblos, 225; in Peru, 79–82, 84, 89, 94, 97, 105–6; as strategy of the Spanish, 69, 199; and the Yucatán, 177

Reed, Paul and Lori, 242n7

Reeve, Frank, 229

Reglamento, 1772, 247

Reichard, Gladys, 230

religious conversion: of Apache nation, 223; and built environment, 99; and church placement, 110; Eurocentric perspective of, 6; by Franciscans, 77–81, 85; of the Maya, 177; of Native Americans (Hispaniola), 43, 46–47; of Native Americans (La Florida), 43, 50–51; of Native Americans (NC Piedmont), 23–24; of Native Californians, 246, 252, 254–55; of the Navajo, 223, 226, 233; of NM Pueblos, 199, 204, 213, 223–26, 231–33; in Peru, 70–71, 74; rejection of, 51–52, 78, 254;

Spanish policies for, 46–51, 78–81, 110; through documents, 119

repartimiento system, 46, 49, 177, 192, 199, 225

resistance concept, 17–18; case studies of, 10–17, 108–22; complexity of, 10, 195, 199–201, 244; de-centering of, 219–20; definition of, 5, 45–46; and dominance dichotomy, 19–21; popularity of, 44; romanticizing of, 9–10, 45, 219; study of, 6–10, 44–46, 195, 199–201, 218–20

Rímac Valley (Peru), 58, 60, 62, 68

Río de Ulúa (Honduras), 152–56, 158, 164, 168

rituals: and alcohol, 187; Andean, 116–19; of Aztecs, 122; Christian, 52, 86, 110, 160–61, 177; dominated by Spanish, 108; honoring the dead, 57–58, 69; indigenous, 15, 157, 177; of the Navajo, 238–41; of NM Pueblos, 205, 210, 213, 220, 232, 238–40; pagan, 53–54; paraphernalia for, 85; and processionals, 98; public, 80, 100; shamanic, 122; spaces for, 14, 53, 85, 89, 98–100, 110; state organized (Peru), 85–86. *See also* kivas

rock art, 239–41

Rodríguez-Alegría, Enrique, 134

Russian American Company, 250

Saints, images of, 159–61, 167, 169

Sal, Hermenegildo, 247, 254

San Antonio site (Peru), 85, 87

San Diego de la Congregación mission (Jemez Pueblo, NM), 207–9

San Felipe Pueblo (New Mexico), 226, 235

San Francisco Bay region, 246, 250, 254, 260–62

San Ildefonso Pueblo (New Mexico), 231, 234–35

San José Mission (California), 255

San José Yalbac (British Honduras), 176, 178–79, 183, 185, 187, 189, 191–93, 195

San Juan Pueblo (New Mexico), 231–32, 234–35

San Lázaro Pueblo (New Mexico), 231

San Pedro (Honduras), 151, 156, 158, 164–68, 170

San Pedro Maya (British Honduras), 173–75, 178, 180–85, 187–89, 191–93

San Pedro Sirís (British Honduras), 175–76, 178–79, 181–94, 196n1

Sandia Pueblo (New Mexico), 207, 235

Santa Ana Pueblo (New Mexico), 202–3, 209, 213, 234–35

Santa Clara Pueblo (New Mexico), 231, 235

Santa Elena (Parris Island, SC), 21–22, 24, 26, 36–38, 49–50, 54

Santa Fe, New Mexico, 203, 206–7, 234

Index

Santiago de Tlatelolco (Mexico). *See* Tlatelolco (Mexico)
Santiago Posta (Honduras), 161
Santo Domingo, 62
Santo Domingo Pueblo (Kewa Pueblo, NM), 202–3, 207, 209, 213, 234–35
Schaafsma, Curtis, 238
Schaafsma, Polly, 239–40
School for Advanced Research (SAR), 11, 76n2
Scolari, Paul, 262
Scott, James C., 7
Seven Years' War, 246
Sewell, William Jr., 20, 27–28, 33
sexual politics/violence, 37–38, 225
shells, 60, 116–18, 251
Silliman, Stephen, 174, 245
slavery, 8, 13, 51, 170, 263–64. *See also* Africans; labor
Smithsonian Institution, 31, 38
social: action, 119; agents, 174; change, 18, 237; divisions, 130, 168; dynamics, 103; engineering, 80; hierarchy, 187; histories, 17; identity, 43, 111, 180; landscapes, 23, 52, 149, 154, 176, 246; life, 7–10; networks, 164; order, 80, 99, 181; practices, 170, 236–37, 241; relations, 9, 15, 253, 259; strategies, 123; structures, 28; upheaval, 178
Society for American Archaeology, 10–11
Sonoma, California, 246, 252
Soto, Hernando de, 21–23, 25–26, 30–31, 38
South America, 74. *See also* Peru
Spanish colonial heritage sites, 244, 259–65
Spanish conquerors: brutal nature of, 7, 218; failutres of, 19–21, 26, 38–39, 49, 175, 202; goals of, 41; introduced cultural practices, 165; and peace, 48, 54, 229–31; resist own caciques, 55–56; retaliation by, 54, 56, 152, 226, 254, 257; romanticizing of, 6–7. *See also* specific names of individuals
Spanish historical documents, 3–5, 15, 21–24, 35, 38, 51–52, 74, 156, 164, 172, 224–25
Spanish imperial project, 12, 15, 43
Spanish legal system, 165–67
Spanish–native relations, 12–13; of accommodation, 41, 48, 54–55, 73, 80, 110–11; ambiguity/variability of, 123–24; and ambivalence, 218; and built environment, 82; in California, 251; complexity of, 199–201, 218; of cooperation, 20, 35–36; and gift exchange, 31–32, 37–38; sexual, 37–38; violent, 74–75; weakening of, 33–34
Spanish pottery, 48, 132, 135, 148, 171
Spanish Reconquest of New Mexico, 201–3, 210, 214–20, 229–30
Spondylus shell, 60, 116–18
St. Augustine, Florida, 21, 49–52, 245
statues, of indigenous leaders, 194–95
status, 13, 32, 140, 168, 170, 194, 258
Stein, Gil J., 174
Stern, Steve, 124
Suárez de Peralta, Juan, 138, 141–43
subaltern peoples, 4–5, 8, 11, 16, 44, 173, 220
survival, 9, 50, 199–200, 218, 224, 240, 244, 262, 265

Taínos (Hispaniola), 3–4, 14, 42, 46–49
Taki Onqoy movement (Peru), 4, 86, 124
Taos Pueblo (New Mexico), 206, 216, 226, 234–36
taxation, 51, 86, 161, 188, 199, 204–5, 225
Tehuma (Honduras), 164–65
tejas (clay roof tile), 248–50, 255
Tennessee, 19, 24–25, 32
Tenochtitlan (Mexico), 4, 15, 127–31, 133, 135–36, 141, 145–47
Tesuque Pueblo (New Mexico), 232, 234–36
Tewa-speaking Pueblos (New Mexico), 216–20, 230–31, 238, 241
Texas, 135, 146
Texcoco (Mexico), 129, 131, 134
textiles, 15, 31, 51, 60, 69, 73, 97, 108, 111–16. *See also* weaving
Thomas, Cyrus, 38
Thompson, E. P., 5
Thompson, J. Eric S., 191–94
Ticamaya (Honduras), 151–57, 163–65, 167–72, 197n3
Timucua people (La Florida), 49–50, 54
Tlatelolco (Mexico), 128–30, 133–35, 138–39, 145, 147
tobacco, 120, 185
Toledo, Francisco de, 69–70, 74, 81–82, 100, 124
tools, 31–32, 35, 60, 97, 107, 157, 161, 163, 188, 195, 251. *See also* obsidian
Toribio de Mogrovejo, Alfonso, 107–8
Torquemada, Juan de, 141, 143
Torres, Naomi, 262
Towner, Ronald, 228–31, 240
Towton, England, 66
toys, 189–90, 194
trade: and British Honduras, 181, 185, 187; disrupted by Spanish, 223–24; global system of, 258; illicit, 164; inter-tribal (New Mexico), 208–9, 216, 223–24, 226; prohibitions against, 56; of the Yucatán, 154–55
trade goods, 194; cacao, 152, 154; ceramics, 132; contraband, 164; European, 31–32, 37, 47, 51

tribute, 46; and ceramics, 132–33; and *encomiendas*, 136, 139; in Honduras, 156–59, 161, 170; lists, 132, 136, 165; of the Maya, 188; and NM Pueblos, 204–5; payment of, 30, 168; of the Taínos, 37
Tringham, Ruth, 253

Ulúa River (Honduras). *See* Río de Ulúa
Ulúa Valley (Honduras), 152, 154, 156, 160, 163, 165, 169
United States, 185, 246
urban: planning, 93–94, 97, 105–6, 184; settlements, 80–82; societies, 130, 135, 144
Urban III, Pope, 223
Utes, 224, 229–30, 240

Vallejo, Mariano, 258
Valley of Oaxaca (Mexico), 140–41
VanderVeen, James, 49
Vargas, Diego de, 202, 209–10, 214, 219, 229, 231
Vásquez de Ayllón, Lucas, 21
Velasco, Luis de, 139, 143, 225
Venezuela, 48, 89
violent conflicts, 26–27, 32–34, 50, 54–55, 63–64, 74–75, 155–56, 178, 187, 202, 225–26, 252, 258. *See also* Pueblo revolts; warfare
Virgin of Candelaria, 167
Virginia, 24, 32, 38
visitas, 205, 208

Warfare, 41, 47–48, 62–63, 65, 68, 155, 175–76, 220, 231. *See also* Lima, Siege of
Wateree-Catawba Valley (South Carolina), 23, 25
weapons, 155; British, 180–81, 192–93; European, 14, 63, 65–68, 75; firearms, 165, 182–83, 187, 192–93, 196n2; machetes, 194–95; medieval, 67; Spanish, 65–67
weaving, 60, 97, 111–12, 115, 224, 232. *See also* textiles

Weber, David, 43, 56
Wilson, John, 230
women, native, 230; as chiefs, 23, 26; marriage to Spanish men, 37, 45; and sexual politics/violence, 37–38, 232; traditional clothing of, 112; traumatic injuries of, 63

Xenome, Diego, 226

Yadkin River (North Carolina), 25, 31–32, 38
Yamala (Honduras), 151, 161–63, 165
Yamane, Linda, 262
Yanque (Peru), 85–86
Yé'i ceremonialism, 238–41
Yerba Buena Pueblo (California), 252
Ylasi (North Carolina), 25, 31
Ylasi Orata, 30
Yrigoyen, José, 233
Yucatán, 4, 77, 152, 154–55, 177–78, 180, 182, 186–88, 192

Zia Pueblo (New Mexico): allied with Pueblos, 201–3, 206–7, 209, 218; allied with Spanish, 201–3, 209–10, 213–15, 218; ambivalence towards religion, 213; architecture of, 210–14, 221n1; armed resistance of, 201–3, 206, 210, 213; ceramics of, 216–18; demographics of, 235; execution of its leaders, 213–15, 219–20; during independence, 208–9; and inter-Pueblo politics, 216–20; and missions, 204–6, 208; ritual life of, 213; society of, 210, 213; strategies of, 16, 218; and the Tewas, 216–17, 219. *See also* Cerro Colorado village
Zuni Pueblo (New Mexico), 206, 226–27, 231, 234–36
Zúñiga, Diego de, 166
Zúñiga, Juana de, 140

# School for Advanced Research Advanced Seminar Series

PUBLISHED BY SAR PRESS

CHACO & HOHOKAM: PREHISTORIC REGIONAL SYSTEMS IN THE AMERICAN SOUTHWEST
Patricia L. Crown & W. James Judge, eds.

RECAPTURING ANTHROPOLOGY: WORKING IN THE PRESENT
Richard G. Fox, ed.

WAR IN THE TRIBAL ZONE: EXPANDING STATES AND INDIGENOUS WARFARE
R. Brian Ferguson & Neil L. Whitehead, eds.

IDEOLOGY AND PRE-COLUMBIAN CIVILIZATIONS
Arthur A. Demarest & Geoffrey W. Conrad, eds.

DREAMING: ANTHROPOLOGICAL AND PSYCHOLOGICAL INTERPRETATIONS
Barbara Tedlock, ed.

HISTORICAL ECOLOGY: CULTURAL KNOWLEDGE AND CHANGING LANDSCAPES
Carole L. Crumley, ed.

THEMES IN SOUTHWEST PREHISTORY
George J. Gumerman, ed.

MEMORY, HISTORY, AND OPPOSITION UNDER STATE SOCIALISM
Rubie S. Watson, ed.

OTHER INTENTIONS: CULTURAL CONTEXTS AND THE ATTRIBUTION OF INNER STATES
Lawrence Rosen, ed.

LAST HUNTERS–FIRST FARMERS: NEW PERSPECTIVES ON THE PREHISTORIC TRANSITION TO AGRICULTURE
T. Douglas Price & Anne Birgitte Gebauer, eds.

MAKING ALTERNATIVE HISTORIES: THE PRACTICE OF ARCHAEOLOGY AND HISTORY IN NON-WESTERN SETTINGS
Peter R. Schmidt & Thomas C. Patterson, eds.

CYBORGS & CITADELS: ANTHROPOLOGICAL INTERVENTIONS IN EMERGING SCIENCES AND TECHNOLOGIES
Gary Lee Downey & Joseph Dumit, eds.

SENSES OF PLACE
Steven Feld & Keith H. Basso, eds.

THE ORIGINS OF LANGUAGE: WHAT NONHUMAN PRIMATES CAN TELL US
Barbara J. King, ed.

CRITICAL ANTHROPOLOGY NOW: UNEXPECTED CONTEXTS, SHIFTING CONSTITUENCIES, CHANGING AGENDAS
George E. Marcus, ed.

ARCHAIC STATES
Gary M. Feinman & Joyce Marcus, eds.

REGIMES OF LANGUAGE: IDEOLOGIES, POLITIES, AND IDENTITIES
Paul V. Kroskrity, ed.

BIOLOGY, BRAINS, AND BEHAVIOR: THE EVOLUTION OF HUMAN DEVELOPMENT
Sue Taylor Parker, Jonas Langer, & Michael L. McKinney, eds.

WOMEN & MEN IN THE PREHISPANIC SOUTHWEST: LABOR, POWER, & PRESTIGE
Patricia L. Crown, ed.

HISTORY IN PERSON: ENDURING STRUGGLES, CONTENTIOUS PRACTICE, INTIMATE IDENTITIES
Dorothy Holland & Jean Lave, eds.

THE EMPIRE OF THINGS: REGIMES OF VALUE AND MATERIAL CULTURE
Fred R. Myers, ed.

CATASTROPHE & CULTURE: THE ANTHROPOLOGY OF DISASTER
Susanna M. Hoffman & Anthony Oliver-Smith, eds.

URUK MESOPOTAMIA & ITS NEIGHBORS: CROSS-CULTURAL INTERACTIONS IN THE ERA OF STATE FORMATION
Mitchell S. Rothman, ed.

REMAKING LIFE & DEATH: TOWARD AN ANTHROPOLOGY OF THE BIOSCIENCES
Sarah Franklin & Margaret Lock, eds.

TIKAL: DYNASTIES, FOREIGNERS, & AFFAIRS OF STATE: ADVANCING MAYA ARCHAEOLOGY
Jeremy A. Sabloff, ed.

Published by SAR Press

Gray Areas: Ethnographic Encounters
with Nursing Home Culture
Philip B. Stafford, ed.

Pluralizing Ethnography: Comparison
and Representation in Maya Cultures,
Histories, and Identities
John M. Watanabe & Edward F. Fischer, eds.

American Arrivals: Anthropology
Engages the New Immigration
Nancy Foner, ed.

Violence
Neil L. Whitehead, ed.

Law & Empire in the Pacific:
Fiji and Hawai'i
Sally Engle Merry & Donald Brenneis, eds.

Anthropology in the Margins
of the State
Veena Das & Deborah Poole, eds.

The Archaeology of Colonial
Encounters: Comparative Perspectives
Gil J. Stein, ed.

Globalization, Water, & Health:
Resource Management in Times of
Scarcity
Linda Whiteford & Scott Whiteford, eds.

A Catalyst for Ideas: Anthropological
Archaeology and the Legacy of
Douglas W. Schwartz
Vernon L. Scarborough, ed.

The Archaeology of Chaco Canyon: An
Eleventh-Century Pueblo Regional
Center
Stephen H. Lekson, ed.

Community Building in the Twenty-
First Century
Stanley E. Hyland, ed.

Afro-Atlantic Dialogues:
Anthropology in the Diaspora
Kevin A. Yelvington, ed.

Copán: The History of an Ancient Maya
Kingdom
E. Wyllys Andrews & William L. Fash, eds.

The Evolution of Human Life History
Kristen Hawkes & Richard R. Paine, eds.

The Seductions of Community:
Emancipations, Oppressions, Quandaries
Gerald W. Creed, ed.

The Gender of Globalization: Women
Navigating Cultural and Economic
Marginalities
Nandini Gunewardena & Ann Kingsolver, eds.

New Landscapes of Inequality:
Neoliberalism and the Erosion of
Democracy in America
*Jane L. Collins, Micaela di Leonardo,
& Brett Williams, eds.*

Imperial Formations
*Ann Laura Stoler, Carole McGranahan,
& Peter C. Perdue, eds.*

Opening Archaeology: Repatriation's
Impact on Contemporary Research and
Practice
Thomas W. Killion, ed.

Small Worlds: Method, Meaning, &
Narrative in Microhistory
*James F. Brooks, Christopher R. N. DeCorse,
& John Walton, eds.*

Memory Work: Archaeologies of
Material Practices
Barbara J. Mills & William H. Walker, eds.

Figuring the Future: Globalization
and the Temporalities of Children and
Youth
Jennifer Cole & Deborah Durham, eds.

Timely Assets: The Politics of
Resources and Their Temporalities
*Elizabeth Emma Ferry &
Mandana E. Limbert, eds.*

Democracy: Anthropological
Approaches
Julia Paley, ed.

Confronting Cancer: Metaphors,
Inequality, and Advocacy
Juliet McMullin & Diane Weiner, eds.

Published by SAR Press

Development & Dispossession: The Crisis of Forced Displacement and Resettlement
  Anthony Oliver-Smith, ed.

Global Health in Times of Violence
  Barbara Rylko-Bauer, Linda Whiteford, & Paul Farmer, eds.

The Evolution of Leadership: Transitions in Decision Making from Small-Scale to Middle-Range Societies
  Kevin J. Vaughn, Jelmer W. Eerkins, & John Kantner, eds.

Archaeology & Cultural Resource Management: Visions for the Future
  Lynne Sebastian & William D. Lipe, eds.

Archaic State Interaction: The Eastern Mediterranean in the Bronze Age
  William A. Parkinson & Michael L. Galaty, eds.

Indians & Energy: Exploitation and Opportunity in the American Southwest
  Sherry L. Smith & Brian Frehner, eds.

Roots of Conflict: Soils, Agriculture, and Sociopolitical Complexity in Ancient Hawai'i
  Patrick V. Kirch, ed.

Pharmaceutical Self: The Global Shaping of Experience in an Age of Psychopharmacology
  Janis Jenkins, ed.

Forces of Compassion: Humanitarianism Between Ethics and Politics
  Erica Bornstein & Peter Redfield, eds.

Now available from SAR Press

The Archaeology of Lower Central America
  Frederick W. Lange & Doris Z. Stone, eds.

Chan Chan: Andean Desert City
  Michael E. Moseley & Kent C. Day, eds.

Demographic Anthropology: Quantitative Approaches
  Ezra B. W. Zubrow, ed.

The Dying Community
  Art Gallaher, Jr. & Harlan Padfield, eds.

Elites: Ethnographic Issues
  George E. Marcus, ed.

Entrepreneurs in Cultural Context
  Sidney M. Greenfield, Arnold Strickon, & Robert T. Aubey, eds.

Lowland Maya Settlement Patterns
  Wendy Ashmore, ed.

Methods and Theories of Anthropological Genetics
  M. H. Crawford & P. L. Workman, eds.

The Origins of Maya Civilization
  Richard E. W. Adams, ed.

Structure and Process in Latin America
  Arnold Strickon & Sidney M. Greenfield, eds.

Published by Cambridge University Press

The Anasazi in a Changing Environment
George J. Gumerman, ed.

Regional Perspectives on the Olmec
Robert J. Sharer & David C. Grove, eds.

The Chemistry of Prehistoric Human Bone
T. Douglas Price, ed.

The Emergence of Modern Humans: Biocultural Adaptations in the Later Pleistocene
Erik Trinkaus, ed.

The Anthropology of War
Jonathan Haas, ed.

The Evolution of Political Systems
Steadman Upham, ed.

Classic Maya Political History: Hieroglyphic and Archaeological Evidence
T. Patrick Culbert, ed.

Turko-Persia in Historical Perspective
Robert L. Canfield, ed.

Chiefdoms: Power, Economy, and Ideology
Timothy Earle, ed.

Reconstructing Prehistoric Pueblo Societies
William A. Longacre, ed.

Published by University of New Mexico Press

New Perspectives on the Pueblos
Alfonso Ortiz, ed.

The Classic Maya Collapse
T. Patrick Culbert, ed.

Sixteenth-Century Mexico: The Work of Sahagun
Munro S. Edmonson, ed.

Ancient Civilization and Trade
*Jeremy A. Sabloff &
C. C. Lamberg-Karlovsky, eds.*

Photography in Archaeological Research
Elmer Harp, Jr., ed.

The Valley of Mexico: Studies in Pre-Hispanic Ecology and Society
Eric R. Wolf, ed.

Explanation of Prehistoric Change
James N. Hill, ed.

Meaning in Anthropology
Keith H. Basso & Henry A. Selby, eds.

Explorations in Ethnoarchaeology
Richard A. Gould, ed.

Southwestern Indian Ritual Drama
Charlotte J. Frisbie, ed.

Simulations in Archaeology
Jeremy A. Sabloff, ed.

Shipwreck Anthropology
Richard A. Gould, ed.

Late Lowland Maya Civilization: Classic to Postclassic
Jeremy A. Sabloff & E. Wyllys Andrews V, eds.

Published by University of California Press

Writing Culture: The Poetics and Politics of Ethnography
*James Clifford &
George E. Marcus, eds.*

Published by University of Arizona Press

The Collapse of Ancient States and Civilizations
*Norman Yoffee &
George L. Cowgill, eds.*

Participants in the School for Advanced Research short seminar "The Archaeology of Indigenous Resistance to the Spanish Conquest" co-chaired by Matthew Liebmann and Melissa S. Murphy, November 5–6, 2008. *Standing, from left:* Robin A. Beck Jr., Patricia Fournier, Robert W. Preucel, Russell N. Sheptak, Steven A. Wernke, Jeffrey Quilter, Barbara L. Voss, Minette C. Church; *seated, from left:* Matthew Liebmann, Melissa S. Murphy. Photograph by Jason S. Ordaz.

www.ingramcontent.com/pod-product-compliance
Lightning Source LLC
Chambersburg PA
CBHW030520230426
43665CB00010B/702